Around the Book

Around the Book

Systems and Literacy

Henry Sussman

FORDHAM UNIVERSITY PRESS

NEW YORK 2011

Fordham University Press has no responsibility for the persistence or accuracy of URLs for external or third-party Internet websites referred to in this publication and does not guarantee that any content on such websites is, or will remain, accurate or appropriate.

Fordham University Press also publishes its books in a variety of electronic formats. Some content that appears in print may not be available in electronic books.

Sussman, Henry.
    Around the book : systems and literacy / Henry Sussman.
        p.   cm.
    Includes bibliographical references and index.
    ISBN 978-0-8232-3283-3 (alk. paper)
    ISBN 978-0-8232-3284-0 (pbk. : alk. paper)
    ISBN 978-0-8232-3285-7 (ebook)
    1. Criticism.   2. Social systems.   3. Literature—
Philosophy.   4. Books—History.   5. Books and reading—
Sociological aspects.   I. Title.
PN98.S6S87   2011
002.09—dc22

                                        2010033985

Printed in the United States of America
13 12 11   5 4 3 2 1
First edition

To the students of Yale University at all levels,
in solidarity and with deep appreciation.

CONTENTS

ILLUSTRATIONS

The book you are about to read is the product of a lifetime spent both in freely consorting with other books and in negotiating a rich and diverse, if not comprehensive panoply of systems. The latter have included systems primarily familial or communal, legal, technological, and cultural in their primary impact and thrust. They have been organized over time in order to regulate, within the jurisdictions I have inhabited, such phenomena as political and economic life and opportunity, travel and residence, public order, domestic cohabitation, education, and aesthetic and sexual expression.

The intense and volatile loop in which books and systems are involved in mutual communications, feedback, and revision and adaptation is by no means obvious or intuitive. Systems would at first glance seem inimical to books, especially to ones of cultural elucidation and critique. In their very architecture, they would seem to foreclose the expansive proliferation of logical, speculative, scientific, imaginary, informational, and skeptical possibilities that such books barely manage to contain within their bindings. Systems, by the same token, would seem to annex books among the other things and phenomena that they regulate, characterize, order, select, and, through multifarious methods, efficiently or not, bring under control. This striking dissonance, which is also a communications highway for needed messaging, is both the starting point for the following study and an investigative topography that it will not abandon.

I spend a disproportionate amount of my time and life's blood (*qi*, in Chinese medicine, as we shall see in Chapter 8) in circulating among and between various systems. I am hardly alone or unique in this regard. These in turn play a decisive if not absolute role in calibrating the possible qualities and outcomes of the interactions in which I am involved. Time and experience have conditioned me, in no irrevocable way, concerning what to expect from my systemic interchanges. Some obvious examples of systematically nuanced interactions with the world include: the parameters of collegiality and friendship, where these relations, stemming from very different sectors, overlap and interchange, as well as where they do not; the role of professionalization, not only in structuring my interactions with my colleagues and the work we share but as a template, submerged or not, for other associations I entertain but do not associate with vocation and livelihood; what my acknowledged role vis-à-vis the cycle of (biological) reproduction both demands and withholds from me, whether this relation is defined by marriage or not, whether it is legal or not.

My shuffling or scrolling between the particular social subsystems crystallizing around and impinging on my "official" or documented life in large measure defines me and any singularity or distinction I can claim. This relentless surfing also perforce earmarks me as nomadic, homeless in the broadest sense of the term. Regardless of the extent of my real-estate holdings, of my claim or lack of it to a fixed abode or address, I am congenitally homeless to the degree that I rarely, if ever, dwell in the convergence of the communicative and sociocultural systems with which I chiefly and characteristically interact. The sheer multiplication and dissonance of the respective systems renders me an alien, transient, a "temporary," without benefits, within each system with which I intersect. As I have elsewhere suggested, this drift in my systemic interactions, whether accompanied by physical travel or dislocation or not, combined with my ongoing cybernetic hookup to all time zones in the world, places me in a permanent state of jet lag.[1] Jetlag, along with its signature jarring senses of dissociation and dislocation, becomes one of the most compelling figures for contemporary consciousness.

All the while wandering from system to system, I spend a substantial portion of every working day occupied with the storage and translation into different electronic file formats, whether text, photo, video, or audio, of material that I either compose myself or download from that immense brain or database known as the Worldwide Web. The brunt and authentic significance of memory and translation has, in recent years and by dint of this technological evolution, shifted from being between national languages, dialects, and other linguistic idioms to residing between, on the interface between different operating systems, media languages, and displays. I cannot overlook the compelling parallelism between my personal homelessness, the significant periods of time I spend in transition, negotiating the *sequence* of the significant subsystems of my existence while plainly residing in *none* of them, and the endemic homelessness of the data I access and program in my personal effort to come to terms with and make sense of the experiences and artifacts of cultural devising I have happened to encounter. The data, material, or text that I generate, assemble, and archive hovers, as I do, between a range of potential media and applications, resting squarely or definitively in none of them. If the foregoing has established anything, it should be the considerable time and effort we collectively marshal, whether by necessity or choice, to deal with the systematic dimension and organizations of our interchanges with the world.

My particular reaction to the systems defining, placing, supporting, and impinging upon me is the generation, collation, and production of a book, something that could not begin to transpire without the concerted and most welcome assistance and collusion of a publisher, an editor, and readers. As will become clearer in Chapters 8 and 9, every concerted book of poetry, fiction, philosophy, history, theory, and critique can only derive its rationale from serving as a release valve installed contrary to the intransigence of a closed system or systems. My book, like any other in its domain, justifies itself through the freshness and defamiliarization it hopes to introduce into established traffic patterns of epistemological organization and interpretative and rhetorico-linguistic usage. Any creative interpretation or reassessment surfacing in my book hovers at a cusp between the confirmation and violation of well-established theoretical and methodological contracts.

The set of codes and understandings militating for the scoring, compilation, and dissemination of my book may well be "creative" or improvisational, within the framework of the academic institution that spawns it. The social foundation of such an institution largely inheres in the ethos of creative problem solving and innovation it instills in its students and reinforces on the part of its faculty, researchers, and staff. This does not, however, make my book, as it travels outward from its immanent scene of writing and reception, immune to constraints emanating from systems different from the one that accords universities their hegemonic role. My book may be offensive, not only because of its subject matter or approach, but because of its potential reverberations with the social networks to which I belong. It may be an intellectual coup but a social, political, moral, or aesthetic disaster. The book embodies the potential for instigating an opening or release

in too established and entrenched systems, but as an informational and social phenomenon, it is liable to judgment, sanction, or oblivion as rendered
by every system on whose sensors or screens it registers.

★

It is only a few weeks since we lost J. D. Salinger—who incited several
generations' dedication to the book medium. That his public profile has
again captured the spotlight saves me from "all that David Copperfield kind
of crap" regarding my own relationship to books. I have been preceded in
my lifelong obsession with them by the likes of Laurence Sterne, Marcel
Proust, James Joyce, and Walter Benjamin. I have been taught on too many
registers to name by Richard Macksey, a book collector whose rapport with
Walter Benjamin, had an encounter ever taken place, would have been intense and immediate. Macksey's own collection, lovingly arrayed in his library in a house on a quiet street to the north of the Johns Hopkins
University campus, gave me a graphic sense of the networks of books that
form once the lines of one's interests and preoccupations are drawn. In the
wake of all this, does the world really need another detailed rendition of
how books, during one's early years, became magical companions and transitional objects of the most inspiring and later productive pedigree?

My own initiation into the interconnected community (or network, or
rhizome) of books therefore needs little in the way of telling. I remember
rainy evenings at the Lovett Branch of the Free Library of Philadelphia, on
Germantown Avenue, in the company of Hugh Lofting's Dr. Doolittle, the
Victorian Harry Potter. I had been ferried there by my single mom, as she
gathered and dropped off her own ongoing reading. The unforgettable aura
that pervaded my early readings and that has persisted since was indubitably
heightened by the failure of one of the great social systems, marriage, at
least in terms of its impact on our particular family. We lived on the margins
of that great historical U.S. city, not far from the branch library.

The hub of the Philadelphia library system, on Logan Circle, was the
site of my first semi-serious research and the reports that grew out of it.
The central branch of the Free Library was a bookish kind of place; the
highest tech it offered was an immense globe in the monumental history
and social sciences reading room. The Free Library, as I first surveyed and
took advantage of its archival and informational riches, was above all analog.
I look forward to my next visit home in order to discover the high-tech

addition that has been planned for the central branch, which was, along with other collections and museums in Philadelphia, among my earliest homes away from home.

I spent a lot of time on my own during those years of growing up. The urban density of Philadelphia was on a manageable scale for a fourteen-and fifteen-year-old, who could explore the riches of Center City at all hours of the day and night. Beginning with those years, I was catching the monuments of global art cinema, from *Rashomon* to *Blow-Up*, in houses strung along those downtown streets. My activities as a young *flâneur* suited me well to the academic life, a regime calling for a split personality, at least in one basic sense of the word: the need to flourish amid rapid alternations between the amiability demanded by teaching and collegial and administrative life, and long periods of the isolation and silence, in several senses of this word, requisite to thinking and writing, particularly as these processes became embroidered by the wonderful philosophy, critical theory, and psychoanalytical theory to which I was exposed during my graduate studies.

At an intellectually vibrant state university, over a twenty-year period I performed every administrative function, from student recruitment to acting as dean. Apart from teaching itself and its implicit demand to recast complex aesthetic and theoretical material in an intelligible but still open and suggestive way, my intellectual life was sustained by withdrawing into books and into my running commentary on issues and artifacts that I found compelling during research leaves furnished by a number of sponsors, among them NEH, the Rockefeller Foundation, the Fulbright Commission, and the Camargo Foundation, and by the sabbatical leaves provided by the University at Buffalo. Wherever I happened to be during these leaves, including Camargo's amazing residence in Cassis, Bouches-du-Rhône, I was always also, to some degree, in downtown Philadelphia, wandering in and out of the Free Library.

I would improvise, over the years, odd images for this meandering, often interrupted, and radically nonlinear encounter with auratic books, films, and paintings that was the leading thread of my life. I thought of this encounter, and the ongoing voice-over that it produced, as an open-ended bicycle ride.

As I withdrew, about the beginning of the current century, from twenty years as chair of a small but dynamic comparative literature department and service in the dean's office that administered it, the trajectory, modus operandi, and writings of Benjamin reemerged as the model of what I had left to produce. I had been introduced to them years before, as a beginning graduate student, by Carol Jacobs, who herself had encountered them in a seminar of Paul de Man in Zurich in the late sixties. Benjamin, of course, by submitting and then preemptively withdrawing a somewhat incomprehensible overview of Baroque tragedy and the allegory that powered it to the philosophy faculty at Frankfurt as his Habilitation thesis in 1925, was deprived thereafter of the stability and concentration that would have accrued, along with institutional service and forced collegiality, from a conventional academic career. In the wake of this certain rejection and involuntary recalibration of plans, Benjamin embarked on an unbroken, inspired illumination of his age and the compelling artifacts that were its primary symptoms. He wrote about Western core concepts, food, fashion, and forgotten children's books. He submitted stunning—because largely unpredictable—critique on a vast range of literary and critical producers. He explored, in a philosophically rigorous way, the potentials embedded in the emergent mass media of the twentieth century—including books. Once exiled for good in Paris, he wandered into Proust's favored brothels and nightspots. Never once imagining that his writings would someday occasion a vast collective enterprise of scholarship, commentary, and even adaptation, he scored his meandering urban trajectory with the most telling, that is, shocking commentary that he could muster. His concentration and critical integrity derived from the trajectory he had launched and was sustaining, not from academic or related institutional affiliations.

In a certain sense, all works of literary criticism are books about books. The present one is odd only in that it circles around exceptional instances in this history, and in so doing inquires into the current limit cases and prospects for the book medium. It sets out from a sense that books cannot productively be studied in isolation from other media, whether material or electronic, analog or digital. Indeed, if the long-standing tradition of the book as a leaved folio with inscription, engraving, or printing on its surfaces finds itself currently in a state of radical and rapid transformation, it is equally true that the template of the book, its relation to the reader of being grasped physically, gazed at, and radiating back a textual display remains the core architecture of our encounter with electronic media. We thus exist in a double bind in our passionate, bemused, and long-standing relation to the book. My present endeavor is, I believe, a constructive and hopeful version of this double bind, whose architecture and fallout will be explored in relation to Gregory Bateson's seminal systems theory. The book medium, as the preeminent format or display of information and thinking, being often of an "inconvenient" or disconcerting nature for its readership, is always in a state of crisis, of immanent disappearance or hostile restructuring, yet we are not about to give it up, above all its transfer of information and its face-to-face communication, deeply mobilizing linguistic, visual, and cognitive faculties all at once, anytime soon.

Books, even before the Gutenberg revolution in printing, had largely foreseen and explored their graphic potential and limits as a medium. A visit to any of the great European monastic libraries, in Dublin or St. Gall, for example, will make this clear. These privileged repositories include among their holdings works composed in columns and with marginal annotation, also with super- and subscript, works with charts, illustrations, ornamental calligraphy, footnotes, endnotes, indices, and bibliographies. The books leaving the most indelible imprint on the following essays tend to be ones already at the far reaches of book technology and book culture. This is because of the rich theoretical complexity that they embody. Sei Shōnagon's early work *The Pillow Book*, as well as the film version by Peter Greenaway that it engendered, Mallarmé's radically new poetic page, Benjamin's *The Arcades Project*, Derrida's *Glas*, and the comix art inspired by Franz Kafka all make cameo appearances in the following pages. Precisely because they both perform and test the limits of books and book culture, none of these works is particularly easy to read. But they radiate, through and through, "the fascination of what's difficult."

The following chapters are unavoidably affected and structured by the theories of criticism and of books that I personally encountered during my long education and training as a literary critic. I've been exposed to: the Frankfurt School; Freudian, Lacanian, and object-relations psychoanalysis; structuralism; post-structuralism; rhetorical reading; and, above all, deconstruction. From them I extrapolate a critical project in which there is a pointed engagement between the language of the Prevailing Operating System (more on which in the following chapters) and the crystallizations of artifacts so telling and auratic as to be symptomatic, whether literary, conceptual, or discursive in nature. Critical work, over the decades of my involvement in it, has staged a clean and suggestive followthrough from the language-critical elucidation of artifacts to the parameters of certain conceptual models or operating systems (hence the subtext of systems theory prevailing throughout the following book). In several senses, the following study hinges upon the feedback loop, circular, but with digressions, direct, but also indirect, between books and systems. The approach to this core problem is of necessity recursive. I have already broached it in this Preface. We encounter it again in Chapter 1 and in Chapters 7 through 9.

Not only are the artifacts I have selected as the topics of this investigation at the limits of books and therefore at the limits of comprehensibility; the philosophers and other theorists on whom I rely for their respective "takes" on or snapshots of the Prevailing Operating System in its stately but unavoidable progression often make difficult reading. Philosophical work standing up to the test of time often does so by dint of its clarifications of the key terms and wiring facilitating the Prevailing Operating System at distinctive moments of its configuration. Memorable theory tinkers with the POS while exposing hitherto neglected sources and models. These come particularly to the fore as cultural history retrospectively tracks the POS's often jarring mutations, upgrades, or downgrades. Epoch-making philosophers such as Derrida, Deleuze, Guattari, Anthony Wilden, Niklas Luhmann, and Bateson sometimes make exasperating reading, but a contemporary status report on the prospects for the book medium relies heavily on the daring of their uncanny insights and vision. In the following pages, I will ask readers to contend with such theoretical constructs as faciality, the rhizome, the supplement, and digital as opposed to analog organization, in the assurance that there are tangible repercussions to these and other theoretical constructs in the architecture of and prospects for books, including the ones that we might still simply pick up and take by hand. The intentional eccentricity of some of the theoretical terminology I invoke is essential to the full continuity between conceptualization and cultural exegesis defining theoretical performance at the present moment.

As I go forward with my own longstanding critical intervention, I find it easier to group larger segments of work under fewer theoretical operating principles. In retrospect, I cannot overestimate the centrality of Marshal McLuhan's "the medium is the message"—or rather, an extension of this dictum leveraged by the great traditions of contemporary critical theory —to the following book. Beginning in the initial chapter, I will argue "the display's the thing." The display in which information and its script are configured—with irreducible visual among other components—is as crucial to its impact and outcomes as anything substantial it might have to import. As I've argued earlier in my 2005 *The Task of the Critic*, script's display, whether as handwriting, printing, graphic icons, or electronic traces, is, more often than not, more pivotal to its meaning and signification than its argumentation or conceptual engineering, or its placement within the marketplace of academic paradigms. In this vein, I would argue as well that the transposition and translation between diverse media operating systems is currently, willy-nilly, more at the heart of any comparative literature discipline than interactions between different national languages or ethnic, theological, or national cultural traditions.

If there is a second overarching viewfinder in the current project, it tracks the sea changes and directional shifts accruing from many current theoretical paradigms. The suspects include deconstruction, psychoanalysis, gender studies, postcolonial theory, and cultural studies, viewed from the domain of systems theory. Extrapolating to the level of systematic organization allows investigation to focus in two ways: either on the overarching constitution of diverse systems, the factors of continuity and variance tempering their persistence and their rapport with the surrounding environment (as in the work of Bateson and the theorists of turbulence and chaos); or on the possibilities for mutation and reconfiguration allowed by such dynamics as autopoiesis, artificial intelligence, and virtual reality (this in a second generation or reprise of general systems theory).

Groping toward the level of systematic dynamics allows the rigorous testing of one of the great predictive observations of the current age, made by Bateson, in the environmental studies he conducted toward the end of his career. He brilliantly argued that the simultaneous ratcheting up of the major developmental subsystems in any culture (e.g., economic, industrial, and urban development, military aggression) will result in the overheating—and eventual implosion—of the overall organization, say, a national state. The ethics of systems management, then, entails the installation of release valves, the application of brakes, to the exploitative and extractive motives that will overheat society in its socioeconomic, political, and diplomatic spheres. I think it fair to assert that the great waves or paradigm shifts in theoretical thought over the past half-century have held in common the ethos of implanting release valves in *conceptual* systems and simulacra in process of burnout or implosion, on the verge of devolving into "white dwarfs." This is, precisely, what could align such diverse theoretical climates as rhetorical reading, deconstruction, gender theory, and postcolonial theory in parallel impact, as in common cause.

Surely such large collective endeavors as psychoanalytical theory or deconstruction devote a considerable share of their activity and findings to the meticulous testing, exegesis, and dissemination of the diverse cultural materials on which they found themselves. But in assuming the task of this rigorous analysis, this penetration to the level of the programmatic language animating different artifacts and arenas of cultural striving, such enterprises as deconstruction, gender studies, and postcolonial theory share one major bearing in common: they configure themselves as release valves for social and cultural systems only too capable of totalization, hyper-regimentation, exploitation, overextension, and repression. This is precisely the interstice at which the fate of the book medium, as the still-preeminent zone of cultural programming and inscription, grafts onto systems analysis. It is within the purview and under the auspices of the book that the noise of the system, "the rustle of language," and the static generated by the machine as unavoidably as its repetitive order achieve their annotation and enter the archive of cultural recognition and memory.

The third overarching torque in the present project is a belief that it is highly advisable for those who engage in critical encounters with the broader cultural environment to access the "cybernetic unconscious" accruing from the countless hours they spend online, surfing the Web, and translating different databases into electronic impulses. These activities, especially the time we spend in uploading, downloading, and saving textual, mathematical, visual, and musical information and data, are in themselves rich in theoretical apprehension and nuance. The rendering explicit of the conceptual operations we perform while working on computers is yet another challenge that cultural psychoanalysis, particularly as performed in universities, museums, and other public collections and archives, would do well to address. Wherever possible, the following chapters attempt to extract the figurative richness already embedded in the cybernetic operations we repeat so often and so mechanically that their deeper conceptual implications disappear. From "Prevailing Operating System"—my contribution to a list that would include Antonio Gramsci's and Ernesto Laclau's "hegemony," Louis Althusser's "Ideological State Apparatus," and Foucault's "episteme"—to a rhetoric of displays, screens, scrolling, feedback loops, information, input, and output, which I deploy wherever possible, the following chapters are motivated by a design to render cybernetic processes explicit in reading, writing, and critique, to harvest the nuances made possible by technological parlance and imagery.

★

This book has benefited from the inspiration and support of innovative colleagues, from leaves furnished in spring 2008 and spring 2010 by the University at Buffalo, and from the encouragement and support given freely by Fordham University Press, particularly by its Editorial Director, Helen Tartar, whose good offices and efforts have been decisive in the appearance of my last three books. I am deeply fortunate that my collaborative relationship with her has deepened with each of these projects. There are several chapters in the present volume that simply did not achieve their final form and full potential until she, with unflagging acuity, insight, and creativity, significantly reformatted them. That this could happen is only by dint of her involvement in the full spectrum of publishing, from her fascination with the source texts and theoretical frameworks involved to her commitment to specifications of design and lucidity of style. All this sets the standard in humanities publishing.

The wider ecological and systematic dimensions of the book have been immeasurably illuminated and qualified by my collaborative work, with Tom Cohen and Mary Valentis, in establishing the Institute for Critical Climate Change (IC3). Cohen, in particular, has positioned the forums and publications of IC3 on the strategic cutting edge of contemporary critical theory, a dynamic and to some degree unpredictable place, where theoretical turbulence and unpredictability can intervene in the open-ended string of catastrophes—ecological, economic, resource related, demographic, technological, informational—defining our historical moment. Under the auspices of IC3, I have seen or heard work surely decisive to the perspective of *Around the Book*, by, among others, Cohen, Valentis, J. Hillis Miller, Eduardo Cadava, Joan Copjec, Rey Chow, Catherine Malabou, Sarah Elder, Chris Hedges, David Pitt, Randy Martin, Haun Saussy, Samuel Weber, Gil Anidjar, Robert Markley, Bruce Clarke, Justin Read, Alan Shelton, Jim Swan, James H. Bunn, Mike Hill, and Thomas Bass.

I continue to learn and profit in invaluable ways from teachers who have assisted me intellectually since the outset of my career. I somehow manage to keep up with J. Hillis Miller's astonishing rate of cultural and critical production. I learn significantly from each of his new publications. Richard Macksey continues to accord me the personal as well as intellectual welcome that became my primary model for pedagogy, my ongoing ideal of what a university can offer. On too many fronts to name, Carol Jacobs continues to teach me, as ever. The University at Buffalo Comparative Literature Department and the Yale German Department have been nurturing, stable intellectual homes from which to navigate a multiplicity of theoretical and cultural tacks.

One of the most illuminating and surprising tangents in my program as a life-long learner has been the studies I did over the late 1990s and into the first decade of the century at the Ohashi Institute, New York City. Under the spiritually uplifting as well as mind-expanding guidance of Sensei Wataru Ohashi, the Institute trains its students in a particularly mindful and delicate form of shiatsu massage, grounded in the traditional meridians and points of Chinese acupuncture. Not only was I able to gain insight into and mastery over some of my physical manifestations through these studies, the discipline's emphasis on flow and gentleness of movement introduced me to a system of knowledge and intellectual practice markedly different from any with which I was already familiar. The practice demanded constant stretching, crouching, crawling, and sitting patiently in a cross-legged position. I can't say that the practice came easily to a fifty-something man from a culture in which movement and flexibility are not exactly core values. But my studies, by dint of Sensei Ohashi's mastery, patience, and deep intuition into the human condition, and also through the profound curiosity and tolerance of his students, who wonderfully helped each other learn, were nothing less than revelatory. My initiation into Ohashiatsu will be particularly evident in Chapters 8 and 9, but as an encounter with systems of knowing, health, and spiritual value markedly other than the Western philosophy, theology, and literature into which I was inculcated, I owe my training at the Ohashi Institute, as well as practice conducted over many years at the Himalayan Institute, Buffalo, a great deal in the very *possibility* for the present book.

It should not surprise the readers of this book that, even given the unbelievable archival and bibliographic resources now available online, I continue to frequent libraries. The James Blackstone Memorial Library in Branford, Connecticut, is, in its charm, successor to the Lovett Branch as a

book-filled substitute home. On a material level, I have consistently benefited and drawn considerable support from the University Libraries at the
University at Buffalo and from the Sterling Memorial Library and Beinecke
Library at Yale. I have found their staffs to consist, uniformly, of highly
resourceful and unrepentant cultural literacy workers.

★

A version of Chapter 5 has been published in *Diacritics* 39 (2010); of Chapter
6 in Stuart Barnett, ed., *Hegel after Derrida* (London: Routledge, 1998); and
of Chapter 7 in *Modern Language Notes* 122 (2007). An abbreviated German
translation of Chapter 3 has appeared in the *Kafka-Handbuch*, ed. Bettina
von Jagow and Oliver Jahrhaus (Göttingen: Vandenhoeck & Ruprecht,
2008).

Around the Book

ONE

Introduction: Around the Book

Holding Patterns

There is something congenitally troubled about the history of the book. Always at its wit's (if not virtual) end, the book is forever actively engaged in its own disappearing act. Even in its various heydays (the papyrus scroll, the illuminated manuscript, the movable-type imprint, the mass paperback), the book informs of, even illustrates, its immanent outmoding. The reader is free to speculate along with the rest of us about the full cultural and environmental impact of Amazon's Kindle and related electronic reading and scrolling systems: whether these spell a definitive break in the history of the book or a cybernetic extension and supplement. Yet there is some persistent core (or binding) to the book, and its storied history holds on. Might this tenacious trunk or tree-line of the book be material? Perceptual? Cognitive? Textual? Whatever its exact nature, the book persists, through all the medium's technological updatings, through all the theologico-political regimes in which it appears, each with a distinctive ideology of representation, information, communication, and archiving.

Or is it rather that we—creatures of culture—can't let go of it? Over the generations of structured communal life, amid civilizations of astonishing diversity, the book has become a good object, a magical thing, a fetish, an information source, and a commodity. When the book is publicly burned during political upheavals, civility and its very possibility have gone awry.

There is something irreducibly tactile in our relation to the book[1] It confronts us at eye level. It addresses us face-to-face. The oppositions, repetitions, and incipient madness of a dissipated, textual counter or interlocutor, characterized by Gilles Deleuze and Félix Guattari as a face, are written into it. The book into which we gaze is a mirror with no silvering, whose readout is as diffuse and unfathomable as our familiar images of ourselves—and identities—are not.

The face, to Deleuze/Guattari in their Capitalism and Schizophrenia diptych, the face poised opposite the book in the process of reading, while the book is held in the hands, is the insignia of a decisive break with animality, one coinciding with regimes of subject-formation and representation centered in the signifier. The face, as a mega-anthropological index and icon, marks a particular formation they associate with the overall relegation of minorities of many stripes, whether by their outsider, ethnic, racial, economic, chemical, or zoological status, to bare or marginal being. In this case, what they call deterritorialization underscores a devolution of human traits into animal ones, such as snout and mouth: "Once again, a whole intensive map must be accounted for: the mouth as a deterritorialization of the snout (the whole 'conflict between the mouth and the brain,' as Perrier called it); the lips as a deterritorialization of the mouth (only humans have lips, in other words . . . only human females have breasts, in other words, deterritorialized mammary glands."[2] Note that even here, the deterritorialization by which the nose is no longer the snout runs right over the body: the face is by no means limited to the head.[3] On the surface, the centrality of the face seems to be but another element in the spectral mapping that Deleuze/ Guattari effect of the decisive flows propelling late capitalism onto its overarching double binds, inducing its volatile defense mechanisms to attack its own infrastructure and configurations. But in view of our interest in the book, both as culture's evolving and unwinding papyrus scroll and an embattled institution always on the verge of annihilation, the pivotal role assigned faces and hands in labor and production as well as in reading, marks these corporeal elements as uncanny signifiers, as Lacanian *objets petit a*,[4] whose trajectory it is incumbent upon us to pursue.

One of the striking early lessons that Deleuze/Guattari's exposition of faces teaches us is that a face doesn't have to look like one in order to assert a quasi-universal specter of surveillance and integrated psychological processing. It may indeed be at the threshold level, where faces reduce to graphic icons or schematic caricatures of themselves, that they attain their full symbolic value: "the face is part of a surface—holes, holey surface, system."[5]

> Significance is never without a white wall upon which it inscribes its signs and redundancies. Subjectification is never without a black hole in which it lodges its consciousness, passion, and redundancies. Since all semiotics are mixed and strata come at least in twos, it should come as no surprise that a very special mechanism is situated at their intersection. Oddly enough, it is a face: the *white wall/black hole* system. A broad face with white cheeks, a chalk face with eyes cut in for a black hole. Clown head, white clown, moon-white mime, angel of death, Holy Shroud.[6]

Even, and perhaps all the more so, at the level of an iconic visual infrastructure the face is a format for contrast and a *zone* of totalization and propriety: "Faces are not basically individual: they define zones of frequency or probability, delimit a field that neutralizes in advance any expressions or connections unamenable to the appropriate significations."[7] We take readerly delight in the radical migration and displacement of such constructs as faciality and flow itself, to new and ever-surprising contexts of elucidation that they make possible. The poetic fragmentation at the end of the citation immediately above signals the invasion of the face, both as indexical icon and as modality of signification and subjectification to cultural constructions as far afield as ghosts in general, Pierrot, and the Holy Spirit. In their discursive design, Deleuze/Guattari practice the flow that they teach. The interconnectedness of the world that they are in a constant practice of deconcealing harkens back to an epoch when schizo disorientation and drug-induced oceanic sensibility left their mark on the public sphere: "Each morning we would wake up, and each of us would ask himself what plateau he was going to tackle, writing five lines here, ten lines there. We had hallucinatory experiences, we watched lines leave one plateau and proceed to another like columns of tiny ants. We made circles of convergence."⁸ We will have occasion below to survey why Deleuze/Guattari recast the book into a rhizomatic map or assemblage as part of their effort to configure a systems theory animated by flows of information, desire, materials, and money—as crucial factors of motion and process—working in tandem (or in serial), with permeable membranes or interfaces between them. (This as opposed to centralized psychoanalytical and socioeconomic processing, determined by unitary critical features, such as capital or sexuality.) What intrigues us at the present juncture is how the materiality as well as the inscriptive dimensions of the book, as something that we hold and as something that grasps us back, something that physically addresses and oddly mirrors us, belong to culture's uncanny face-to-face (not tête-à-tête) with itself, as Deleuze/Guattari choreograph it.

It is in its struggles of alienation and overshadowing with its own head that the face, the very face up to which we hold the book, which in turn does nothing if not stare back, reveals its true mettle:

> Although the head, even the human head, is not necessarily a face, the face is produced in humanity. But it is produced by a necessity that does not apply to human beings "in general." The face is not animal, but neither is it human in general; there is even something absolutely inhuman about the face. It would be an error to proceed as though the face became inhuman only beyond a certain threshold: close-up, extreme magnification, recondite expression, etc. The inhuman in human beings: that is what the face is from the start. It is by nature a close-up, with its inanimate white surfaces, its shining black holes, its emptiness and boredom. Bunker-face. To the point that if human beings have a destiny, it is rather to escape the face, to dismantle the face and facializations, to become imperceptible, to become clandestine, not by returning to animality, or even returning to the head, but by quite spiritual and special becomings-animal, by strange true becomings that get past the wall and get out of black holes, that make *faciality traits* themselves finally elude the organization of the face.⁹

Uncanny specter of the face as it outstrips and overruns the very head that it is attached to, both addressing the animal and barring the path back to the animality with which it might otherwise be conflated! The "white wall/black hole system" is not merely a schematic of the face increasing in its uncanniness the farther it travels, whether culturally or referentially. It marks the "becoming-writing"¹⁰ of the feature, rendered in graphic shorthand marking us as "most human" or, in the bankruptcy of this trope, connecting us to our evolutionary "home" or origin in the biosphere, the animal domain. Deleuze/Guattari's figure of the face resides, then, in the interstice between the Lacanian insignia of psychic otherness and the deconstructive spectrality of writing. It peers out, beckons, and threatens from every possible angle and dissolves every reassurance that we might pose, like Perseus's shield against Medusa, against it, whether the familiarity of the human or the essential sympathy, goodwill, and protection of animals. The face, then, is not only the icon of the *facet* of the human anatomy that *reads*, taking in information in all its flows; it is a cipher of *writing*, of what is, in its multifarious notations and registers, being taken in and processed.

Deleuze/Guattari are by no means unmindful of the hand-eye coordination without which the curious process of reading would not occur. The hand not only holds or positions the book, or information display, face-to-face with the visual sensor or input. The hand has followed a line of descent analogous to that of the face. It has been deterritorialized from the tangible rapport with the physical world it maintained as claw. As bionic tool, as the preeminent "natural" anatomical feature to have assumed instrumental (or implemental) functions, it inputs the information that is now the domain of work and striving. The hand has become digital in multiple respects:

> In this context, the hand must not be thought of simply as an organ but instead as coding (the digital code), a dynamic structuration, a dynamic formation (the manual form, or manual formal traits). The hand as a general form of content is extended in tools, which are themselves active forms implying substances, or formed matters; finally, products are formed matters, or substances, which in turn serve as tools. . . . For with the hand as a formal trait or general form of content a major threshold of deterritorialization is reached and opens, an accelerator that in itself permits a shifting interplay of comparative deterritorializations and reterritorializations—what makes this acceleration possible is, precisely, phenomena of "retarded development" in the organic strata. Not only is the hand a deterritorialized front paw; the hand thus freed is itself deterritorialized in relation to the grasping and locomotive hand of the monkey.[11]

The hand grasps the book that is the database, the tablet where the flow of information has been temporarily stratified and suspended, so that it can be taken in by the face. The spectral face of the book demonically stares back at the visage decoding its flows, an iconic configuration marking a hopeless alienation from the human as well as the animal. The face of the book and the face of the reader glare back at one another in the uncanniness of undecidable reciprocity. The reader might imagine that she can pick up or put down the book at will, but in fact the facial configuration of its reciprocal attentiveness is on duty 24/7. The book grasps us at least as firmly, unrelentingly, and inhumanly as we grasp it.

Books *hold back*, they take us by force, they will not let us go. We access them by reaching out for them. They surely touch us back at some profound and visceral register, or they would not have enjoyed their storied, detailed, technologically rich, and still undiminished run.

Now and seemingly forever, books have us in a quandary. In order for us rigorously to take it in, the book detains and isolates us to a degree for which we are never fully prepared. At recurrent intervals, we are done with the discomfort and other importunities demanded by books. We casually toss them out, as Freud's grandson Ernst does the spool toy at the outset of *Beyond the Pleasure Principle*, only to retrieve them, and this with no small degree of anxiety. It is a game of *fort-da*, here today, gone tomorrow, that we parry with books, at considerable cost, as the deeply engrained conventions of sociability forever remind us.

Like little Ernst, we are forever pushing the book away, stupefied by its tedium, overwhelmed by its sheer informational mass, inured to its unrelenting incitement, taken aback by its minute detail. At the same time, the book never lets us go: it lures us with unintended tangents and wrinkles; it intrigues by strategically holding back the information it would take to satisfy the curiosity it has piqued; it captivates us with the inexhaustible figures and tropes that it sets into play; it generates the astonishment enabling us to prevail, from time to time at least, in the unbearable attentiveness it has demanded of us. In the violent, unmarked segues between the derision and rapture it draws out of us, the book is a classic instance of the uncanny object, Melanie Klein's breast to the infant, somehow both very good and very horrid at the very same time.[12] The terms of this meta-ambivalence, a doublethink in the very engine room of doubling, have been rendered meticulously explicit to us since Jacques Derrida's seminal and signature extrapolations of logocentrism, in such texts as *Of Grammatology* and "Plato's Pharmacy."

As Derrida notes in the former work, to which we will have occasion to return, the book is constitutionally poised between its ethical and political bankruptcy as the "good book," what he calls "the book of Nature and

God's writing"[13]—the codex of ideology, both in its idealist and moral facets—and its ongoing reconfiguration as the prevailing display case of linguistic dynamics and processes. There is a direct follow-through between the mixed emotions to which a work of extended linguistico-cultural articulation gives rise in its readership, in those who literally hold it in their hands, and an about-face, a terminal double bind, transpiring at the far reaches and amid the deep structures of time itself, as this dimension is grasped by the likes of Proust and Heidegger. The book has always reached its abject ending, epitomized by the Hunger Artist's progressive deterritorialization to the outer margins of the circus midway in Kafka's parable.[14] But it is just as constantly positioned in the avant-garde of a new medium, one that will, with messianic fervor, redeem its lapsed promises. It is not by accident that Derrida announced the turn to a project of rigorous grammatology, a rerun of the history of ideas with a critical difference, from the perspective of linguistic priority, contingency, singularity, materiality, and disfiguration, as "The End of the Book and the Beginning of the Letter":

> The end of linear writing is indeed the end of the book, even if, even today, it is within the form of the book that new writings—literary or theoretical—allow themselves to be, for better or worse, encased. It is less a question of confiding new writings to the envelope of a new book than of finally reading what wrote itself between the lines in the volumes. That is why, beginning to write without the line, one begins also to reread past writing according to a different organization of space. If today the problem of reading occupies the forefront of science, it is because of this suspense between two ages of writing. Because we are beginning to write, to write differently, we must reread differently.[15]

The book is, at the outer reaches of its cultural mission, both signal and vehicle of a relentless feedback loop implanted in time itself. At the moment of yet another crisis in the history of the book, it is incumbent on us to explore the current book system in whatever specific openness it affords.

Binding

Even with its polymorphous variety, then, and the full spectrum of its bearings or tendencies—ranging from orthodoxy, canonicity, and ideological authority, on the one hand, to poetic invention, pornography, and critique, on the other—the book, as an element of cultural infrastructure as well as an informational object or scored thing, remains *binding*.[16] It is one binding element within the overall contractual understandings making up a culture, while also being a scriptural or print-culture data store architecturally buttressed and in certain respects sequenced by a physical binding. As an artifact of cultural memory and invention, the book stands at the convergence of its sociological status as an embodiment of cultural relations to history, science, and the Imaginary, and its technology as an informational compendium, a material thing, or possibly a system. So deeply imbricated are the book's design and other technical features in its sociocultural impact as a medium that the results of any attempt to precipitate these two bibliographic dimensions out from one another could only be reductive or obfuscatory.

Wherever the book plays, then—and in its cultural dimensions this can be in societies with little documented history of formal book making—its tradition and culture are *binding* in several senses. Perhaps by dint of the concerted sociocultural collaboration that book production, dissemination, reception, distribution, and storage demand, there is no dearth in the bibliographical subcategory known as the history of the book. The ongoing chronicle of the book's history and evolution, its production and technical conditions in varying places, continues unperturbed through whatever fluctuations the book medium undergoes on the stock markets of cultural interest and utility. Like U.S. show business and comics art (I refer here to the tradition of collation volumes), the ongoing general culture of the book is in a strong position to earmark and document its crowning developments, achievements, and transformations.

Here I do not want to recapitulate the impressive and growing body of scholarly treatments of the history of the book in its multiple (aesthetic, technical, material, media, sociological, epistemological, and ontological) dimensions.[17] Rather, I hope to inquire into the dimensions and contours of the book under the prevalent sociocultural and technological conditions within which I write—as it happens, from Berlin at the outset of 2008.

It seems to me binding, in other words, incumbent upon me to reformulate the umbrella under which the conceptualization, writing, production, dissemination, and reception of the book transpire in the current constellation of conditions, especially cybernetic technology. I realize that this is at most the virtual configuration of the understandings and metaphors converging on the book, which will no doubt be supplanted by further evolutions in a long and formidable, although in certain respects binding, history. When I consider to what degree this recapitulation or recasting of the book consists in merely a semantic or syntactical translation, a hopefully felicitous importing into the actuality and culture of the book the languages of cybernetics, cognitive science, and systems theory, I haphazardly gain some significant insights into the workings of cultural history itself. To adapt or update is to translate, in Benjamin's sense of the term, effecting linguistic defamiliarization and freshness rather than a seamless transition, whether between media or national languages and dialects, an activity prevalent in the margins and other apparatuses of illuminated manuscripts and other multiregister and hypertextual books.

So what, then, is the status of books at the current moment of inscription? Under actual conditions, a book counts first and foremost as a zone of intensity in textual processing, effecting both the scrambling of its input and the possibility of surprise or uncertainty in its output.[18] The input into the book is itself a conjunction: between the books and other data serving as a baseline for its synthesis, regardless of the degree of authorial consciousness or deliberateness involved, and the reader's uploaded programmatic power (i.e., methodological paradigms, philosophical and critical theories) and erudition (or reading store) allowing for its decoding. The book's output is the open set of mutations—thoroughly accidental recombinants, inferences, hitherto unthinkable hybridizations and coincidences—first rendered possible by the scramblings and other reformattings that have managed to transpire under its aegis, that is to say, within the idiomatic neighborhood or zone of its intervention.

The effectiveness of the book, its moment, is then tantamount to the mutations or the surprises that it leaves in its wake. In terms of contemporary systems theory, the book, having submitted to the architecture and social and aesthetic contracts of its binding, and having therefore capitulated to some central organization or operating system (even only implied) and to some linear sequence, is a closed system fanning out into an open one. No one has been more attentive to the simultaneous, multiple pressures bearing down upon the systems of writing, technology, and society, including the book, than Anthony Wilden. Indeed, the contrary forces that he tracks and decodes in his communications theory both push systems toward contraction and withdrawal and militate for their learning and adaptation. In Wilden's account of the flows of systematic inputs and outputs, negative feedback is not only a source of likely thwarting and suppression, it is also a potential interface to the Real. Positive feedback, by the same token, not only offers reinforcement and encouragement, it can add to the simultaneous pressures for expansion and accumulation, pushing an otherwise viable system over the brink into implosion. If there is any ethical thrust to Wilden's principled pursuit of the vicissitudes of systems, it is toward the "open" as opposed to the "closed" (book or) system. Yet Wilden is too astute a philosopher and critic to advocate a linear or monolithic opening:

> In order to characterize this process, we can use the methodological distinction between the closed system and the (reproducible) open system to set up the following circular definition: All systems produced by any form of evolution are (1) reproductive (capable of supplication with or without errors), and (2) adaptive (they have memory and are capable of learning at the homeorhetic level and of evolution at the morphogenic level). Such systems are characterized by emergence in two senses: (1) the emergence of new characteristics as the system follows the "program" of its instructions (e.g., the child's coming to speak, sexual maturity, the "working-through" of mercantilism), or (2) the evolution of the system to a stage of complexity or organization not forming part of its "program" (industrial, technological, political revolution).[19]

This paragraph nevertheless offers a blueprint for Wilden's particular model of an "open book": one that learns its alternatives and future prospects even in the process of its inscription; one that evolves the *épistème* of which it forms part; one that adapts to its environment as multiple interpretations and critical bearings spin out from between its covers. With uncanny prescience, Wilden ushered in the age in which such innovations as cybernetic databases and the Worldwide Web would supplant the book as the reference instrument of record. Even in its electronic constitution, the Worldwide Web is contained, on one flank, by a binding. This could be considered either the "hardware," in its arbitrary materiality, by means of which we access, enter, and store information, or the code of social conventions determining our electronic personae and our online behavior. The Worldwide Web and its allied cybernetic phenomena may be bound to the same degree as a traditional paginated book, but the rhizomatic electronic universe that a computing device accesses is vaster and even more "open," in terms of data capacity and storage, also in the ramification of links *between* pieces and stores of information, than the most elaborate encyclopedia ever printed.

This is the juncture at which to broach the peculiar resonance or feedback by which the fate of books is deeply and inextricably wired into systems. When we think of systems, such features as distance and mechanical repetition, an overarching, often accumulative generality and impersonality, unrelenting momentum, and obliviousness to environmental or local repercussions almost invariably come to mind. What systematic features or qualities could invade and co-opt the book, both as cultural phenomenon and as tradition, given the book's own pronounced momentum—starting from the fact of its binding—toward complexity, labyrinthine proliferation, and involution of themes, motifs, storylines, and implications? Vice versa, what perverse tendencies or opportunistic viruses could bring the precise design, rigorous logic, and ethos of disinterest and impartiality underlying the very architecture of systems to a debilitating halt? How might books figure in this? Have we not witnessed, throughout the twentieth century and into the current decade, an opening within the most pretentious and overdetermined systems in the form of a *turbulence* blurring the very outlines and boundaries of bureaucratic and conceptual processes, an *undecidability* pre-empting the very possibility of definitive outcomes, and a multiplicative *scrambling* of the messages and communications that systems purportedly route and decode? We encounter this opening to systematic structure and function, this salutary destabilization in the momentum of large-scale social and logistical organization, as systems embrace their "second-order" components and epiphenomena: autopoeisis, turbulence, even, to a certain degree, chaos.[20] The destabilizations in the system of global finance are merely one of the most glaring current instances of "first-order" systematic presumptions, whether of "free" markets or "equilibrium," being bracketed or left in the lurch. We can regard this large-scale economic drift, with its disastrous impact on employment and labor, either as the aftermath of turbulences and X-factors hitherto unaccounted for or as the surfacing of unsound financial practices that have outlasted their protective camouflage. The book, contained by nothing more physically or symbolically daunting than its binding, has from its outset embraced the contingencies and proliferating network of possibilities now unavoidably invading, disrupting, and tempering large-scale systematic organization.

Literature emerges as the unlikely suspect defining the common stake in which books and systems explicitly and indirectly share. A literature happens when a body of cultural interventions, linked through adherence and reference to shared aesthetic, technical, conceptual, and referential contracts, aspires to the dimensions and parameters of a *medium*. My assumption here, one that I have explored in detail in earlier work, is that innovative and improvisational work, in such spheres as science and environmental design as well as in the arts, operates as the limit case to contractual understandings through which cultural productions and their practitioners obtain indispensable comprehension and recognition, through which they are spared obscurity.[21] Both theoretically and historico-culturally, literature furnishes the display or screen affording the dominant systems of ideology, might, social administration, and technology, what might be termed the Prevailing Operating Systems[22] of their place and moment, their most vivid and unfettered registration or tracing. Literatures, then, are not merely the basis for a broad range of institutions configured around cultural and aesthetic contracts, those concerning, for instance, sciences, technologies, historical phenomena, and art forms and their notable practitioners. They open the very arena, platform, or space for the critical registration, recapitulation, analysis, and reimagination or supplementation of the prevailing systems of actuality.

Yet it is within the binding of the book that a constant, desperate, and hopefully *critical* grappling with systems of power, ideology, technology, and the social administration of goods and resources can transpire. In them, critical and theoretical bearings can come to coincide with books' transmission, display, and registration of Prevailing Operating Systems.

The core irony of the uncanny, almost unspeakable coincidence and collusion between systematic ordering and domination and the open-ended textual-theoretical proliferation of possibility within the framework and medium of the book was not lost on the enduring literary programmers of the twentieth century. I think especially of those, from Conrad through Kafka, Proust, and Joyce to Borges, who addressed an increasing regulation and systematization prevalent in the subcomponents within and between technologically "advanced" and economically exploitative societies.

Concerning meditation on the charged and fated interplay between books and systems on the plane of literature—in this case, the literature of fictive improvisation—I think first of Kafka, then of Borges. Within the framework of this inaugural chapter, I ask only: What could the representations of corrupt institutions (say, the Law in *The Trial*), of broken machinery littering the fictive landscape (the instrument of execution in "In the Penal Colony"), or of hopelessly incoherent communications media, such as the Castle telephone network, be if *not* figures for the shambles of contemporary social and technological systems? Only within the binding and the contract of the book can these elaborated figures of pronounced incoherence, indeterminacy, and inefficiency—deep-lying constituents of the social and ideological systems from which they derive—find their disclosure and display.

As I see it, the phenomenon and tradition of the book mark and house the convergence between open-ended fictive invention and entrenched systematic homeostasis or self-perpetuation. The following chapters revel in the different playful interventions a series of dedicated writers—from Mallarmé to Derrida and the contemporary literature of the graphic novel—have improvised and ponder a range of systemic impasses, extending from Gregory Bateson's double binds to how the selections inevitably executed by Niklas Luhmann's social systems are used in their processing of differentiation.

Perhaps no programmer of fiction has ever pointed to the divide at which systems cannibalize the books that are their only possibility for expression and display—while books, wittingly or not, aspire to the rigor and compass of systems—more compellingly and inventively than Jorge Luis Borges.[23] Borges's *ficción* "Tlön, Uqbar, Orbis Tertius" can serve as an elaborate introduction to his labyrinthine fictive universe, engaged in a constant calculus of literature's expansive performances and possibilities. If my long-standing fascination with a single figure from "Tlön, Uqbar, Orbis Tertius," a heavy metal cone that a character encounters at the culmination of a series of "intrusion[s] of the fantastic world into the real one," has never abated, it is because of the pointed particularity and open-ended expansion coinciding in the very geometry of the cone. The architecture of Borges's Library of Babel, which houses not only every book but every possible articulation of nonsense as well as sense, is by design absurdly arbitrary and overdetermined.

The book, in view of its strategic place in an entire tradition of media and communications and of its complex, to say the least, rapport with systems and their theory, has entered an age of expanded opening and openness.

Deleuze/Guattari, as they usher in a contrapuntal movement to the centralized administration, logics of accumulation, and proliferating subjectification at the heart of late capitalism, anoint the book as a rhizome, not a hegemonic system but an "acentered" one.[24] Such an arrangement, what they call an assemblage, is

> a short-term memory, or antimemory. The rhizome operates by variation, expansion, conquest, capture, offshoots. Unlike the graphic arts, drawing, or photography, unlike tracings, the rhizome pertains to a map that must be produced, constructed, a map that is always detachable, connectable, reversible, modifiable, and has multiple entryways and exits and its own lines of flight. It is tracings that must be put on the map, not the opposite. In contrast to centered (even polycentric) systems with hierarchical modes of communication and preestablished paths, the rhizome is an acentered, nonhierarchical, nonsignifying system without a General and without an organizing memory or centralized automaton, defined solely by a circulation of states.[25]

Deleuze/Guattari conjure up a conspicuously phantasmatic rhetoric of systems as they configure the rhizomatic networking one of whose tangible artifacts is books. This scenario may seem a far cry from the musty branches of large urban library systems and from the reduced-price bins at bookstores where we may have experienced some of our most intimate and memorable encounters with books. But Deleuze/Guattari's blatantly contrived language of assemblages and rhizomes allows them to launch a parasitic counter-history of the book, one tinged by digital organization, virtual reality, and cyberspace. Annoying as their rhetoric of systemic assemblages and strata may be, as a capitulation to the lifestyle and regime imposed by computers, machines whose highest virtue is their versatility as complex appliances, this contrived language marks a constellation of factors and phenomena that cannot be overlooked in any viable status report on books at the present moment.

Processing. Zones. Intensity. Display. Translation, as Benjamin developed the term, meaning as much a hopeless interlinear predicament between media, between linguistic operating systems, as between languages, whether ascribed to nations or to other geographical divisions. Drafts, never in a final form, always as adaptations, between one version of formulation and another, unknown one yet to come, in a state of endless revision. These are among the terms in which the prospects for the book may be couched at the present juncture.

Before Deleuze/Guattari appeal to the machinic assemblage, with its parastrata, epistrata, and ecumenical processor (*ecumenon*) as an architecture allowing for the mapping of late capitalism's schizo inclinations and flows, they invoke the book as the paradigmatic instance of a rhizomatic cultural construct. The book is nothing less, to them, than culture's capacity to extricate itself from the domination and hegemony of the face. "Dismantling the face is the same as breaking through the wall of the signifier and getting out of the hole of subjectivity."[26] Their type of book distinguishes itself from the "root-book,"[27] the canon of lineages, seats of power or centrality, patrimonies, and declensions, whether of political rule, logic, or grammar. A rhizome is an open-ended site of expansion and processing, whose power is measured by its moments of intensification. Their long-standing interest in the philosophy of Henri Bergson is in part motivated by a critical transformation that he effected in the conceptual hardware driving the systematic machines of German idealism, which I characterize in Chapter 7 below as "computers without hardware," from a hierarchy into the wiring of ongoing processing, continuous feedback loops, and the self-reference of artificial intelligence. Deleuze/Guattari's notion of the rhizomatic book follows Bergson's suit in shifting emphasis from the conceptual agents operating within experience and the division of labor over which they preside to the constant programming and reprogramming in which the cognitive processors are engaged, above all, in the provisional pictures and memory stores that they generate.[28]

Bergson is by no means above redeploying, in his accounts of memory and the role that perception and images play within it, some of the conceptual usual suspects on which Kant and Hegel, albeit differently, have poised considerable architectural weight: entities including perception, understanding, and experience. We'll also be exploring the rhythmic, tonal, and geographic differences between the wiring of the Kantian and Hegelian systems in Chapter 7. What becomes palpable in Bergson's reprogramming of these entities is their role in a far more fluid circuitry:

> Thus there is supposed to be a rectilinear process, by which the mind goes further and further from the object, never to return to it. We maintain, on the contrary, that reflective perception is a *circuit*, in which all the elements, including the perceived object itself, hold each other in a state of mutual tension as in an electric circuit, so that no disturbance starting from the object can stop on its

way and remain in the depths of the mind: it must always find its way back to the object from where it proceeds.[29]

In recasting what he calls here "reflective perception" as circuitry, Bergson has taken on an epochal task, one that he goes about fulfilling with the multiperspectival insight and poetic delicacy of Proust, whose *Remembrance of Things Past* conspicuously displays his thinking in a narrative showcase. In both Kant and Hegel, perception (*Wahrnehmung*) betokens a major transition between the extremely low-level, possibly nonexistent processing at the level of sensation (*Sinn, sinnliche Gewißheit*) and the dazzling achievements of inference and theorization that can be made just one level up, in understanding (*Verstand*). Especially as Hegel orchestrates the transition, perception, at its peak, precipitates out of itself "smart sensation"; this is the foothold for all subsequent achievements of *Verstand* in the realms of abstraction and theorization. With a modicum of abstract conceptualization implemented perceptually, in other words, the panoply of "higher" achievements in Western science—medicine, law, religion, morality, government, art, and so on—are free to kick in. When Bergson declares that the tradition of "reflective perception" can be rewired as circuitry, he is taking on, with a modesty bespeaking Proust's exemplary composer Vinteuil, a monumental piece of the nineteenth century's epistemologico-historical baggage, the evolution from utterly unschooled sensation to the highest confections of reason, whether these conceptual stations of the cross exhibit their "pure" or their worldly emanations.

There are specific features to the circuitry that Bergson inaugurates within the machinery of Western epistemology, ontology, and phenomenology. It is continuous and self-referential, the last in the sense that it closes upon itself in what we now call feedback loops. Paradoxically, Bergson's move toward an open system of phenomenology is rooted in cognitive circuitry's capacity to close, to form self-referential, that is, feedback relations. Whether Bergson successfully accounts for the creative dimensions of perception and memory or not, the circuitry of his two-phase memory system incorporates its other in the form of lower-level processing. Environmentally, Bergson's cognitive circuitry recycles: it refuses to divest the lower levels of processing, which become, in effect, templates for the creativity that his philosophy dares to embrace and celebrate. The tendency of Bergson's processes, whether of perception or memory, to break down into counterposed phases or subsystems may be a carryover from German ideal-ism's dialectical thrust. But what is crucial in the rewired circuitry that Bergson announces is that the opposed models, say, rote learning and mem-ory-based intuition, are held in suspended, dynamic tension; relatively open and closed models of thought keep learning from one another. The results of this confrontation between differential models of perception, recollec-tion, and storage held in suspended animation by Bergson's circuitry may well be unpredictable. It is in this sense that Bergson's counter to the Kan-tian, Hegelian, and systematic architectures reaches out toward artificial in-telligence, toward circuitry's capacity, in the continuous flux, reiteration, and critical review that it sustains, to improvise creative mutations:

> It must not be thought that this is a mere matter of words. We have two radically different concepts of the intellectual process. According to the first, things hap-pen mechanically and by a merely accidental series of successive additions. At each moment of an attentive perception, for example, new elements sent up from a deeper stratum of the mind might join the earlier elements, without thereby creating a general disturbance and without bringing about a transformation of the whole system. In the second, on the contrary, an act of attention implies such a solidarity between the mind and its object, it is a circuit so well closed that we cannot pass to higher states of consciousness without creating, whole and entire, so many new circuits which envelop the first and have nothing in common be-tween them but the perceived object.[30]

As he continues to find words for the updated and streamlined circuitry that he installs in existing conceptual architectures, Bergson couches the crucial encounter between closed and archaic models of memory, perception, and thinking as the mutual infiltration of relatively deeper and more superficial strata of processing. Indeed, where Bergson opts for the relative disinterest of an above all philosophical account of memory and experience, his thought veers closest to psychoanalysis in its meticulous attention to cogni-tive "deep roots." Bergson's circuitry, having plumbed (as in psychoanalyti-cal working though) to the very foundations of thinking and memory, resolves itself in what Deleuze/Guattari will call the "smooth space" of asys-tematic apprehension. In advance of Deleuze/Guattari, then, Bergson brings his writings to the plane of smooth space, having retraced the entire vertical sweep of striation. In this passage, a fluid modality of attention, what Bergson calls "attentive perception," bubbles up, allowing new cir-cuitry to form in what had been a mechanical chain of associations. It is precisely at the point of the crystallization of new circuitry within established systems themselves, whether under the auspices of feedback, autopoeisis, artificial intelligence, or, in Luhmann's theory, the difference between system and environment,[31] that critical theory's concerns with inscription, supplementarity, and archiving mainline into the discourses and investigations of cognitive science. There is no more critical interface for literary studies and the humanities in general to survey and elaborate as their attention is increasingly drawn to the frontiers not so much between national languages and traditions as between media, systems of representation and communications, and the operating systems that power them.

The prospects and format of the book are central to a sequence of systems formats (or discursive computer simulacrums) arising in the positivism and hardwiring (hard in every respect) in Kant and Hegel and culminating in Deleuze/Guattari's polymorphic strain and resistance to the intersecting centrisms and overdeterminations of late capitalism. This project of cognitive and phenomenological modeling has surely also passed by way of Bergson's rigorous yet poetic dynamism, philosophy's embrace of its own recursive processes of recollection, creative feedback, and autopoiesis. Within this sequence of speculations, projections, and corrections, the book no longer needs to be a manufactured thing, made mostly of paper and cloth. It needn't be a physical object. Its relation to people needn't be determined by their touching or grasping it. They needn't turn its pages. The book will, rather, be defined by the processing going on within its compass or its zone. And its impact will be articulated or gauged according to the levels of intensity encountered by psychic process, aesthetic experience, or the unfolding of being. Bergson's recalibration of metaphysics toward creative processing and programming will reorient the viewfinder of philosophical sensibility toward such phenomena as the vividness of a memory or the rapt intensity of an aesthetic encounter with an artifact. We who have been uplifted by following a sequence of readings on interpretation and exegesis, whether by Adorno, Benjamin, Gadamer, Blanchot, Barthes, de Man, Derrida, or Miller, can add to this list of book recalibrations the following proviso: in the wake of Bergson's shifting the field of phenomenology and the linguistically acute corrections to his corrections added first by Husserl, then by Heidegger, the awakening of metaphysics to the dynamism and evanescence of experience also inheres in the closeness of close reading, the intensity of the reader's engagement with the book. Everything that

Bergson says about the relation between perception and recollection under conditions of "pure perception," for him an out-of-body experience, applies to the encounter between reader and book, particularly when the latter's impact and effectiveness is defined by the pitch of the processing that it prompts: "There is only a difference of intensity, or more generally of degree, between perception and recollection."[32] As time capsules both of creative improvisation and cultural memory, books only gain in intensity as they persist beyond perception, as they enter the critical phases of their processing.

To Deleuze/Guattari, intensity—of reading and decoding as much of flow and acceleration—remains a pivotal parameter of the rhizomatic assemblage characterizing information as well as market forces and migrations under the umbrella of late capitalism. The architecture of parastrata and epistrata that they devise to describe late capitalism's assemblage, its intersection of counterforces at full throttle, sounds whimsical, yet monitoring and decoding the intensity of the flow, tracking its play within the inconceivably expansive and open-ended manifold of forces, is one of the primary functions that they attach to the assemblage's autopoietic architecture. Late capitalism, even at the extreme of its violent and incoherent expansion, is a book, whose indeterminacies demand to be read, among other things, as intensities and accelerations:

> Nomadic waves or flows of deterritorialization go from the central layer to the periphery, then from the new center to the new periphery, falling back to the old center and launching forth to the new. The organization of the epistrata moves in the direction of increasing deterritorialization. . . . The more interior milieus an organism has on its own stratum, assuming its autonomy and bringing it into a set of aleatory relations with the exterior, the more deterritorialized it is. . . . Every voyage is intensive, and occurs in relation to thresholds of intensity between which it evolves or that it crosses. One travels by intensity: displacements and spatial figures depend on intensive thresholds of nomadic deterritorialization (and thus on differential relations). . . . Every stratum operates this way: by grasping in its pincers a maximum number of intensities or intensive particles, over which it spreads its forms and substances, constituting determinate gradients and thresholds of resonance.[33]

Late capitalism, as Deleuze/Guattari figure it in the above citation, is an organism, whose skin and deep layers communicate with one another, whose DNA is not oblivious to environmental factors. The reference book to the terrestrial mega-system is an atlas in which the marginalizations and stampedes of disposable persons, seasonal labor, outcasts by dint of unforeseen changes in political regimes, can be registered. The legibility of this map, flowchart, and visual display, which is perforce a book, is contingent on a readout of shifts and differences in intensity. The power of the reading or decoding of the flow, whether of people or signifiers, can be ascertained only at and above a minimum threshold of intensity.

Deleuze/Guattari's figure of the rhizomatic book thus stands at a way station between Bergson's radical rewiring of hierarchical and rigidly evolutionary models of perception and cognition and the challenge facing us today: to understand our own processes of exegesis, critique, and inscription in terms of the wiring, circuitry, and architecture of the Prevailing Operating Systems under which we think, work, process, and collectively devise political solutions to the conditions and problems besetting us. The prevalent thrust of their recasting of the book in the direction of what we currently call "open systems" is unmistakable:

> A book has neither object nor subject: it is made of variously formed matters, and very different dates and speeds. To attribute the book to a subject is to overlook this working of matters and the exteriority of their relations. It is to fabricate a beneficent God to explain geological movements. In a book, as in all things, there are lines of articulation or segmentarity, strata and territories; but also lines of flight, movements of deterritorialization and destratification. Comparative rates of flow on these lines produce phenomena of relative slowness and viscosity, or, on the contrary, of acceleration and rupture. All this, lines and measurable speeds, constitutes an *assemblage*. A book is an assemblage of this kind, and as such is unattributable. It is a multiplicity—but we don't know yet what the multiple entails when it is no longer attributed, that is, after it has been elevated to the level of a substantive. One kind of a machinic assemblage faces the strata, which doubtless make it a kind of organism, or signifying totality, or determination attributable to a subject; it also has a side facing a *body without organs*, which is continually dismantling the organism, causing asignifying particles or pure intensities to pass or circulate, and attributing to itself subjects that it leaves with nothing more than a name as the trace of an intensity.[34]

This passage acknowledges the profound debt that contemporary intellectual work owes to the book, not only for its historically accruing contents and materials but as a rubric, a format, under which current reconfigurations of knowledge, pedagogy, archiving, and communications transpire.

Reaching outward to the epistemological mutations proceeding from the cybernetic sphere, this particular reformatting of the book is not only imaginative but timely. Within it is imprinted the entire set of cognitive, epistemological, phenomenological, and even physical conditions that we enter and negotiate in our multifarious daily encounters with computers, digital organization, and virtual reality. As apt and intuitive as Deleuze/Guattari's readout of the book under cybernetic metaphysics may be, it is merely today's chapter in an ongoing and open-ended history. The book medium will continue to challenge critics to register its transformations even while, under field conditions, they synthesize and post their interventions. To writing taking into the fullest possible account its own media and design parameters, strengths, and liabilities will fall the spoils of memory.

The passage is also a card catalogue or map of themes that in Deleuze/ Guattari's unique constellation of philosophical motives and flows configure around the book. Deleuze/Guattari appeal above all to the book as the blueprint for a database, what they call an assemblage, somehow incorporating the great processes of history, geology, and biology under the sway of a dynamic intellectual architecture. Deleuze/Guattari take upon themselves the task of devising an assemblage that can incorporate nomadic invasions, respond to the ebb and flow of historical deterritorializations and reterritorializations, and sustain a bewildering multiplicity of differential accelerations and intensities (e.g., of the sort that Marx first noticed coinciding amid the economies of large-scale industry).[35]

The book, as they set it out in this passage, is a Janus figure, facing at once its own dismemberment and the orders and totalities that it summons into being. The book, speaking out of both sides of its mouth (an instance of Deleuze/Guattari's own faciality), addresses at the same time the strata of hierarchy and the state of abject disarray (they attribute it to the body without organs) to which we regress when we penetrate to the far side of social convention, the redundant propositions of identity, the familial division of labor, and the communal attitude and bigotry that make us who we are. (Indeed, full-blown schizophrenia, to the degree that it can be intuited by those capable of rendering an account of it, and drug-induced delirium are two of their prime examples of the experience of the body without organs.)

Deleuze/Guattari introduce us to the dynamics and cross-currents prevailing on both sides of the book binding and coming to a crux in the reader's grasping hands. Their rewiring of the prevailing motives and momentums of Western philosophy has been prescient. At the same time, new forces, figures, metaphorics, and factors have entered the fray since the inscription of Capitalism and Schizophrenia. A number of these loom particularly large as of the present critical notation: the theories of systems, games, and chaos; the outreach of the Worldwide Web and the incredible storage capacity afforded by computers; evolution, hybridization, and mutation in the mass media; a number of environmental contingencies, whether Hurricane Katrina or global warming, indicating that geology is not so stable and critical resources not so plentiful as during the lives of Deleuze/ Guattari; such human factors as endless war and the corporatization of what were once governmental functions. These developments, too, need to be added to the mix. Slowly, incrementally, perhaps with the deliberation of geological time, the architecture, wiring, and assemblage of the book advance, always departing from themselves.

Parchment, Skin

It could be argued that Walter Benjamin's Angel of History not only barrels headlong into the historical bad weather incessantly proceeding from Paradise.[36] It situates itself precisely in the binding of the book, one of whose pages displays the impossible sequence of cultural transformations it has undergone simply to come into being. En face is the page that would deliver all the secrets of the continuously emergent prevailing system of flows, production, and material allocations under which we labor, if we could only decipher it. It is in the very nature of this Prevailing Operating System (some have called it capital; others the world economy; still others Empire[37]) that its full disclosure requires more critical discernment than can be collectively marshaled at any given moment. Yet this system, for all the furious labor emanating from the full panoply of disciplines and fields struggling to decode it, always reserves at its margins the uncertainty and chaos forcing its "users," wherever their home on the social spectrum, into a reactive stance. In these figures, criticism is the life-or-death rearguard battle to unveil and illuminate the Prevailing Operating System that cannot—by dint of its irreducible margin of illegibility—ever be completely won. In its unfolding, the system whose constraints work a tangible impact upon the lives, aspirations, knowledge, and processing of everyone, animals as well as people, implicated by it, *strategically* withholds elements of the data required for its discerning exegesis.

The British filmmaker Peter Greenaway's *The Pillow Book*, a screen adaptation of Sei Shōnagon's courtly work of the same title, dating from the Heian period of Japan, deftly sits astride the multiple divides that it straddles: (1) the "classical," if not ancient, in narrative and the postmodern in fictive experimentation; (2) the heyday of book culture in the Heian court as merely one of the shifting moments of its glory and the ongoing demise of books or their transition into something else (Greenaway underscores the novel's translation not only into cinema but into the computer-generated "moving windows" that are a hallmark of his cinematographic style); and (3) the manners of propriety and deference indispensable to the functioning of a cloistered ruling elite—even in a polygamous context—and the sexual free-for-all that is the contemporary counterpart to the Heian empire. As a cadre of gifted scholars and readers has indicated, notable among them Norma Field and Edith Sarra, the intense mannerism and varied palette of sexual relationships in the Heian court made it first and foremost a visual panorama and generator of critical sensibility.[38] As elucidated by the above critics and others, Murasaki Shikibu's *Tales of Genji* and *The Pillow Book* are social panoramas in which relations of seeing and being seen, voyeurism and exhibitionism, are of supreme importance, no doubt fueling the courtly obsession with fashion, fabric, and the design of domestic implements and ornaments. The politico-sexual pyrotechnics of the gaze in these enduring memoirs, one worthy of elucidation, in a distant age, by Lacan or Girard, suggests a profusion of sociosexual attitudes, postures, and alternatives in the Heian court. The interaction between men and women within its domain remains a complex partnership and dance. The proliferation of roles played by court ladies, like the elaborate hierarchy of official ranks and functions, in no categorical way relegates women to the status of sexual pawns. *The Pillow Book* takes elaborate pains to establish the indispensability of the feminine sensibility in the interpretation and critique of courtly mores and conventions and of Japanese culture (particularly against the backdrop of Chinese civilization, from which it heavily borrowed), and in establishing an affirmative metaphysics of nature and life. As we shall see below, the intense visual sensibility already embedded in this protonovel of the Heian court deals Peter Greenaway an unusually strong hand as he sets about the cinematographic adaptation—with significant shifts of theme and motif—of Shōnagon's text and the socio-visual scenes from which it emanates.

In the Heian court, pillow books were a hybrid genre: field notes and social reminiscences composed by the courtesans who embodied the cloistered coterie's claim to distinction through detached observation. It is not by chance that freer than normal sexual expression, in an experimental social environment, would lead to a fascination with the inscriptive process and with the media of writing. The Heian pillow book is what we would now call a cybernetic notepad, wired into a scene of intense social regulation and scrutiny whose outgrowth is the experimental testing of conventional sociosexual mores. The theoretical program through which we can understand our sexual activity as a *medium of expression* as opposed to the essence or stamp of identity, the hard and fast correlative to social affiliation, or as the defining feature of subjectivity has long been available. We can with perfect legitimacy articulate our erotic behavior as semiological exchanges within the field of the sexual sign, negotiations within the scene of the Derridean trace, or, as fluctuations within the global reach and tidal rhythms of Deleuze/Guattari's flow. Polygamy afforded great latitude for sexual coupling in the Heian court, but, oddly, lines of communication between men and women not formally affiliated with one another were not always open. In many acts of communication, as chronicled in *The Pillow Book*, men and women relied on oblique means of expression: costume and sharing poetic citations, for example. The very medium of the pillow book indicates Heian courtiers' sophisticated understanding that writing and its media are as integral to sexual expression, whether falling within or outside the binding of official registry, as the erotic ministrations themselves.

In several senses, then, it is by no means accidental that Greenaway makes Shōnagon's classical novel the occasion for his fullest filmic exploration of and elaboration upon the book medium,[39] or that the configuration of the film, cinematographically and technically encompassing the book's transformation into the contemporary (i.e., computer-enhanced) other, corresponds precisely to the ongoing historical predicament and teletechnic format of the book. The reading of this film, then, is highly symptomatic of the current stresses and strains, impasses, and, yes, crying needs encountered by the book medium.[40]

In its firsthand account of the doings and predicaments of a lady-in-waiting to Teishi, a Heian empress who had risen from the position of consort, *The Pillow Book* brings into play three crucial elements that will be of considerable moment to Greenaway's screen adaptation. The first is an elaboration of the codes, stylistic as well as moral, instrumental to the distinction, power, and mutually affirming self-reference of the ruling elite. The most striking instance of the novelistic account of the spectacle as well as the systematic parameters of the Heian court is the exquisite attention the narrative lavishes on official costume, ranging from the pointed hats worn by the courtiers to the color-coded layering of the robes befitting certain ranks, courtly functions, and events. The description in Section 99 of Her Majesty's ensemble on the occasion of the visit by the Shigeisa (Genshi, her younger sister) sets the tone for several of the extended costume descriptions, with special attention to the effects of layering and the interplay of tints:

> Her Majesty wore two plum-pink cloaks, one a heavy brocade and the other with a raised brocade pattern, draped over three scarlet robes of glossed silk. "Plum-pink is really best when set off with deep purple," she remarked. "It's a pity I can't wear it. No doubt at this stage of the season it would be better not to wear plum-pink, but on the other hand I think a colour such as spring-shoot green would be awful. Does this go with the scarlet, do you think?" Despite these concerns, she looked utterly splendid.[41]

Teishi's character comes alive in this section in a way not always permitted by Shōnagon's scenographic narrative. She joins Proust's Duchesse de Guermantes and Mme Verdurin as one of the grandes dames of literature.

The meticulously composed and described color-coordinated ensembles transform their wearers into ciphers or characters in the unfolding message or text transpiring around them, in which they constitute merely one seme or thread. Surely in different ways, Roland Barthes, when he offers an account of Japan as a culture inflected by a particularly high level of semiological acuity in *The Empire of Signs* and Derrida, in noting the extreme sensitivity to veils, webs, tissues, fabrics, and texts in Mallarmé's poetics, echo Shōnagon's intuition of the continuous Möbius strip linking dress to the synthesis of texts throughout *The Pillow Book*.[42] A precise attention to fabrics and their function and interrelation links the book's service as an aesthetic record of the Heian court's inner workings and imprint to a second key component, a celebration of the written medium as the consummate refinement that "wires" the court, facilitating both its internal functions (e.g., marking events and rituals of imperial significance, establishing itself as a bastion of culture at once exemplary and utopian), and driving relations of a domestic and foreign nature within the parameters of a feudal state. Poetry—both Chinese source texts and their Japanese adaptations—functions throughout the novel both as a database of shared knowledge and as a shorthand—a meta-language if you will—that can abbreviate and accelerate what might otherwise devolve into ambiguous messaging. The novel takes great care to point out the multiplicity of situations, often of a complex and delicate nature, that are resolved, adjudicated, or otherwise resolved simply through the application of script technology. One is reminded of how, in section 77, the character Shōnagon restores her reputation, gratuitously smeared by Captain Secretary Tadanobu, by dashing off at the end of his letter, with a piece of charcoal, a classical line of Chinese poetry: "Who shall come visiting this grass-thatched hut?" The line derives from a classical Chinese poem, Bo Juyi's "Alone at Night in a Grass-thatched Hut Beneath Lu Shan Mountain." Directed to a lady of the court, this classic line is at best a double-edged message: the solitary humble abode may well be a figure of sexual yearning, but the sexual availability of the real-life woman identified—literally and figuratively—with the hut makes her vulnerable to innuendo and prurient speculation. The recipient of the grass-thatched hut epithet, the Shōnagon surrogate, is, furthermore, constrained on several sides in her response to Captain Secretary Tadanobu's catty courtly innuendo. She is, for example, by Heian conventions of female deference enjoined from quoting the poem in its original Chinese, this language being designated as a male gender-specific medium of official transactions and communications. The fictive Shōnagon improvises a hybrid solution to her unduly bound speech act: she cites the classical poem, but in Japanese. This response catches its collective audience off guard (there is not even a pretense of confidentiality in Heian court correspondence). Not only does it set off a scramble on the part of her male interlocutors to recall the entire verse of which the line forms part; it transforms a tense situation, prompted by the invariably troubled phenomenon of communal gossip, possibly leading to the cessation "of all relations" between Shōnagon and Tadanobu, into a comic anecdote added to the court lore.[43]

> "So she sent it back!" he said, but as he spoke he looked more closely, and the next instant he cried, "Oh! How extraordinary! Whatever's this?" Everyone gathered round to look, and he made a great fuss. "What a clever rogue she is!" we said. "No, you can't really give her up."

"We then set about trying to add the first three lines of your poem, everyone urging me to take on the challenge, and we racked our brains over the task till it grew so late we finally had to give up the task. We decided that it would make a fine tale for future telling, at any rate," he concluded. "Your name has become 'Grass-thatched Hut,'" he added, and off he hastened.[44]

In its sustained attention to the shorthand that poetry affords the court, the novel configures itself as the "voice" or house organ of the written medium, which powers a prodigious refinement in sensibility that distinguishes the court as its ultimate raison d'être. Let one citation, albeit a striking one, characterizing "Startling and Disconcerting Things" (section 92), serve as an umbrella for the full-fledged, unmotivated eloquence repeatedly breaking forth in the text, its poetic compression itself evidencing its speaker's posture of detached and informed critique:

> It's horribly startling and disconcerting to stay up all night waiting, certain that someone will come, and then finally begin to give up thought of him as dawn breaks, and drift off to sleep—only to wake up with a start when a crow caws suddenly outside and discover that it's broad daylight.
>
> Someone with a letter that's to be delivered somewhere shows it to a person who shouldn't see it.
>
> Someone pins you down and commences laying down the law about something that means absolutely nothing to you, without your being able to get a word in edgeways.
>
> Spilling something is always very startling and disconcerting.[45]

The catalogue of poignantly observed exasperations here is artfully composed, linking sexual longing to the violation of discretion, to the coercive application of pat morality, to unavoidable physical mishaps. The impromptu list bemoans physical, sexual, communicative, and moral contingencies, particularly ones resulting in discomfiture, if not outright shame. Yet in setting this miniature tour de force of articulation on display, the persona Sei Shōnagon places "her" voice at the service of a major paradigm shift in sensibility, conflates her "self" with the emergence of a critical discourse within writing technology. Sei Shōnagon is also unabashed that the femininity both of her purview and of the literary genre with which she is interacting plays a substantial and irreducible role in the emergence of a critical discourse of courtly culture and life.

A third inescapably prominent feature in the work's landscape or perspective is, then, its enunciation of an irreducibly feminine counterpart to the male exercise of governmental power and sexual initiative. With considerable rigor, the book pursues certain of the upshots (or shadow events) to happenings on the male stage of power in the feminine sphere. "Stage" is a by no means gratuitous designation for the setting of many of the court's interactions. Shōnagon's architectural evocations of the curtains and sliding doors dividing up the women's quarters along the outside corridors of the palace are unforgettable (sections 5, 20, 230). Such permeable dividers, preventing any possibility of privacy and putting discretion to a severe test, imply that women's housing, indeed the court in general, is by its very nature provisional. The preoccupations of the female retainers during their free time and the impact that royal movements have on their lives are depicted with particular vividness in sections 20 and 259, the latter detailing the various impacts of Her Majesty's move to the Nijō Palace on her household and retinue. In Section 178, we read how beside the point and tedious the formal question of social rank, a central concern among the male courtiers, becomes when applied to women:

> [178] Nothing is more splendid than rank. . . .
> Women, on the other hand, are certainly less impressive. Certainly an imperial nurse who attains third rank or the title High gentlewoman is of considerable importance, but she's already past her best, and what's so good about it after all? And most women never even get that far.

By giving voice to the feminine interests in the Heian court, Shōnagon articulates the supplemental configuration in which women—and their polymorphous relations of propinquity with male royalty and officials of the court—although subordinate, are indispensable to the court's very possibility. They literally reproduce the court on the bio-political level and are therefore key pawns in the complex kinship machinations through which Foucaultian biopower is exercised.[46] Indeed, the Heian court is an excellent example of how history in large measure inheres in the accounts of those who have serviced its sexual whims.[47] The persona Shōnagon lends voice to a constituency whose running account fades in and out of the official national and cultural histories. In so doing, Shōnagon reorients history and the narrative that is its software around the viewpoint of those who attend to ideology's manners, who service its current sexual tastes, and who write—particularly under the aegis of autonomy and disinterest.

Shōnagon's account of life in the Heian court is not a conventional narrative that progresses via the development of its characters but a nonsequential choral accompaniment to a way of life structured and even overdetermined by ritual. When we ask ourselves what makes *The Pillow Book* particularly rich for Peter Greenaway's cinematic adaptation and embroidery, the answer may well reside in its vibrant vocal and introjective qualities. The film adaptation rises to the challenge of translating the voices of aesthetico-perceptual refinement, achieved sexual expression, and scriptural finitude and diversity into a graphic cinematographic idiom. Even with the considerable twists that Greenaway introduces into the movie's story line, much of its achievement inheres in the polyphonic resonance that it establishes between book and film, between film and skin, and between film, skin, and letter, reminiscent of a tribute that Christian Metz paid to Alain Resnais: "In *Last Year at Marienbad*, the image and the text play a sort of game of hide-and-seek in which they give each other passing caresses. The sides are equal: Text becomes image, and image turns into text. This interplay of texts gives the film its particular contexture."[48]

Coining a term at the outset of semiotic film theory, *contexture*, Christian Metz gives notice that cinema, for all its visual formatting, its linear progression, the smooth surface of the film material, and the distance between the film image and the spectator is a medium very much concerned with and invested in textures and depths.

If we were to generalize Greenaway's lifetime achievement, we might say, among other things, of films such as *Prospero's Dream* and *The Cook, the Thief, His Wife, and Her Lover*, as well as *The Pillow Book*, that he introduced into the cinematographic image a depth and layering carried over from texts and fabrics and powered by cybernetic capabilities for windowing and hypertext. He synthesized a cinematographic practice, in other words, that spliced the full potentialities of book technology together with emergent facets and capabilities of cybernetics. He thus bracketed cinema between its foundations in the book and illuminated manuscript and the spectral simulation that these receive thanks to computer language. Since Greenaway's signature features, there have been more stunning achievements of special effects and more technologically advanced claims of cinema verisimilitude, yet for the moment, at least, we remain indebted to his consummate montage linking the medium paradigms contributing to textual sensibility and its critical articulation. In this sense, his work spans the deep historical structures of the book and its uncertain future.

Greenaway's film adaptation extends and deepens Shōnagon's earlier celebration of scriptural technology, while radically altering its narrative framework. Shōnagon's picture of Heian court life—her narrative repeatedly draws attention to its mission and capacity to evoke scenes[49]—is divided between several discursive functions, themselves abruptly and some would say chaotically spliced together. (This is a work that unapologetically puts on display its own internal montage.) Shōnagon's famous lists, comprising lyrical disruptions to a story line, irregularly alternate with the recounting of specific episodes, some fleeting, some elaborate, and many punctuated by narrative exclamations both reveling in aesthetic refinement and offering critical discriminations. The openness of this irregular, discontinuous, and to some degree fragmentary book medium, which we now situate at the epicenter of textual capability, does not necessarily make for an effective screen scenario. (The closest Western parallels to the Shōnagon classic might be some of the experiments in heterogeneous textual media of the eighteenth and nineteenth centuries, ranging from Swift's Menippean satire and Sterne's *Tristram Shandy* to the *Fragments* by the Schlegels and their *Athenaeum* cohort. The typographical improvisation in which, in different ways, James Joyce, Gertrude Stein, and the Surrealists luxuriate would rank high among the twentieth-century embellishments of this tradition.)

In order to effect the translation of an ancient work conspicuously about books and scriptural technology into a full-length commercial dramatic feature, Greenaway structures the film around a central love story. Nagiko Kishihara, a modern-day Shōnagon whose social milieu is the fashion world rather than the court, and her bisexual lover Jerome, who does translation work in Hong Kong, are the central couple. Nagiko's fascination with calligraphy, the link that she corporeally experiences and acts out between body writing and erotic experience, is not merely an attribute of her personality, as it is for the narrator of the Shōnagon classic. Her obsessions are, rather, a patrimony. They come to her by way of her father, a master calligrapher and book artist, whose initiation (or rather inscription) of her into a tradition of writing occurs at the outset of the film, when she is a young child. The film begins with his painting *congi* on her face, declaring human creation and gender differentiation an act of inscription. The father's recitation of a creation myth in which God inscribes each major feature of the human anatomy as he creates it is capped with a signature applied to the nape of her neck. According to the film-translation's framing myth, then, inscription, with all its beauty and complexity, is tantamount to creation. There is no more impressive *imitatio dei* than serving as a scribe and participating in the creation of books. This sacred body-inscription scene will be repeated twice in the film: as a celebration of the kickoff of Nagiko's deeply erotic liaison with Jerome and as the heritage that she bequeaths to her own young daughter as the action ends.

Not only does Greenaway galvanize the otherwise meandering reminiscences and impressions of the Shōnagon classic with a love story.[50] He insists on dramatic tension at every turn by ratcheting this up with a multifaceted and dialectically twisting revenge plot. It turns out that a powerful Japanese book publisher working out of Kowloon, also proprietor of Swindon Book Co. Ltd—identified in the film only as Yagi-san—has been Nagiko's nemesis throughout the film. Though in no way resembling the emperor of Shōnagon's *The Pillow Book*, Yagi-san occupies a central (Lacan would say phallic) position of power analogous to royal majesty. His sexual coercion of Nagiko's father early on cannot be concealed from the family. It becomes a homosexual primary scene that will be of critical moment to Nagiko's love relationship with Jerome. As a result of this exploitative and humiliating relationship, the father takes his own life during Nagiko's late childhood. Yagi-san goes on to conduct an affair with Jerome that will complicate and ultimately destroy her relationship with the latter. At the end of a film that challenges its audience with its relentless reversals and turns, Yagi-san steals Jerome's body after he has faked his own death by poison in a failed Romeo and Juliet death plot. This maudlin act is a punishment meted out to Nagiko in response to her spirited brush-off. Yagi-san skins Jerome's corpse and has it inscribed, so that it can become his personal pillow book of his most enthralling lover.

Greenaway ultimately has Nagiko's revenge plot—to destroy Yagi-san by sending him a series of men made irresistible to him through the beauty of the calligraphy and poetry scored all over their bodies—backfire. The story line opens up a battle of contemporary sexual lifestyles, gay and straight, that might well, given a strong tradition of homosocial bonding in Japanese culture, have been uncontroversial to Shōnagon's readers. As strikingly beautiful and seductive as she may be, Nagiko cannot seduce Yagi-san on her own. The first in a series of lavishly inscribed and illustrated male living books that she sends to Yagi-san is Jerome, at a moment when her passion for him is in full bloom. Jerome, already a habitué of Yagi-san, never returns from this mission of sexual reconnaissance. His demission is the core tragedy of the film, from Nagiko's point of view. It lends the film, almost up to its final frames, the kind of dramatic tension indispensable to narrative feature films, at least at present.[51]

As freewheeling as Greenaway's liberties may be, not only with the events of the Shōnagon classic but even more so with its atmosphere and tone, the screen translation establishes several connections crucial to an aesthetic exploration of the foundations and parameters and of the contemporary prospects for books.

First and most basic is an apprehension going back to Derrida's early grammatological insight: cinema, with all its devices, along with musical notes and computer languages, is a variety of script.[52] Shōnagon's discovery that writing is the wiring at the basis of the court's administrative capability, advanced communications, aesthetic judgment, and critical acuity is the revelation lending her formulations their power, what makes them both trenchant and acute. Greenaway gives ample indication of the fusion that he effects between writing and his own erotic cinema language when he has the historical Sei Shōnagon, say, at the end of the extended erotic reverie between Nagiko and Jerome, "I am certain there are two things which are dependable, the delights of the flesh and the delights of literature. I have had the good fortune to enjoy them equally." Writing and steamy sex not only share intensity, interactivity, intimacy, and pleasure; they are polymorphous in their expression. There is little need to catalogue here the variety of settings, positions, and stimulations to sexual pleasure that Nagiko shares with Jerome and that publisher Yagi-san experiences with the long succession of his sexual partners in the film. The vital point is that the incursions made by writing into the film's visual panorama and the multi-media variations that Greenaway devises for its display are as pervasive and multifarious as its erotic allures and its moments of sexual expression. In this sense, *The Pillow Book* is a splendid moving display case for writing at one of several pivotal historical junctures of its theorization, celebration, and performance.

If I follow Shōnagon in cobbling together an invariably imperfect list of the cine-manifestations of writing that Greenaway devises in his dual celebration of scriptural culture and sensibility and of uninhibited sexual expression, it is in exploration of the rich future for the book that Greenaway uploads into the film. Even at a moment when we quite legitimately worry whether reading on computer screens or in printouts affords the same intensity and lucidity as holding a book in hand, whether our cognitive capacities for discursive decoding are being distracted and otherwise debilitated by the flood of visual and aural information to which we are constantly exposed, the plethora of inscriptions and visual display techniques that Greenaway improvises, in this film and others, all remain options within the evolving phenomenon of book production. The cinematic adaptation of *The Pillow Book* is, in effect, a handbook of the resources, formats, and displays already in play in the book's ongoing updating and retrofitting.

It remains for each reader to determine whether Greenaway's cinematographic extensions of book technologies and book-induced cognitive processing result in a cultural experience as satisfactory as intense reading. My goal here is simply to survey the channels—between book archaeology and book teleology, between text-based and electronic literatures—that he establishes in a specific screen adaptation. Surely the baseline in this transcriptive crossover are the calligraphic screens in Japanese characters with apposite seal imprints either deriving from Shōnagon's text or attributed to Nagiko, her contemporary emanation. Greenaway is surely not the first to discover the screen appeal of striking calligraphy. In this film, however, he drives the point home with particular aesthetic ferocity.

Not only do written *congi* appear against a white background, composing what are, in effect, screen pages. They are projected as light beams against a variety of surfaces throughout the film, the most sensational of which is the human body. Two large *congi* are projected behind Nagiko, for example, as she languishes in her tub after her first inconsequential scene of body writing with Jerome at the Café Tiepolo. Jerome's mediocrity both as a calligrapher and a writer are apparent to her from the outset. "You're not a writer. You're a scribbler!" she rightly accuses him. "I've watched you with your typewriter go click, click, clack." But he vastly increases in her interest and esteem when he offers his own skin to serve as her writing surface. "Use my body like the pages of a book, your book." In so doing he has unknowingly situated himself center stage in the truncated plot of Nagiko's paternal heritage and her shadow identity as the contemporary Shōnagon. It is a backdrop of Western script projected first onto a close-up of Nagiko, then onto a dialogue between her and her maid, after her first pillow book, instigated and photographed by her lovesick admirer Hoki, has been summarily rejected by Yagi-san.

It is one thing for light-writing (photography in its literal sense) to glance over the human epidermis. Especially in view of the collaboration between writing technology and aesthetics cultivated by the Heian court, the conjugation between what I have elsewhere called "the writing of the nerves" and full-service textuality raises the ante on the central role of inscription in the film.[53] Greenaway is justly famous for generating techniques of writing, subscript, hypertext, and self-commentary within conventional (if cybernetically powered) filmmaking techniques. I am referring here particularly to the significant mileage he derives in this work and others from photographic inlays and the split screen (by the latter, I mean sustaining two or more simultaneous registers of screen action by means of film windows). These techniques are quite distinct from one another, and their success is contingent not only on superb photography and cinematography but also on pinpoint editing and synchronization.

Although the photographic insets that proliferate throughout the film often serve an illustrative purpose, they are by no means limited to this role. In the widest sense, Greenaway's visual inlays open depth and texture within the film and screen surfaces. They serve, if you will, as a picture gallery or visual display space imported into the film.

In Borgesian fashion, they suggest alternative thematics or plots open to the film at the moment of their "posting." They introduce book technology and power into the cinema experience by furnishing examples of what is semantically at hand (e.g., in *The Pillow Book*, "things that irritate," and "anything that is indigo is splendid"). The photographic inlays set into the surface of the film, in other words, simulate a range of indexical functions served by devices that include marginal illumination, allegorically embellished letters, footnotes, endnotes, parentheses, dashes, italicization, and boldface print. They are a text-intensive extension to the famous long shot introduced by Welles and others in the sense that they open a panorama of simultaneous registers of signification. Greenaway is predictably polymorphous in the backdrops that the photographic inlays punctuate, puncture, and open up. He's just as happy for insets to break out against pages of calligraphy as he is for them to offer a visual counterpoint to realistic cinematography.

Surely increased visual depth and density of images, coding, and their processing by the viewer also result from a closely related technique, Greenaway's practice of introducing into what had previously been a single narrative progression, and then withdrawing, simultaneous "lines of action." Through this practice, Greenaway allows his film story to diverge, divaricate, distract from or echo, loop around, and feed back into the dominant strand of storytelling. By means of these simultaneous splittings or multiplications in its storytelling, the film morphs from a closed system, constrained by the uninterrupted sequentiality of its development, into an open one.[54] The supplemental "feedback loop" that the film develops is free to challenge prevailing interpretations or to multiply the perspectives from which the events may be viewed. Sensing that she has lost Jerome to Yagi-san at the very outset of the conspiracy to bring the publisher down by bringing him into the clutches of a series of living pornographic volumes, Nagiko becomes Orpheus in search of Euridice. At a moment of excruciating pain to her, her approach to the primal scene of the male lovers' tender attentions to one another, the screen splits. We see her in various stages of her efforts to gain entry into the "hell" of Swindon Book Co. Ltd, even resorting to the side entrance. As Jerome, at a later phase in the plot's development, devastated by Nagiko's rejection, returns to her apartment to overdose on a cocktail of unwise drugs, simultaneous windows of action show him ransacking the supply closets. It is at the peaks of its dramatic tension, as it reaches the boiling point of its own narrative and emotional intensity, that the film breaks down into perspectival multiplicity and the simultaneity of parallel narratives.

Greenaway's radical technological as well as aesthetic experimentation with the depth and layering of the cinematic narrative surface surely has an impact on *The Pillow Book*'s extended elaboration on images of skin, film, and other membranes. By the time the film reaches its conclusion, we have observed virtually every contour of the human anatomy, from the broader surfaces to the top of the skull, the eyelids, and verging on the anal cavity—in an inscribed condition. Let's pause for a moment over this pivotal trope, as leveraged as is language itself between utter intimacy and protracted impersonality.

In terms of the film's plot of sexual coercion, betrayal, and revenge, painting or tattooing the skin's surface only increases the sexual aura emanating from the potential love partner, both for the one s/he arouses and for haphazard visual bystanders. (Freud would describe this as a rise in nervous excitation or sexual tension.) The logic here is that the impersonality of the inscription (the congenital irony inhering at the semantic level, whatever the phraseology) comprises a relaxation or break in the sexual tedium (in the Proustian idiom, *habitude*) accruing to erotic exchange as a repetitive medium. (Yes, on a mega-sociological level, the erotic dimension of the visual, as explored in painting, film, and other media, spurs us on in our devotions to the reproductive cycle through the variation they promise and in the very specific agents and doses of visual pharmacology that they deliver.)

On the expansive but taut torso of a Sumo wrestler, Nagiko has inscribed the text of book 13, the last in the series of living books addressed to Yagi-san: "This is the writing of Nagiko Ukigino,[55] and I know you blackmailed, violated, and humiliated my father. I suspect you of ruining my husband. You have now committed the greatest crime. You have desecrated the body of my lover. You and I now know that you have lived long enough." Couched as the formula of Yagi-san's death sentence, Nagiko's body inscription assumes the role of a speaking character in its own right. In the wake not only of her father's self-inflicted loss but the publisher's theft, tanning, and customizing of Jerome's pelt into his personal collectible, Nagiko has lured her tormentor to his ultimate sexual adventure through inscriptive decoration promising sexual novelty as *différance*, difference not only for its own sake but even begging to differ from itself.

Whatever its particular sexual preference, the entire audience joins Yagi-san, a jaded libertine whose sexual will and hunger can only be sustained by embellishing skin, that is, by the promise of intimate touch already marked by intrinsic variation. And as Greenaway has retrofitted the cinematographic medium in his adaptation of the Shōnagon classic, film is the skin, on a cultural level, that enables its spectators to labor on, having been party to the sexual transgressions that make both the tedium of life and ongoing participation in the diffuse collectivity of film, in its codes and discoveries, not only bearable but edifying.

It is no accident that the French term for film stock, the tape or band that will be transformed into photo negatives and cinema and slide positives, is *pellicule*, whose closest English cognate may be *pelt*. In Greenaway's cine-matography, with its mythic tracking shots, akin to extremely broad brush or pen strokes, its filmic inlays, and its split or double screens, film reaches its closest proximity to skin, both as the promise of tactile sensual satisfac-tion and as the written page of parchment or vellum. Twice Nagiko achieves masturbatory pleasure by caressing her skin with a written surface. Her touching (in fact, gluing) writing to skin is a declaration of reclaiming her calligraphic heritage in the midst of several low-end jobs that she takes in Kowloon directly after the breakup of her conventional Japanese marriage, precisely over the issue of her bibliographic and scriptural activities. Late in the film, after Jerome's demise, Yagi-san achieves the closest access possible to his departed lover by wrapping himself in the pillow book that he has fashioned of Jerome's purloined skin. By way of the writing and other mes-saging that they convey, film and skin are indeed tightly interlaced on sev-eral levels throughout. Both as the medium of writing in its multifarious forms and as the promise of sensory-cognitive variety overcoming the te-dium of time, film serves as a permeable membrane allowing us to patch together a truce, however tenuous, with our own hides.

In fetishizing the many forms of skin contact rendered visible in the course of *The Pillow Book*, Greenaway's film adaptation underscores the col-lusion between touch and taste. (The latter sensory domain may receive its fullest cinematic treatment in Greenaway's *The Cook, the Thief, His Wife, and Her Lover*.) Shōnagon, along with the other courtiers and court ladies, may be held in thrall to the whims of Her Majesty's comings and goings and to the multifaceted arbitrariness of aristocratic decorum and political ritual. But her perch in the court also affords her an unparalleled degree of critical detachment and autonomy. Especially in an environment of poly-morphous sexual expression, pervasive occasions for skin-to-skin touch eas-ily morph into an aggravated sense of taste, in terms of aesthetic judgment as well as gustatory experience. Greenaway's placement of Nagiko in the heart of the Far East branch of global haute couture, as she breaks from her severely dyslexic and logocentric Japanese spouse, is a stunning stroke. The fashion world is distinguished precisely by the arbitrariness, short duration, and costliness of its judgments and taste.

Shōnagon's self-appointed task of critic within her milieu bodes well for the socio-aesthetic critique that Greenaway's film, situating itself on the membrane between touch and taste, can render. Long before the role of critic would be carved out of a discursive division of labor negotiated by a tradition at some remove from Japan, Shōnagon's commentary extends to splendid things, to things that fall, and to clouds, as well as to fashions in dress, manners, and the ethics of language. Concerning the last, she is especially farsighted and precocious. Indeed, on no topic in her wide-ranging gloss on her culture is she more diligent and discreet than the decorum of language:

> *I particularly despise people who express themselves poorly in writing.* How horrible it is to read language that rides roughshod over manners and social conventions. It's also poor to be very over-polite with people who should rightly be treated less formally. It's bad enough to receive poorly written letters oneself, and it's just as disgraceful when they're sent to others.
>
> Generally speaking, even when you hear someone use language in this sort of slovenly way when talking face to face, you wince and wonder yourself how they can say such things, and it's even more appalling when it's directed to someone eminent.[56]

The acute critical sense characterizing Shōnagon's entire discourse, one she displays in response to plants and natural scenery as well as dress, ceremony, and decorum, finds no more powerful expression than in her pronouncements on style.[57] The aesthetics of writing, in the above lines, is tantamount to whatever sociopolitical and ethical force communication can claim. Although Shōnagon's "self"-presentation may veer toward the ceremonial, the ornamental, and the tritely feminine, her overarching sense of language as the ultimate arbiter of social as well as ethical values affords her a powerful claim to the position of the operative critic within her milieu.

There is a crucial breaking point in the domain of aesthetic values at which transgression allows an influx of fresh sensibility and innovative power. Whatever liberties Greenaway may have taken with the story line and other traits of the original court classic, his cinematic adaptation retains Shōnagon's devotion to books as the medium, surface, and texture of cultural sensibility and transmission. The moment late in the film when the camera meticulously follows Jerome's transformation from a painted corpse into the unique copy of an artist's illuminated book on human parchment surely constitutes the culmination of its transgressive allegory: the violation and disqualification of conventional morality at the hand of textual values and practices. Through his trademark cinema inlays, Greenaway uses the occasion to put the full technical virtuosity of Japanese book art on display. Yagi-san personally dons a surgeon's gown to make the first cut into Jerome's body, adorned with the completed design. We see the skin measured, cut, and folded into the segments of a continuous scroll. We witness the design and production of a cover just for this book. We wonder at the precision of the measurement, cutting, coloring, folding, sewing, and pasting involved in these processes. We see Jerome's discarded flesh amass in a straw basket; we observe how the garbage truck, on its conventional pickup, drives away with the offal. The very next shot allows us to observe how, in a state of postorgasmic relaxation, Yagi-san touches the scroll to his living torso. This assures the intimacy of the contact between lover and beloved, writing and body, film and skin, and writing and film: it will all be skin to skin.

In this state, Jerome has once again become a book, in this case, book 6, "The Book of the Lover." The aim of all subsequent human books sent to the publisher, Nagiko informs us in the voiceover, will be her retrieval of this volume, both sacred and illicit. Yet as the camera pans up the torso of book 7, "The Book of the Seducer," a succession of odd riddles appears as a caption on the screen. Apropos of a film very much about the lives and deaths of books, the questions are reminiscent of the baited queries regarding human reproduction that young children pose to their parents. But these questions—as the camera, surveying Yagi-san's next lover, pauses at his cock—are about the birth of books:

> Where is a book before it is born?
> Who are its parents?
> Does a book need two parents—a mother and a father?
> Can a book be born inside another book?
> Where is the parent book of books?
> How old does a book have to be before it can give birth?

The moment of greatest transgression is indeed the moment of greatest innovation, at least within the obverse genealogy of books. It is precisely the birth of a new book, in its format and outreach, that we witness in the film version of *The Pillow Book*. This is an artifact mobilizing, at least at the threshold level, the full panoply of cognitive processing skills requisite to cultural empowerment and literacy at the present juncture. The film, in its cinematographic technique and strategy of adaptation, constructs an allegory of the conditions for its own decoding and reception. In many respects, this highly nuanced and articulate cinematographic artifact lays claim to being a book in its own right, yet Greenaway has meticulously retrofitted it to the cybernetic and visual software powering the current flow of information and its communications media.

Display Case, or Display's the Thing

An obscure tract of materials and observations on nineteenth-century Paris by Benjamin entitled *The Arcades Project* transformed the very notion underlying all the books coming after it. In the wake of this highly diverse print-medium website, whose items chronicle the history of Euro-American modernization as well as of Paris, the book is as much a *display*, with a full array of visual design features, as it is an agglomeration or compendium of materials.[58] The significance of the book's visual design parameters can hardly be overestimated. The book medium is itself a modality of visual display, with a particular history and technology. Leaving aside the meta-demarcation between poetic and prosaic typographies, each of the discursive subgenres—say, fiction, criticism, philosophy, and history—entails an embedded visual design and distinctive display features. The difference between the ways theory, criticism, history, and philosophy *say* something is often less a matter of ideology, conviction, or intellectual crystallization than a matter of its *modality as a display screen*, however indistinguishable from its counterparts any single prosaic subdiscourse may seem.

The history, draft, and drift of the book are reducible to no single technology. The second generation of the Kindle, which Amazon, Inc. has already issued, speaks no more authoritatively to the tradition and prospects for the book than did papyrus, engraving, or movable type. The perdurance of the book transcends the specificity of any particular mutation or configuration in which the book may find itself. A visit to a distinguished medieval archive, whether at Trinity College, Dublin, or the Stiftsbibliothek in St. Gall, Switzerland, indicates that the book underwent a steady development of several centuries in order to arrive at the full panoply of its internal technological engines.[59] This was hardly an eternity. Marginalia, subscript, superscript, footnotes, endnotes, charts, outlines, and indices are in full evidence in hand-written volumes by the end of the eleventh century. The devising of the display technologies immanent to the book in no way needed to await "the Gutenberg revolution."

The book is, then, neither a specific medium nor a technology, though it of necessity delves in both.[60] It arises at the interface, on the page or screen, between ongoing, pervasive inscriptive activity and public expression or display. A book is a folio or compendium of one or more inscriptive processes or scenes of writing, carried to their invariably inconclusive interruptions or terminations.

Benjamin arrayed a vast mass of materials he began collecting in 1927 into a thematically organized series of convolutes or files.

Convolutes may well be regarded as a subgenre of discursive prose in their own right. While each convolute is invariably "convened" by a thematic subtext, the genre, as an accretion of sources of highly diverse provenance, sets in play a characteristic drift or topical wide berth. The author's motives or point of view, in this case Benjamin's interjected comments, clearly play second fiddle to the nonlinear reverberations and unexpected sequiturs arising from the incorporated materials. In the sense that the juxtaposition of the materials and their drift begin to generate their own critical commentary on the historico-cultural phenomena under consideration, the convolute as an art form is interactive, in technological as well as temporal senses, generations before its most powerful successor, the cybernetic website. Each reading of a convolute, even by the same reader, is therefore a completely discrete and singular artifact of cognitive processing and of time. The spontaneous quality of each encounter with the convolute, the quick turnaround between assimilating the materials and reading out their critical commentary on the age and its telling phenomena, endows the convolute with an irreducible performative dimension.

Those who would fashion convolutes and/or websites are therefore Deleuzians before the fact: they monitor and direct the flow patterns crystallizing around certain artifacts, historical actualities, and technological developments. The art of the convolute has in common with music and poetry that it is a compositional art in multiple respects, drawing upon and incorporating the contingencies of real time.

When Benjamin's initial convolutes, those addressing the most obvious features of nineteenth-century Parisian life surfacing in the historical viewfinder, approached unwieldiness or redundancy, he placed related materials in spin-off convolutes, and these he sequenced further back in the queue. These subsequent collations of materials related to earlier investigations became, in effect, the overflow stacks in a book configured as a virtual library of modernization in Paris and by implication the advanced Euro-American world. The imprint of the library or archive, in particular the Bibliothèque nationale, where Benjamin spent increasing amounts of time in exile from 1933 to 1940, may be said to be all over *The Arcades Project*, to haunt its organizational format as well as its topical substance.

In keeping with the full-throttled practice of critique that he developed, particularly when an academic career was no longer in the picture, applying the full brunt of his erudition and theoretical power to any artifact that culture placed in his trajectory, for several of the convolutes Benjamin chose topics that are counterintuitive. In any account of the sweep of modernization overtaking Paris, London, Milan, and New York in the nineteenth century, we would expect to find major sections on the city's streets (Convolute P), iron and glass construction (F), subterranean Paris and Haussmann's demolitions (C), and prostitution and gambling (O), and we do. Yet we owe the choice of other directions in which Benjamin turned the cinematographic eye of his conspicuously hybrid, cubist, and Surrealist book form to his singular critical sensibility and sense of historical timing. Their prominent place in what he would call the panorama of the aesthetic and sociopolitical urban landscape is also a credo regarding the task and viewfinder of the cultural critic.

It is not a terrible stretch of credulity or imagination for contemporary readers to find that Benjamin placed convolutes dedicated to Charles Baudelaire (J), Victor Hugo (d), and Karl Marx (X) in a sequence otherwise dedicated to urban phenomena (e.g., "Arcades, *Magazins de nouveauté*, Sales Clerks" [A]). In this fashion, Benjamin closes a Möbius strip allowing literary or cultural "properties" to exert a sociocultural impact every bit as tangible and material as mass-transit vehicles, building materials, advertisement posters, and storefronts. This insistence on including texts and memorable formulations in the mix of powerful historical influences in no way weakens his commitment, inspired by the Marxist side of his readings and values, to historical materialism and to dialectical historiography.

We can even stand by Benjamin's side as he devotes certain of his internal collations of materials to personifications or mascots, such as the *flâneur* (M), who index the new behaviors and patterns—for example, of locomotion, consumption, and entertainment—arising amid urban modernity. Each February, the reappearance on *The New Yorker*'s cover of its mascot, emblematic nineteenth-century dandy Eustace Tilley, creates a minor stir. The convolute on the apartment (I, "The Interior, The Trace") as the privatized interior countering the monumental public spaces encroaching on greater segments of the city mobilizes the figures of the collector and the allegorist, whose contrasting attitudes toward the accumulation and display of artifacts have been elaborated one convolute earlier. Benjamin sees the prototypes of the contemporary apartment arising in nineteenth-century metropolises as sheaths or display cases for the commodities acquired in unprecedented opportunities for shopping.

The second convolute is devoted to fashion. Convolute D achieves an odd conflation between the prominent place of the weather in a collation of nineteenth-century materials including Charles Meryon's engravings and the turbulences of mood. And Benjamin makes a foray into the zone of mass psychology when he orients two central convolutes, K and L, around the dream house, both as an element of the dream city and in relation to the museum as a regulated display case of collectibles (whose regime bears significant resemblances to Michel Foucault's notion of archaeology).[61] Mood is the most elusive possible target for a historically formatted cultural exegesis. Benjamin even declares, by the end of Convolute B, that the succession of fashion styles and fetishes is his preferred paradigm for history. "For the philosopher, the most interesting thing about fashion is its extraordinary anticipations [*Antizipationen*]. It is well known that art will often—for example, in pictures—precede the perceptible reality by years. . . . Yet fashion is in much steadier, much more precise contact with the coming thing, thanks to the incomparable nose which the feminine collective has for what lies waiting in the future [*kraft der unvergleichlichen Witterung, die das weibliche Kollektiv für das hat, was in der zukunft bereitliegt*]."[62] Pursuing such lines of inquiry as fashion and mood are indicative of pointed and unpredictable choices that Benjamin made in the orientation of his compilation-volume on Paris. On one of its flanks, *The Arcades Project* might be construed as a particularly diffuse historical text or source book, perhaps, of urban modernization. Yet in another of its emanations it is a multidimensional display of textual citations suspended in book space, if you will, an installation of citations that we take in as we traverse the convolutes. It is in such seemingly long-shot or oddball points of view as weather or fashion that we can discern the full play of aesthetics and poetics that is indispensable to *The Arcade Project*'s intervention and design. It is in this respect that *The Arcades*

Project sets in action a phrase that Benjamin has lifted from Baudelaire's dedication to Arsène Houssaye in *Paris Spleen* on more than one occasion:[63] it establishes the indispensable role of poetic prose and indeed of overall discursive hybridity in memorable and informed critique.

If *The Arcades Project* is a time capsule of urban modernity assembled and sent out under horrendous conditions of cultural neglect and disenfranchisement, we cannot avoid Benjamin's exhortation to the effect that the inchoate, the intangible, and the downright disreputable belong to the amalgam that the critic negotiates as much as the big-ticket items: whether the obvious sectors of historical activity and investment or the "unavoidable" literary and cultural "properties." This is indeed the place for one of the unforgettable nuggets of Benjamin's ongoing critical intervention, which is peppered among the fragments of extracts composing the bulk of the convolutes: "Method of this project: literary montage. I needn't *say* anything. Merely show. I shall purloin no valuables, appropriate no ingenious formulations. But the rags, the refuse—these I will not inventory but allow, in the only way possible, to come into their own: by making use of them."[64] If in its methodological thrusts and improvisations *The Arcades Project* amounts to a scrambling of critical practice, as Benjamin demonstrates (not asserts) here, it is in a pronounced direction of writerly *performance*, indeed, one particularly (though not exclusively) calibrated to the *visual*. He "needn't *say*. . . . Merely show." It's particularly noteworthy that in this powerful aphorism, culled from Convolute N, "On the Theory of Knowledge, Theory of Progress," arguably the work's theoretical engine room, the downbeat on the performative mode of enunciation, as opposed to the constative, is conflated with an *allegorical* (as opposed to historicist, proprietary) relation to, hold on, the materials. A ventriloquism of "letting the materials speak for themselves" is therefore more apposite to the core program of *The Arcades Project* than taking prisoners, that is, "purloining" the cultural properties under scrutiny. Benjamin is also suggesting in this truly pivotal snippet of his formulation that the splicing in of authoritative theoretical formulations from elsewhere, through a habit of appropriative paraphrase, is less relevant to his project than memorable improvisational phrasing: "appropriate no ingenious formulations." This is phrasing that will stop us dead in our tracks in the midst of the "dialectical image": "wherein what has been comes together in a flash with the now to form a constellation. In other words, image is dialectics at a standstill."[65] Benjamin's dialectical image stands at the apogee of the critical insight that can be conveyed by writerly performance, one whose radicality is measured in its poetry and surreal unpredictability.

The intervention deposited by *The Arcades Project* into the library stacks of history and time is made more distinctive by the relative paucity and brevity of Benjamin's own critical interpellations. That is to say, he has strongly democratized the process of reading a historico-cultural retrospective emanating from a particular epoch by severely restricting and largely relinquishing the argumentative and narrative control that are part and parcel of a running commentary. Benjamin achieves participatory readerly democracy in many ways, aiding and abetting readers in drawing their own conclusions from the materials comprising the vast main part of the text.

That main part largely comprises citations culled from a broad range of sources: not only contemporary accounts of Paris and historical and sociological retrospective overviews, but poems, advertising copy, texts from signage over stores and boutiques, posters, advertising prospectuses, and proclamations with and without the force of law. So pervasive are the citations that play the predominant role within most convolutes that the brief "bullet-statements" in which Benjamin sets most of his own comments, rarely exceeding more than a few paragraphs, also approach our own readerly sensibilities with the otherness and the truncated, packaged feeling of citations.

Benjamin lends his voice to the citations that he has gathered with a collector's obsession and an allegorist's sense of irony and incommensurability; his own words emerge from their display on the pages of *The Arcades Project* on the far side of "the alienation effect." Thus *The Arcades Project* turns out to be a work written entirely in citations, even when certain of the fragments have been written by the author himself. And of course such a work, culled from preexisting materials that its textual maker has arranged, sets into play a notion of authorship strikingly different from the received idea of the author as writer, synthesizer, or composer.

Benjamin distributes the cultural fragments and remains that he has gathered from his vast reading and sustained aesthetico-cultural attentiveness in *space*. But this space, like so many design parameters accompanying the aesthetic contracts of modernism, is multifaceted. On the most tangible level, the space in which Benjamin distributes the materials of *The Arcades*

Project is the bound facets of the pages making up the book. At the level of the virtual space opened out by the book pages, Benjamin can hedge his bets. He knows that the sequential order of the convolutes will establish certain priorities, will in effect orchestrate certain movements and counter-movements, certain rises and falls in tension, intensity, and lucidity, whose development will approximate the fluctuations in drama and mood common to music and cinema. It is a fascinating curiosity for further meditation that Benjamin holds a good measure of his theoretical fire in *The Arcades Project* for Convolute N. I personally believe that he reserves his highest and most trenchant theoretical formulations for a moment *after* the reader has been privy to his updated notions of dialectical and materialist histories, after she has been introduced to pivotal personae such as Baudelaire, the collector, the allegorist, and the *flâneur*, after she has swerved in and out among the city's streets, its centers of entertainment and commerce, and its protected interiors.

Yet at the same time Benjamin knows that the dazzling gems that he has mined in the long course of his reading shimmer simultaneously in sustained fascination. This particular mystique or aura comes to him in part via the experiments in poetic prose made by the Romantics, a quality to which they attached the label of *parabasis*, a memorable formulation by Friedrich Schlegel: this phenomenon as poetic reflection achieves the multiplication effect of "an endless succession of mirrors."[66] Benjamin knows full well that the arresting fascination set off in the display case by his densest, most memorable citations countermands the linear sequence in which the materials have been chained. The free rein with which Benjamin composes bibliographic space, in other words, by distributing citations throughout it enables him to exploit features of readerly and exegetical time.

Yet it can be argued that the book space, the virtual space established by the bound defile of pages in all books, is unavoidably a simulacrum of mental space, of space as one of the few givens or a prioris that Kant allowed within the architecture of the human faculties, whether perception, understanding, or reason, and the processing that they accomplish within their tight division of labor. In Chapter 7, we will be pursuing the sequence of circuitries structuring thought machines from the "computers without hardware" of German idealism to contemporary theories of systems and chaos. Indeed, it is precisely this simulation, the smooth transition from psychological process to the tablet of the printed page, the heightened ability of images, events, and logical sequences decoded from printed pages to be psychologically downloaded, that would at least in part explain the hold of books upon their audience during the epoch of their predominance as a medium. In this sense, though, the effectiveness and verisimilitude of the book page as a psychological screen comprises an ongoing potential for mental simulation at only one moment, albeit a rich and enduring one, in the history of media. We can point to the immense power that cinema and video each wielded, in the moment of their appearance and broad dissemination, as the latest and most virtual analogons to mental and cognitive display. The potential of the computer screen and of such applications as virtual reality has barely begun to be exploited.

It is in a sublime space both mental and virtual that Jorge Luis Borges distributes the contingent volumes making up his "Library of Babel" and elaborates the principles of the archive's architecture. The architecture of this imaginary repository of phantasmatic books, based on the maniacal repetition of hexagons, communicates directly with the assemblages of strata and parastrata that Deleuze/Guattari configure as the housing for an acentered decoding of the flows and schizoid madness unleashed by late capitalism. *The Arcades Project*, had Borges been aware of it when he wrote *Ficciones*, would have occupied a preeminent place in the reference section of the Library of Babel. On which strata of hexagons it would have been placed, I cannot tell you. My point here is that Benjamin installs his heterogeneous collection of extracts within the same mental and cognitive simulation that accounts for some of the draw and staying power not only of Borges's *Ficciones* but of the speculative fiction that has brilliantly drawn on the features of textual involution and permutation in geology and architecture. The geological inscription in Edgar Allen Poe's "Eureka" and Court architecture in Franz Kafka's *The Trial* come immediately to mind. One of the explanations for the relevance and appeal of the cognitive sciences at the present juncture is that they occupy many of the vital intersections anticipated in different ways by Borges's Library and Benjamin's labyrinthine study of the Parisian Arcades.

In *The Arcades Project*, Benjamin has programmed or composed a work in which the process of citation, the extraction and arrangement in textual space of fragments notable in their vividness and irreducibility, exercises unprecedented creative and architectural control. On bibliographical terrain, citations often play the role of references. The making of *The Arcades Project* documents a transition in citation from "external," allo-oriented reference depending on sources situated "elsewhere" to self-reference. In a work consisting entirely of citations (we have already reviewed how Benjamin's own interpellations are transformed, willy-nilly, into citations), the process of citation is invariably self-referential: it refers the extrinsic sources of the materials back to the very body of the text. In its corporeal features, simulating the arrangement of a rhizome, *The Arcades Project* is an instance of Deleuze/Guattari's body without organs. The text assimilates—anything but integrally—the extracts making it up. It has literally incorporated its contents. The sustained self-reference of the book as it devours new materials is a feedback loop transforming the conventional reference work, whether a dictionary or an encyclopedia, from a machine of dyadic pairings into an open system, capable of autopoiesis,[67] at least in some measure, homeostatic in the face of cultural turbulence,[68] and in a dynamic and porous relationship with its surrounding environment.

The book in the wake of *The Arcades Project*—as an auto-referential display of materials, and regardless of the extent to which it is inflected, as it inevitably is, by photography, cinema, video, and cybernetics—is a very different animal from what it was before. It is never more than a draft, a provisional proof photo, of what it might be. It never comes close to its "definitive edition." Its processing, the mutual interplay in its output or printout of input, editing, formatting, random memory, and long-term memory, is relentless and unending. A published book at the present moment in media history and cybernetic tele-technics is at most a snapshot, a very important one, of a process that preceded it and continues in the wake of its formal appearance. The best books are those that have set out the most inviting welcome mats to the ghosts and specters of thinking, reworking, and revision that can abide within their invariably provisional architecture. We have our hands on these books; they have trained the glare of their lifeless eyes on us. They will never go away.

Extraterrestrial Kafka: Ahead to the Graphic Novel

Amid the Flows

There is always something out of this world, by which we probably mean radically weird and inexhaustible, about Kafka. The weirdness arrives in broad strokes and tiny splashes. It encompasses the earth-shaking fictive premises of *The Trial*, "The Metamorphosis," and "The Burrow," which have given rise to innumerable extensions and adaptations in fantastic literature, sci-fi, and the graphic novel, but also such specific touches as the servants' uniforms in *The Castle* and the hum of the Castle telephone system. Often in Kafka's writing there is no greater weirdness than a minor detail. Or a creature that may not exactly be human but that thinks and generates discourse, not only obscuring the boundaries between the human and the animal but inquiring, at the most elemental level, into the nature, qualities, domain, and pertinence of consciousness and cognition.[1]

Kafka was uncannily attuned to the systematic restructuring ensuing from nineteenth-century colonialism and military science, from twentieth-century corporate organization and bureaucracy, and from the vastly enlarged scale, acceleration, and range of mass communications facilitated by such technologies as the telephone, radio transmission, and photojournalism. Such striking depictions as the Court in *The Trial* attest to Kafka's being, as much as any of his agents, servants, or facilitators of the Law, an unrepentant (and we would have to say *bound*) creature of the book. But the book medium that can be extrapolated from diverse snatches of his fiction, like the institutions of legal impartiality, personal freedom, and corporeal respect and integrity (as in habeas corpus), is also under seismic stress, in the process of morphing into something else, into something, like Gregor Samsa at the outset of "The Metamorphosis," not quite what it was before.

Whether Kafka intuited or not the future of his script in the medium of the graphic novel is beyond the scope of the present chapter. But that a discernible elective affinity prevails between Kafka's imagination of systems and of urban and bureaucratic space under advanced capitalism and what would become the formal specifications and constitutive aesthetics and ethos of contemporary graphic fiction is the taking-off point and basic assertion of the following exposition. This meditation demands that we not only paraphrase and catalogue the substantive messages surfacing throughout Kafka's prose. It requires that we explicitly address the irreducibly *visual* component in Kafka's imagination, that we extrapolate its features and potentials outward toward powerful and memorable innovations in book, newspaper, and magazine publishing, and, for that matter, in painting, photography, and cinema, developments that it indirectly inaugurated and facilitated. The completion of this exercise will demand an acknowledgment necessary even in the face of the demonstrable superiority that the rigorous deployment of tropes and bearings emanating from philosophy and contemporary critical theory has afforded the reading of literature in general and indeed that of consummately difficult and autopoietically generative authors, including Kafka, Proust, Joyce, Woolf, and Borges: namely, that a host of visual, graphic, performative, and decorative art forms and media could be tangibly marked and reformatted by contributions and innovations filed by literary artists; furthermore, that these nonlinear aftershocks and repercussions of literary performances did not require discursive or conceptual legitimation, mediation, or intervention in order to transpire.

We can watch in bemused awe as the overarching skew and strangeness in his fiction ricochet beyond his written corpus into entire orders of speculative and conceptual derangement. I think in particular of the degree to which Kafka's writing, more than any other single factor, occasions Deleuze/Guattari's notion of deterritorialization,[2] a general category of social and psychic alienation and displacement amid global flows of money, goods, migration, sexual traffic, and signs (the latter accorded the same status by the mega-trope of flow), amid current hegemonic incursions by war machines on a greater than continental scale. Deterritorialization, of which Kafka is the exemplary visionary and poet, is for Deleuze/Guattari always the consequence of a crisis of encoding and decoding that has resulted in mutations:

> The modern theory of mutations has clearly demonstrated that a code, which necessarily relates to a population, has an essential margin of decoding: not only does every code have supplements capable of free variation, but a single segment may be copied twice, the second copy left free for variation. In addition, fragments of code may be transferred from the cells of one species to those of another, Man and Mouse, Monkey and Cat, by viruses or through other procedures. This involves not translations between codes . . . but a single phenomenon we call surplus value of code, or side-communication. . . . Every code is affected by a margin of decoding due to these supplements and surplus values—supplements in the order of a multiplicity, surplus values in the order of a rhizome.[3]

This sample passage, in which Deleuze/Guattari begin to characterize deterritorialization as the aftermath of a crisis in the transmission of a program or code, is redolent of the overarching wish spanning their combined project: to place an array of cultural, biological, semiological, and sociopolitical processes, all involving the transfer and decoding of signs, in parallel. The great enigma still hovering at the outreaches of their combined project is whether the exchanges of language, on the Lacanian Symbolic order, comprise one flow among others, translating unproblematically into movements of goods, money, and bodily fluids, say, or whether, as deconstruction would have it, language is the very possibility of all the movements or exchanges.[4]

But these lines set the stage for a dynamic in which deterritorialization experienced as a putative outside, that is, tangibly and substantially, occasions a scrambling or reconfiguration of the codes programming the immanent behavior and possibility of the affected entities, whether individuals, communities, or biological species:

Nomadic flows or waves of deterritorialization go from the central layer to the periphery, then from the new center to the new periphery, falling back to the old center and launching forth to the new. The organization of epistrata moves in the direction of increasing deterritorialization. . . . Not only are physical particles characterized by speeds of deterritorialization . . . but a single chemical substance (sulphur or carbon, for example) has a number of more or less deterritorialized states. The more interior milieus an organism has on its own stratum, assuring its autonomy and bringing it into a set of aleatory relations with the exterior, the more deterritorialized it is. That is why degrees of development must be understood relatively. . . . Deterritorialization must be thought of as a perfectly positive power that has degrees and thresholds (epistrata), is always relative, and has reterritorialization as its flipside or complement. An organism that is deterritorialized in relation to the exterior necessarily reterritorializes on its interior milieus.[5]

Kafka emerges as the poet and prophet of deterritorialization in his relentless pursuit of the collapse of regimes of order and the radical mutations these constitutional crises occasion at the infrastructural level. Deterritorialization signals the undermining and collapse of the political systems of imperial and national sovereignty, national self-assertion and interest, and territorial integrity, with all the subregimes of immigration, naturalization, and selection (e.g., racial, ethnic, and religious profiling and control) attached to the latter. Kafka's relentless pursuit of this phenomenon, all the more outrageous and horrifying in its literary precision and realism, may track Gregor and his social world after he has suddenly and radically switched species, flipping out (or into) our beloved giant insect with alien genetic coding, or the colonial war machine after its instrument of torture, whose program is indistinguishable from the power and justice claimed by the Judaic god, has totaled itself. The aftermath of the devastating crisis of incomprehensibility, of superannuation at the level of code, well illustrated when Gregor as family secret is lured by his sister's playing into the public eye of the boarders, is invariably a frenetic effort of scrambling and improvisation (as in jazz) within the sphere of the immanent or underlying operating system.

The book, as we have been elaborating its specifications and parameters in an age of cybernetic technology and comprehensive overload in the systems and infrastructure of communications, demographics, and critical resources, is the primary screen or display on which the flows and deterritorializations to which Kafka was so uncannily attuned are charted and registered. The instability and immanent collapse that Kafka intuited in imperial, national, and even municipal institutions of his day also had tangible repercussions for the book, both as a communications medium and as an institution. Benjamin's *The Arcades Project*, to which we've already had recourse, may be characterized as a concrete retrofitting of the book, and certain of its definitive and long-standing conventions of authority/authorship, coherence, and unity of perspective or framework, in keeping with the seismic cultural instabilities that Kafka was so acute in sensing and articulating.

Institutional and Typographical Architectures

Kafka is the avatar, prophet, and bureaucrat of an alterity and resulting waves of deterritorialization that are complexly too unmotivated and unremitting ever to be resolved, rationalized, domesticated, territorialized, or disciplined, in the academic sense. So unremitting are the conditions of unabashed strangeness and architectural disorientation that Kafka infuses into his characters and the predicaments besetting them that he trespasses terrestrial limits, not only rendering national boundaries of language and culture tenuous, but circumventing the notion and economy of globalization before it achieved currency.

It has long proven more fruitful to think of Kafka as an atelier or worksite of textual programming rather than as a specific author, producer, or franchiser of a limited or closed body of works. The "complex art-games" that Kafka disfigures in the process of inventing others can surely walk, and in many cases do so, far afield, not in the mechanized march of iterability but in the improvised postures of modern dance.[6]

This is ultimately a retracing of Kafka's cosmic journey, into fields remaining disturbingly open, even if they have been charted. Among the multiple distinctive features of his fictive and inscriptive landscapes, we will focus on his spatial disorientation, the sordid involution of his architectural settings; on the prepossessing failure of the communications media and traffic systems that his domain encompasses; and on the blurred gender lines on which his human, animal, and mythological creatures interact, taking each other's places and forming hybrids difficult to place, perhaps, but inexhaustible in their suggestiveness. Kafka's uncanny architecture, decisive as it was for the twentieth-century Imaginaries of literature and the visual arts, incorporates the threshold between the human and the animal, under his administration a particularly active and generative interface.

The cumulative effect of the calculated weird effects coinciding in this field and defining it is a relentlessly open frontier or borderline, one that has never been and never will be completely filled in. It is the paradoxical instability of architectural involution and interspecies hybridization that delineates the hinge between the global and the extraterrestrial. The Baedecker to this realm might well begin with the following blueprint of one of the Court's installations, though it would surely go on to catalogue Mr. Pollunder's house, the superhighway on the way to Ramses, and the image and structure of the Castle:

> "Just look at this waiting room." It was a long passage, a lobby communicating by ill-fitting doors with the different offices on the floor. Although there was no window to admit light, it was not entirely dark, for some of the offices were not properly boarded off from the passage but had an open frontage of wooden rails, reaching, however, to the roof [*denn manche Abteilungen hatten gegen den Gang zu statt einheitliche Bretterwände bloße, allerdings bis zur Decke reichende Holzgitter*], through which a little light penetrated and through which one could see a few officials as well, some writing at their desks, and some standing close to the rails peering through the interstices at the people in the lobby [*und durch die Lücken die Leute auf dem Gang beobachteten*]. There were only a few people in the lobby.[7]

Kafka's architectural blueprints of the Court are highly ambiguous: here the language of structural description and the rhetoric of bureaucratic organization and rule become indistinguishable. The Court lobby combines intrusive panoptical monitoring—the civil servants can peer down at its current occupants—with a ramshackle architectural inefficiency: the incomplete compartmental walls allow whatever illumination might enlighten this rendition of the Law accidentally to filter through. The space of this particular installation is made unbearably oppressive both by a dearth of windows and by the sunlight that the windows do permit, because they refuse to open. This may well be a nightmare from the perspective of all the room's fictive users, yet it also a presents a visual artist, whether of the comics variety or not, with a rich opportunity.

Since all spaces in the novel, even the Church, where the pivotal Parable of the Doorkeeper is read to Joseph K. as his ultimate sentence, "belong to the Court," it is no surprise that our protagonist has wandered into a setting with similar features when he rushes up a residential staircase past child prostitutes, some with physical deformities, for his consultation with artist Titorelli, who delivers a semiotically knowing playback of his legal fiasco.

> When he reached the third floor he had to moderate his pace, he was quite out of breath, both the stairs and the stories were disproportionately high, and the painter was said to live quite at the top, in an attic. The air was stifling; there was no well for these narrow stairs, which were enclosed on either side by blank walls, showing only at rare intervals a tiny window very high up. [*Auch war die Luft sehr drückend, es gab keinen Treppenhof, die enge Treppe war auf beiden Seiten von Mauern eingeschlossen, in denen nur hier und da fast nach oben kleine Fenster angebracht waren.*][8]

Yet this now characteristic architecture is most disturbing in its complete coincidence with regimes of power, discipline, and punishment. Kafka's architectural blueprint extends into the organization and strategic operations of the Law as a system of philosophical speculation that has eventuated in its practicality, its tangible application. The narrative's tangential remarks on the Law, delivered by a wide range of knowing insiders, men and women, privileged cognoscenti and peons, thus hovers on the cusp between Kant's first and second *Critiques*:

> The ranks of officials in this judiciary system mounted endlessly, so that not even the initiated could survey the hierarchy as a whole. [*Die Rangordnung and Steigerung des Gerichtes sei unendlich und selbst für den Eingeweihten nicht absehbar.*] And the proceedings of the Court were generally kept secret from subordinate officials; consequently they could hardly ever quite follow in their further progress the cases on which they had worked; any particular case thus appeared in their jurisdiction often without their knowing whence it came, and passed from it they knew not whither.[9]

In this passage, architectural survey and description have made a sharp swerve into sociological mapping. The upper echelons of power in this social system are as remote and inaccessible as the Kantian Transcendental, whether in its "good" emanation, as the highest authority, purified by detachment and disinterest, or in its malevolent configuration as barren nature, retaining at all times the potential of devastating outbreaks against humanity. The hierarchy of officials, in this passage, ascends toward an utterly desolate and unforgiving *human* polar region.

Galactic Mood Climates

Our tracking of Kafka's meteoric and commodious swerves toward the universe of fantastic literature and the graphic novel begins in the panoply of dimensions in which Benjamin set his virtual simulation, in *The Arcades Project*, of nineteenth-century Paris. One of the astonishing things about this print-medium website of more than we could possibly wish to apprehend or know about Paris as the portal and capital city of global modernization is that Benjamin attends even to its modal parameters, the backdrop of cosmic ennui, inscribed in sources extending from Balzac's *Human Comedy*, to Baudelaire's lyrics, to Meryon's misty engravings, to Grandville's galactic cartoons. It is against this backdrop of world-weary fatigue that the culture of the moment works up a voracious appetite for the cornucopia of new commodities and entertainments, in an overall addiction to sensory overload that Benjamin argues, through a display of textual materials rather than logic, are the mainstays of European modernity.

> Only someone who has grown up in the big city can appreciate its rainy weather [*Städtisches Regenwetter mit seiner ganz durchtriebenen Lockung*], which altogether slyly sets one dreaming back to early childhood. Rain makes everything more hidden, makes days not only gray but uniform. From morning until evening, one can do the same thing—play chess, read, engage in argument—whereas sunshine by contrast shades the hours and discountenances the dreamer. The latter, therefore, must get around the day with subterfuges—above all, must rise quite early, like the great idlers, the waterfront loafers and the vagabonds. The dreamer must get up before the sun itself.[10]

> Blanqui's last work [*Critique sociale*, 1885], written during his imprisonment, has remained entirely unnoticed up to now, so far as I can see. It is a cosmological speculation. Granted it appears, in its opening pages, tasteless [*abgeschmackt*] and banal. But the awkward deliberations of the autodidact are merely the prelude to a speculation that only this revolutionary could develop. . . . In fact the cosmic vision of the world which Blanqui lays out, taking his data from the mechanistic natural science of bourgeois society, is an infernal vision. At the same time it is a complement of the society to which Blanqui, in his old age, was forced to concede victory. What is so unsettling is that the presentation is so lacking in irony. It is an unconditional surrender [*eine vorbehaltlose Unterwerfung*], but it is simultaneously the most terrible indictment of a society that projects this image of the cosmos—understood as an image of itself—across the heavens. With its trenchant style [*sprachlich von sehr starker Prägung ist*], this work displays the most

remarkable similarities both to Baudelaire and Nietzsche. (Letter of January 6, 1938, to Horkheimer)[11]

In the idea of eternal recurrence, the historicism of the nineteenth century capsizes. As a result, every tradition, even the most recent, becomes the legacy of something that has run its course in the immemorial night of the ages. Tradition henceforth assumes the character of a phantasmagoria in which primal history enters the scene in ultramodern get-up [*in modernster Ausstoffierung*].[12]

Life within the magic circle [*Bannkreis*] of eternal return makes for an existence that never emerges from the auratic.[13]

Benjamin's weather-central for nineteenth-century Paris, or twentieth-century Berlin, for that matter, combines the resignation and making do of rainy days, often an edifying experience of self-discovery and interpersonal intimacy, with the programmed inevitability of the Nietzschean eternal return. On those seemingly lost days of climatic infelicity, locating their cultural capital city in the nineteenth century, play joins up with fatalism. These are days of improvised activities, trivial pursuits, and silly games. They are also the ideal moment for breaking the comic-book collection out, with its piled leaves of disintegrating newsprint.

It doesn't surprise us that in Convolute C Benjamin plumbs to the foundations of Paris's vertical configuration, where he encounters ancient springs, sewers, metro tunnels, and the dungeons under the Châtelet in Victor Hugo's phantasmagoria of *Les misérables*, where slave labor for the Mediterranean galleys was sequestered and the argot song born, or that in Convolute F he assembles textual materials illuminating iron and glass, the new smart materials liberating function from form in architecture and urban planning and allowing both the buildings (e.g., the grand train stations, the Eiffel tower) and the infrastructure (e.g., railroad tracks) to usher in production, consumption, movement, and acceleration on an unprecedented scale. We might find it a little bit odd, but marvelous, that Benjamin devotes Convolute B to fashion—not only as a paradigmatic consumer industry of the age but as the very model for the evolution of culture in time, even if by the end of this mixed portfolio of materials he incriminates himself by suggesting that women persisted later in anthropological history than men in their horizontal positions for perambulation and related functions. The precise anthropological context in which the early twentieth-century public deliberated on the gender sociobiology underlying fashion behavior is and will remain obscure to us.

Reports on the Baron Haussmann's demolitions, contemporary prospectuses for major development projects, statutes regarding the employment of *filles publiques*, or prostitutes, reports on the political swings occasioned by such events as the uprisings of 1848 and the Commune, modern-day speculations on architecture and public transportation and related topics by Le Courbousier, Georg Simmel, Sigfried Giedion, and Sigfried Kracauer: all these comprise the *matériel* and camera angles that we would expect to be followed by Benjamin's unabashedly cinematographic critico-historical photographic apparatus: "Method of this project: literary montage. I needn't *say* anything. Merely show [*Ich habe nichts zu sagen. Nur zu zeigen*]."[14] Yet *The Arcades Project* takes no less seriously—and documents no less tangibly—dimensions of modernization of a far different nature: its tempos, its moods, even its collective dreams. In this more speculative outreach, Benjamin demonstrates his solidarity with an ongoing Frankfurt School project whose simultaneous purviews would be phenomenological, anthropological, mass psychological, and multimedia, as well as historical, literary, critical, psychoanalytical, and sociological. The literary montage that informed critique brings about effects a near-simultaneous panning from one of these discursive frameworks or perches to the next. In this virtually simultaneous overload of contrasting perspectives, the materials of *The Arcades Project* allegorically enact the desperate temporalities of expansion, consumption, and perception of the historical moment. (Marx's core passages on the simultaneity of industrial manufacturing process from *Capital*, volume 1 are among the materials of Convolute K [K3.1–2].) In daring to assemble the moment's collective dream or in reconstructing its distinctive moods and mood swings, Benjamin displays a more democratic receptivity to incompatible or minority reports on the mega-phenomenon of modernization than we are inclined to under our contemporary division of labor of professional academic subspecializations. Which hip psychoanalytical critic engaged in spinning out the present-day dream-phantasmagoria do you know who currently entertains Jung? Benjamin certainly did.

The modal parameters of modernization, as they are assembled and extrapolated above all in Convolute D, incorporate boredom, sublime world-weariness, indeed, exhaustion in general, set within an urban landscape engulfed by clouds and other atmospheric downers. The externally projected sociopsychological scene of depressive "learned helplessness"[15] is undergirded, as Benjamin's extracts chronicle, by a manic release always about to

break out. We can, indeed, argue that the nineteenth-century visual prece-
dents to the *noir* aesthetic are the visual objective correlative to this collective
mood of urban Parisian funk: that is, a depopulated urban landscape, ripe for
the solitary wanderings of the *flâneur*, whose somber tone is accentuated by
clouds and other soft visual filters, on the verge of an outbreak of the grotesque. (For the sake of the present discussion, we will define the modern
grotesque as an atmosphere of always-immanent invasion of the city by the
monsters, mutants, and extraterrestrials accessed by scientists and other scholars whose insider knowledge and duty calls them to the very brink of the
Kantian Transcendental. Baudelairean spleen in this sense incorporates the
troubled expectation that Frankenstein's monster is going to wander into
Paris from the Swiss Jura as an advance party for mutants such as postnuclear
Japan's Godzilla.)

Time Regained in Graphic Panels

In what follows, we will see, in a number of related sectors or screens, how
Kafka traveled into the populist literatures of comics art and fantastic fiction—despite his solid bourgeois upbringing, the small cadre of Prague intellectuals with whom he interacted, and the learned erudition clearly in
evidence throughout his writings. While a variety of formats of literary and
intellectual history allow us to trace such influences, the challenge before
us here is to appreciate the unrelenting, ongoing openness that Kafka configured for twentieth-century culture, the specific ways in which it remains
a screen on which turbulent and autopoietic cultural force fields can still be
charted. Key factors in this demonstration are the meticulous detail that
Kafka infused into his serial portraits of strangeness, whether the furrows
on Sortini's forehead or the conflation of mechanics and semantics programmed into the Penal Colony execution machine, and the original techniques by which he realized spatial disorientation. We should bear in mind,
though, that Kafka's entirely deranged spatial maps ultimately segue into a
time frame at once definitively empty and unachieved, in which motion
stutters, like the shutter on a movie camera, between definitive arrest and
open-ended continuity. This is a temporality in which repetitions are mutations, in which motion vacillates between time-lapse photography and slow
motion, in which the outlines of the body multiply into the shadows of an
image endlessly retaken and retraced. The temporal possibilities that Kafka

opened up for fiction form a Bermuda Triangle with Marcel Duchamp's "Nude Descending a Staircase" (Figure 1) and the odd temporal solutions found by the contemporary *bande dessinée* (comic book, literally "drawn volume"). This is something other than the magisterial but also monstrous and deeply unsettling reprise that Proust fashions for his cosmic plan of remembrance and inscription in *Time Regained*, even if Proustian melancholy and recollection claim a significant role in the demographics of mood that Benjamin extracts and assembles. Kafka's truest extraterrestriality consists in the persistent openness with which mutations can be scored within his permutations of alterity, the compulsive involution of his spatial zones, and the time frame of a motion never quite realized and never quite virtual.

The architectural implications of the Court in Kafka's *The Trial*, its involuted passageways, spatially compromised compartments, and unmarked conduits to the halls of greatest power, find a native land in the domain of sequential graphic narrative. Benjamin has, once again, through his immersion in the *matériel* of modernization and his insistence on a history discovering its truth only amid the flash of dialectical tensions impinging on the present, accessed nineteenth-century visual sources, above all Grandville and Charles Meryon. In his pivotal Baudelaire Convolute (J), he cites Gustave Geffroy on the atmospheric features of the latter artist's urban landscape, which translates particularly well into the graphic novel:

> I have rarely seen the natural solemnity of an immense city more poetically reproduced. Those majestic accumulations of stone; those spires "whose fingers point to heaven"; those obelisks of industry, spewing forth their conglomerations of smoke against the firmament; those prodigies of scaffolding 'round buildings under repair, applying their openwork architecture, so paradoxically beautiful, upon architecture's solid body; that tumultuous sky, charged with anger and spite; those limitless perspectives, only increased by the thought of all the drama they contain;—he forgot not one of the complex elements.[16]

Comics art is constantly beset by the demand to open up panoramas of "mystery and the imagination" within a medium constantly conforming to the constraints and architecture of frames and framing. Kafka and theoretically astute twentieth-century comics art intersect at the framework where his parody of power, elaborating through fictive figuration not only the antinomies but also the absurdities of the Law and its banal abuses as they derive from a universe of speculation (perhaps best exemplified by Kant),

1. Marcel Duchamp, *Nude Descending a Staircase*. An iconic moment of modernist painting when the "still" of portraiture opens up to incorporate sequential movement and through it, time.

segues into the cartoonist's unremitting struggle against the law of the frame, its structure, and its sequence. One could argue, then, that the architecture of Kafka's Castle as well as Court is already comics art embedded into the medium of discursive fictive narrative.

The comics artist, by contrast, is a master of the laws and gymnastics of the line. Against the narrative imperatives of discernible sequence and developments, she orchestrates a shibboleth between the line as principle of continuity and assertion and the line as trace of physical accident. All comics art registers as the slapstick collision, as in the clash, in Kafka's "A Common Confusion," between the linear logic and progressive constructions of speculative thinking and the accidents of line as a physical phenomenon or Deleuzian "line of flight."

Because we are dealing here with structural affinities between some of Kafka's investigations along the time-space-language discontinuum in fictive narrative art and some of the exigencies imposed on comics artists by their medium, it is no surprise that the traits of Kafka's extraterrestrial investigations migrate well to very different graphic settings, whether the illustrative style of the old Classic Comics, the *cités obscures* of the Belgian *bande dessinée*, or the rich if slightly maudlin New York cityscapes of Ben Katchor. The migratory range of the grotesque urban climate and aesthetic documented in *The Arcades Project* and elaborated throughout Kafka's novels extends well beyond the print medium. This comes home with particular force when we trace the impact of the Belgian *cités obscures* on the recent French-Canadian contribution to big-time, full-length animation, "The Triplets of Belleville."[17]

I will begin this demonstration of the endurance and scrambling of a distinctive climate or mood of inscription with the comics art of Ben Katchor, whose daily strips for the *Jewish Daily Forward* furnished the material for such volumes as *Julius Knipl Real Estate Photographer: Stories* and *Julius Knipl Real Estate Photographer: The Beauty Supply District*. Even in a framed and paneled world of muted realism, one accentuated tangibly by the daily fluctuations in the real estate market, the allegorical melancholy of nineteenth-century Paris persists and the uncanny involutions of Kafkan architecture find an extension. Indeed, Katchor exploits the somber style in which he depicts the neighborhood settings of the purely local and small-scale real estate transactions that take place there as the ho-hum, customary backdrop to the relentless productions of his wit. Knipl surveys, along Ornamental Avenue, "that broad, tree-lined thoroughfare originating at Beukelson Circle," in the section leading off *The Beauty Supply District*, such public architecture as "a monument to the inventor of pickled herring," "Arterial Hall, a legitimate surgical theater," "the Halitosis Society and the Museum of Insect Art," and "the Municipal Laxative Garden and the Katsigh Collection of Worn Shoe and Broken Laces."[18] Some modest introduction to the world of perverse humor might be useful in order to appreciate these jokes fully. Katchor manages to make them flash out, like Benjamin's dialectical image in Convolute N of *The Arcades Project*, against the backdrop of the drab urban surroundings. The dialectical image is Benjamin's consummate figure, an image so stunningly compressing the telling sociopolitical anomalies of the moment that it stops readers dead in their tracks.

In other words, a thread links the graphic novel to the Parisian arcades, even when its mode of delivery is realism and its subject real estate. This point is already evident in the sweepingly panoramic perspective depicted on the cover of *Julius Knipl Real Estate Photographer: Stories*,[19] (Figure 2). As Knipl enters a crowded Brooklyn intersection from stage left, his gaze continues a visual pan initiated by the El tracks and station in the upper right-hand corner. His gaze has moved leftward from the urban density at right toward a horizon still largely open. Comics art's affinity for panoramic sweeps through the horizontal panels of comics gutters plays a decisive role in the design of *The Beauty Supply District*, the sequel to *Julius Knipl: Stories*. The front enpapers (Figure 3) seem at first glance a continuous montage of the fronts of three contiguous streets, beginning at left with Sensum's Symmetry Shop, sitting atop the Synthetic Apriori Corp., whose storefront signage advertises "Mindwork." But the endpapers also incorporate a collage element: two theater tickets peer out from the strip of 1950s foldout real estate snaps. The back endpapers to the volume (Figure 4) exploit the collage motif initiated at the front. Here a theater seating plan and a perfume-sample strip (this is the beauty supply district), are affixed around a waterproof urban map of puddles. A gutter, presumably like those running alongside the blocks of storefronts on the front endpapers, has, in this map, taken on the scale of a whole neighborhood.

Katchor thus appropriates in his practice of the graphic novel the visual tradition of collage, both in the multiregister, fragmented surfaces of cubism and in the playful assemblages of Surrealism. It is nigh impossible to

2. Ben Katchor, *Julius Knipl Real Estate Photographer*: *Stories* (Boston: Little Brown, 1996), cover.

overestimate the centrality of Surrealism to Benjamin, as the aesthetic sensibility and *technē* most closely accompanying the jarring collisions of the modern cityscape and approximating the disjunctions of allegory. Louis Aragon's *Paris Peasant* may well serve as *The Arcades Project*'s preeminent contemporary fictive talisman, and not only in shuttling between the centrally located Parisian arcades and the artists' colonies gathered at the periphery around such sites as the Parc des Buttes Chaumont and the Canal St-Martin: its narrative is structured by the arcades' architectural configuration, by the linear progression of boutiques, the parallelism between storefront and covered passageway, and the vertical layering of legitimate and illegitimate business zones. It is no accident, then, that Katchor's collages in the endpapers of *The Beauty Supply District* is strikingly similar to that incorporated by Aragon into his exemplary urban surrealist novel, whether consisting of ads spliced onto the pages of fictive exposition (Figure 5), or the inscriptions on the official buildings and monuments of the nineteenth arrondissement, reproduced in the narrative with perfect typographical fidelity (Figure 6).[20]

The play of architecture—its fantastic exaggeration, its emergence from linear structures of the sort schematized in blueprints, the modal shadows, canyons, and clearings cast by the profiles of skyscrapers—is even more decisive in the Belgian *bande dessinée* than in Katchor's atmospheric evocations of the real estate market. If Katchor's productions hold Kafka at bay as an implicit demiurge of their relentless, maudlin wit, he is an in-your-face business partner of the Schuiten brothers, Luc and François, who, sometimes with and sometimes without Benoît Peeters, invented the apocalyptic and grotesque urban landscape of the Belgian books. Of particular interest for the influence of Kafka on popular visual media are two series of comics art volumes produced by these artists, *Dark Cities* and *Hollow Earths*. Both of these, in turn, fall under the marvelously sordid rubric *Confederated Humanoids*. Kafka is in serious cahoots with these comics artists, both as a supplier of narrative themes and as an unofficial city planner. The conceptual gutter or margin of humanoids holds itself invitingly open to the multifarious experimentation with animals (cognitive, narratological, characterological) that Kafka implanted within a literary framework.

Who but Kafka could have inspired the Schuitens' postnuclear holocaust tale—entitled *Carapaces*—of two lovers who, hungry for direct contact, strip off their prophylactic carapaces (this is a fable deriving from the age of AIDS) only to be devoured by the insects who now dominate the world (Figures 7 and 8)?[21] Kafka's Gregor has indeed been fruitful and multiplied. The central image of this book is no longer his quite particular shell but a mutant exoskeleton so dominating the biosphere that the remaining human stragglers are forced to devise a parallel covering for themselves.

Moving into an explicitly urban environment, the denizens of the *cités obscures* devote considerable labor and newsprint to chronicling their own projects and initiatives, generating a massive archive filled with the blueprints and textual remains of the various themed and styled architectural sites. The internal archivists of the *cités obscures* are good businessmen, as well: compilations based on the most striking graphics from each prior book can be added to the series. Unapologetic *bande dessinée* fans will snap them up. We meet Kafka as well (not to mention the Melville of "Bartleby the Scrivener") in the pages of *L'archiviste*,[22] specifically, in the figures of the stooped-over archivists who, amid the mad symmetry of a Borgesian library gone shabby, transfer disintegrating volumes of architectural plans from one crumbling floor of the archive to the next (Figures 9 and 10).

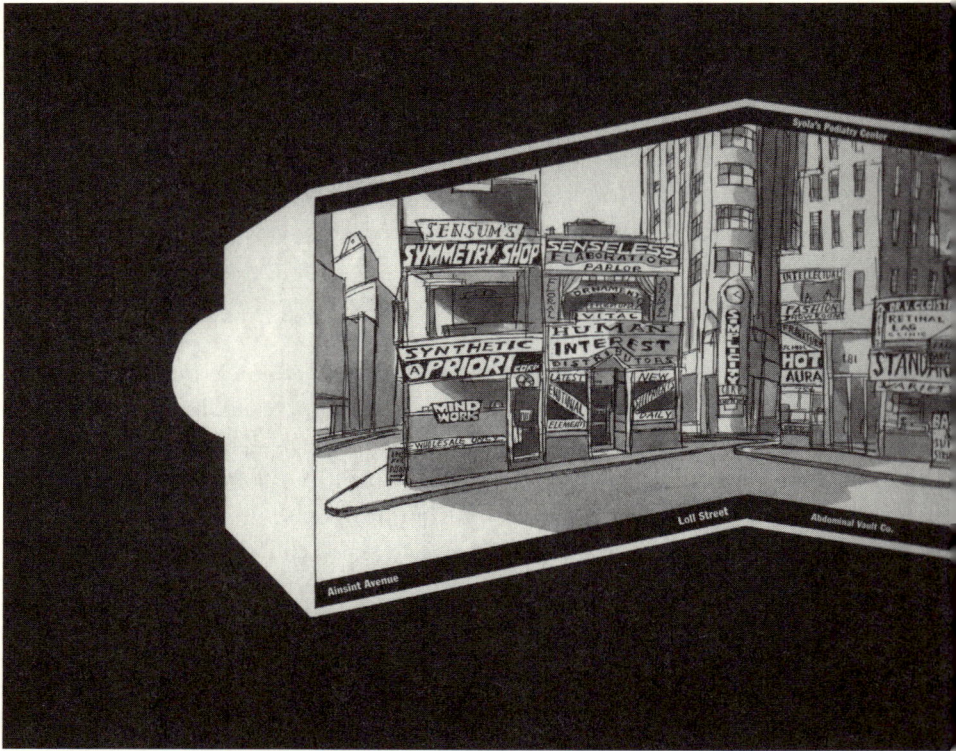

3. Ben Katchor, *Julius Knipl Real Estate Photographer*: *The Beauty Supply District* (New York: Pantheon, 2003), endpapers, front, with storefronts, including "Sensum's Symmetry Shop" and "Synthetic Apriori Corp."

With respect to the grotesque architectural setting of these volumes, the key point to bear in mind is the rich interface between Kafka's conceptual and rhetorical dismantling of the Law and the graphic novel's capability to tease out, elaborate, and structurally analyze the infrastructures as well as exoskeletons of buildings and other constructed spaces. We can achieve an appreciation of the full richness of registers of signification, rhetoric, and performance embedded by this medium in the act and material of writing not merely by interposing a comic book in the space of what the Examining Magistrate had been reading during Joseph K.'s notorious preliminary hearing on a Sunday, a porn novel entitled *The Degradations Grete Suffered from Her Husband Hans*.[23] This is the title Joseph K. comes upon a week after the initial deliberation, when he approaches the dais of justice.

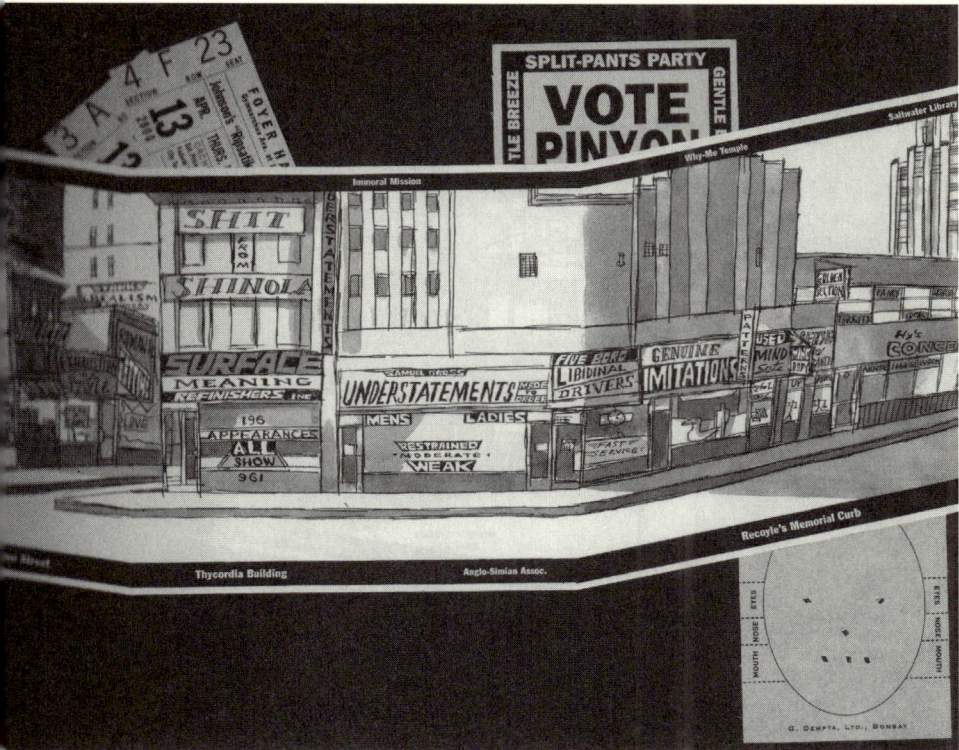

It is precisely at the law of the line that the authoritarian and closed systems of the Law, whether that of *The Trial* or the Commandant's parodic Mosaic law in "In the Penal Colony,"[24] segue into the hyper-detailed architectural schemata that have been the matter of lithography and prints for some time now. The line is the mark or scoring where the ideational elements of communications and the accidents of physical linearity converge. The sheer arbitrariness of the line, which I can make swerve anywhere I want to on the reasonably flat, two-dimensional *tabula* before me, snuffs out the mannered distinctions between conceptualization and materiality, between reflection and graphic arbitrariness. The attenuated materiality of the line, its unmarked swerves between word and sentence formation, including the semantic burden they bear, and unmitigated visual accident preempts a full range of exasperating confusions—between medium and meaning, between message and unintended resonance—taking up so much of critical-exegetical deliberation. It's far less absurd than you might think

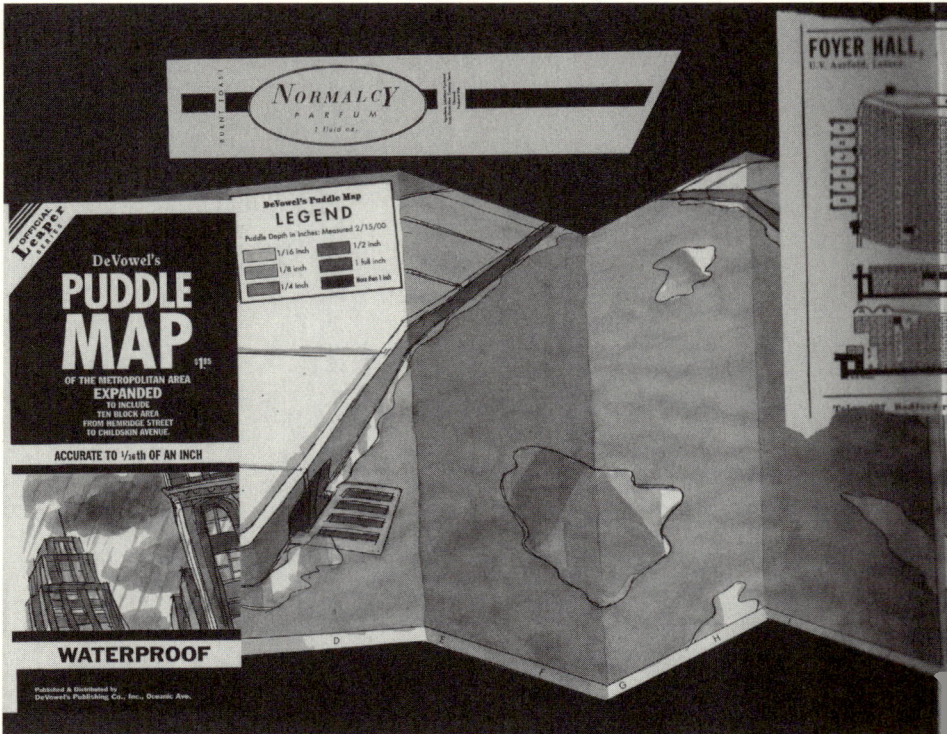

4. Ben Katchor, *The Beauty Supply District*, endpapers, rear, with collage, including theater seating plan and "De Vowel's Puddle Map."

to imagine that the actual pulp reading of Kafka's Examining Magistrate was a comic book.

To the degree that I myself have stepped into of the attorney's role in the utterly spurious and corrupt Court of Kafkan Law, let me begin to rest my case.

Exhibit #1 is the case of an architectural virus, a cube form, that erupts and madly proliferates in the *bande dessinée* volume *The Fever of Vrbicande*, something like killer-weed, within the architectural projects of one Eugène Robick, imploding them from within (Figure 11).[25] The virus is another mutation filtering into the world of utopian-apocalyptic graphics from the world of AIDS. Robick, whose name resonates well with Rubik's Cube, a mind-bending geometrical puzzle in its ascendancy in 1992, when these volumes were produced, is yet another advanced male protagonist who ends up paired

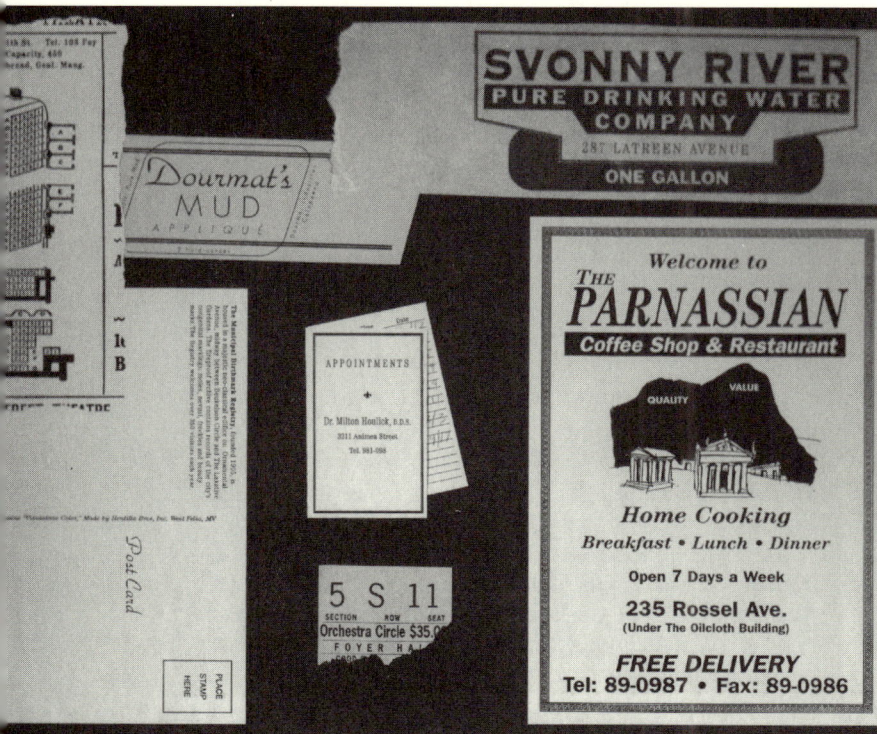

with a much younger female possessor of pornographic aura. Yes indeed, another fertile field of exploration in the law of the line, particularly in its open-ended graphic *flânerie* over the smooth space of the page, is exquisite effigies of fantasized sexual objects, whichever genders or modes of dress and other aspects of presentation are dictated by fashion. Via auto-affection—to which Husserl assigned a pivotal role as a constitutive element of personal experience and to which Derrida subsequently appealed as the very dynamic of representation's effect and power, given the absence of the signified—the graphic novel possesses an irreducible pornographic dimension, as the *auteurs* of the Belgian *bande dessinée* make sure to remind us at every turn.[26] The long-standing graphic tradition of vivid sexual caricature prominent within the art repositories of so many cultures and civilizations remains at the disposal of contemporary comics artists. Those such as R. Crumb, the Schuiten Brothers, and Peeters freely draw upon its visual power and in so doing illustrate Derrida's object lesson in the driving force of what is absent.

BONJOUR, CHER AMI !

Avez-vous pris
vos biscuits

MOLASSINE ?

et ces commentaires :

MOLASSINE { dogs & puppy } { biscuits }

Après l'armurier vient le fournisseur en champagne de S.A.R. le duc d'Orléans. Il possède
quatre vitrines que nous suivrons des boulevards
au fond du passage : la première contient du
Chianti, du Lacrima Christi, et de la Malvoisie;
la deuxième contient du Chianti, du Lacrima
Christi et de l'Asti; la troisième contient des
radiateurs électriques en cuivre rouge. La qua-
trième, de l'autre côté de la porte, ne contient
que du champagne aux armes des rois de France.
Dans la devanture aux radiateurs, il y a des
plans et dessins de villas situés à Domfront-
en-Champagne (Sarthe), à trois minutes de la
gare, sur la grande ligne de Paris au Mans. Enfin
une pancarte annonce à l'amateur :

UNE RARETÉ : CALVADOS 1893
Mis en bouteille
APRÈS DIX-HUIT ANNÉES DE FÛT !

5. Louis Aragon, *Le paysan de Paris* (Paris: Gallimard, 1953), 122. Here and elsewhere, Aragon incorporates signage from the boutiques of the Parisian arcades into his text.

cinéma, humanité appliquée et mal récompen-
sée, éprise du bonheur du dimanche et soûle des
connaissances acquises à l'école du soir :

> ### 19e ARRONDISSEMENT
>
> PAR AUTORISATION BIENVEILLANTE
> DE L'ADMINISTRATION MUNICIPALE
> CET OBÉLISQUE-INDICATEUR
> A ÉTÉ ÉRIGÉ LE 14 JUILLET 1883,
> PAR L'INVENTEUR
> **EUG. PAYART**, VOYAGEUR DE COMMERCE
> AVEC LE CONCOURS DE :
> **MM. A. BOUILLANT**, FONDEUR,
> **DUMESNIL**, CIMENTIER,
> **COLLIN**, HORLOGER,
> **RICHARD** F^res, FAB^ts DE BAROMÈTRES,
> **DELAFOLIE, BASTIDE,**
> **CASTOUL** AÎNÉ ET Cie
> FAB^ts D'APPAREILS A GAZ
>
> ### BOUILLANT
> FONDEUR-CONSTRUCTEUR
> ### PARIS

La face ouest de la colonne porte haut les
initiales laurées de la République, affrontées
d'une étoile; elles surmontent un baromètre
rond, sur le cadran duquel on apprend l'adresse
de la Société anonyme des Établissements Jules
Richard : 25, rue Mélingue, Paris. Les cœurs

6. Aragon, *Le paysan de Paris*, 196. In this passage, Aragon reproduces
official municipal inscriptions from the city hall of the nineteenth
arrondisement into his text.

The cube virus, in *The Fever of Vrbicande*, is relatively more primitive,
more closed, in terms of contemporary systems theory; more analog, in
terms of Wilden's *System and Structure*.[27] The graphic artists thus establish
a tension between the style of their phantasmatic intervention and the structural elements into which their graphic arabesques break down.

7. Luc and François Schuiten, *Carapaces* (Geneva: Humanos, 1980), 6. A couple, wearing prophylactic body armor against insect swarms, prepares for sexual intercourse.

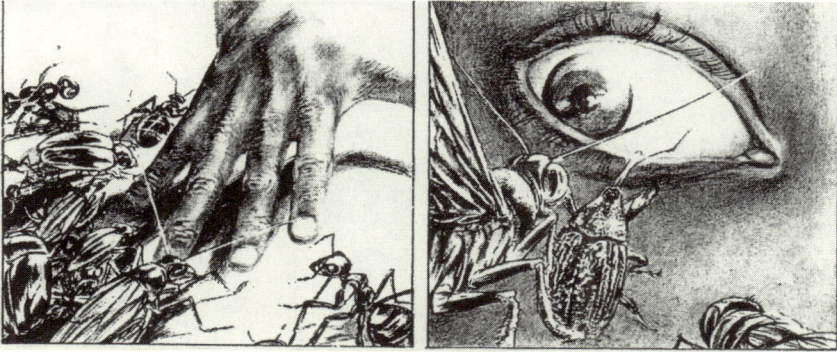

8. Schuiten brothers, *Carapaces*, 10. One of the sexual partners realizes the consequences of having removed protective garb.

Exhibit #2 will demonstrate that their ultimate loyalty is to the phantasmagoria that they can summon forth, in conjunction with suggestive theories of representation, from the graphic line. An interior landscape from the volume entitled *The Tower* refers explicitly to some of Escher's most notorious graphic tricks.[28] We look down from our perch in an antiquated gothic tower, but all at once we also glimpse architectural shapes head on, which are in turn on a Möbius strip, with other elements we are staring at from below (Figure 12). Kafka's explorations of temporal-spatial anomalies are notorious, not only the trip from village to village in "A Common Confusion"—which lasts, in separate transversals, ten minutes, ten hours, and "practically . . . an instant"—but also the wild juxtaposition of divergent paces of activity in *Amerika* and *The Castle*. I think particularly of how excruciatingly long it takes the aged paterfamilias of the Barnabas family, in the latter novel, to cross the parlor, while K. marvels at his sleekness and gains an introduction to his ostracized family.[29]

As has been noted by so many commentators, Kafka's visual world resides in a shabby neighborhood of architectural decay and superannuation, where basic infrastructure has fallen into disuse and disrepair, and inhabitants have long disabused themselves of their pretentions of keeping up appearances. The irreversible decline evident throughout the domain of this particular visual imaginary may well constitute Kafka's enduring debt to the seedier corners of Dostoyevsky's St. Petersburg. This aesthetic is a natural hinge or interface between Kafka's imagined cities and their residential and bureaucratic installations and the grotesque flank of contemporary comics

9. Luc & François Schuiten and Benoît Peeters, *L'archiviste* (Casterman, 2000), jacket. A figure almost from the pages of Melville's "Bartleby the Scrivener" assumes the burden of cultural memory, with all its archiving tasks.

10. Schuiten brothers and Peeters, *L'archiviste*, cover. Here the archivist hides in a compartment reminiscent of the madly symmetrical architecture prevalent in Borges's "The Library of Babel."

art, particularly as it emerges in the hilarious antics of R. Crumb. It is by no means an overstatement to assert that Crumb's invariably unkempt human figures, punctuated by the detail furnished by their hair and bodily secretions, combined with the Schuiten Brothers' grimly overbearing, even if soaring, architectural fantasies, could be characterized as "Kafka made graphic."

11. Schuiten brothers and Peeters, *La fièvre d'Vrbicande* (Casterman, 1992), 38. The virus of proliferating cubes begins to expand around its architect, Eugène Robick.

Comics art, while its radical combination of framed enclosure and open-ended panoramic perspective initiates serious explorations of represented space, maintains a vividly operatic relation to time. Exhibit #3, our last from the *bande dessinée*, details how a theoretically motivated comics art deals with its own status, in Scott McCloud's terms, as "sequential fiction."[30] The title of *Nogegon* is a long palindrome, suggesting a closed feedback loop.[31] The volume details some work Nelle, an artistic as well as pornographic model, does for a master of a futuristic art medium, "art-trace." By leaping from a balcony to the ground in a simulated flying posture, Nelle allows her image both to be fragmented, photographically dissected into the separate moments of her fall, and to bring sculpture into

12. Schuiten brothers and Peeters, *La tour* (Casterman, 1987), 6. Giovanni Battista, master of the tower, enters an Escher-like perspective, in which he gazes at the internal gothic trappings of the structure simultaneously head on, from above, and from below.

a new paradigm of poetic fluidity (Figure 13). Nelle's leap, captured in multiple outlines like the cinematic image, claims a canonical source in twentieth-century visual experimentation: nothing less than Marcel Duchamp's nude negotiating a downward staircase.

We don't really need to go into the rapport with her artistic master that Nelle enters into when the relationship turns personal. Through this fantasy, the comics art of the *bande dessinée* indicates the horizon of its own rapport with time, imagining the acceleration of its progressive sequence of frames until it achieves a blur, the sustained, continuous trace of movement in space. It is no accident that Convolute Y of *The Arcades Project*, "Photography," becomes an overall survey of the technology of image-transfer made possible by nineteenth-century innovations.[32] It may not anticipate artrace, but it encompasses, in addition to photography, the phenakistiscope, the pantograph, the physionotrace, and photosculpture. (Indeed, it is the latter of these technologies that probably most closely approximates the futuristic master's sculptures.)

At the moment when comics art theorizes its possible relations to time, it commits itself anew to its status as writing or trace. It is precisely when the graphic mark achieves the contours of a continuous if blurred profile that the possibility of graphic narrative is born. The possibility and indeed

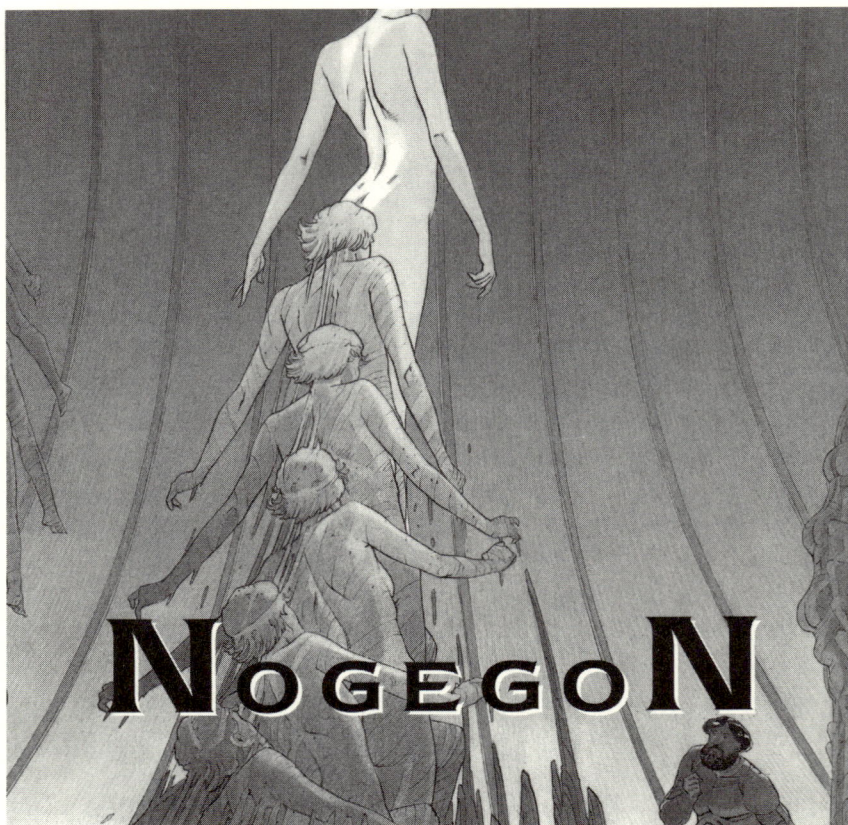

13. Schuiten brothers and Peeters, *Nogegon* (Casterman, 1990), rear cover, indicating the multiple-image trail left by the model Olive in the futuristic sculptural artform "artrace."

imperative to narrative development inheres in the ocular progression from frame to frame along the gutter, which also marks a progression in time (even in view of a rich disparity between the subgenres of comics art as to the rigidity of the gutter structure and the temporal composition of individual frames.) There is a tedious repetitiveness to the necessity of moving from one framed image to the next, a tedium like that of splenetic rainy days of the Second Empire in Paris. Like *flânerie* in the city, or strolling along the boutiques of the arcades, the linear progression from one visual frame to the next reaches toward the acceleration of cinema and all the manipulations that can be achieved through montage. The graphic novel knows that it is cinema in the making, or already happening, on the page. Through the blurred extension of figures such as Nelle, at once fast-forward graphics and freeze-frame, comics art reveals its status as a cinema that has invaded and taken over reading, the private experience of the defile of words, icon, and other signifiers along the gutters and other passageways of the screen or page.

Conclusion

Through their graphic effigies, cultural programmers perforce become meteorologists, charting the very climate of writing: its parameters, the laws of the line, panel, and gutter, its enabling and disabling conditions. Graphic fiction can be read as a weather map of inscriptive possibilities from one historical moment or epistemological configuration to another.

This becomes clear in the encounter that Leo Leonhard and Otto Jägersberg stage, in *Rüssel in Komikland*,[33] between shapes and characters emerging from Hieronymus Bosch's apocalyptic landscapes and the gaudy colors and forms that dominate contemporary advertising and other forms of hard sell. The shapes that Rüssel and Schrüssel, the central characters, assume and the landscape through which they wander derive from a specific apocalyptic work by Bosch, *The Garden of Earthly Delights*, in a comics-art translation Leonhard and Jägersberg insert late in the volume (Figure 14).[34] The tale of *Rüssel in Komikland* is a simple one: two characters in every sense of the word, Rüssel and Schrüssel, every bit as "animal" as they are "human," wander further and further from their home in an environment reminiscent of late-medieval/early Renaissance Flemish landscape painting, depicted in a severe style of monochromatic etching, until they encounter Flabby Jack, a knockoff of Disney's Goofy, but with the outrageous hair of the 1970s and an the unmistakable residue of profound recent chemical experiences (Figure 15). They are flown in a helicopter called the "Red Pill" to Komikland, while Flabby Jack sleeps off some of the toxins still circulating in his blood system. There they meet bubblegum executive Al Bosso, dressed in the costume of a 1930s mafia don but speaking the patois of aggressive capitalism under conditions of expansion so rapid that it becomes blurred (Figure 16). This is Al Bosso's discourse:

14. Leo Leonhard and Otto Jägersberg, *Rüssel in Komikland* (Darmstadt: Melzer, 1972), detail, 44–45. Fountain, graphic caricature of Bosch, *The Garden of Earthly Delights*.

We need to feature the Chinese. This is our new market. The Chinese should be chewing bubblegum, the devil with them. That's what we need to push, so that the stock goes up. Chop chop! BANG! BANG! [*Wir müssen die Chineschen fietschern. Das ist die neue Markt für uns. Die Chinesen sollen Babbelgamm kauen, zum Geier. Da müssen wir zuschlagen, daß die Aktien steigen, racker, racker, ZACK, ZACK!*][35]

The overall didactic thrust of this volume is a warning about the cultural environmental impact of voracious global capitalism and the creeping

Americanization of global mass culture, which has the effect of sweetening the pill. But what powers this line of thought and critique is above all a multiregister and multifaceted contrast of styles: first between the narrative density and rich mythological and allusive traditions underscoring European culture, as embodied in the paintings of a Bosch or a Poussin and the utter bluntness of U.S. mass culture of the 1960s and 1970s, its multifaceted and frank testing of rules, boundaries, and prevailing social convention, devoid of a sequential history of modulation and qualification. *Rüssel in Komikland* orchestrates this cultural divergence above all in a visual sense: through the contrast between the intricate detail of Brueghel or Dürer and the dayglo colors and paisley shapes colonizing the late-capitalist mind by way of

15. Leonhard and Jägersberg, *Rüssel in Komikland*, 31. Contemporary Flabby Jack finds distorted playmates from the graphic universe of Bosch's imaginary creatures.

16. Leonhard and Jägersberg, *Rüssel in Komikland*, 35. Al Bosso, mob godfather, at home in the seat of his power.

psychedelic culture. This isn't to suggest that living in a Brueghelian apocalypse of hyperactive mass superego would be any more edifying than kowtowing to the staccato business orders of Al Bosso. But through the medium of graphic narrative, Leonhard and Jägersberg have brilliantly seized an opportunity to couch a sociopolitical and critical argument in vivid visual terms.

We need to remember that psychedelic humor, achieved with or without the deployment of chemical substances, is another by-product of Kafka's imaginative intervention. The imaginary expanse opened by Kafka's literary dismantling of the prevailing systems of law and authority, possibly extending, in contemporary terms, to extraterrestrial domains, is in fact a drug with chemical aftereffects. Kafka's personal readings from *The Trial* and

"The Metamorphosis" kept his close circle of friends in stitches. This laughter did not require the stimulation of hemp or hashish. In certain of its emanations, the dawning of the extraterrestrial as the framing environment to global schemes of commerce and exploitation may cast an ominous shadow, but its mood is a rollicking, furious, and unremitting Nietzschean laughter that resounds in the Open cleared out by critique and the radical deployment of aesthetic variation.

THREE

Kafka's Imaginary: A Cognitive Psychology Footnote

Imaginary Ventures

This was an even poorer neighborhood, the houses were still darker, the streets filled with sludge oozing about slowly on top of the melting snow. In the tenement where the painter lived only the wing of the great double door stood open, and beneath the other wing, in the masonry near the ground, there was a gaping hole [*war . . . eine Lücke gebrochen*] out of which, just as K. approached, issued a disgusting yellow liquid [*eine widerliche, gelbe, rauchende Flüssigkeit harausschoß*], steaming hot, from which some rats fled into the adjoining canal. At the foot of the stairs an infant lay face down on the ground bawling.[1]

What do we mean when we say that an author, in her relentless cultural reprogramming, has not only added to or reconfigured the conventions surrounding a genre or a discourse, but has facilitated the incursion of a different Imaginary? How can an Imaginary,[2] owing something both to Kantian imagination (*Einbildungskraft*)[3] and to the visualizing faculty with which

Lacan replaces the Freudian superego, evolve, change, or be different from itself? Psychoanalysis, along with the philosophical infrastructures making it possible, pushes us toward an apprehension of the Imaginary as a hard-wired human facility of mental processing, which changes only with difficulty and reluctance over the centuries and generations. Yet cultural history places a high premium on the cognitive and epistemological changes—even on the profound level of processing—made possible by significant technological and communicative developments and by demographic, commercial, and political arrangements. At what point does the Imaginary cease being a more or less permanent faculty, as situated by Kant in the configuration of knowing and other human capabilities, and become susceptible, in its ongoing negotiations with the Symbolic and the Real, to events and developments marking both a specific moment and a way of life?[4] Can we say that we remember Kafka so vividly, that we accept him as a taking-off point for projects by artists as diverse as Samuel Beckett,[5] Albert Camus,[6] Ingmar Bergman,[7] Orson Welles,[8] György Ligeti,[9] Thomas Bernhard,[10] Orhan Pamuk,[11] and Haruki Marukami,[12] in part because he furnishes a demographically specific site for tangible developments in the aesthetico-cultural Imaginary?

Kafka's penchant for improvising such epoch-changing as well as vivid figures as Gregor Samsa and Odradek, the execution machine in "In the Penal Colony," the telephone systems of *The Castle* and the Hotel Occidental of *Amerika*, the friendly Oklahoma detention center at the conclusion of the latter novel, and the expansive yet claustrophobic underground warren of predation and compulsive rumination in "The Burrow" has been documented by a vast and still-growing community of commentators. Surely an author who managed, in the radical fictive imbalance he sustained over the course of his writing, to crystallize stunning hybrids at the outer limits of figuration left a palpable and enduring environmental impact upon the book, the medium of his writerly commerce or traffic. A powerful case could be made, I believe, for *The Trial's* not only housing Kafka's most extended textual allegories but *being* the very book implicated by the unanticipated figurations orchestrated by the mutations of his Imaginary. The parable "Before the Law" establishes an exegetical house of exchange in which every episode in the novel renders an interpretation of every other, successively disqualifying every plausible explanation for Josef K.'s inexplicable

predicament tendered by the narrative.[13] The novel as a whole is the labyrinthine medium in which mutually disqualifying perspectives, inferences,
and explanations coexist in a condition of growing dissonance and unease.
It is no accident that Borges was an avid reader and interpreter of Kafka.
He recognized in his predecessor the designer of a new paradigm of books,
"different from our own. Their fiction has a single plot, with every imaginable permutation. Their works of a philosophical nature invariably contain
both the thesis and the antithesis, the rigorous *pro and contra* of every argument. A book that does not contain its counterbook is considered
incomplete."[14]

Surely if any author can claim to usher in a new Imaginary, it is Kafka.
The ways in which his literary critics have rehearsed this claim, whether
making it explicitly or not, are legion. Whether they have treated Kafka as
an author who placed sublimity, as it emerged in Romanticism and over the
broader modernity, head-on against the bureaucratic social programming
of the late nineteenth and twentieth centuries; or as the avatar of cultural
minority and deterritorialization emerging on the margins of speculative
systems and the nation-states modeled on their functioning; or as a fictive
author whose works convey, with unusual lucidity and power, the traits and
possibilities of a universe existing in an a priori state of deconstruction,
critics have responded to the epoch-making repercussions of his work. It
remains an open question whether Kafka's singular attentiveness to the
techno-socio-politico-aesthetic developments taking place around him, experienced from the relative insularity of Prague, is tantamount to the configuration of a new Imaginary. But surely in his moment he had few peers
in the enterprise of reconfiguring not only how the reading constituency
experiences politics, communications, representation, and cultural history
but how it dreams: Joyce, surely, in the drive toward a global language of
cultural attainment and sharing; perhaps Proust as well. In the nineteenth
century we look toward Hoffmann (a material witness in Freud's discourse
regarding the uncanny), Dostoyevsky, and Melville as belonging to a very
small cadre of authors—perhaps, indeed, by dint of their unique acuity concerning contemporary developments transpiring at the level of the philosophical operating system—who tampered with or contributed to the sway
and very possibilities of the Imaginary.

I would postulate that truly memorable literature—literary composition
and display uncanny both in its summation of past and prevailing cultural

conditions and in its extrapolation of the drifts of the future—can cognitively transform and reprogram its audience. We can think of the cultural
transformations enacted by literature as *epistemological* ones, modifying what
and how the public knows; as *cognitive* ones, affecting how its public then
processes its world and the data ensuing from this world; or as *inscriptive*[15]
or *programmatic* ones, adding new options to existing modes of noting,
transmitting, displaying, composing, recording, and archiving information
and thinking. In a sense, the literature whose inevitability is a sustained
performance as well as an assertion is also a drug, a chemical compound, in
whose aftermath readers process perception, experience, and the Real itself
in a slightly different way than before. History is as much a sequence of
perceptual and cognitive thresholds as anything else. We return to certain
authors with the craving of addicts and the twinges of reformed criminals
because their works open panoramas on the evolution of cognition itself, on
epistemological ruptures in whose wake people operated on different registers and in untried ways. In the absolutely mysterious fashion in which
Kafka anticipated in his fiction the tumult of twentieth-century communications and cybernetics, the waves of its deterritorializations and the industrialization of its death, he exemplifies the epoch-making writer. And surely,
the magnitude and diversity of the adaptations of his signal, singular works
is one indication of the cognitive reprogramming that they imaginarily effected. But while Kafka may have few peers in the fatal homing instincts of
his intuition, when we entertain the criterion of cognitive restructuring and
rewiring as a decisive mechanism of cultural persistence and innovation and
admit cognitive processes and possibilities into the engine room of cultural
history, he is joined there by a rich and diverse list of fellow-programmers,
including Aristophanes, Plato, Petronius, Shōnagon, Cervantes, Baudelaire,
Nietzsche, Proust, Eisenstein, Welles, and Disney. We need to at least consider the possibility that signal instances of cultural reprogramming—from
Lascaux to the Palladian perspective to the cybernetics-inspired (if not powered) cinematography of Peter Greenaway—are as much at play in any tendency toward species evolution as the usually suspected factors, whether
geological catastrophes, technological and industrial revolutions, or massive
political realignments.

The quotation that opens the present section is hardly extraordinary in
the concentration of its fictive innovations. Yet it encompasses, like many
other examples that could have been selected from the stories and novels,

the odd combinations at the basis of an improvisational imaginary recon-figuration. Reiterating Joseph K.'s initial foray into the *banlieu* of housing projects on the day of his preliminary interrogation in *The Trial*, it describes his entry to the tenement where Court artist Titorelli lives and has his ate-lier. This will be the scene of the artist's elucidation of the labyrinth of mutually intertwined and mutually exclusive legal-bureaucratic alternatives from which Joseph K. will never escape. Notable in the passage is its precise architectural attention to an overall scene of misery.[16]

It is a shoddy and ramshackle architecture that houses the economically marginal, whose numbers have skyrocketed in the latter years of the Haps-burg Empire. The most shocking indication that the construction fails in its function of housing and protecting its inhabitants is the disgusting yellow fluid of unspecified composition and provenance emanating from its breaches. This is as direct an encounter with the Lacanian Real as we are afforded in the body of Kafka's fiction. As in the case of the inarticulate screeching that emanates from Gregor's bedroom in the aftermath of his metamorphosis, we know that something is terribly amiss here, but we can't say exactly what the fluid means or is. It is in such an abject setting, one whose misery and divorce from conventionality (the Symbolic) cannot be fully processed or made articulate, that we encounter a bawling baby face-down in the mire. The yet-unsocialized creature is an avatar both of the animals whose ontogenetic difference from humans is left fluid in the world of Kafka's fiction and of the child prostitutes who storm Titorelli's apart-ment and violate every possible social convention.[17] Kafka's animals and his children both travel in Deleuzian packs:[18] they wreak havoc with any clear-cut margin between the individual and the composite grouping, between the personal psychology of the drive, its expression, and its repression and the asocial psychology of flows,[19] whether of money, commodities, aggres-sion, or sexuality, winding in impersonal waves through amorphous popula-tions or masses.

The vividness of this sample from Kafka's fictive embroidery can be mapped both on the evolving network of literary history and in terms of creative deployment of conventional literary tools and resources: innova-tions in imagery, style, narrative splicing, and so on. Yet something in the panorama (first and foremost a *visual* scene) that it opens and the linguis-tico-social forces that it marshals and coordinates implicates the manner in which its readers are capable of *processing* (in the sense in which cognitive psychology would deploy this term) the evolving state of affairs around them. When I propose that Kafka, along with very few writers at any particular moment (and invariably by means of a special acuity to contemporaneous developments in philosophy and the philosophically driven social sciences) emends the Imaginary enabling culture and current events to be processed, I am gravitating toward the interface at which aesthetics intersects with cognition and cognitive psychology.

Recourse to Lacan

In very general terms, I want to dwell a bit on the ramifications of the substitution for the triad of the classical psychoanalytical agencies—Id, ego, and superego—of the Lacanian faculties, Real, Symbolic, and Imaginary (here we find a strong appeal to Kant).[20] As I've had occasion to argue in much earlier work, the subject that Lacan inherits from Freudian discourse is perhaps most productively characterized as both: (1) a homunculus of subjective traits and functions extrapolated from the history of Western metaphysics, from Greek to German idealist philosophy; and (2) the small-scale replica of an autonomous system of intellectual work whose mechanics owe more to Hegelian dialectics than to Kantian mapping.[21] In such pivotal early works as "The Function and Field of Speech and Language in Psychoanalysis" and "The Freudian Thing,"[22] Lacan meticulously orchestrated a shift from subjective metaphysics to linguistic mediation and processing as the decisive phenomenon within the psychoanalytic field. In his core reconfiguration, the Freudian emphasis on the schooling and tempering of the drive, the work of ego congenitally whipsawed between immoderate impulses and equally excessive restraints, is supplanted by a focus on the accommodations effected by the subject as a user and programmer of language. The interactions and negotiations brokered, successfully or not, by the Lacanian subject implicate the full panoply of linguistic negotiations and operations. (Lacan characterizes them, first and foremost, as *symbolic* abstractions and substitutions.) Through this intervention, the focus of psychology shifts away from the age-old psychomachy of the soul, charged with judgment, moral torment, and bipolar valuation, to a more neutral scene (Derrida might call it a scene of writing),[23] in which an agent or operator negotiates her fate across the multiple registers of symbolic forms or notations. Not only does the picture of the subject radically change through this modification (how it is composed, what it does, how it operates), so does its social bearing or address toward subjectivity (its moral reception, if you will). The subject becomes a programmer or writer instead of a defendant in a cosmic trial—implicitly overseen by the monotheistic Abrahamic deity—concurrent with existence. (This point is not lost on Kafka. It can be argued that all Joseph K. gains in the course of *The Trial*, a novel in which he loses friends, family, and work, and in which his options as a sexual being are foreclosed, is a pronounced acuity as a reader and decoder of pronouncements, narratives, and messages.)

It is no less earth-shaking (and I say this sincerely) that Lacan could expand the fulcrum of bipolar thinking, judgment, and moral rumination concentrated, within the Freudian subjective homunculus, in the superego, into the full constellation of functions and activities related to visualization. This is, I believe, the Imaginary's broader orientation. It is by no means intuitive that the needs, at least under conditions of modernity, for internalized moral and behavioral restraints and self-regulation, effected in large measure by the imaginary visualization of negative repercussions accruing from one's thinking and behavior, evolve into a vast spectrum of visual processes and artifacts, including, dreams, daydreams, waking fantasies, and the full array of the visual, graphic, and media arts.

Those who dwell on these paradigm shifts, as we are doing briefly now, cannot help but be benefited by a good measure of therapeutic healing, at least in the domain of cultural psychoanalysis. The inevitable Day of Judgment, the Dark Night of the Soul, a scenario as intrinsic to the system of psychoanalysis (as Freud formally enunciated it) as to the monotheistic religions and the philosophy of subjective metaphysics, has been suspended or lifted in favor of a scene of cultural programming (whether in language or in images, a distinction Lacan programs into his map of consciousness but that we don't need to). Psychoanalysis becomes less a course in self-improvement and more the acquisition of greater facility on the plane of discursive, visual, and critico-interpretative experience.

It is obvious that the Real, the Lacanian stand-in for the Freudian Id, is not an intrapsychic agency, even one relegated to the status of the subject's bad boy, the primitive selfhood refusing the restraints and sublimations of adulthood. Lacan metamorphoses the superego into a dimension or a site (in this respect it is the only element in the psychoanalytical triad not expressing itself as a faculty or mode of processing). The Real is, rather, both the arbitrary condition of unmediated and non-negotiable thrown-ness[24] (or sublimity, or uncanniness, or silence, or death) from which psychoanalytical thinking sets out and the very possibility of being or articulation toward which the therapeutic encounter might lead.

The Real, as a *khōra* or site,[25] may not issue a solicitation to open-ended improvisation or production that a faculty does. It may not provide the enabling legislation (or wiring) for linguistic articulation or visualization. But it renders just as indispensable a service: it situates encounters with the intractable, death, ecstasy, inspiration, loss, and utter futility, which might pass as only the surprises, discoveries, or even results of thinking and experience. From a psychoanalytical perspective, experience has been atrophied and stunted when withheld from the open incursion of the Real. The Real is the Platonic cave where existence's revelations are projected. It is the scene into which the improvisations of language and the imagination are projected in order to be registered, in order to realize their energy and labor. The Lacanian Real is the utterly overwhelming and intractable *given*, which nevertheless sets us on the course to whatever it is we might discover, in whatever form it might assume: as a Heideggerian being toward death (*Sein zum Tode*),[26] as a conversation "without alibi" with a therapist,[27] as an apprenticeship in an inscriptive process—encompassing the panoply of discourses and media—imbued with the relentless intensity and play of Derridean *écriture*. The disgusting yellow gutter fluid that spews out when Joseph K. approaches the tenement building in which the visual artist Titorelli will gloss the impenetrabilities of the Law as a legal code and as a pretext for the institutions that purportedly administer it grabs us as a particularly graphic instance of Kafka's accessing the Real through the agency of an epistemologically radical novel.

Real Concerns

Given these somewhat crude postulates regarding the architecture and function of a faculty and articulation-based picture of our psychological experience, in what senses does Kafka open new resources for the Imaginary at the same time that he leaves an indelible imprint on twentieth-century aesthetics? It might be said on the most general level that, albeit on a fictive plane, Kafka withdraws the cushioning protecting his readership from a variety of relatively recent and pervasive manifestations of the Real. Among these would surely number the following. First is a mechanical Real, inaugurated by the deployment of automatic apparatuses in every sphere of communal and personal life. In Kafka's work, we look to the execution machine in "In the Penal Colony"; its parodic counterpart is the feeding machine surfacing a bit later in Chaplin's *Modern Times*. Second is a bureaucratic Real, embedded in European societies at least since the modernization of urban policing techniques in the nineteenth century.[28] Third is a Real of demographic saturation and corresponding mass movements and displacements related to such historical phenomena as industrialization and ensuing housing shortages in the major urban centers. At the outer limits of these at times seemingly unfounded mass-movements is the genocidal potential that can be read between the lines, in different ways, of the "good" concentration camp to which Karl Rossmann finds his way by the Nature Theater episode of *Amerika* (*The Man Who Disappeared*) or the antics of the mouse pack led by "Josephine, the Singer," title character of Kafka's late animal parable.[29] Fourth is a corporeal Real (akin to the Deleuzian "body without organs"),[30] in which physical experience is neither detached from the world beyond the body nor lent coherence or structure by the central processing of consciousness. The body serves as a pawn for the absurdities of the social code, whose strictures are literally inscribed upon its surface by the execution machine in "In the Penal Colony." It proves unable to resist the willed manipulations of a host of grasping and controlling characters, whose hands and hand operations on the protagonists of the novels proliferate from every corner. In *Anti-Oedipus* and elsewhere, Deleuze/Guattari offer the corporeal experience of heroin addiction as a tangible instance of the "body without organs." A clinical forerunner to this experience would surely be the system of corporeal connectors (rays, nerves) linking Senatspräsident Schreber to God in Freud's *Psychoanalytc Notes upon an Autobiographical Account of a Case of Paranoia (Dementia paranoides)*. Finally, fifth is an evolutionary Real under whose aegis animality is not an exclusively other ontological state or a long-discarded evolutionary stage on the way to anthropocentric destiny and hegemony but a collective potential for spontaneous regressive behavior at any moment and under any sociopolitical formation. There might well be additional variations to the contemporary modifications in the Real of "advanced" European societies to which

Kafka's fiction accommodated itself, but to focus the present discussion, let's confine ourselves to these five.

It can be said in general of Kafka's fiction that imaginarily, under the aegis of the Imaginary, it withdrew the curtain separating its readers from these particular outcroppings of the Real. In the service of the Imaginary (and according to the Symbolic functions of literary language), the corpus of Kafka's fiction facilitated a new alliance (and discomfort) with the Real. The Real that Kafka's fiction accessed included not only material features (the stones of the Great Wall of China, the knife ripping though Josef K.'s chest at the end of *The Trial*, the yellow liquid abomination near the entrance to Titorelli's tenement house). The Real to which Kafka's fiction imaginarily connects perhaps even more interestingly leads to a host of new sociopolitical relationships that have become *virtual*: the nausea-evoking potential of denunciation by one's unfamiliar neighbors; bureaucratic processes as vague and interminable in their resolution as potentially devastating in their outcome; relations of power and control camouflaged (as in the Castle village) by the trappings of home-spun intimacy and familiarity; the spontaneous formation of impersonal crowds, whether migratory work-seekers, participants at an urban political rally, or packs of lemminglike, subterranean thinking rodents. It can be said of Kafka's fiction that it withdrew the diverting disguises from all these emanations of the Real at the same time as it became an artifact of fantastic literature in its own right. It joined the very aesthetic image formation and condensation whose fantasies it deconstructed. In this respect it forms a vast, encompassing dialectical image, as Benjamin, in his *The Arcades Project*, unveils this telling figure of our age.[31] Kafka launched this figure into mercurial orbit above the Parisian skies that Benjamin would go on to scan, during the years of *The Arcades Project*, for signs of reason and hope. His fiction thus heralded this consummate Benjaminian construct: so shockingly does the dialectical image manage to coalesce the ironies and counterforces of a moment or configuration that the reading process stops dead in its tracks, pausing in a caesura of stunned realization.

Four Versions of the Imaginary

What follows are four brief vignettes characterizing, over a broad swathe of Kafka's literary production, the fatal attraction in his work—thanks to the

Lacanian Imaginary—between fictive embroidery and a disquieting encounter with the Real. It interests me in retrospect that I draw in this demonstration as much on the shorter fiction, perhaps in its focused imagery and what Freud would call its condensation,[32] as much as I do on the extended figurative elaboration in the novels. These extended passages allow Kafka's style and his multiple fictive innovations (culminating in an Imaginary, as I am arguing) to speak for themselves. This is a critical practice I have evolved in recent years in keeping with the "mosaic technique" that Benjamin theorized in his *The Origin of German Tragic Drama*,[33] amply in evidence throughout *The Arcades Project*.

> This principle of piecemeal construction [*System des Teilbaues*] was also applied on a smaller scale by the two great armies of labor, the eastern and the western. It was done in this way: gangs of some twenty workers were formed [*gebildet wurden*] who had to accomplish a length, say, of five hundred yards of wall, while a similar gang built a similar stretch of the same length to meet the first. But after the junction [*Vereinigung*] had been made, the construction of the wall was not carried on from the point. . . . Naturally in this way many great gaps [*viele grosse Lücken*] were left, which were only filled in gradually and bit by bit. . . . In fact it is said that there are gaps which have never been filled in at all, an assertion, however, that is probably merely one of the many legends to which the building of the wall gave rise.[34]

> Now one of the most obscure of our institutions is that of the Empire itself. In Peking, naturally, at the imperial court, there is some clarity to be found on this subject, though even that is more illusive than real. . . .
>
> So vast is our land that no fable could do justice to its vastness [*kein Märchen reicht an seine Größe*], the heavens can scarcely span it—and Peking is only a dot [*nur ein Pünktchen*] in it, and the imperial palace less than a dot. The Emperor as such, on the other hand, is mighty throughout all the hierarchies of the world: admitted. But the existent Emperor, a man like us, lies much like us on a couch which is of generous proportions, perhaps, and yet very possibly may be quite narrow and short. . . . The Empire is immortal, but the Emperor himself totters and falls from his throne, yes, whole dynasties sink in the end and breathe their last in one death rattle. Of these struggles and sufferings the people will never know; like tardy arrivals [*wie Zu-spät-Gekommende*], like strangers in a city, they stand at the end of some densely thronged side street peacefully munching the food they have brought with them, while far away in front, in the Market square at the heart of the city, the execution of their ruler is proceeding [*die Hinrichtung ihres Heern vor sich geht*].[35]

Kafka is hardly the first post-Romantic author who, in a fable like "The Great Wall of China," places the figurative resources of the sublime and fragmentation at the service of fantastic literature. In a manner reminiscent of the Poe of "Eureka" and related texts, Kafka enters a nimble dance with the Real of the Great Wall's materiality, the incomprehensibility to the common people of its day in the fragmentary design for its erection, its dwarfing the proportions of past historical and even present architecture, and the irrationality of the riddle that it poses to its modern-day onlookers.[36] Kafka invents an occasion for marveling at the sublime qualities and conundrum that the Wall embodies, and, in the process, he dissolves the protective distance that would otherwise insulate us from the violence of the Qin Dynasty's defenses and the forced labor used to erect the Wall; the sheer scale of the unnamed masses marshaled in its construction and the underlying coercion coordinating their labor. There is, in other words, a clear connection between the Romantic poetics of the sublime and the fragment in Kafka's figurative meditation and the political in the broadest sense: more specifically, the politics of constituitively skewed communications between the nodes of power and the periphery, the bizarre spatiotemporal anomalies inevitably resulting from such governmental oversize, and the migrations and deployments of masses undercutting the dominion of the metaphysics of subjectivity and individual agency in whatever cultural milieu it emerges. Although the Great Wall, like any particular cultural artifact, emerges in a particular historical moment, Kafka deliberately leaves the fable's time frame unspecified and murky. The massive public works project built by forced labor coexists both in the moment of its creation and in our day. The elaborated figure of the Wall itself becomes a subtle time switch leading from distant Chinese chronicles to the actualities of the Hapsburg Empire. The detail with which Kafka builds up the empire's aspirations for imperial hegemony, the phenomenon of vast populations both easily movable and dispensable, and the power in a chain of command extending from the capital city to the barbaric hinterlands links, with stunning force, the Qin dynasty to modern Europe. Even in assuming the role of a lightning-rod for fantasy, Kafka can only offer us, in defense against the forces of sublime political power and industrial-scale death, a wall or defensive shield hopelessly riddled in its incompletion and antiquation.

The fable is surely the cornerstone to a reading of Kafka as an important political theorist, by and large a neglected narrative save in Deleuze/

Guattari's hybrid account, in the Capitalism and Schizophrenia diptych and elsewhere, of thinking, perception, and corporeal experience under the regime of late capitalism. A good measure of the virtuosity in this blueprint for a politico-fictive critique inheres in the smooth follow-through in its internalized accounts of Chinese political process and cultural invention. In the first of our extracts from the story, the verb *entstehen* characterizes both the inevitable gaps in the construction and the legends arising around it. Kafka graphically demonstrates both that the political capability to carry out such a project encounters unforeseen resistances and indirections in the exigencies and media of communication and that the imaginary public representations of the process are conditioned by prevalent power configurations in very Real terms. Poetic invention cannot utterly exonerate itself from the imprint of power, which, however, loses much of its brute force in the media of inscription, resulting in the anomalies lending Kafka's parable so much of its aura and charm. Through an elaborate visual figure, in other words, Kafka renders accessible in Symbolic terms a configuration of current or actual sociopolitical conditions first evident to him in his pitched encounter, by means of history and narrative, with the Real: the immobile arbitrariness of the stones, the lost spectacle of forced migration and labor, and imperial might attached to them as a residue. The scanning and print-out of this hidden, inarticulate drama is not unlike the passionate Greek revelry that Keats delineates in "Ode on a Grecian Urn."

★

"Yes, the Harrow," said the officer, "a good name for it. The needles are set in like the teeth of a harrow and the whole thing works something like a harrow, although its action is limited to one place and conceived with much more artistic skill. Anyhow, you'll soon understand it. On the bed here the condemned man is laid—I'm going to describe the apparatus first before I set it in motion. Then you'll be able to follow the proceedings better. Besides, one of the cogwheels in the Designer is badly worn; it creaks a lot when it's working; you can hardly hear yourself speak; spare parts, unfortunately, are difficult to get here.[37]

As soon as the man is strapped down, the Bed is set in motion. It quivers in minute, very rapid vibrations, both from side to side and up and down. [*Es zittert in winzigen, sehr schnellen Zuckungen gleichzeitig seitlich wie auf und ab.*] You will have seen similar apparatus in hospitals; but in our Bed the movements are all precisely calculated; you see, they have to correspond very exactly to the movements of the Harrow. [*Sie müssen nämlich peinlich auf die Bewegungen der Egge abgestimmt sein.*] And the Harrow is the instrument for the actual execution of the sentence.

"And how does the sentence run?" asked the explorer.

"You don't know that either?" said the officer in amazement, and bit his lips. . . .

Then he drew out a small leather wallet and said: "Our sentence does not sound severe. Whatever commandment the prisoner has disobeyed is written upon his body by the Harrow [*dem Verurteilten wird das Gebot, daß er übertreten hat, mit der Egge auf dem Leib geschrieben*]. This prisoner, for instance"—the officer indicated the man—will have written on his body: HONOR THY SUPERIORS!". . .

Many questions were troubling the explorer, but at the sight of the prisoner, he asked only: "Does he know his sentence?" "No," said the officer, eager to go on with his exposition, but the explorer interrupted him: "He doesn't know the sentence that has been passed on him?" "No," said the officer again, pausing a moment as if to let the explorer elaborate his question, and said: "There would be no point in telling him. He'll learn it on his body. [*Er erfährt es ja auf seinem Leib.*]" . . . "But surely he knows that he has been sentenced?' "Not that either," said the officer, smiling at the explorer as if expecting him to make further surprising remarks.[38]

The snapshot of very tangible twentieth-century political relations with which Kafka is furnishing his readers gravitates—in "In the Penal Colony"—closer to the explicit technology of a machine. Foreign policy has become far more sophisticated in this fable: what the colonial adventure or the erection of a physical barrier (the Great Wall) cannot accomplish will be finished off precisely by an apparatus complicated in its mechanics. There will be a tight and striking analogy between the absolute and a priori nature of the *thinking* mobilized by the Criminal Code (what Derrida will call the Law of Genre)[39] and the *mechanics* of the machines conjured up by Kafka's play of figuration. And indeed, the execution machine's affinity to the mechanical printing machines of its day (typewriters, teletypes) and its anticipation of digital technology have been noted by many commentators.[40] (In the latter case, the machine's operating system is a particularly simplistic version of the Mosaic Law: its *input* is the particular sentence declared by the colonial kangaroo court, and its *output* is the lethal scoring of this imperative on the body of the accused.)

When the traveler (*Reisende*: we would now say "anthropologist") inquires as to whether the most basic rights as they have evolved in the history of Western jurisprudence apply to the condemned man (e.g., habeas corpus, formal procedures of charging with legal violations, explanation of procedure and punishment), he is informed by the officer that these measures do not apply to colonial justice. The Symbolic—in other words, the articulate and measured modulation of drive, violence, and punitive impulses—has been completely extruded from this justice machine. It is in this sense that the phantasmagoria of the execution machine in the penal colony furnishes a detailed close-up shot of colonial power in its contemporary Reality.

It is no accident, then, that in this fantasy there is a complete collusion between power and writing. Writing, in the context of civil society the most delicate and articulate medium of modulation, is in this tale completely subordinate to the regime of absolute power. To be used in a deadly body piercing is so blunt and stultified a deployment of script that, in this particular fantasy, writing eludes the civil sphere of the Symbolic, the domain of manners, consensus, and compromise, and enters the unthinkable violence of the Real.[41] Kafka has in this fable conjured up an instance of what I have elsewhere called the Real of language.[42] Through the agency of this parable, language assumes certain of the arbitrary and inchoate powers ascribed, under conditions of "normalcy," to despotism or fate. On the microscopic level, Kafka formulates the diabolical coordination between the Bed's vibrations and the victim's body as "simultaneously sideways," or *gleichzeitlich seitlich*. It could be argued that the multiple resonances between the German words, an aural echoing of uncontrolled mechanical extension, is almost as ominous as the punishment by scriptural incision.

★

In addition, there was direct commerce [*noch ein unmittelbarer Verkehr*] between the porter's lodge and the lobby, because of the two sliding windows which were manned by under-porters, who were uninterruptedly engaged in giving out information on all kinds of subjects [*Auskünfte in den verschiedenen Angelegenheiten zu erteilen*]. These men were really overburdened [*Das waren geradezu übergebürdete Leute*], and Karl could have sworn that the Head Porter, as he knew him, must have gotten around this job in his past career. These two information dispensers had—you couldn't get a sense of it from outside—at least ten inquiring faces at the windows in front of them. These ten questioners, who were continually changing, spoke in a babble of different languages [*war oft ein Durcheinander von Sprachen*], as though each of them had been sent from a different country.

There were always some asking their questions at the same time, while some others were talking among themselves. For the most part, they wanted to collect something from the porter's lodge or leave something there, so you could always see hands waving impatiently out of the mass of people.[43]

For instance there were six under-porters manning six telephones. The principle, you could see at a glance, was that one would jot down conversations, while from his notes, the man next to him would pass on the orders by telephone. They were the very latest type of telephone that needed no telephone cubicles, for the ringing was no louder than a cheep, you could whisper into the mouthpiece, and, thanks to special electrical amplification, your voice would boom out at the other end. And so one could barely hear the three speakers on their telephones, and might have supposed they were murmuringly observing some process in the telephone mouthpiece, while the other three drooped their heads over the paper it was their job to cover, as though stunned by deafening volume in their ears that was inaudible to everyone else in the room [*wie betäubt von auf dem auf sie heran-dringenden, für die Ungebung in übrigen unhörbarer Lärm*]. Once again there was a boy standing by each of the three speakers; these boys did nothing but crane their necks to listen to their masters, and then hurriedly, as though stung, look up telephone numbers in enormous yellow books—the rustling of the volumes of paper easily drowning out all the noise of the telephones.[44]

The above paragraphs intervene, in the heart of *Amerika*, just as Robinson, one of the two vagabonds who pursue and to some degree enslave protagonist Karl Rossmann throughout the novel, succeeds, by association, in getting his dupe blamed for his own misdeeds and sacked from his job at the Hotel Occidental. Karl has wandered away, in a drunken state, from the trial scene in which he is charged by the hotel management with Robinson's trespass. What he discovers—in an instance of narrative escape from the story line and internalized reverie and in the Hotel's lobby, no less—is an updated version of the technology at work in the variably programmable death machine in the penal colony. We pass in this vignette from the fictive idea of ineluctable mechanics rooted in writing to the crisis of the Information Age. An unremitting and overwhelming stream of questions, in the service of the vast human traffic circulating on the highways in and out of Ramses, threatens to crush, literally as well as figuratively, the hotel employees charged with satisfying its inquiries and other demands. The speed and availability of information serve to create an inexhaustible market for more information. Information is as indispensable to the traveling babblers, who hail from every point of the compass and every language area of the world, as is the food, also dispensed with the latest industrial efficiency, at the Hotel Occidental's buffet. The Hotel information dispensers are beset by the same acceleration pervading the factory system as Marx characterizes it in *Capital*. Instead of dealing with ever-faster rates of material production extended over an increasingly attenuated work day, Kafka's information workers struggle to keep pace with bundles of inquiries and corresponding responses, arriving more quickly than they can be dispatched. Kafka infuses this scene with the comedy that also pervades the out-of-control assembly line in Chaplin's "Modern Times."

Karl ushers this world of movement and information, so immense and sublime as to seem unmotivated, just as he is about to be forcibly expelled from it. (Deleuze and Guattari, in their Capitalism and Schizophrenia diptych, apply the term *flow* to this vast barrage of energy and activity, whether it involves language, information, money, goods, or sexuality. This parallelism, or wiring in parallel, turns out to be a linchpin of their theoretical intervention.) Proust and Joyce, as well as Kafka, note the full range of spectral qualities attending telephonic communications. It is no accident that the Hotel's communications hub should also house the bank of telephones described in our second passage. As opposed to the narrator of Proust's *Remembrance of Things Past*, who is devastated by the ghostly voice emanating from his beloved *grand-mère* on the phone (a character by dint of age and health already in a state of worldly withdrawal),[45] in Kafka's rendition the telephone occasions a series of absurd bureaucratic measures in the hope of controlling the uncontrollable, whether we designate it "language" or "information." The problems underscored in the extract above may well boil down to storage: the Hotel employs functionaries to effect a transcription from the electronic impulses channeled by even early telephone systems into handwritten notes. Given the qualities of the burgeoning information chronicled by the novelistic episode, the effort to manage electronic information by storage in handwriting is patently absurd. This moment in the novel is on the cusp of a fundamental transformation in the world of work: the physical movement of people and information is on the way out (Karl worked in a high-industrial relay of elevator operators before the incriminating invasion of Robinson); the storage and management of information is on the way in. Electronics is the energy system and medium in which the new work and knowledge relations take place. (Here and in

The Castle, Kafka explicitly traces out the uncanny hums, static, and other epiphenomena characterizing electronic communications.

We find ourselves once again in the crux of the Benjaminian dialectical image. In its pictures of the road to Ramses (a contemporary superhighway punctuated by periodic surveillance towers) and of the Hotel's information control room, *Amerika* places itself on the threshold of science-fiction whimsy and playfulness. Yet the invention, at the level of an as yet unaccustomed Imaginary, also serves to draw its public closer to a set of new informational, communicative, and bureaucratic conditions in fact already in place. Indeed the alreadiness of these relations is no small measure of their sublime uncanniness.

★

The applicant wrings from us in the night, as the robber does in the forest, sacrifices of which we should otherwise never be capable; well, all right, that is the way it is now when the applicant is still there, strengthening us and compelling us and spurring us on, and while everything is still half consciously under way; but how it will be afterwards, when it is all over, when, sated and carefree, the applicant leaves us and there we are, alone, defenseless in the face of our misuse of official power [*die Partei, gesättigt und unbekummert, uns verläßt und wir da dastehen, allein, wehrlos in Angesicht unsers Amstsmißbrauches*]—that does not bear thinking of! Nevertheless, we are happy. How suicidal happiness can be! We might, of course, exert ourselves to conceal the true position from the applicant. He himself will scarcely notice anything of his own accord. He has, after all, in his own opinion probably only for some indifferent, accidental reasons— being overtired, disappointed, ruthless, and indifferent from overfatigue and disappointment [*übermüdet, enttäuscht, rücksichtslos und gleichgültig aus Übermüdung und Enttäuschung*]—pushed his way into a room other than the one he wanted to enter, he sits there in ignorance, occupied with his thoughts, if he is occupied at all, with his mistake, or with his fatigue. Could one not leave him in that situation? One cannot. With the loquacity of those who are happy, one has to explain everything to him. Without being able to spare oneself in the slightest one must show him in detail what has happened, how extraordinarily rare and uniquely great the opportunity is, one must show how the applicant, though he has stumbled into this opportunity in utter helplessness such as no other being is capable of than precisely an applicant, can, however, now, if he wants to, Land-Surveyor, dominate everything and to that end has to do nothing but in some way or other put forward his plea, for which fulfillment is already waiting, which indeed it is already coming to meet; all this one must show; it is the official's hour of travail.[46]

We begin, I hope, to get the gist of how it would be possible to value Kafka not merely as a literary innovator on the aesthetic plane but as a visionary who brought certain unprecedented possibilities within the range of the Imaginary. It is not excessive to claim, I believe, that the samples we have examined thus far not only demarcate the interstitial zones in which Kafka was willing to stretch the reality principle as well as novelistic convention, they index and perform updated formats for linguistico-cognitive processing that would accompany current Imaginary thresholds. Such Kafkan inventions as the Hotel Occidental and Castle telephones, Uncle Jacob's telegraph room, the political rally near the end of *Amerika*, and the execution machine in the penal colony allegorically perform new relations with language and the communicative media at the same time that they access, with shocking as well as enthralling vividness, the Real of the power relations at the basis of the current socioeconomic matrix. Creative input at the level of the Imaginary carries with it a linguistico-cognitive reprogramming that will materially facilitate new formats of seeing, hearing, and thinking.

Our final sample passage, from the end of *The Castle*, when Bürgel rehashes the bureaucratic eventualities that would and would not have been possible in light of K.'s mistaken summons to the village and his experiences upon his arrival, seems remarkably impoverished (in Marshall McLuhan's terms, "cool") in comparison with some of the instances of tele-technic pandemonium and human expendability that we've been exploring. Indeed, all the passage offers us is Bürgel's circumlocutions about the transformation of a bureaucratic impasse into an unanticipated window of opportunity. K.'s conventional and overt efforts to attain recognition, to secure some semiological valuation and status within the community through petitions, meetings, and confrontations, have all ended in a standoff. But intruding into just the right bureaucrat's living quarters in the middle of the night, explains Bürgel, may prove just the ticket for removing obstacles and achieving a felicitous outcome. The passage becomes a meditation on the status and efficacy of volition (critics say intentionality) within an artifact of writing. Consequences indeed ensue from initiatives and compositional designs. They are, simply, never the results of explicit desires on the part of agents equipped with subjectivity. Bürgel, as the voice of the involuted and dysfunctional system over which he presides, enunciates the parameters of action within a textually configured organization. So excruciating have K.'s interactions with such a counterintuitive and asystematic social network proven that he is oblivious to the world by the time he is apprised of this turnabout in his prospects.

How could a self-sustaining, self-modulating, and self-correcting discourse become the only reality, the encompassing reality, the ultimate reality, the only field in which change or development will transpire? Our relation to death, horror, ecstasy, the sublime, the absolute can be negotiated only within an ongoing semiological network in which we ourselves already comprise signifiers. As in Borges's *ficción* "Death and the Compass," in which the ultimate labyrinth, amid a proliferation of geographically related murders, is the one "that consists of a single straight line that is invisible and endless,"[47] the most compelling snapshots of Kafka's Imaginary may well be the passages in which language and the Real most materially intertwine and coincide. Our ultimate snapshot of the Kafkan Imaginary is the one in which *less* in the way of technological and distraction and thematic stage props and window dressing means *more*. The all-embracing, self-sustaining discourses of Bürgel near the end of *The Castle* and the paranoic subterranean creature throughout "The Burrow" comprise the Reality—of articulation sustained and embellished for nothing more than its own sake—to which Kafka's fictive invention ultimately acclimates us. This is a Reality unearthed amid the rigors of inscription that occur in very different ways in Proust, the late Joyce, Stein, Woolf, Beckett, Faulkner, and Bernhard, as well. In this sense, Kafka's Imaginary, translated into the operating language of the Symbolic, affords us a memorable access to a Real with a virtual objectivity. The sociopolitical, demographic, and linguistic realities to which Kafka acclimates his readers communicated themselves to other authors as well. The accessibility of key elements of a distinctly Kafkan Imaginary to other writers in no way detracts from its singularity and invention.

Language exposed in its rawness, materiality, and unapologetic contingencies may be the ultimate Real that Kafka, by means of a battery of imaginative measures, including his fictions, style, ironies, and spatiotemporal anomalies, makes bearable to a certain aggregate of readers.

Kafka's Imaginary Legacy

In bringing this ultimately tentative inquiry into Kafka's Imaginary to a close, I want to return to the general question of what constitutes an authentic contribution to this psychoanalytical domain. We say then, that an author (or other aesthetic producer) revises, corrects, or in some other fashion contributes to the prevailing (i.e., culturally recognizable) Imaginary when the work augments how its audience will henceforth see, think, or process images and words, and when the work facilitates cultural access to new conditions with fundamental bearing on climatic and sociopolitical experience. In this sense, Kafka, as the harbinger of striking new sociocultural relations absorbed into the Real, may be a stronger candidate for this initiatory status than, say, Zola or Dreiser, who successfully adapted preexisting novelistic conventions to the ends of measured interventions. Along these lines, it may be possible for a relatively minor novelist, say, Witold Gombrowicz, with his surreal landscapes sprinkled with enigmatic markers and other inconsequential signs, to lay a greater claim to initiating a distinctive Imaginary than such a monumental novelist as Dickens, with all the vividness of his characters and their Victorian surroundings. Flaubert, in the sustained ambiguity he creates between his characters' fantasies and the actualities around them, in the realism that he initiates through an ironic debunking performed by the narrative voice itself (as opposed to objective reportage), ends up, in this regard, trumping Dickens, and for that matter Balzac.

We could say, by the same token, that Orson Welles, in *Citizen Kane*, both ushers in a cinematography, with its famous long shots and low-angle perspectives, that affects the way its audience sees, both in and out of the movie theater, and (like Kafka in *Amerika*) accounts for states of affairs, some ominous, in the mass and speed of communications and in mass political movements. *Citizen Kane* pursues, for example, a vast proliferation of print and news media (prominently displayed in the newsreel spliced into the film covering Kane's death and biography). The Imaginaries both of twentieth-century U.S. culture and of cinema in general will never be quite the same.

A pair of films directed by Ingmar Bergman in the late 1960s, in the heyday of his own inventiveness and psychological torment, first *Persona* (1967) and then *The Hour of the Wolf* (1968), effect a similar deep-seated and widespread reprogramming of cultural resources and experience. Both films accentuate the contrivance of cinematic characterization at the same time, in Kafkan fashion, as they withdraw the pretenses that give us reassurance against the monstrosity of the Real. In *Persona*, Bergman makes certain to remind us not only that the individuality of actress Elisabet Vogler and her separateness from Alma, her psychiatric nurse, are highly tenuous. Through close-ups in which the characters' paired visages morph into one another, Bergman endows them with an aura of uncanny doubling of the sort intimated by Kafka between Georg Bendemann and his lifelong friend in Russia in "The Judgment." Bergman furnishes the cinematic audience with a Doppelgänger in the film itself: the son with whom Elisabet, by virtue of her immersion in acting, in self-impersonation and surrogation, cannot fully bond. The narrative observed in *Persona* is as much a screen sequence or memory for the son as it is for the audience. By incorporating at the beginning and end of the film a celluloid meltdown, as was once endemic to film projection, whose flickering shots are a montage of horrific, thematically related scenes and snaps from the history of cinema, Bergman achieves an alienation effect distanciating the disconcerting revelations in the story. By invoking the technological Real of cinema, its fragmentation, jarring rhythm, and sudden flashes and cuts, Bergman creates a climate conducive to the even more disturbing Real of human relations: the assaults on personal singularity, the transformations from affection to hatred transpiring with lightning speed. In several instances, Bergman makes the audience privy to the same internalized screen that the lost son, whose uncontained affection for his mother is a sad irony, also observes. This eruption of strongly backlit, auratic shots (as when Elisabeth wanders into Alma's room while she is sleeping) leads first away from, but then eventually toward the abyss of human separation and misrecognition. This *fort-da* relation to the Real,[48] first away by means of contrivance and artifice, then toward, in unaccustomed clarity and detail, is also achieved by the gothic stage set, replete with ominous ravens and Draculalike secondary characters, in *The Hour of the Wolf.* Here the madness that sustained aesthetic creation entails—its hyper-suggestiveness, the hovering influence of culture's specters and phantasms, always close at hand—is made ever more pervasive by means of film's accentuated mannerism and artificiality. Welles and Bergman, by virtue of their receptiveness to the most disturbing and submerged conditions of the Real and the explicitness of their placement of cinema at the service of verbal and imagistic representation, belong to the significant group of directors managing to jar, however slightly, the range and prospects for the cinematic Imaginary.

FOUR

Booking Benjamin: The Fate of a Medium

It's time, as we say in English, to throw the book at that polymorphous miscreant of reading and writing, Walter Benjamin, to book him, in the patois of American film noir. We can see already that in English there are some hang-ups between the book, whether a material object or a volume or space of writing, and the notion and conventions of legality. But in German a bookseller, the manager of a market or trading place in which the historical Benjamin spent a good number of his happier hours, is a *Buchhandler*, someone who handles and touches books—it might not be excessive to say, who fondles them. By contrast, in French, the culture of books is caught up both in their physical weight, *gravitas*, and burden, and also in the promises in their de*liv*ery of what they, in the expanse of their open-ended and en-gendering space, *convey*, the democracy to come in language that they affirm and promise.

Let us ponder, today, the vertiginous convergence of designs in books and the text that they encompass. Each text consequent and invasive enough to be memorable as a book is as much the result of a design—above all of a visual nature—as it is the residue of the traces of thinking. When we enter the domain of stylistics, when we take into account the conditions of verbal density, the span and fluidity of inscription, the familiarity or surprise of semantics, diction, and syntax, which also add meaning and significance both to a singular text and to a body of works, even when we enlarge the scope to encompass the expectations surrounding the aesthetic genres in play, we are characterizing the discourse design in effect for that text.

Contributing to schooled discourse, today as in Benjamin's time, entails a crisis of discursive models or subgenres. As I detail in a recent book, *The Task of the Critic*, the contemporary cultural critic unavoidably trucks simultaneously in several discursive designs, at the very least in what is recognizable as poetics, philosophy, close reading, and critique.[1] It is no exaggeration to assert, as I do in that volume, that German Romanticism inscribed the enabling legislation for what we continue to recognize as cosmopolitan criticism, distinguishable by its abrupt turns and linkages, its fragmentary constitution, and its irony or multiple, simultaneous levels of signification, in large measure by underscoring the discursive elements of this critique appropriated from the existing genres and media of culture—among them poetry, drama, fiction, and other narrative art, and even the fine arts. In such collations as the *Athenaeum* and *Philosophical Fragments*, German Romanticism launches modern cultural commentary, in other words, with a multifarious inquest into text or discourse design. As Benjamin devised specific and distinctive styles for his interventions, he was taking the Schlegels, Novalis, Tieck, and compeers both at their word and a step beyond. To decode and elucidate such diverse texts as "Goethe's *Elective Affinities*," "The Critique of Violence," "Food Fair," "Franz Kafka," *One-Way Street*,[2] and *The Arcades Project* is to a significant degree an exercise, with a full visual component, in the discernment and teasing out of textual design. The plurality of styles mobilized by the invariably occasional writing projects we score, whether concertedly designed or not, constitutes our fullest exercise of the freedom available to us.

Benjamin was a creature of the book at once voracious and overwhelmed by devotion. We all know this. This commonplace of cultural history can only make Benjamin endearing to us, just as we are endearing to ourselves by clinging to this eccentric medium, whose decisiveness in the storage and delivery or transmission of culture is already in question. A book encompasses a certain volume of text, itself, as we have already seen, the product of a certain process of design. The text's material or content is embodied in a book medium with certain design features of its own: typography, scale and layout of pages, binding, contents and design of the cover, and so forth. Yet in the sense that a book is a free-standing structure, we can also say that it has been modeled after an architectural blueprint. We can speak more compellingly of the architecture of books than of the architecture of discourse or text. Yet books, architecture, and even discourse itself are all inflected and imbued with significance by the elements and choices of design.

Just a word, if I may, on certain features of comparative discourse design that draw Arendt close to Benjamin and then apart. Assuming that all the works I keep coming back to again and again derive something from Derrida's notion, in *Specters of Marx*, of deconstruction as the experience of the impossible, the amalgam of textual functions that Arendt assembles and coordinates in *The Origins of Totalitarianism* as emblematic of her later works, is as impressive in its rhetorical tact and diversity as in its didactic thrust. Although technically a well-trained philosopher, she largely forgoes her discourse by formation and preference in favor of a distinctive blend of the social history of the Jews in European modernity, the social psychology of mobs and their manipulators, and the sociology of class allegiances and rivalries.[3] Like Marx in *Capital*, she moves between the diverse registers of her discursive amalgam almost seamlessly. To the extent that, at least in its day, the Frankfurt School was an *Institut für Soziale Forschung*, an Institute for Social Research, Arendt presses a more compelling claim for membership than Benjamin, whose writing wanders into autobiographical memoir and seemingly inchoate collages of citations.

Arendt's brilliant analyses of such phenomena as totalitarian alliances between elites and mobs, the liquidation of entire classes, and the easy expendability of human rights would lose much of their power without their extensive historical backdrop of the experience of the Jews and other expendable minorities in modernity. She fills in the occulted stages of modern European and Jewish histories in a fashion not unlike Deleuze/Guattari's demonstration of the persistence of antiquated stages of social formation—such as barbaric nomadism and feudalism—at the periphery of contemporary liberal experience. Her backdrop to the precipitous intensification of anti-Semitism in the twentieth century encompasses such phenomena as the

Jewish involvement in the scandals surrounding the construction of the Suez Canal and the mascoting of exotic Jews in certain Parisian salons on the eve of the Dreyfus case. In effect, she performs the work of cultural psychoanalysis by reconstituting—at the level of philosophically driven cultural studies—the stages that could have rendered the Jews so expendable at a fateful juncture of social forces in the twentieth century.

We can say that Arendt designs a discourse markedly different from Benjamin's. Benjamin is too taken up with the project of a critical redemption of contemporary culture, his allegiance is too invested in the transformations of the book and the vicissitudes of the book medium, to accede to her historicism and work of psychosocial reconstruction.

Benjamin was, before all else, a citizen, habitué, cognoscente, and transgressor of the history and tradition of the book. It will emerge, as we pursue this impassioned lifelong liaison, that the book is not the fading lily or lameduck politician that it is often taken to be, in view of such phenomena as the overwhelming burgeoning of visual and cybernetic messaging and media, often blamed for a precipitous decline in the concentration and other cognitive faculties requisite for the decoding and comprehension of books. In the wider and virtual sense in which Benjamin and such contemporaries and *semblables* as Proust and Joyce also took the book, the book is a volume of cultural process and understanding, binding together a community of neighbors and readers. For these writers and the sociologists who theorized the wider implications of their contributions, the community itself, insofar as it exists, is tantamount to the readership of certain texts and discourses. Even as we shift over to digital databases and as discourse is disseminated as much over the Worldwide Web as between the covers of books, it will not be easy to dispense with the communities and binding understandings and conventions ensuing from the medium of books. We can place the book in the wider history of tele-technics, as Derrida and Tom Cohen do,[4] or we can begin to imagine a history of the book that has already embarked on its digital future, where it is as much a game as an authoritative canon.

Given their architectural program, it could be said that books are the buildings in a virtual ecology or a climate experienced as an urban landscape. Surely the work of Benjamin traces a confluence between the labyrinthine configurations of both textual constellations and modern cities. The excitement in the subgenre of Benjamin's work that might be characterized as urban memoir (I refer to such works as *One-Way Street* and *Berlin Child-hood around 1900*[5]) surely in large measure inheres in the close parallels, traces almost indistinguishable, between the experience of discovering a city and the homecoming, by those already tainted by the instincts of the omniv-orous reader, to the world of books. The return extends to that *côté du chez Swann* so aptly demarcated as a zone, landscape, or climate characterized by the global meandering and interconnection of the sign and by the distinc-tive Proustian dissolve of the surface of appearance, Law, and convention into a subtext of smooth, fluid semiological resonance. For Benjamin, the discoveries, experiences, and shocks encountered in reading and in the modernized city, the city realized in the Paris of the Second Empire and afterwards, are inseparable.[6] Yet the history and tradition of the book as a medium leave a slightly different imprint and thrust than the bold adventure into the city orchestrated by Walter the hipster Benjamin, the city as the nexus of modern circulation, perception, cognition, experience, and shock. The history and covenant of the book are too binding, in several senses. I want to initiate the present exploration in keeping with a broader notion of the book, one that I believe was studied and advanced by Benjamin, not merely as one medium for the dissemination and storage of script among others but as the very volume, space, forum, foyer, scene, and abyss for cultural articulation and public discussion and for critical apprehension. This longer trajectory of the book will continue to haunt us, in the sense of Hamlet's ghost, to rouse us to critical discrimination and in some cases resistance, to prod us with the relentless stirrings of being and thinking, regardless of the techno-political regime under which information happens to be registered, stored, disseminated, withheld, or obliterated.

Benjamin was nevertheless savvy enough a dialectician of media to know that the book medium to which he was so devoted, at least in its time-honored forms, would not last forever. The book medium is surely suscepti-ble to the progression that Benjamin sets out in "The Work of Art in the Age of Its Technological Reproducibility," one in which even the most ex-perimental and transgressive art forms and technologies of representation claim a foundation in prior media.[7] The thrust of this meditation allows Benjamin assiduously to imagine the end of the very book tradition he has served, with an even ascetic devotion. In several senses, *The Arcades Project* is his Book of the Future, his draft for the future of the book, a time capsule addressed to the future from a moment of unheralded achievement in socio-political, logistical, hegemonic, administrative, and informational control, and by this I mean the cosmopolitan, urban nineteenth-century city, with its backdrop of global commerce and trade. This extended work, which occupied him from 1927 until his death in 1940, can be described as a text-medium website of Paris in the nineteenth century: Paris both as the fore-runner of certain repressive political conditions that would dog and outlive him and as the world of quintessential modern aesthetic innovation, the imaginary universe of his personal and creative escape.

It may be no accident that, in their different ways, Proust and Joyce joined Benjamin in telegraphing scrambled messages concerning the book, anticipating its future history. The time-warp implied by this messaging is itself complex and, to a certain extent, paradoxical. It evokes Benjamin's Angel of History: "His face is turned toward the past. . . . This storm drives him irresistibly into the future, to which his back is turned, while the pile of debris before him grows toward the sky."[8] As Benjamin presciently notes, Proust dissolved the conventional novel into a genre sensitive and welcom-ing to the catastrophes in authority, certainty, objectivity, the stability of the physical world, the integrity of media and art forms, and the exclusive-ness and duration of selfhood and identity that had come to pervade the fields of knowledge, perception, and cognition. Hovering above the hybrid narrative form, the polyglot linguistic medium, the nearly illegible seman-tic, syntactic, and grammatical discourse that Joyce devised for *Finnegans Wake*, his ultimate novel, as its bibliographical talisman, is a singular and unforgettable book, *The Book of Kells*, a work that surely, much as in Benja-min's words about Proust, both makes and breaks tradition.[9] As Joyce tarries at the limit of the bibliographic forms, traditions, and conventions that he has unleashed and unraveled in the modernist experimentation of *Ulysses*, he too experiences a state of crisis, appealing to *The Odyssey*, one of the notable fundaments and exceptions in the book's long and storied run.

★

We are heading toward an inventory and census of the Benjaminian library. We ask not so much which books Benjamin encountered and read, for his own works are quite explicit about their raw materials, and the remarkable scholarship that has grown up around Benjamin has been persistent in ex-ploring his sources. We ask ourselves instead which books, not only the notable exceptions comprising *The Origin of German Tragic Drama* and *The Arcades Project*,[10] did Benjamin's practices of reading and writing predicate? What are the scale, design, architecture, and other salient features of the books, as much hypothetical as actual, that have been shelved both in Borges's Library of Babel and in the Parisian Bibliothèque nationale? It was in the latter archive, of course, that Benjamin, when Paris no longer provided any cover for him, deposited the manuscript of *The Arcades Project*, leaving it with Georges Bataille, who fulfilled his custodial charge, the obligation of the Talmudic *shomair ḥinam* ("unremunerated watchperson"). In what senses are the books comprising Benjamin's virtual library both the highest syntheses in the history of their medium and the departure points for as yet unrealized and unmastered programs of inscription and information? The assayer of the Benjaminian library would surely have to base his or her inventory on at least the following major categories of volumes: the illustrated or illuminated book, the Talmudic book or hypertext, the mystical book, the compendium or encyclopedia, and the dissolving or interstitial book, the volume inscribed with the traits of its own future. Each of these collections arises at a particular conjunction of discourse design with book design; we need to constantly remind ourselves that these two items are not exactly the same matter. Because of my earlier encounters with *The Arcades Project* as a radical book-experiment complying with parameters of Talmudic work, the hypertext, and the encyclopedia in Benjamin's collection,[11] I will be unpacking, in my overview of books of the Benjaminian library, only the illuminated book, its mystical counterpart, and the dissolving variety that opens up the entire tradition.

The Illuminated Book

As Benjamin initiates his life-long nomadic quest for a discourse in which he is definitively at home, a search perhaps futile in the end but on the way unearthing the bewildering profusion of dialects in which he became proficient, among them philosophy-based literary critique, travel literature, food criticism, personal memoir, and radio talk, he is aware of the profound synergy initiated by the incursion of images into text, particularly in the sphere of children's literature. The picture book is an indispensable element of the Benjaminian library from the moment that he openly assumes the guise of a book collector, a real one, a role delineated from that of a seller or even a writer.[12]

The encounter with Benjamin transpiring in a truly inventive library or collection may well be as instructive as the illuminations gained from acts of reading his prose. Anyone fortunate enough to have wandered into Richard Macksey's library in the Guilford section of Baltimore, a collection in the letters, arts, and sciences never at rest, has gained an even more tangible access to the real collector's devotion and discipline than the reader of Benjamin's "Unpacking My Library." The line from the obsessions, dissimulations, and triumphs encountered in book collecting and chronicled in that essay, one of Benjamin's most elegant and compelling, to Macksey's book-filled house, is direct. The rare privilege of witnessing, over the years, the development of this collection, the rhizomatic growth and movement of its subsections toward one another and into more and more sections of the house, has been the purest possible Benjaminian experience.

The window that the illustration introduces into the printed medium bears a privileged relation to childhood, which for Benjamin is less a zero point of human development than the initiation of perception and sensibility into the wonders of language and reading. Childhood sensibility, in other words, is the initial encounter with variants of color, touch, sound, and play that will persist under siege during the later phases of life but in childhood comprise the basis and structure of aesthetico-cultural experience. The illuminated book is not merely the vestige of a childhood whose magical evanescence is first invoked and commodified by the Romantics; it is, in its many guises—from the *Shah-nameh* and the *Book of Kells* to *The Magic Umbrella: A Story*[13]—a window on the particular propensities to linguistic play and dissonance hardwired into the individual. It is in this sense that Proust's *Recherche*, setting out with a scene of bedtime reading between a little boy and his mother, a scene emblematic of the profound intimacy, wonder, distraction, separation, and suffering accruing from the encounter with signs, was, as its multiple volumes appeared during the 1910s and 20s, already primed with one of its most astute readers, Benjamin.

Benjamin may draw our attention, in "Unpacking My Library," to the "childlike element which, in a collector, mingles with the element of old age."[14] But the world of *Old Forgotten Children's Books*,[15] the title of a book by collector and exhibitor Karl Hobrecker that Benjamin reviewed in the

Illustrated Newspaper in 1924, is not a domain of antiquated and outmoded relics. It is, rather, a riot-house of colors, games, and mixtures:

> Since the Enlightenment, this has been one of the mustiest speculations of the pedagogues. Their infatuation with psychology keeps them from perceiving that the world is full of the most unrivaled objects for children's attention and use. For children are particularly fond of haunting any site where things are being visibly worked on [*geneigt, jedwede Arbeitsstätte aufzusuchen, wo sichtbare Betätigung an den Dingen vor sich geht*]. They are irresistibly drawn by the detritus generated by building, gardening, housework, tailoring, or carpentry. In waste products they recognize the face that the world of things turns directly and solely to them. [*In diesen Abfallprodukten, erkennen sie das Gesicht, das die Dingwelt gerade ihnen, ihnen allein zukehrt.*] In using these things, they do not so much imitate the works of adults as bring together, in the artifacts produced in play, materials of widely differing kinds in a new, intuitive relationship. [*Mit diesen bilden sie die Werke von Erwachsenen nicht sowohl nach als daß diese Rest- und Abfallstoffe in eine sprunghafte neue Beziehung zueinander setzen.*][16]

Children serve Benjamin, in this brief passage, as vehicles for two of his prized hobbyhorses: they defy the pedagogical heritage of Rousseau and the Enlightenment, which would treat them as miniature men and women, prematurely overburdened with the baggage of reason and, by implication, the moral imperative; and their play has an open-ended, combinatorial thrust, making them proto-modernists of the first order. In preparing his culture to receive and welcome the innovations of modernism, Benjamin enlists a *Kinderbrigade* of fellow urban explorers and innovators. In their intuitive relation to matter and materials and their inborn gift of improvisation, the children of Benjamin are already, in their sensibilities, structural anthropologists of mythology, visual cubists, editors of film montage, and jazz musicians, even if, in 1924, Benjamin does not yet venture all these connections. The children of Benjamin are less imprinted with intuitive senses of purpose and rectitude than they are with the marks of modernist sensibility and improvisation, including a susceptibility to what Benjamin will later call shock. Benjamin already circles about this link between childhood and shock in his review of *Old Forgotten Children's Books* by tracing the heritage of illustrated books back to the Baroque period, when it was, in its representational program, infused by an allegorical shorthand and violence. The value of any future education for these children would be to prolong and interrelate these predilections to radical juxtaposition and experiment, not to eventuate in the well-tempered man or woman.

In keeping with his work in the Youth Movement and his emerging political philosophy, Benjamin deduces the artifacts of child culture, including the illustrated book, from the habits and relations of childhood, not the reverse:

> Children thus produce their own small world of things within the greater one. The fairy tale is such a waste product—perhaps the most powerful one to be found in the spiritual life of humanity; a waste product that emerges from the growth and decay of the saga. Children are able to manipulate fairy tales with the same ease and lack of inhibition that they display in playing with pieces of cloth and combining its various elements. [*Kinder bilden sich damit ihre Dingwelt, eine kleine in der großen, selbst. Ein solches Abfallprodukt is das Märchen, das gewaltigste vielleicht, das im geistigen Leben der Menschheit sich findet: Abfall im Entstehungs- und Verfallsprozeß der Sage.*] The same is true of songs. And the fable. . . . We may question whether young readers admire the fable for the moral tagged on at the end or whether they use it to school their understanding, as was the traditional wisdom. . . . Children enjoy the spectacle of animals that talk and act like people far more than they enjoy any text overburdened with good thoughts. . . .
>
> One thing redeems even the most old-fashioned and self-conscious products of their era: their illustrations. . . . The collections with fables show that related formulas recur in the remotest places with larger or smaller variations. In like fashion, picture-books go back even further, as we can see from the way in which, for example, illustrations of the Seven Wonders of the World can be traced back to the copper engravings of the seventeenth century, and perhaps to earlier times. We may perhaps venture to surmise that the illustrations of these works have some connection with the emblem books of the Baroque period.[17]

In his apprehension that children in effect carry over material relations and tactile habits to become intellectual (or mythical, or narrative) "property," Benjamin radically preempts Lévi-Strauss's approach to science, experimentation, and classification as conducted by so-called primitive peoples. Moral fables spin or tease out the permutational play of formulas and fragments of narrative sequences in which children are particularly adept. Children's books, forgotten or not, illustrate—literally—this playful repetition with *différance*. The Baroque, among many things, is a site where the putative child, the unabashed learner from repetition and trial and error, the by no means naïve exploiter of the materials at hand, interfaces with the studied tedium of adulthood, the latter perspective one that any cultural critique approaching the thresholds of its own spontaneity and its own impossibility wishes to avoid.

Benjamin's encounter with Karl Hobrecker as a purveyor and historian of children's literature serves him well in his engagement with the perception and sensibility of the child. The Benjaminian child, for example, enjoys a privileged experience of and rapport with color, which for Benjamin infuses the world, cutting through its spatial, authoritarian, and logical compartments. It is a form of interconnectedness that Deleuze/Guattari associate both with the schizo mentality and with the experience of the "body without organs." Benjamin distinguishes the coloring in paintings from that in children's books:

> When in paintings the colors, the transparent or glowing motley of tones, interfere with the design, they come perilously close to effects for their own sake. But in the pictures in children's books, the objects depicted and the independence of the graphic design usually exclude any synthesis of color and drawing. In this play of colors, the imagination runs riot. [*Bei den Bildern der Kinderbücher bewirkt es jedoch noch meist der Gegenstand und die Selbstständigkeit der graphischen Unterlage, daß an eine Synthese von Farbe und Fläche nicht gedacht werden kann. In diesen Farbenspielen ergeht sich aller Verantwortung entbunden die bloße Phantasie*]. After all, the role of children's books is not to induct their readers directly into the world of objects, animals, and peoples—in other words, into so-called life. Very gradually their meaning is discovered in the outside world, but only in proportion as they are found to correspond to what children already possess within themselves.[18]

The meaning of color, as children encounter it in illustrated books, is unbound: its fidelity to the known features of objects in the empirical world is limited. The worldly place and context of the objects represented in the illustrated book will dawn upon the youthful reader only as his or her experience evolves. As Benjamin characterizes the impact of color on the childhood imagination, his description is akin to that of a developmentally specific Derridean archi-trace, the irreducible mark of articulation that conditions all further thinking and expression. Indeed, the play of color in the illustrated book stages an early symbolic encounter between the imagination and the law. The color "not confined to illustrating objects . . . must be full of light and shade, full of movement, arbitrary and always beautiful," writes Benjamin in "A Child's View of Color." The completely absorbing, fully entrancing childhood experience of color plays around and against the symbolic order, the division of labor between form and function. Whereas color occupies a specific place in the "world order" that it is incumbent on the adult to furnish, "In a child's life, color is the pure expression of the child's pure receptivity. . . . The concern of color with objects is not based on their form. . . . It cancels out the intellectual-cross-references of the soul and creates a pure mood [*Sie hebt die intellectualle Verbindungen der Seele auf und schaffte die reine Stimmung ohne darum die Welt aufzugeben*]."[19]

Color is a primary medium for the child's playful and ultimately short-lived resistance to the adult law. There is a magical, if not mystical quality to the child's encounter with color: "The order of art is paradisiacal because there is no thought of the dissolution of boundaries—from excitement—in the object of experience. Instead the world is full of color in a state of identity, innocence, and harmony. Children are not ashamed, since they do not reflect but only see."[20] It is precisely a quasi-mystical phenomenon, "the struggle between light and darkness," that Benjamin discloses in Goethe's Romantic account of color in *The Theory of Colors*:

> The *Theory of Colors* takes up a position diametrically opposed to Newton's optics. The basic disagreement underlying Goethe's often bitter polemic, prolonged over many years, is this: whereas Newton explained white light as the composite of the different colors, Goethe declared it to be the simplest, most indivisible and homogenous phenomenon known to us. [*Newton erklärt das weiße Licht als eine Zusammensetzung aus farbigen Lichtern, Goethe dagegen, als das einfachste, unzerlegbarste, homogenste Wesen, das wir kennen.*] . . . The *Theory of Colors* regards the colors as metamorphoses of light, as phenomena which are formed in the course of the struggle between light and darkness. Together with the idea of metamorphosis, the concept of polarity, which runs like a thread through Goethe's entire scientific enterprise, is of decisive importance here. Darkness is not merely the absence of light. [*Die* Farbenlehre *nimmt die Farben für Metamorphosen des Lichtes, für Erscheinungen, die im Kampf des Lichtes mit dem Dunkel sich bilden. Neben dem Gedanken der Metamorphose ist hier für Goethe bestimmend der der Polarität, der sein ganzes Forschen durchzieht. Dunkel ist nicht bloße Abwesenheit des Lichtes.*][21]

Goethe's treatment of color is infused by a cosmic struggle between darkness and light. In its transformation from the completely absorbing and entrancing medium of childhood apprehension into an interstice at which

Goethe's incipient Romanticism arrives at a mystical worldview, color gathers momentum as a force of sociocultural reform and redemption. Toward the end of his full-fledged early work of philosophically inspired literary criticism, "Goethe's *Elective Affinities*," Benjamin becomes obsessed by the hope that "shot across the sky above their [the novelistic characters'] heads like a falling star. . . . That most paradoxical, most fleeting hope finally emerges from the semblance of reconciliation, just as, at twilight, as the sun is extinguished, rises the evening star which outlasts the night."[22] Benjamin discerns, in other words, the workings of the possibilities for a messianic redemption of the world at the stratospheric limits of Goethe's chemical and alchemical novel of erotic affiliations, set amid the trappings of neoclassical architecture. In degraded form, the falling star that Benjamin tracks in Goethe's novel of the displacements and limits of erotic possibility continues its trajectory across the sky of Benjamin's Second Empire capital, where it is ironically transformed from the vehicle of the wish in folktale into the white ball on the roulette wheel of the gambling casino.[23] More importantly, Goethe emerges from a figural network in which childhood is both a mystical fascination with play and color and a prefiguration of radical modernist experimentation as the legitimizing vehicle of mystical apprehension in German letters.

Throughout his treatment of Goethe's novel, Benjamin is attentive to the play of *Schein*—semblance, appearance, but also glimmer—within it. *Schein* is a term with impeccable credentials in German idealist philosophy. In Hegel's *Phenomenology of Mind*, for instance, *Schein* is the semblance at the heart of the *Erscheinung* or manifestation, by which *Geist*, spirit or mind, in heavily onto-theological fashion, makes its presence known and felt in the world. In Benjamin's approach to Goethe's novel, *Schein* is a swing term, what Derrida would call a hinge,[24] linking literature to philosophy, enabling "all genuine works" to find "their siblings in the realm of philosophy [*Und alle echten Werke haben ihre Geschwister im Bereiche der Philosophie*]."[25] In a fashion that we will pursue later in this inventory, Benjamin somehow manages to add a mystical resonance to the glittering play of Christian, idealist semblance, one emerging from far afield. Against the backdrop of the childhood apprehension of color in illuminated books, Benjamin enlists Goethe, whose invention and exemplarity encompass both Enlightenment and Romantic ages, in the service of a redemption of the world both mystical and messianic, one grounded, among other sources, in the literature of Jewish

mysticism. The yearning for a graft between the Judaic messianic imagination and the mainstream of German letters is acted out in a dream recorded
in *One-Way Street*, in which Goethe's hospitality to Benjamin's relatives
brings him to tears. "Goethe rose to his feet and accompanied me to an
adjoining chamber, where a table was set for my relatives. . . . Doubtless
there were places for my ancestors, too. . . . When the meal was over, he
rose with difficulty, and by gesturing I sought leave to support him. Touching his elbow, I began to weep with emotion."²⁶ It is precisely at this juncture that the illuminated Benjaminian book is shelved in the holdings in
mystical literature, a register we have yet to explore.

Although residing at the very gateway to reading and informed cultural
discourse, the illustrated books in the Benjaminian library are a far from
simple matter. If they serve as primers, they already sustain a colloquy of
different voices and mixed messages—the aesthetic, the modern, the Ger-
manic, the Judaic, and the messianic—to which I add the program of radical
change, exemplified best of all by the Marxian analysis of and proposal for
capital. Not only an adept practicing modernist, the Benjaminian child is,
willy-nilly, a proto-Marxist. Children's book illustrator Johan Peter Lyser
figures in *Old Forgotten Children's Books* as "a bohemian from those days"
who effects "a merging of all intellectual classes and modes of action [*Das
Ineinandersinken aller geistigen Schichten und Aktionsweisen*]."²⁷ Under the
stewardship of artists such as Lyser, children's literature becomes a site for
challenging the division of labor between classes and the effects of the Derridean "Law of Genre."²⁸

As Marx set about decrying the debilitating sociocultural changes
wrought by the factory system, nothing inspired him to purer outrage than
child labor as a squandering of human potential by impairing its development. Like the Benjaminian child, Marx, in his own dance among the discourses of algebraic calculation, detached sociological observation,
evolutionary history, outraged polemic, and theoretical speculation, violates
the laws of order and good sense. When he addresses the impact of child
labor under the factory system, Marx metamorphoses from the revolutionary social thinker with whom we are most familiar and comfortable into a
developmental psychologist:

> It appears, for example, in the frightful fact that a great part of the children
> employed in modern factories and manufactures are from their earliest years

riveted to the most simple manipulations, and exploited for years, without being taught a single kind of skill that would afterwards make them of use, even in the same factory. In the English letter-press printing trade, there formerly existed a system . . . of advancing the apprentices from easy to more and more difficult work. They went through a course of teaching until they were finished printers. To read and write was for every one of them a requirement of their trade. All this was changed by the printing machine. It employs two sorts of worker. On the one hand, there are adults, tenters, and on the other hand there are boys . . . whose sole occupation is either to spread the sheets under the machine, or to take from it the printed sheets. They perform this weary task, in London especially, for 14, 15 and 16 hours at a stretch. . . . A great proportion of them cannot read, and they are, as a rule, utter savages and very extraordinary creatures. . . . As soon as they get too old for such children's work, that is at about 17 years old, at the latest, they are discharged from the printing establishments. They become recruits for crime.[29]

We must not overlook the Marxian impulse behind Benjamin's reverence for the child, to whatever degree it is also inflected by a Romantic aura and by the child's pivotal placement in the process of messianic repair and correction. The child is not only a playful resistor of norms and an endlessly inventive player. The child is potential for human realization and progress, ravaged and subjected to irreversible degradation once reconfigured as the ward of voracious capitalism. When Benjamin introduces the illustrated children's book to his readership, his aim is as much to spare the unborn victims of capital as it is to fetishize the auratic freshness of early experience. Romanticism, Marx, Jewish mysticism, and modernistic improvisation converge here. However playful its provenance, under Benjamin's stewardship, the illustrated book attains a certain gravity in advance of its age. He assigns it a daunting and strategic role in the extension of culture.

The Mystical Book

We discover the placement of the mystical book in Benjamin's library when we address key anomalies in some of his most liminal and haunting works. Why would he devote so much material, in the Kafka essay commemorating the tenth anniversary of the Czech author's death—an author who did so much to translate into the modes and formats of twentieth-century configurations of power and signification—to Kafka's totemism, his relation to prehistory, and his human and animal ancestors? Why, in "Critique of Violence," in which Benjamin investigates the rationale for violent proletarian insurrection, would he elaborate the position of divine violence, which, although arbitrary and always at the extreme limit of credulity, furnishes an alternative to mythic violence? We are familiar with the latter form of unrest, the mythic, which expresses itself externally as warfare and internally as state repression, from its basis in an ideological constriction and fetishization imposed upon the free play of signs. This process, for Benjamin, is as old as recorded history; it is what Roland Barthes, in the 1950s, taking a cue from his predecessor, whether blindly or explicitly, referred to as mythology.

It is when such questions arise that the gates (or covers) of the mystical book in the Benjaminian library swing open. In the background to this literature are mysticism in general and Jewish mysticism in particular, including the Zohar, which opens a sublime Judaic afterlife whose spectral landscape found a receptive European home in German letters, particularly during the Romantic moment. Moreover, Benjamin enjoyed a lifelong collaboration and commiseration with Gershom Scholem, who, whereas Benjamin confined his critico-cultural interventions to the secular sphere, blazed a trail backward from twentieth-century Zionism to the literatures of the Kabbalah and Zohar. The supplemental tension in which Benjamin places the Judaic, on the one hand, and the Greco-Christian, on the other, is not unlike a parallel pulsation that Derrida pursues, particularly in such early works as *Of Grammatology*, "Plato's Pharmacy," and "The Double Session," the latter his study of the poetics of Mallarmé, between the discourse of philosophy and its literary sibling. In general, we can say that for Benjamin the Judaic, particularly in its mystical aspect, implicates a vaster time scheme than the history of dialectical movements, developments, and structures emerging from the doubled sources of Greek mythology and idealist philosophy and Christian theology.

The Judaic, furthermore, in the hope that it holds out for the redemption of a morally polarized and intrinsically flawed world—not entirely unlike certain aspects of Indian and Chinese civilizations—also encompasses the possibility of circumventing certain rationalist dynamics and eventualities. This is not to suggest that the Judaic, in its exceptions to the dialectical, as Benjamin can discern it in the writings of Buber and Rosenzweig as well as of Scholem, is entirely devoid of the arbitrary. On the contrary, the Judaic gains a good measure of its sublimity, achieving a particular intensity in writers ranging from Kleist and Büchner to Celan, precisely in furnishing a place for an arbitrariness that will not submit to reason.

It is in this context that Benjamin, at the outset of dire conditions of political repression, in "Critique of Violence," his inquiry into legitimate grounds for the general proletarian strike, one that might extend from figural to actual violence, goes to the extreme lengths of articulating and invoking "divine violence." Benjamin takes Georges Sorel at his word—to the effect that "the proletarian general strike sets itself the sole task of destroying state power. It 'nullifies all the ideological consequences of every possible social policy. . . . The revolution appears as a clear, simple revolt, and no place is reserved either for the sociologists or the elegant amateurs of social reform or for the intellectuals.' "[30] But against the grain of Sorel's "rejection of every kind of program, of utopia . . . for the revolutionary movement," Benjamin disallows "any objection . . . that seeks, on grounds of its possibly catastrophic consequences, to brand such a general strike as violent."[31]

"Critique of Violence" not only spells out, through meticulous argumentation, conditions under which the particular violence of the general proletarian strike would be warranted, it furnishes a methodological template for the "critique of all legal violence."[32] Benjamin examines the variations linking and separating such social controls as militarism, universal conscription, and the death penalty. His reasonings take up the gauntlet that Sorel has thrown down to "intellectuals who have made it their profession to think for the proletariat."[33] The general proletarian strike becomes viable only through a concerted labor of distinction making: between the "natural law, which regards violence as a natural datum" and furnishes a critique of ends, and positive law, which lays the blame for violence at the feet of history and delivers the critique of means; between the law-making and law-preserving functions of violence (the one the inaugural event in the formulation of laws; the latter an incipient violence always in potentia from the state). The ignominy of police brutality consists in its suspension of the distinction between law-making and law-preserving violence:

> It is law-making, because its characteristic function is not the promulgation of laws but the assertion of legal claims for any decree; and law-preserving, because it is at the disposal of these ends. [*Sie ist rechtsetzende—denn deren charakteristische*

Function ist ja nicht die Promulgation von Gesetzen, sondern jedweder Erlaß, den sie mit Rechtsanspruch ergehen läßt—und sie ist rechtserhaltende, weil sie sich jenen Zwecken zur Verfügung stellt.] The assertion that the ends of police violence are always identical or even connected to those of general law is equally untrue. Rather, the "law" of the police really marks the point at which the state, whether from impotence or because of the immanent connections within any legal system, can no longer guarantee through the legal system the empirical ends that it desires at any price to attain. Therefore the police intervene "for security reasons" in countless cases where no legal situation exists. [*Daher greift "der Sicherheit wegen" der Polizei in zahllosen Fällen ein, wo keine klare Reschtslage vorliegt.*][34]

Benjamin has initiated his own chess game with systems of law and justice that allow escalating abuses by the state; this as much by dint of as in opposition to the law's own logico-rational underpinnings. Even in the logical construction and disposition of his own essay, Benjamin demonstrates that there is an ample scaffolding of logical operations and moral principles for the negotiation of violence by civil society. Police rule, as he indicates in the above citation, sets in not by bypassing the abundant legal literature of natural law versus positive law, the relative validities of ends versus means, and so forth, but by short-circuiting this substantial defensive apparatus. In moments of authoritarian repression, the system of the law does not so much void itself or cancel itself out as implode under the inertia and equilibrium wrought by its distinctions. In this sense, the legal crisis resulting in police violence, which includes the suppression of workers' resistance, is a practical instance of the proliferation of insubstantial "differences that are not differences" marking the limit of Hegelian understanding, or *Verstand.*[35]

The proletarian general strike emerges in Benjamin's parlance not merely as a recourse to justice unavailable through any other means but as the expansion of a system as repressively closed off and involuted as it is corrupt. The proletarian general strike, in other words, opens up the conceptual-structural configuration in which the class interests of workers are systematically devalued and underrepresented. By the time of "Critique of Violence," Benjamin is already beginning to discern the historical coherence and perdurance of this gridlocked system, lending it something of the cohesion that Derrida will extrapolate in his notion of "Western metaphysics." The grounding of the proletarian general strike will demand an expansion—historical, conceptual, and literary—of the logical grid arising in

myth and prevailing through the only too familiar cycles of absolutist tyr-
anny, revolution, civil adjudications of violence, and abuses of civil law by
the very state agencies of moderation. In this piece of writing, Benjamin has
anticipated the ploy of the rigorous deconstructionist; he is riding logic to
its very ends to demonstrate how arbitrary and illogical these eventualities
are. It is precisely here in Benjamin's argument that he appeals to the divine
violence whose sublime arbitrariness circumvents mythic violence, which
lends itself only too well to the various outcomes of the play of force and
law; it is at this point that he opens up the temporal framework of Greco-
Christian metaphysics and law to the somewhat wider (indeed, on some
level timeless) horizon of Judaic creation.

Both subsequent history and Derrida, in "Force of Law," will demonstrate that the appeal to a divine violence, "without warning, without
threat" and not stopping "short of annihilation," can be a double-edged
sword.[36] It can, indeed, be directed against those whose interests it might
otherwise protect. At a moment in history when the ordeal of reading a
newspaper is exacerbated in no small measure by near-global inroads of
religious fundamentalism and proliferations of ethnic strife, we need to underscore the irresponsibility and risk of invoking "divine violence."

Much as mythic violence may initiate cycles of casuistry and bad faith in
government and the civil sphere, in Benjamin's account, divine violence is
not exactly unproblematical, either: it is abrupt, bloody, disproportionate,
and hyper-arbitrary. It shows no mercy and may exact inexplicably vast tolls
in sacrifice. Benjamin situates the educational system under the aegis of
divine violence: his first political activity was dedicated to the Youth Movement's program of educational reform. With respect to such phenomena as
the recalibration of laws in the wake of military treaties, Benjamin demonstrated striking acuity with regard to his particular historical moment. But
like the rest of us, he was blind addressing the future. Within the framework
of "Critique of Violence," such moves as the bracketing of the Niobe myth
by the biblical account of Korah give an early indication of where the mystical book, particularly the book conditioned by the Jewish mysticism of
which Scholem was such a powerful avatar, is placed within the body of
Benjamin's writing:

> The mythic manifestation of immediate violence shows itself fundamentally
> identical with all legal violence [*zeigt die mythische Manifestation der unmittelbaren*

Gewalt sich im tiefsten mit aller Rechtsgewalt identisch]. . . . Just as in all spheres God opposes myth, mythic violence is confronted by the divine. And the latter constitutes its antithesis in all respects. If mythic violence is lawmaking, divine violence is law-destroying; if the former sets boundaries, the latter boundlessly destroys them; if mythic violence brings at once guilt and retribution, divine power only expiates; if the former threatens, the latter strikes; if the former is bloody, the latter is lethal without spilling blood. The legend of Niobe may be contrasted with God's judgment on the company of Korah. . . . Mythic violence is bloody power over mere life for its own sake; divine violence is pure power over all life for the sake of the living. The first demands sacrifice; the second accepts it. [*Die mythische Gewalt ist Blutgewalt über das bloße Leben um ihrer selbst, die göttliche reine Gewalt über alles Leben des Lebendigen willen. Die erste fordert Opfer, die zweite nimmt sie an.*][37]

In seeking a framework and pretext for the general proletarian strike, even at the cost of his own logical inconsistency (for the configuration in which he places mythical and divine violence here is nothing if not stringently dialectical), Benjamin is willing, to borrow a phrasing from his major Kafka essay, to "move divine time." The general proletarian strike comprises a severe challenge to the Western tradition of conceptualizing, making, and adjudicating laws and punishment for their violation. Yet it is backed, in the logic of Benjamin's argument, by an alternate tradition, one characterized, if by nothing else, by a sublime arbitrariness, one capable of suspending the rule of logic, and by cosmic time.

This alternate tradition subtends the manifest wish, in the dream recounted in *One-Way Street*, for an intimacy between Judaic and German letters (parallel to the graft that Faust makes onto the very bedrock of Greek culture when, in *Faust II*, he marries Helen of Troy), and it makes its influence felt, often surprisingly and with seeming irrelevance, in a wide range of Benjamin's addresses to cultural artifacts.

In view of the preceding discussion and its distinction between mythical and divine violence, and the time frames whence they proceed, it is perhaps not difficult to understand why Benjamin, in his 1934 Kafka essay, discerns Chinese, Greek, Judaic, and even Indian forerunners—his term is "ancestors"—to Kafka's fiction making. In this line of inquiry, Benjamin of course takes his cues from Kafka, whose Poseidon sits "at his desk, going over the accounts,"[38] a twentieth-century bureaucrat, and whose Abraham appears "with the promptness of a waiter."[39] In one respect, Kafka continues the ploy, along the lines of Baudelaire's angel in "Lost Halo," of inserting cultural figures of venerable pedigree into a contemporary setting, depicted in all its realistic wrinkles. But Benjamin figures the complementary side to this temporal reversal or metalepsis as a case of premature cosmic old age:

> To speak of any order or hierarchy here is impossible. Even the world of myth, which comes to mind in this context, is incomparably younger than Kafka's world, which has been promised redemption by myth. But if we can be sure of one thing, it is this: Kafka did not succumb to this temptation. . . . Among Kafka's ancestors in the ancient world, the Jews and the Chinese (whom we shall encounter later), this Greek one should not be forgotten. Ulysses, after all, stands at the dividing line between myth and fairy tale. Reason and cunning have inserted tricks into myths, and fairy tales for dialecticians are what Kafka wrote when he went to work on legends. He inserted little tricks into them [*Und Märchen für Dialektiker schrieb Kafka, wenn er sich Sagen vornahm. Er setzte kleine Tricks in sie hinein*]; then he used them as proof "that inadequate, even childish measures may also serve as a means of rescue." With these words, he begins his story "Das Schweigen der Sirenen" ("The Silence of the Sirens"). For Kafka's Sirens are silent. [*Sie schweigen nämlich bei ihm.*][40]

Although the expression is as stunningly trenchant as Benjamin can often be, we can well understand how Kafka could have devised "fairy tales for dialecticians." Kafka's fictive ploys of logic, spatiality, and temporality are indeed legendary and unavoidable. But Kafka's cosmic time frame remains a puzzle unless Kafka's fiction occupies a cosmic sweep of time, the eons of mystical apprehension: "Kafka did not consider the age in which he lived as an advance over the beginnings of time. His novels are set in a swamp world."[41]

We remember how, in "Critique of Violence," the dialectical operations of mythical violence and justice are both meticulous in their distinctions and constrictive in their compulsion. In the citation immediately above, Ulysses is an interstitial figure, hovering "at the dividing line between myth and fairy tale." He thus claims a dual citizenship in the progression of myth into civil law instrumented by dialectical logic and resulting in mythical violence but also in the incomparably broader scope, international and intercultural as well as historical, claimed by fairy tale and legend. That literature, of course, like the particular aura of colorful illustrations, enjoys a particular intimacy with children, their play, and their culture. I would suggest that the aspects of Ulysses that make him an emissary to the world of

Old Forgotten Children's Books also make him figure in the cosmic universe of Benjamin's mystical book holdings, a world proceeding, among other sources, from the literature of Jewish mysticism as penetrated and purveyed by Scholem. Where Ulysses belongs to both myth and fairy tale, the dialectical does commerce with the mystical, and the Greek joins the Judaic, as in Joyce's trenchant phrase from *Ulysses*, "Jewgreek Greekjew."[42]

In an act of authentic critical impossibility and creation, Benjamin links Kafka's dealings with the prehistorical pretext to world literature to the sordid bureaucratic spaces that fill his novels. "We do not know the makeup" of the suffocating, phantasmatic family from Kafka's very early "He feels as though he were living and thinking under the constraints of a family," writes Benjamin, "composed of human beings and animals. But this much is clear: it is this family that forces Kafka to move cosmic ages in his writings. Doing this family's bidding, he moves the mass of historical happenings the way Sisyphus moved his stone."[43] It is with bemused admiration that Benjamin characterizes Kafka's Archimedean feat of moving, with his imagination, the building blocks of a broader, more anthropologically resonant tradition than the Western canon alone. The women in the world literature mobilized by Kafka's imaginary, like the vague and innocent sister of "The Knock on the Manor Gate," do not stand out clearly, like Penelope, heroically devising to restore the unity of her world. They are, like Leni of *The Castle*, "swamp creatures," who arise from "swampy soil."[44]

The communication with the prehistoric and animal worlds that distinguishes Kafka's modernist innovation embarks him, in Benjamin's scenario, on an exploration of oblivion itself, of the collective and cosmic unconscious. Kafka becomes the psychoanalytic explorer of prehistory in its anthropological as well as cultural dimensions. It is no accident that Benjamin cites Rosenzweig on the Chinese ancestor cult in illuminating Kafka's uncanny gravitation toward oblivion. In the passage that inspired Benjamin to this particular thrust, Rosenzweig, in *The Star of Redemption*, an overview of the tradition of redemptive history in Judaism, accounts for the transformation of spirit, or *Geist* in its Hegelian sense, into spirits. In Rosenzweig's terms: "All spirit must be concrete, particularized, in order to have its place and *raison d'être*. The spiritual, if it plays a role at all, turns into spirits. These spirits become definite individuals, with names and a very special connection with the name of the worshipper. . . . Unhesitatingly, the fullness of the world is filled to overflowing with their fullness."[45] Kafka's special relation to the amorphous creatures who teem out of this inchoate history, in Benjamin's scenario, marks him as a partner in a cosmic process of the redemption of the world, *tikkun olam*, in a framework whose application and potential surpass its grounding in Judaic texts:

> What has been forgotten—and with this insight we stand before another threshold in Kafka's work—is never something purely individual. Everything forgotten mingles with what has been forgotten of the prehistoric world, forms countless uncertain and unchanging compounds, yielding a constant flow of new, strange products. Oblivion is the container from which the inexhaustible intermediate world in Kafka's world presses toward the light. . . . To Kafka, the world of his ancestors was as unfathomable as the world of realities was important, and we may be sure that, like the totem poles of primitive peoples, the world of ancestors took him down to the animals.[46]

As Benjamin sees him, Kafka looks backward to a past of sublime number, scale, and nondefinition. The oblivion with which Kafka trucks is reminiscent of the uncanny afterlife through which the rabbis wander in pairs throughout the Zohar, often under cover of night, looking backward upon a world they have departed, as they deliver elucidations of the Torah whose thrust is more poetic than legalistic (even when the same rabbis have figured earlier in the Talmud as legalists). It can be argued, I believe, as I do elsewhere,[47] that the legends of the Zohar not only mark a new relation between Judaic theology and the afterlife but also a premodern Judaic receptivity to literature itself, to literature as literature. Scholem even went so far as to collect some of the most compelling of the anecdotal and allegorical rabbinic commentaries in the Zohar into a slim volume.[48] The uncanny aura pervading Kafka's "Parable of the Doorkeeper" lends this decisive allegory of the Law and its unresolved aporias the traits of the afterlife as it is imagined in the Zohar: "From hall to hall keepers stand at every door, one more powerful than the next. And the sight of the third man is even more than I can stand."[49] Benjamin's poetic compression and condensation shift into high gear as he undertakes to formulate a singularly Kafkan oblivion.

The dimension of cosmic time that Benjamin associates with divine violence does not extend only backwards. The dimension of Jewish mysticism in Kafka's work becomes most explicit when it figures, even ironically, the possible redemption of the swamp world out of which so many of the characters press. At the moment when it allows for the repair or redemption of the world, the cosmic time of children's literature, of fairy tale and legend, becomes messianic time. In the world of Kafka, we would, of course, expect the agents of the messiah, the Judeo-Christian counterparts to bodhisattvas, to be screwball in some quintessential way. From the students common to *Amerika* and *The Trial* to the bumbling assistants of *The Castle*, the agents of redemption are not who we expect them to be. As Benjamin characterizes them in two related passages:

> In Indian mythology there are the *gandharvas*, mist-bound creatures, beings in an unfinished state. Kafka's assistants are of that kind: neither members of, nor strangers to, any of the other groups of figures, but, rather, messengers busy moving between them. Kafka tells us that they resemble Barnabas, who is a messenger. They have not been completely released from the womb of nature.[50]
>
> The gate to justice is study. Yet Kafka doesn't dare attach to this study the promises which tradition has attached to the study of the Torah. His assistants are sextons who have lost their house of prayer; his students are pupils who have lost the Holy Writ [*Schrift*]. Now there is nothing to support them on their "untrammeled, happy journey."[51]

Whether the agents of redemption elicit our laughter or our longing, they are messengers from the domain of mystical thinking and figuration, without which, according to Benjamin, the full sweep of Kafka's imagination and writing cannot be taken into account. In militating for this dimension of Kafka criticism, Benjamin continues in his role as an agent provocateur for the instatement of the Judaic in its full role in German letters and for the contrary movement, recognition by Jewish authors of the hospitableness to key elements of the Judaic imaginary shown by German literature. This is a major file in his ongoing, self-delegated portfolio. The role demands that he plumb to the innermost depths of Goethe, Schiller, Hölderlin, Kleist, Schlegel, Hebbel, Keller, George, Hofmannsthal, Brecht, and others, so that he can read them both as concretions of ongoing Western and European curricula and in a second light. Exegeses underwritten by such a split identity inevitably are scored with a hidden secret or a shibboleth, one into which Scholem delves deeply in his surveys of the messianic literature. Celan, at certain pivotal moments in his poetic composition, acknowledges the cryptic side of his linguistico-existential predicament and the messages with which he responds to it, a point not lost on Derrida in his Celan elucidations.[52]

Benjamin casts a mystical *Schein*, or light, upon Goethe's *Elective Affinities*, even while he rigorously sets about the task of a philosophically trained critic in the sphere of German letters. He reminds us that Goethe himself has launched "Hope . . . against the sky above their [the characters'] heads like a falling star," hope even in the face of the constitutional indirections and failures of love, intimacy, and commiseration. The hope toward which Benjamin gazes as much for his own edification as that of his readers is only comprehensible in terms of the messianic dream of the end of *Galut*, or exile: "That most paradoxical, most fleeting hope emerges from the semblance of reconciliation, just as, at twilight, as the sun is extinguished, rises the evening star which outlasts the night. Its glimmer, of course, is imparted by Venus. And upon the slightest such glimmer all hope rests."[53] Benjamin's wish for a synthesis between the major strands of his study and his most compelling interests is embedded in the fragmentary phrase "semblance of reconciliation [*Schein der Versöhnung*]." This briefest of genitive constructions merges the *Schein* of semblance and appearance, the facilitating link in the transition between sensible and supersensible worlds in systems as far-reaching as Kant's and Hegel's, to the mystical yearning for a connectedness to the universe made possible by the undoing of exile. In the "system" of Lurianic Kabbalah, according to Scholem the second major phase in the Jewish mystical adventure:

> redemption is synonymous with emendation or restoration. After we have fulfilled our duty and the emendation is completed, all things occupy their appropriate places in the universal scheme, then redemption will come *of itself*. Redemption merely signifies the perfect state, a flawless and harmonious world in which everything occupies its proper place. Hence the Messianic ideal, the ideal of redemption, receives a wholly new aspect. We all work, or are at least expected to work, for the amendment of the world and the "selection" of good and evil.[54]

In Benjamin's account, such a world of mystical harmony and reconciliation flashes above the horizon of Goethe's *Elective Affinities*. His appeal to the semblance of reconciliation furnishes the exception to Plato's dictum "that it is absurd to desire the semblance of the good." Once again, the experiment of Western idealism finds a certain culmination and fulfillment among the reaches and reconciliations of cosmic space.

Between the twelfth century and the expulsion of the Jews from Spain in 1492, Scholem argues, Kabbalists could hope for a particular and mystical redemption for each individual, to be achieved by escaping from the turbulence, perplexity, chaos, and storms of the actual course of history.

These early Kabbalists assigned special importance to such questions as "What is the nature of Creation?" and "Whence have we come?" For they believed that to know . . . the secret of our beginnings, whence the imperfections of this distorted and dark world in which we are stranded, with all the storms and perturbations and afflictions within it—to know all this would teach us the way back to "our inward home."

The Zohar follows Talmudic Aggadah in seeing redemption not as the product of inward progress in the historical world, but as a supernatural miracle involving the gradual illumination of the world by the light of the Messiah.[55]

The Zohar itself takes the bold step of imagining a messianic redemption taking place amid the relative objectivity of the external world. The messiah's work is redemption by means of illumination, a Judaic spin on the spiritual centrality of acts of exegesis and criticism, one that could not have been lost on Benjamin or Scholem.

The postexilic picture of the universe, as we might imagine, was not nearly as rosy for the Kabbalists. Once again they contended with exile or *Galut*, the loss of a discursive as well as a geographical community. Those who stayed behind in Spain submitted to the circumlocutions of feigned, doubled, and secret identity. Under such conditions, the mission of the messiah himself took on untoward complexity. The redemption of the world might just as well be achieved through messianic apostasy as through impossible perfection and exemplarity. In the wake of 1492, the stage, in Scholem's account, gradually became set for the actual messianic adventures and catastrophes, in the seventeenth and eighteenth centuries, surrounding Sabbatai Zevi and Jacob Frank, among others. Sabbatai Zevi (1626–76) achieved notoriety at a moment of apocalyptic expectation in several religious communities in the Levant and Balkans by declaring himself messiah. He received alternately spirited condemnation and adulation until his conversion to Islam, in 1666, under dire conditions. Jacob Frank (1726–91) was a Polish apostate. A merchant before claiming to be the messiah, Frank invoked the tradition of Zevi but scandalized the Jewish establishment by converting to Christianity and exhorting his followers to do the same. The transgressive undercurrent that entered Jewish messianism in the aftermath of the early modern exile from Spain (1492), itself an imaginary replay of

parallel events in Biblical times, is not without interpretative repercussions
for a commentator such as Benjamin, invested for long stretches of his critical run in a modern Judeo-Germanic graft. The Jewish mystics "began to
seek explanations" for the 1492 expulsion. They posed such questions as:

> What had happened? What brought on the affliction and suffering? What is the
> nature of the gloomy world of Galut? They sought an answer to such questions
> in terms of their basic mystical outlook. . . . And by connecting the notions of
> Galut and redemption with the central question of the essence of the universe,
> they managed to elaborate a system which transformed the exile of the people of
> Israel into an exile of the whole world, and the redemption of their people into
> a universal, cosmic redemption.[56]

It fell to the Lurianic messianism of the decades following 1540 to meld
the dream of messianic redemption with the destructive forces at play in a
world of *Galut*. According to the Lurianic Kabbalah, this is "a terrible and
pitiless state permeating and embittering all of Jewish life . . . but . . . also
the condition of the universe of the whole, even the deity."[57] Scholem pegs
this as "an extremely bold idea," demanding destructive action along with
creativity, forming a context for the notorious Kabbalistic *shevira ha-kelim*,
or "breaking of the vessels," in which the divine attributes have been dis-
bursed.[58] Lurianic Kabbalism thus adds a strain of violence to the mystical
imperatives to repair and redemption. We can recognize it in the more
disruptive features of Benjaminian shock, not only a condition of an industrial landscape increasingly under the sway of the assembly line and its spasmodic gestures,[59] but also in the storm that has gotten caught in the Angel
of History's wings, drawing him "irresistibly into the future, to which his
back is turned, while the pile of debris before him grows toward the sky.
What we call progress is *this* storm."[60]

Within the aura of the mystical book in Benjamin's library, exegesis
needs to keep its eye on cultural repair and correction. It needs at the same
time to calibrate its interventions of system-scrambling disruption. Does
this sound at all familiar? Lurianic Kabbalism, according to Scholem, ushered in a new twist to "an old rabbinic concept . . . 'a commandment which
is fulfilled by means of a transgression.' . . . We know that even before his
apostasy, Sabbatai Zevi violated several of the commandments."[61] There
is no more distinctive signature to Benjamin's imprint than the sustained
coordination between redemptive exegetical striving and twentieth-century

violence throughout his script. So much of his commentary emanates from the obscure writing desk shared by the angel of interpretation and the avatar of shock. The mystical books in his library may well serve as a commanding context from which he incorporates one additional Talmudic legend into his celebratory essay on Kafka, one explaining "why Jews prepare a festive meal on Fridays":

> The legend is about a princess languishing in exile, a village whose language she does not understand, far from her compatriots. One day this princess receives a letter saying that her fiancé has not forgotten her and is on his way to her. The fiancé, so says the rabbi, is the Messiah; the princess is the soul; the village in which she lives is in exile is the body. She prepares a meal for him because this is the only way in which she can express her joy in a village whose language she does not know.—This village of the Talmud is right in Kafka's world. For just as K. lives in the village on Castle Hill, modern man lives in his own body; the body slips away from him; is hostile toward him. It may happen that a man wakes up one day and finds himself transformed into vermin. Strangeness—his own strangeness—has gained control over him. [*Denn so wie K. im Dorf am Schloßberg lebt der heutige Mensch in seinem Körper; er entgleitet ihm, ist ihm feindlich. Es kann geschehen, daß der Mensch eines Morgens erwacht, und er ist in ein Ungeziefer verwandelt. Die Fremde—seine Fremde—ist seiner Herr geworden*].[62]

The Dissolving Book

> It has rightly been said that all great works of literature establish a genre or dissolve one—that they are, in other words, special cases.
>
> —WALTER BENJAMIN, "On the Image of Proust"[63]

No one with Benjamin's exquisite attunement to the destructive as well as generative forces and flows released by modernization could be accused of a facile conviction in the permanence of books, whether as a medium or as a culture. Some books are acquired only to be released again into the general flow of printed matter, even by the "genuine" collector. The forces of commerce, capital, industrialization, and mass production, as well as the regimentation of the masses, all of which make *The Flowers of Evil* "the last lyric work" with "a broad European reception,"[64] affect not only communities of folktale and the ritual calendar but community as such, including the implicit community crystallizing around each book. When the community of the book is dismembered, when each book abandons its potential to become a quasi-institution of discourse, then the prospects for the book as a medium of information and thinking has undergone a detrimental reversal. History is replete with instances and explanations of the crisis of the book during the last two decades of Benjamin's life. However the ground and pretexts have shifted since that time, perhaps from politics to technology, those of us charged with disseminating the topography, sensibility, and skills of the broader literacy surely today face a constitutional crisis of reading and its potential communities.

To any thinker as sensitive as Benjamin to the vicissitudes of book culture, assaults on the book register in the design, architecture, and volume of actual books. *The Arcades Project*, Benjamin's encyclopedic and hypertextual time capsule of Paris in the Second Empire, obsessed him from 1927 or so until the time of his death in 1940. Itself a resource book (or, as we would now say, a text-medium website) consisting of citations that Benjamin collected from an astonishing range of firsthand, historical, and contemporary accounts and commentaries (social psychology, urban studies, art history, and critical theory number among them), only occasionally interspersed with observations posited by Benjamin himself, *The Arcades Project* subtends some of his most pointed and memorable literary studies, written at the opposite extreme, that of compression and shorthand. *The Arcades Project*, in its omnivorous openness to relevant materials and in the linear progression of its convolutes, is cloudlike in consistency in comparison to such carefully orchestrated essays as "The Storyteller," "Paris, the Capital of the Nineteenth Century" (in both of its versions), and "On Some Motifs in Baudelaire." *The Arcades Project* is Talmudic in its obsession with registers of signification and commentary, in its fascination with the spatial zones, vertical as well as lateral, of Paris, its commerce, and its activities, legitimate or not; it is encyclopedic in the sheer range of factors and materials surrounding Paris's (a.k.a. modernity's) development, achievements, and political vicissitudes; it is hypertextual to the degree to which the individual convolutes supplement and enlarge upon one another. This hypertextual supplementation can transpire even within the compass of a single convolute, as, within Convolute O, "Prostitution and Gambling," the *segues* between the materials related to both of these vices—themselves supplements to the humdrum balance sheets of the legitimate economy, are more telling and suggestive than the nitty-gritty transactions endemic to these spheres.

It is, then, fated, absolutely unavoidable, that *The Arcades Project*, with all the innovation that it brings to the architecture and design of books—its consisting almost entirely of citations, its opening up a display space for its materials as much visual as verbal, the hypertextual mutual referencing of its various sections, its thematic omnivorousness and the internal apparatus of sub-directories that this necessitates—also foretells a devastating constitutional crisis in the medium, culture, community, and consistency of the book. As in the epigraph to this section from "On the Image of Proust," *The Arcades Project* is both the founder, the progenitor of the new electronic book (or whatever name we attach to it), in its rhizomatic configuration, a medium still in the moment of its becoming, and the confirmation of the demise of the book medium as Benjamin encountered it at the outset of his intellectual life and throughout the preponderance of his research.

Benjamin, in other words, is as much the avatar of the dissolving book, the book that provides for its own marginality and dispersion, as he is the champion of the Age of the Book in all its classicism and in all the vitality of its remarkable run. With Benjamin as its ringleader, as the leader of its pack (in its Deleuzian sense),[65] the entire historical production of the book circles around to face its radical reconfiguration, if not its flat-out annihilation. We encounter the dissolving book, whose aftermath remains entirely uncertain, not only in *The Arcades Project*, with its open-ended receptivity and citationality, its soft and amorphous contours, its endless circulation around its motifs and theoretical interests. We run into the dissolving book in a large share of Benjamin's primary inspirations and in generative experimental works that were configured by others within the aura of Benjamin's age. A tragically incomplete list of these manifestations would include: the soft structure, macro- and microcosmic, or the fractal miniaturization making Proust's *Recherche* possible,[66] a gay romance scored between the margins of a straight one, leaving room for an astonishingly broad network of rhizomatically interconnected social relations; the Creole that Joyce fashions for *Finnegans Wake*, a language drawing on national histories and ethnic traditions while paying none of them credence, being the draft, rather, for an incipient global language;[67] fiction, in Borges's counterworld of Tlön, that "has but a single plot, with every imaginable permutation";[68] finally, but not last, as we shall see below in Chapter 6, the crumbling columns of type configured, in *Glas*, by a deconstructive encounter between Hegel and

Genet, a Talmudic work whose demarcated sectors of text have been constructed precisely to fall apart and together.[69] Ever so slightly afield from this body (or perhaps swamp) of intransigent works but thoroughly participating in it is the unique patois that Gertrude Stein devised for works including *Ida* and *Mrs. Reynolds*, a discourse abundantly inventive of grammatical variants and new possibilities for expression at the same time as it suspends and frustrates its reader's addictions to making clear and easy sense.

Benjamin peered over into a future of the book that he would not, having transformed himself into the consummate citizen of its past, fully inhabit. It remains for us to track the flow patterns following in the wake of this inclination and this tradition: by struggling to explore and comprehend them, to furnish them with a memory, however artificial, and, frontally and without a hitch, to embrace their mutants and mutations.

FIVE

Pulsations of Respect, or Winged Impossibility:
Poetic Deconstruction

> Let us suppose that one makes the acquaintance of a person who is handsome
> and attractive but impenetrable, because he carries a secret with him. It would
> be reprehensible to want to pry. Still, it would surely be permissible to inquire
> whether he has any siblings and whether their nature could not perhaps explain
> the enigmatic nature of the stranger. In just this way critique seeks to discover
> siblings of the work of art. And all genuine works have their sibling in the work
> of philosophy.
>
> —WALTER BENJAMIN, "Goethe's *Elective Affinities*"

Among many images for the difficult freedom into which Jacques Derrida
led us by the text is the alternation between the opening up of a vast field
of linguistic transgression and the constraints upon authentically rigorous
decoding and exegesis. The task of interpretation under the aegis of deconstruction is to alternate, like systole and diastole, between the sublime array
of ideological manifestations and aesthetic products placed in mutual communication by the scene of inscription and transgression and a rigorously
limited set of interpretative acts and interventions rendered apt by their
ethical mindfulness of the specific context at hand.

There has always been something provocative about deconstruction.
Arising at a heady moment of psychedelic expansionism coinciding with a
symptomatic limit experience in Western hegemony, the Vietnam War, itself a sequel to the French colonizations of Indochina and Algeria, deconstruction from the outset took a vertiginous leap between radically different
scenes of writing, nonetheless linked by certain always limited and specific

resonances, these always under daunting constraints of semiological, semantic, rhetorical, grammatical, and, yes, logical rigor. To be caught up in the delirious and inebriated momentum of deconstruction is to groove on the vast extent of the connections and associations it makes possible yet to respect the difficulties in positing them; to be slow and meticulous in the gathering of etymological, logical, and rhetorical roots yet blindingly fluent in the moment and act of debriefing.

This skill is akin to the violent pulsations converging upon the Benjaminian dialectical image:[1] the alternation between fluid imagistic balletrics, say, the transformations of falling stars into roulette balls or matches into cameras in "On Some Motifs in Baudelaire,"[2] and the long, wondrous meditation that we enter into when we have been captivated by the dialectical image in its full nuance and density.

Among the many roles that Derrida sustained in the unique elemental balance characteristic of great teachers—between the fire of his interpretations, the wood of his astonishing drive and productivity, the water of his ethical sense and argumentative purity, the earth of his balance and mental stability, and the metal of his logic[3]—was that of a choreographer, someone who could coordinate vastly different tempos of thinking and writing and concentrations of textual density. An earlier version of the present chapter was entitled "The Zen of Deconstruction." Derrida the teacher, writer, and personality was not only characterized by the elemental balance that Eastern medicine associates with vitality, creativity, and circumspection, a somewhat different picture from the uneasy legislative checks and balances between the faculties that Kant schematized for consciousness in general and for aesthetic production and enjoyment in his *Critiques*.[4] In the coordination of literary and philosophical resources into the rhythm of his script, one invariably calibrated toward surprise and impossibility, Derrida opened his prose to the distinctively deliberate breathing rhythm that in Eastern thought is a basic predisposition to meditative thinking. From the early essays on Artaud, Jabès, and Mallarmé to *Sovereignties in Question*, the posthumous English-language compilation of his writings on and around Celan,[5] Derrida orchestrated the mutually generative rapport between literature and philosophy as a yin and yang, as a systole and diastole, as the hospitable relationships binding upon mortal enemies as well as friends.

Derrida's script, very much in keeping with the telling writerly experiments of the century in which he spent the preponderance of his life, verged toward both the diffuse and the supersaturated extremes of scriptural weaving. He was capable both of aerating his prose with the spaces accommodated and incorporated into the resources of writing by French imagist poetry and, when the occasion demanded, of composing with Wittgensteinian spareness and concision.

Derrida was, from the outset of his writing, exquisitely aware of the double potential of books to codify and to facilitate the strictures of ideology, on the one hand, making them binding, and, on the other hand, to fan outward toward impossibility. Already in *Of Grammatology*, the Book, as theocratic, canonical, and juridical instrument, pushes up against its limits by becoming a medium for unfettered and unconditional thinking, for thinking with impunity. In one of its prevalent traditions and ongoing facets, the book facilitates phonetic writing, serving as house organ both to this particular medium and to the metaphysics that it bears with it. Phonetic writing, "the medium of the great metaphysical, scientific, technical, and economic adventure of the West, is limited in space and time and limits itself as it is in the process of imposing its laws upon the cultural areas that escaped it."[6] Derrida's resistance to the Book as a medium of ideological and cultural closure goes hand in hand with his lifelong incredulity with regard to systems—not only to their encompassing totalization but to the iterability (portability and exportation) that their functions, drawing on a particular phrasing of speech-act theory, claim.[7] Derrida's skepticism about systematic regimes and claims also extended to the very existence of systems.

Finalizing and closing out the possibilities for sanctioned cultural production and innovation over a transhistorical timeframe, the book becomes the Book, or the Good Book:

> The good writing has therefore always been *comprehended*. . . . Comprehended, therefore, within a totality, . . . finite or infinite, of the signifier. . . . The idea of the book is the idea of a totality, finite or infinite, of the signifier. . . . The idea of the book, which always refers to a natural totality, is profoundly alien to the sense of writing. It is the encyclopedic protection of theology and of logocentrism against the disruption of writing.[8]

These severe misgivings regarding the book as a transmitter and instrument of categorical, obtuse authority do not undo the fact that Derrida confided the vast majority of his intellectual production to the hybrid medium of what might be termed the philosophical-critical-exegetical book.[9] Despite his pronounced, pointed skepticism about books as canonical instruments, he was an inspired devotee of the book medium, at the open end of its architecture, as showcase and display of writing and text, as an agent of indispensable and salutary rethinking and rephrasing, and, in this sense, as a vehicle of "messianism without messianicity,"[10] his vivid phrase for the reprogramming, reform, therapy (at the level of cultural psychoanalysis), and even healing that theoretical inscription and critique can effect.

The challenge to the tradition and Western metaphysics of the Book that Derrida issues in *Of Grammatology* as part of his overall positioning as a systems theorist in no way writes off the book medium as the prevailing ongoing display of textual programming. In his efforts to reconfigure both the architecture of the book and its graphic design, Derrida accessed an outlet for his spatial sense and visual imagination. In the bicolumnar pages of *Glas* and their typographical evolution in the course of the extended encounter between Hegel and Genet that it stages (see Chapter 6 below), in the structure of frames and corners (another form of binding) that he extrapolates and applies in his commentary on the Kantian aesthetics in *The Truth in Painting*,[11] even in the subgenre of philosophical investigation as epistolary love novel that he invents in *The Post Card* (a work pivoting around a late-medieval British graphic involving Plato and Socrates that he found at Oxford),[12] Derrida expends considerable effort on the innovative redesign of the philosophical-critical-exegetical book. This improvisation can only be taken as an investment in the future of the book, a certain book, perhaps, one whose capacities to mutate, morph, and self-reformat (as in autopoiesis) must painstakingly be built into it: an investment that is also an ongoing participation in the community of writing, however inchoate, dispersed, and rhizomatic it may be.

Yet another telling instance of Derrida's challenge/commitment to the book medium, a distinctly poetic one, is the jarring tattoo of beats, *coups*, the assaults upon representational language and the metaphysics of subjectivity, purity, and propriety that it implies, just as Plato, in *Phaedrus*, prepares to close, both in the senses of finalizing and consummating, his pharmacy:

In this stammering buzz of voices . . . one can sort of make this out but it is hard to hear . . . *pharmakon* means coup . . . "so that *pharmakon* will have meant: that which pertains to an attack of demoniac possession [*un coup démoniaque*] or is used as a curative against such an attack" . . . an armed enforcement of order [*un coup de force*] . . . a shot fired [*un coup tiré*] . . . a planned overthrow [*un coup monté*] . . . but to no avail [*un coup pour rien*] . . . like cutting through water [*un coup dans l'eau*] . . . *en udati grapsei* . . . and a stroke of fate [*un coup de sort*] Theuth who invented writing . . . the calendar . . . dice . . . the calendar trick [*le coup du calendrier*] . . . the unexpected dramatic effect [*le coup du théâtre*] . . . the writing trick [*le coup de l'écriture*] . . . the dice throw [*le coup de dés*] . . . two in one blow [*le coup double*] . . . *colaphos* . . . *gluph* . . . *colpus* . . . *coup* . . . glyph . . . scalpel . . . scalp . . . *khrusos* . . . *chrysolite* . . . *chrysology*. . . .

Plato gags his ears . . . the better to hear-himself-speak, the better to see, the better to analyze.

He means to distinguish, between two repetitions.

He is searching for gold.[13]

In keeping with both the semiotics and aesthetics of dissemination, Derrida does not shy away from opening textual synthesis to the *vides*, voids and intervals of emptiness. He scores the above passage far more in the interest of the rhythm and momentum of its saying than in its substantive addition to a parsing of Plato. The passage's unabashed affinity to poetic dispersion on the page is surely no accident, given Derrida's career-long receptivity to poetics in philosophy, which he gained from, among other sources, his encounter with Nietzsche.

The concatenation of coups in Derrida's passage reminds us of the hatch-marks composed by the birds in Hitchcock's film of the same name, as it has been brilliantly parsed by Tom Cohen.[14] Among the multifarious directions of critical inquiry open in the wake of the particular body English thrown by Derrida's live performance is the one naturally gravitating toward the profound interplay between the grain or texture of his singular style and the possibilities available to contemporary political discourse. Cohen's recent work breaks the delicate equilibrium by which the nostalgic critic and collector and the allegorist are related in Benjamin's "On Some Motifs in Baudelaire" in distinct favor of the allegorist's melancholic premonition. What needs to be mobilized now, Cohen argues, is acceptance of the fact that political reality has already been reprogrammed by hegemonic media spins in the hands of interests as sublimely cynical as they are global and vast. By contrast to the collector, the allegorist "has given up the attempt to elucidate things through research into their properties and relations. He dislodges things from their context and, from the outset, relies on his profundity to illuminate their meaning," Benjamin writes in Convolute H of *The Arcades Project*.[15] Cohen warns us that it may already be too late for us to slip into the more comfortable relations with books, ideas, and their constellations maintained by the counter-persona choreographed by "On Some Motifs in Baudelaire," the collector, who may be something like the public image of the friendly literature professor. Indeed, our compelling need to intervene in ideologically structured and spun images may recast and polarize any benign, repressively tolerant conception of ourselves as literacy workers promulgating general literacy through cultivated intimacy with the book and its culture. This is a tough pill to swallow, and it may militate for the awakening with which Convolute K of *The Arcades Project* begins.

The rich line of thought initiated by Derrida's exposé of language's tele-technic capabilities leads us to apprehend that any political power to which we may presume has a great deal to do with our capacity, as cultural pro-grammers, to isolate and hack the new media programs of ideological ma-nipulation, to break the momentum of existing systems of spin, and to synthesize hybrid languages and media that may mobilize cultural emanci-pation. It is in this sense almost imperative for contemporary students of theory and literature to be inculcated into cybernetic technology and well versed in visual diction and iconography.

Yet the sustained density of writing and thinking for which Derrida was known stems from an ethos of close reading, a conviction that all pro-nouncements and epiphenomena of ideology have been encoded and em-bedded into the specific phrasings of documents in turn invested with cultural memory, authority, and canonicity. This is the very same poet, phi-losopher, close reader, and critic who could, in *The Gift of Death*, interrogate the venerable pathos of the self-sacrifice of one life for another with a blunt-ness and directness as arresting as the *glas* or concatenation of *coups*:

> If something radically impossible is to be conceived of—and everything derives its sense from this impossibility—it is indeed dying *for the other* in the sense of dying *in place of* the other. I can give the other everything except immortality, except this dying for her to the extent of dying in place of her and so freeing her from her own death. I can die for the other in a situation where my dying gives her a little longer to live, I can save someone by throwing myself in the water or fire in order to temporarily snatch him from the jaws of death, I can give her my heart in the literal or figurative sense in order to assure her of a certain longevity.

But I cannot die in her place, I cannot give her my life in exchange for my death. Only a mortal can give, as we said earlier.[16]

Ever vigilant—following Nietzsche—to the incipient sentimentality tinging the West's attitudes toward loss and death, indeed to all blunt incursions of the Real, Derrida here delimits in full rigor the substitutions and compensations that can be claimed for death. In the wake of his own death in 2004, his ethos of textual immanence as the enabling legislation for cultural commentary and as the dynamic for productive exegesis emerges in fuller relief at the fulcrum of the deconstructive bearing. Respect for the highly finite, singular, and specific texts and formulations out of which sociocultural critique emerges is as close to a religious principle as Derrida ever ventures; indeed, this respectful reading, one pervaded by the moderation and modesty inevitably ensuing from the constellated plethora of semiotic markers in a dense text, is fundamental to any prospects for religion that Derrida can imagine. Derrida's theological writings extrapolate the platform of philosophical inquiry, bearing, and conceptual improvisation common to all three major monotheistic, "Abrahamic" religions. A rigorous philosophical, as opposed to sectarian, survey of Judaism, Christianity, and Islam discloses a co-signing of core position and attitude far exceeding the strategic choices regarding canon, liturgy, ritual, custom, and law made by the individual faiths (and their splinter groups) in the name of mutual differentiation and competitive "market share." Derrida's acuity as a systems analyst and as a close reader enables him to isolate the weight-bearing notions and attitudes—including immediacy, purity, awe, secrecy, altruism, and hospitality—creating a confluence between the Abrahamic faiths far exceeding their sectarian differences. Ironically, as I argue in an essay entitled "The Fourth Abrahamic Religion?" the same deconstructive bearings that expose the characteristic biases and attitudinal reflexes shared by the three major monotheistic faiths constitute the most substantial current chance that they might each be able to productively retrofit themselves: (1) in accordance with the intrinsic *diversity* of position and opinion sustained by ongoing theological disputations; and (2) toward the enhancement of their individual abilities to acknowledge and embrace the radical alterity of the other.[17] The at all times problematical but nonetheless promising and exciting interface between deconstruction and religion becomes an explicit framework for one of the cornerstones of Derrida's radical theological thinking, "Faith and Knowledge: The Two Sources of 'Religion' at the Limits of Reason Alone."[18]

★

Literature was, from the very outset, one of the two counterpoised moments in the breathing rhythm of Derrida's prose. The other was, of course, philosophy. Like few others in the history of philosophy (Plato, Kierkegaard, and Nietzsche come immediately to mind), Derrida apprehended what he would brilliantly trope as the supplementarity linking the two modalities of imagination and script. He freely acknowledged the phases of co-creativity, the co-generativity, the co-dependency, and the mutual illumination in which philosophy and literature both ran along the smooth space of a Möbius strip. The close adjacency in temperament as well as approach between Derrida's early teasing out in "Plato's Pharmacy," around the Greek term *pharmakon*, the ambivalence toward writing in Platonic idealism, an essay whose experimentation in literary style has been highlighted above, and his appeal, in "The Double Session," to Mallarmé as a poet of profound philosophical undercurrents and implications is no accident. His pointed hospitality to and affirmation of literature surely numbered among charges consistently pressed against him, over a substantial chunk of his career, to the effect that he was not a philosopher.

In a cultural climate in which there is tremendous pressure to reduce to sound bytes even the most subtle, elaborate, and complex formulations, it is possible that Derrida will be better remembered for some of the hard-hitting legal and sociopolitical formulations he reached toward the end of his oeuvre than for the expansive and circuitous wordplays and reasonings through which he taught us, from the outset, how to access philosophy's seamy and intransigent margins.[19] Precisely because they dare to torque the seeming indirection of Derrida's unrelenting readings toward such recognizable phenomena as the bewilderments of hospitality, the imputation of rogue status to seemingly resistant and free-wheeling states, and the claims of political sovereignty, these accommodations to sociopolitical actuality are particularly memorable. On the basis of meticulous readings of Mallarmé, Artaud, Ponge, Blanchot, Jabès, Joyce, and Kafka, which he performed throughout his career, Derrida was able to venture, on the occasion of an interview or the Q and A at a public seminar, stunning overarching scenarios for the interplay between philosophy and literature:

> I think that literature is argumentative, in another way, with different proce-
> dures. Literature attempts to lead to conclusions, even if they are suspensive or
> undecidable; it is organized discourse that exchanges with the other, needs the
> response of the other, is discursive, and therefore passes through a temporality.
> Such argumentation does not obey the norms of philosophy, even supposing—
> and it is still a presupposition—that within philosophy there is only one type of
> argumentation. All the discussions between philosophers throughout history are
> not only discussions—thus, argumentations—about theses or thetic contents, but
> are also about argumentative norms. . . . Intraphilosophical discussion is a discus-
> sion about argumentation. Aristotle says to Plato: here you are no longer *arguing*.
> If within philosophy itself there is no consensus on the subject of argumentation,
> one has to accept the fact that outside of philosophy the same dissent exists.[20]

This segment from an interview that Derrida held with Maurizio Ferraris
pursues the parallel argumentative course transpiring in literature and philosophy while it affirms some telling differences. Philosophy and literature
both lead to conclusions, but in strikingly divergent ways. Literature, in its
engagement with others and with the very condition of alterity, suggests or
implies conclusions as ambiguous or undecidable as they might be definitive. A good measure of literature's suggestiveness ensues from the undecidability it is capable of sustaining. Philosophy, by contrast, sets its definitive
formulations against the backdrop of a debate on the norms and related
conditions of argumentation itself. The philosophical inference has been
preconditioned, in other words, by an explicit accounting of the presupposi-
tions at play in a viable or felicitous argumentative situation. There is a
critical sense in which time stands still, the scene of philosophical deliberation suspends its temporality, the jarring distractions ensuing from historical actuality are filtered out while philosophy debates the conditions of its
own articulation. Such a conceptual standstill, even if philosophically strategic, is fundamentally inimical to literary unfolding, which proceeds through
a progressive emergence of inferences.[21]

Literature and philosophy pursue markedly different processes in the
above passage, yet they both engage in argumentative process. An unsettling
mutual exchange or transference takes place between them: philosophy, in
shuttling between arguments and the debate on the conditions of argumentation, absorbs some of the undecidability that is part and parcel of literature's claim to fame, while literature, in spite of its constant reference to
the other, displaces and assumes the dissent that philosophy focuses and

sharpens. Derrida's statement introduces an argumentative thrust shared by literature and philosophy and then pursues the slight differences in temporality accruing from varied philosophical and literary bearings on this argumentation. Although broad, as we shall see, this overview of the rapport between counter-discursive and generic modalities is nonetheless founded on careful elaboration of relations of supplementarity and marginality that Derrida conducted in his early work. The logic of the passage runs: with regard to certain shared features, say, argumentativeness and temporality, a textual phenomenon can assume either its literary or its philosophical bearing.

In the wider pronouncements of his later work, Derrida can also dream of a discourse that is *neither/nor*, one not subtending the generic expectations common to both of the discursive modalities that were his lifelong obsession but abdicating membership in either—a discourse, like Derrida himself, canceling his membership in all the predictable communities of affiliation:[22]

> I dream of a writing that would be neither be philosophy nor literature, nor even contaminated by one or the other, while still keeping—I have no desire to abandon this—the memory of literature and philosophy. I am certainly not the only one to have this dream, the dream of a new institution to be precise, of an institution without precedent, without pre-institution. You will say, and quite rightly, that this is the dream of every literary work.[23]

It is nothing less than astonishing that a deconstructive project that began by teasing out the full linguistic underpinnings underlying a host of cultural artifacts, ranging from unwitting ideological vehicles to phenomenological world pictures—as an intervention, therefore, into the philosophy of language—could have culminated in one of the most compelling extant renditions of social theory. By the end of his boisterous run, Derrida pays full heed to institutions that, at the beginning of the project, were too obtuse to be inflected by their full linguistic nuance. An institution, for deconstruction, of course, is not different from the speech acts, performatives, and other linguistic bearings that make it possible. It is in "Ulysses Gramophone" that Derrida first fully acknowledges the institutionality of certain particularly generative (Benjamin would say "genre-founding") artworks, that he measures deconstruction's complex and full rapport with such publicly sustained literary "properties," and that he affirms the constructive contributions and positive fallouts of association with such institutions, whether the Joyceans, the Kafka freaks, the Collège Intérnationale de Philosophie, or the rhizomatic, largely invisible, and worldwide collectivity of deconstructionists.[24] Yet in the dream of a "preinstitutional" discourse registered in this citation, from a 1989 interview with Derek Attridge leading off *Acts of Literature*, one subject to the generic specifications neither of philosophy nor of literature properly defined, Derrida holds out for the possibility of a critical medium free from the gravitational fields generated by such conventions and institutional histories.

As suggestive as Derrida's summative formulations regarding the supplemental *rapport*, the hinged swings between philosophy and literature, have been, as decisive as this broader *mise en jeu* has been to the choices in discursive politics that students of all generations invariably make, it is in his meticulously detailed early position papers that he details, step by step, literature's interests for deconstruction. Mallarmé, a poet's poet, an inveterate explorer and exploiter of aestheticism in its poetic aspects for its own sake, is not an intuitive point of departure for deconstruction's multi-tiered appeal to literature. Far more so are: Antonin Artaud, whose maddened ejaculations added early depth to Derrida's apprehension of psychoanalysis as a scene of reading and writing evolving into a "language without alibi"; Edmond Jabès, whose inscription early on marked Derrida's fascination with and resistance to Judaism as the cornerstone to the overwhelmingly prepossessing edifice of the Abrahamic religions; Francis Ponge, whose truncated, material-intensive prose poems opened a window on the proclivities toward performativity and theatricality (counterparts to Benjaminian allegory) at the heart of deconstruction's take on literature. No, the gravitation toward Mallarmé as an exemplary literary venue for deconstructive reading practice is definitely an out-of-the-way claim for a philosopher demonstrating some of the applications of his innovative and contrary take on philosophical etiquette, a cultural property far off the beaten path.

We would have to say that Mallarmé's poetry, in the etymological and semantic torque that it applies to French signifiers, in its whimsical and seemingly haphazard spacing, in its radical typography, which often varies from page to page, represents the extreme case, the extreme of aesthetic and artsy whimsicality that a modality of rigorous philosophical reading might apply to itself as a test of its relevance and the compelling nature of its takes on the world. The thrust of Derrida's Mallarméan demonstration is to stage the hard-core philosophical interest and relevance of the least overtly logical and conceptual dimensions of poetry, to indicate the volatile margin at which the yin of poetry and the yang of philosophy join in spite of themselves. (In making the hymen the pivotal figure in his Mallarméan exploration, Derrida makes sure to indicate the reversibility of the persistent generic division of labor and valences; this reversibility of gender values indeed becomes a central tenet of Mallarmé's philosophical relevance.)

In order to perform this self-appointed task, Derrida takes the histories of Mallarmé's criticism and reception with utmost seriousness. In the tradition of Lönnrot, the Borgesian detective who studies Judaic arcana so that he can both decode and enmesh himself in a series of Talmudic murders, Derrida joins the literati, *becomes* a close critic of Mallarmé, so that he can specify his profound philosophical significance.[25] It is in the name and interest of this project that Derrida pursues Mallarmé's distinctive vocabulary of images, one encompassing fans, wings, fabrics, and tissues, movements of pulsation, beating, or convulsion, and texts themselves with utmost rigor. "The Double Session," his discursive diptych on Mallarmé, is indicative of the pedagogical devotion characterizing his groundbreaking studies, one never abandoned though sometimes later abbreviated in a shorthand notation of tropes initially synthesized in excruciating detail. In this study Derrida leads us through the minute stitching required for a suture between Mallarmé's hyper-aesthetic poetry and philosophy's historical mega-ambivalence toward the linguistic medium on which it relies and out of which it is fashioned:

> To read Mallarmé's *éventail* [fan] involves not only an inventory of its occurrences (there are hundreds, a very large but finite number if one sticks to the word itself, or an infinite number of diverse possibilities if one includes the many-faceted figure of wings, pages, veils, sails, folds, plumes, scepters, etc., constituting and reconstituting itself as an endless breath of opening and/or closing); it involves not only the description of a phenomenological structure whose complexity is also a challenge; it is also to remark that the fan re-marks itself: no doubt it designates the empirical object one thinks one knows under that name, but then, through a tropic twist (analogy, metaphor, metonymy), it turns toward all the semic units that have been identified (wing, fold, plume, page, rustling, flight, dancer, veil, etc., each one finding itself folding and unfolding, opening/closing with the movement of a fan, etc.); it opens and closes each one, but it

also inscribes *above and beyond* that movement the very movement and structure of the fan-as-text, the deployment and retraction of all its valences; the spacing, fold and hymen *between* all these meaning effects, with writing setting them up in relations of difference and resemblance.[26]

The key surprise in these lines, marking a stunning textual event, is that the fan and its significant variants is at once a figure culled from a literary (or symbolic) vocabulary, an action-figure characterizing the workings (or performance) of specific Mallarméan texts (notably, but not limited to, the "Fan" poems and "A Throw of the Dice"), a shorthand notation for an ecology or climate of action possibly extending to the composite of Mallarmé's poetic output, and even an icon or talisman for the pulsating counterpoint in which poetry and philosophy are joined. With the rigor of a logician, and possibly one-upping the literary critics, Derrida assembles a more or less comprehensive list of terms from Mallarmé's poems exhibiting fan features and behaviors, elements that open and close, fold and unfold. The sleight of hand in this seemingly modest and informal act of collection is the fact that each of the terms in the list is loaded, each leads in the direction of another seismic challenge to the stately persistence of Western metaphysics. The fan as plumes, pages, and folds highlights a privileged relationship between poetic inscription and writing, the latter, in Derrida's parlance, the modality or bearing of language in which the full play of its contingency and intrinsic chaos is registered. There is a series of motion terms in this list—flight, sailing, dancing—a vocabulary underscoring the fact that poetry's resistance to the sanctioned ideological pronouncement that Derrida terms voice assumes above all the form of acting or action. At the juncture where language, through such features as assonance, homonymy, and polysemy, performs the putative content of its messages, it pulls out of the contractual obligations to refer and represent that comprise a disproportionate share of its ideological baggage. Language's performativity is a primary resistance to the closed economy, purpose, give, and play of voice, language that has knuckled under to the constraints of official expression. And finally, at the very point where the Mallarméan fan and its imagistic extensions becomes a hymen, Derrida opens up a critique not only of the vast sway of sexual gender in Western metaphysics but of gender as the broader impulse toward a priori categorical thinking, a line of deconstruction that will guide his commentary on Blanchot. As a figure, the hymen of

"The Double Session" vibrates between two counter-initiatives: whether to install a feminine counter to the patriarchal authority claimed by sanctioned expression, establishing an undecidable generic tension, or to declare thinking in general a female enterprise. The invocation of a tympanic hymen of writing at the moment of Derrida's Mallarmé study coincides with his coming to terms with gender, with the considerable heritage of what he calls phallogocentric thinking involving a major swathe of the writers, from Plato to Freud, whose work has been decisive to his project.[27]

With the dual acuity of an accomplished poet and an authoritative logician, Derrida is able to select from a "buzzing, blooming" corpus of poetry precisely those tropes lending philosophy figural illumination and poetry conceptual rigor. Indeed, this bravura act in the synthesis of discourse is one of selection as much as anything else. The terms that Derrida brings to center stage on the microscopic plate of his exegesis are polyvalent; they function powerfully, even with a certain sense of inevitability, on radically different levels of generality, from the thematic to the performative to the level of systems tracking or analysis. The rhetorics of fanning, inscription, and beating or pulsation that Derrida has accessed in this passage are as exegetically effective in analyzing specific Mallarméan poems as in characterizing the vast, stately, complex, invariably fluid interchanges between poetry and philosophical speculation. There is a kind of alchemy (or, as Derrida will say in relation to Blanchot and Marx, impossibility) in the aptness and far-reaching consequences of Derrida's terminological crystallizations. The impossibility consists in arriving at terms, in the wake of complex deconstructive readings involving hundreds, if not thousands, of signifiers, in arriving at specific terms shedding illumination on texts, artifacts, ideological documents, and social conventions emerging from wildly divergent timeframes and cultural contexts.

The emergence of fans, plumes, wings, and the hymen out of the encounter with Mallarmé is a step by step iteration of a broader and perhaps less traceable distillation through which Derrida's readings of Greek philosophy, Rousseau, and twentieth-century phenomenology, among other literatures, enable him to settle on *voice* and *writing* as the cantilevered, sanctioned, and transgressive modalities of language throughout the duration and extent of Western thought. The generality and scope of these terms may seem vast, yet once the reader has registered the fine nuance with which Derrida has endowed both meta-tropes, their specificity in accounting for the double messages in a range of artifacts extending from Platonic idealism and German idealist philosophy, to Rousseau's improvised anthropology, to the abyssal conditions of dreaming and memory in Freud is nothing less than astonishing.

The process by which Derrida arrives at these key figures and terms is one of crystallization, distillation, and selection. It mobilizes the arbitrary apprehensions of poetry as much as philosophy's systematic bearing. The foldings, unfoldings, pulsations, and tympanic vibrations that Derrida pursues through a wide range of works by Mallarmé not only animate those texts, they characterize and perform the complex interactions between literature and philosophy as vast textual agglomerations. They explain Derrida's appeal to Mallarmé's poetry, among the most intransigent and aesthetic, in the first place. Our citation from "The Double Session" ends on the note of an overarching textual *above and beyond* indicated by the pulsations staged by such Mallarméan works as "Mimique," the "Éventail" poems, and "Un coup de dés." From the dance of Mallarméan signifiers on the page emerges a surplus mark, what Derrida infrastructurally reformulates as the re-mark,[28] a figure both concentrating and performing the "folding and unfolding, opening/closing with the movement of a fan," so that it can serve as an index to the wider margin or blank between the poetic text and its philosophical other:

> This surplus mark, this margin of meaning, is not one valence among others in the series, even though it is *inserted* in there too. It has to be inserted in there to the extent that it does not exist outside the text and has no transcendental privilege; this is why it is always *represented* by a metaphor and a metonymy (page, plume, pleat). But while belonging to the series of valences, it always occupies the position of a supplementary valence, or rather, it marks the structurally necessary position of a supplementary inscription that could always be added to or subtracted from the series. We will try to show that this position of the supplementary mark is in all rigor neither a metaphor nor a metonymy, even though it is always represented by one trope too many or too few.[29]

At a moment of powerful consolidation of attitudes fundamental to deconstruction, conceptual assertions indistinguishable from poetic figures, and with his characteristic modesty, Derrida qualifies the marginality of his own approach, the supplemental relationship in which philosophy and literature fluctuate in a pulsation of wings. The performative textual index culled from the imagistic vocabulary, both of the text and about it, the meta-trope that Derrida here names the re-mark, is neither exactly *in* the text nor *outside* it. (It has been, rather, "inserted.") The re-mark is a valence, that is, it adds value to the exegetical process, and yet the movements or material that it indicates are not definitive or core values. (They are, rather, fluctuating, supplemental ones.) The text cannot be reduced to the meaning of its key words or central tropes. The re-mark culled from the text and indicating strategic elements of its performance might appear to assume the functions assigned to the weight-bearing tropes of classical rhetoric, in the rhetorical division of labor, to figures, including metaphor and metonymy. But this infrastructure, even while adding valence of a certain kind to the texts in which it figures (whether semantic or poetic value), will not submit to inclusion in a closed list of textual functions, is not an element in the rhetorical dictionary of linguistic activities. The re-mark is in excess of the classical tropes of rhetoric; they are always too many or too few for it.

The re-mark is above all, then, a mark or indication of the supplemental relation not only between philosophy and literature but intrinsic to itself as indexical performative figure. The decisive figures in Mallarmé's poetry that Derrida has accessed—fans, folds, blanks, the hymen—shuttle within themselves between their performative dance and their fluctuating conceptual values. It is Derrida's distinction to have tracked at the microscopic level, occasionally invoking even subverbal signifiers, the unmarked morphing of the substantive and performative elements of inscription into one another. The supplement, the broadest figure for the mutual exploitation, appropriation, and affirmation in which philosophy and literature are embroiled, is anything but a margin of excess or superiority claimed by philosophically intensive modalities of reading. It is, rather, a radical fluctuation *between*[30] the concept and the figure, which extends as much to the microclimates of inscription and meaning as to the broader play between poetry and philosophy prompted, in "The Double Session," by the most dispensable poet of needlessly ornate texts.

I would be remiss in this brief backward glance toward Derrida's encounter with Mallarmé as a prefiguration to his extended engagement with the broader body of literature if I did not remark the uncanny appropriateness of this approach to the poems. Deconstruction has never shied away from its ultimate test, the power and specificity of its particular engagements with artifacts.

Even the most perfunctory encounter with Mallarmé's "A Throw of the Dice" will disclose in full vigor the practical benefits of the approach evident throughout "The Double Session." This multifaceted poem is at once a celebration of the contingent aspects of language, the patterned chaos that is the source and basis of poetry, and an extended, self-performing text, allegorical in a relentless and self-recycling way. At the same time as the poem accommodates a Dionysian revelry in the multiple resources of poetry, from sound to spacing on the page, from typography to polysemy, the poem also marshals itself, through such devices as headlines and boldface, into a quasi-scientific (or Apollonian) compendium of what might be called *poetic logic*. The craft of poetry joins with its science in this self-generating, genre-breaking text at the same time as it surges forward as the preeminent period piece of poetic symbolism, imagism, impressionism, and exoticism.

Even for the moment disregarding Derrida's explicit differences with such authoritative practitioners of Mallarmé criticism as Jacques Scherer, Jean-Pierre Richard, and Robert Greer Cohn, "A Throw of the Dice" will never be the same in the wake of Derrida's overall enfolding of its poetics into allegorical or performative inscription, his elucidating it under the active influence of such figures as the fan, the fold, the blank, the plume, and the hymen. "A Throw of the Dice" is a free-verse composition, generally moving from left to right and down the page, but with radical potential for mis- and indirection owing to the unprecedented incorporation of empty spaces (Derrida's blanks) on the page. Each new page of the poem is a unique and singular textual display. Today we would say that each page corresponds to a "new screen" of composition, with its own quasi-system of typographical sub- and super-ordination and its own sequences, whether linear or not, of poetic logic. The whole builds up in magisterial fashion to the mock-syllogistic conclusion of an argument: "Toute Pensée émet un Coup de Dés" ("All Thought emits a Throw of the Dice"). The scaffolding or backbone of this argument has been the phrase, marked by outsized, boldface typography, "JAMAIS . . . N'ABOLIRA . . . LE HASARD" ("NEVER . . . WILL ABOLISH . . . CHANCE"),[31] disseminated over the course of the poem.

Several of the poetic "screens" in the poem are articulated by a longitudinal fold both scrambling and ramifying the reading patterns that have been composed for the page. The poem starts out with a simplified version of this scheme on its second page, beginning "SOIT que l'Abime" ("THOUGH IT BE that the Abyss"), in which the beginning of the text and the upper part of the page fall to the left of the divisive margin or fold, and the remainder of the text falls to the lower right quadrant. The very next (third) page of poetry, beginning "LE MAÎTRE" ("THE MASTER"), achieves the typographical version of a Rorschach blot in the approximate mirroring of the two columns of text structured by the page's central fold. Mallarmé achieves vertical as well as horizontal spatial resonance or compositional mirroring on the sixth page. Here, two more or less balanced vertical columns of text are anchored, top left and lower right, by the capitalized heading, "COMME SI" ("AS IF").

Derrida's detailed attention to the play of fans, folds, sails, plumes, and even tympanic but deeply symbolic anatomical membranes turns out to be the key to any consistent reading of Mallarmé's poetics. The deconstructive reading is anything but a hostile takeover of the corpus by a self-interested philosophical outsider or shyster. Derrida will re-mark his own fascination with the composition of the Mallarméan page, itself a sail, a fabric, a tissue, or a membrane, in the bicolumnar typographical composition of *Glas*,[32] in which he juxtaposes the ethico-metaphysical duplicities attending Hegel's moral pronouncements in his *Philosophy of Right*, the left-hand column on each page, against a picturesque and far more authentic ethos and aesthetic of transgression that he culls from pivotal texts by Jean Genet, among them *Our Lady of the Flowers* and *Miracle of the Rose*. No poet composed more compellingly within the broader textuality than Mallarmé. For Derrida to start out from this premise in distilling Mallarmé's profoundest philosophical resonance is hardly an immodest proposal. This approach indeed culminates in a stunning specificity, what we seek from the best-informed literary criticism.

★

In the supplemental tension that it sustains between concepts and literary images, in the uncanny aptness of the performative figures that it culls from its readings, deconstruction asks nothing less than the impossible from its bearing and notations and from the theoretically astute experience of culture. It is precisely through the intellectual division of labor of the easily possible and the everyday that we become dulled and blinded to what is subliminally at stake in the business of culture, government, education, and social mores. In these modalities we lose sight of such ongoing dramas as the limitations on language and the media to dominant interests and functions (e.g., representation or the theological subtexts to putatively secular discourse); the social imperatives and incentives to think according to a priori categories (a profiling that Derrida associates with genre); the mad and maddening presumptions to purity, everlasting presence, consciousness, and perfect reciprocity embedded in the legal system and in such deeply entrenched social conventions as those surrounding hospitality and monogamous marriage.

Literature is the portal to impossibility implanted within the Western canons of philosophy, religion, and literature, but usually out of radar range. Literature generates the "impossible figures" to which Derrida pays special heed,[33] such as the Mallarméan hymen, the Platonic *pharmakon*, or the Nietzschean heliotrope. In deconstructive apprehension, such figures both disclose, give the lie to, the ideological repression and incipient madness shoring up mainstream moral and metaphysical conventions and illuminate the way, not quite in exemplary fashion, to the interpretative postures and practices through which new possibilities—indeed possibility itself—will emerge. The movement of pulsation that Derrida traces in the Mallarméan text, at once a theme, therefore an element of its material, and an action figure for the motions that it performs, is also a trope for the impossible tension between concepts and images of radically differing registers in poetic and discursive texts, concepts and images occasionally coinciding.

How fantastic, ironic, and thoroughly Derridean it is that the writings of Blanchot could both initiate Derrida's most devastating critique of a priori categorical thinking (one of his most compellingly political interventions, so far as I'm concerned), and render full and touching tribute to Blanchot as a writer whose talent allowed him, repeatedly if not consistently, to lead his readers to the very threshold and abyss of the impossible.

Derrida does not limit himself to literary commentary when he stages the call to action, the constitutional convention, the division of tasks and functions of genre:

"Do," "Do not," says "genre," the word *genre*, the figure, the voice, the law of genre. And this can be said of all genres of genre, be it a question of a generic or general determination of what one calls "nature" or *phusis* . . . or be it a question of a typology. . . . For who would have us believe that we, we two for example, would form a genre or belong to one? Thus, as soon as genre announces itself, one must respect a norm, one must not cross a line of demarcation, one must not risk impurity, anomaly, or monstrosity. . . . If a genre is what it is, or if it is supposed to be what it is destined to be by virtue of its *telos*, then "genres are not to be mixed"; one should not mix genres, one owes it to oneself not to get mixed up in mixing genres. Or, more rigorously, genres should not intermix. And if it should happen that they do intermix, by accident or through transgression, by mistake or through a lapse, then this should confirm, since we are speaking of mixing, the essential purity of their identity. This purity belongs to the typical axiom: it is a law of the law of genre, whether or not the law is, as it is considered justifiable to say, "natural." This normative position and this evaluation are in-scribed and prescribed even at the threshold of "the thing itself," if something of the genre "genre" can be so named. And so it follows that you might have taken the second sentence in the first person, "I will not mix genres," as a vow of obedience, as a docile response to the injunction emanating from the law of genre. In place of a constative description, you would then hear a promise, an oath: you would grasp the following respectful commitment: I promise you that I will not mix genres.[34]

The deconstructive critique of genre arises in an admixture of modalities and forms precisely of the sort proscribed by the law of genre. In this in-stance, the substantive exploration of the law of genre's enabling concept, purity, is interspersed with a mock performance of genre's tenets. Derrida endows the term *genre* with a force and centrality to Western cultural and legal practices that it would not otherwise gain by seeming to reel, haphaz-ardly if not drunkenly, between a constative unmasking of the purity whose interest all categorical prescriptions serve and a staged dialogue between the constative and performative dimensions that genre enfolds, a fault line as decisive to the possibilities for theoretically informed criticism as to the mega-project known as speech-act theory.[35] In Derrida's staging, the law of genre elicits the oath of nonmixture and nonadulteration on the part of its followers, that is, anyone who, knowingly or unknowingly subscribes to Western culture's statutes of purity (whether in eating, dress, monogamous vow and restriction, endogamy, ethnic association, or numerous other spheres). Derrida is not content simply to enumerate the conceptual and social costs of categorical thinking. He meets this deeply wired tendency to sexist, racist, ethnicist, and other forms of purist cognition on the plane of its enactment, its coming into action, its acting out, where the messages of language imperceptibly morph into their social conditions and constraints. This is the effect that Derrida achieves when he puts words, at the beginning of the extract, into the mouth of the word *genre*, or when he formulates, by its end, the law of genre's implied oath.

Derrida has meticulously chosen the literary occasion for his fullest exposé of both genre and categorical thinking. No author better exemplifies the ability to transform concepts and philosophical terms and functions into characters and other literary entities than Blanchot, particularly in his fiction—his narratives (*récits*) and novels. Indeed, in the text that Derrida chooses to illuminate in "The Law of Genre, "The Madness of the Day," the Law, both as a master concept in all world civilizations and as a social reality, assumes the form of the (male) narrator's female interlocutor. Blanchot fits out this fictive text so that it can undertake the impossible task of orchestrating an encounter between two characters that is at the same time an interrogation of the Law's features and qualities by a probing surrogate. A good measure of this text's edifying surprise is the degree to which the intimacy and sexual tension between a male narrator and his female other can be transferred to a staged meditation on the intangibles of the Law. It is in honor of Blanchot's polymorphic lability of posture in the name of articulation itself that Derrida tangibly blurs the boundary between conceptual elaboration, close reading of a compelling text, and a staged dialogic encounter with the text that he is reading.

Through this nuanced performance, Derrida quite simply blows the concept and different ramifications of genre and categorical thinking out of the water. Would that the taking in of the lesson, by Derrida's vast close and not so close, direct and indirect audiences, be as relatively simple a matter as it was to articulate it. But, like the inferences we draw from psychoanalysis, a discourse "without alibi," according to Derrida,[36] precisely by virtue of its unmotivated and undirected trajectory, the lessons of the deconstructive exposure and debunking of the law of genre are forgotten almost as soon as they are learned. The subdivisions of the literary and philosophical professions, our injunctions to our graduate students not to be too overt in their invocation of certain checkered and now discredited theorists, constitute a very clear return of the law of genre. We find ourselves invoking and rein-forcing these imperatives in certain registers of our striving and activity as easily as we hold up to ridicule the latest gaffes of generic profiling commit-ted in and outside of the cloisters of disciplined discourse.

Derrida was too realistic an observer of human nature to be nonplussed by such inevitable losses of rigor. A long-standing defense against this inevi-table backsliding was his couching each of his own critical interventions in terms of the *impossibility* of the conditions that it assembled and addressed. The subjects of Derrida's unabashed tributes—Marx, Mallarmé, Joyce, and Blanchot—are as unpredictable as the gravitation to the impossible that he makes a condition of deconstructive critique. Underlying the "interminable self-critique" in which Marx engaged were surely both a sustained attention to the costs in human potential and facility exacted by capitalism and a messianic affirmation, one modified from its pretexts in Abrahamic religion, whose inspiration Derrida explicitly acknowledges. In addition to Marx's singular critico-affirmative stance, the tribute in *Specters of Marx* thanks him for his attunement to the impossibility of conditions, both intensifying their morass and indicating the way to their correction:

> For, let us speak as "good Marxists," the deconstruction of Marxist ontology does not go after only a theoretico-speculative layer of the Marxist corpus but everything that articulates this corpus with the most concrete history of the appa-ratuses and strategies of the worldwide labor movement. And this deconstruction is not, in the last analysis, a methodical or theoretical procedure. In its possibility as in the experience of the impossible that will always have constituted it, it is never a stranger to the event, that is, very simply, to the coming of that which happens. Certain Soviet philosophers told me, in Moscow a few years ago: the best translation of *perestroika* was still "deconstruction." . . .
>
> To critique, to call for interminable self-critique is still to distinguish between everything and almost everything. Now, if there is a spirit of Marxism which I will never be able to renounce, it is not only the critical idea or the questioning stance (a consistent deconstruction must insist on them even as it also learns that this is not the last or first word). It is even more a certain emancipatory and *messianic* affirmation, a certain experience of the promise that one can try to liberate from any dogmatics and even from any metaphysico-religious determi-nation, from any *messianism*. And a promise must promise to be kept, not to remain "spiritual" or "abstract," but to produce events, new effective forms of action, practice, organization, and so forth. To break with the "party form" or with some form of the State or the International does not mean to give up every

form of practical or effective organization. It is exactly the contrary that matters to us here.[37]

Especially in passages such as these, one is confronted with the alignment in which deconstruction, messianic repair or correction (*tikkun*), and the Marxian revolution, in the sense of an ongoing, never fully realized critical event, a "democracy to come,"[38] are inventively, if not inextricably, linked. However resolute deconstruction may be in its exposure and debunking of the submerged metaphysico-ideological apparatus underlying prevailing social contracts and canonical artifacts, it is not at all indifferent to affirmative energy. Quite the contrary. The affirmation Derrida's commentary gathers as it addresses and is informed by the works of Marx, Mallarmé, Joyce, and Blanchot, a by no means exhaustive list, is the condensed energy of articulation realizing the full sway of its freedom, of articulation reconfiguring prevalent cultural conditions through the poetic power of its figuration and performance, and in the exegetical rigor of the reading and decoding that cultural commentary inevitably entails. Derrida's literary encounters rise in an affirmation of the small revolutions that can be achieved through close philosophico-poetic attentiveness. Deconstructive discourse is at the service of the realization of such exegetical events. These are messianic in the sense that they realize a certain correction or repair, but detached from the teleological redemption of the world specified by Judeo-Christianity and Islam. They are revolutionary in the sense that they bring about a palpable reconfiguration of the experience of prevailing sociopolitical conditions, but not so in the sense of installing yet another political apparatus conditioned by systemic obtuseness and repression.

For a sensibility seemingly endowed with a homing instinct invariably drawing it to the nodes of violence inherent in the multiple systems to which citizens of the contemporary world are unavoidably subjected, Derrida was astonishingly affirmative in his outlook, a perspective no doubt in part facilitated by his engagement with telling literary artifacts. This affirmation, resonating in a different timbre as Derrida plays it in Rousseau, Nietzsche, Marx, Mallarmé, Kafka, Joyce, Ponge, Celan, and Blanchot, brings deconstructive discourse to the very cusp of impossibility. There will be no revolutionary event emanating from the world of culture unless its inscription and commentary belong to the order of the *im*possible. This is a far taller order than the prescription that cultural exegesis make sense, that it be intelligible according to some established subdivision of the disciplinary division of labor. The challenge that Derrida poses to informed discourse, that it gravitate to the limits of its impossibility, is one of deconstruction's two primary ethical commandments. The other is the call to a multifaceted responsibility enunciated best of all in "Faith and Knowledge."

I close my tribute to Derrida's democracy and generosity as a teacher, to his uncanny critical and conceptual instinct and sensibility, and to the uncompromising standards that he applied to his project and then realized in increasingly inventive ways, with two examples of writing. They both happen to stem from Blanchot's "Death Sentence," a work that, in Derrida's terms, finesses the boundary between philosophical exposition and literature, one inherently, therefore, on the wrong side of the law of genre. I cannot tell you whether these passages ever explicitly surfaced in Derrida's Blanchot commentary. That is not the point. The passages are instances of a writing so arbitrary, inventive, and unpredictable that it was, from any empirical or clinical perspective, impossible to write them. Yet Blanchot managed to do so anyway, henceforth upping the ante on our own written traces, if they are to rise to the standards that Derrida specified. In the first, the narrator meditates on his relation to one of his thoughts. The thought to which he relates bears all the glory of the most exalted human ideas, yet is invested with the full materiality of an object, the kind of object of which narratives are composed. This is, to say the least, an impossible set of conditions.

> A persistent thought is completely beyond the reach of its conditions. What has sometimes impressed me about this thought is a sort of hardness, the infinite distance between its respect for me and my respect for it; but hardness is not a fair word: the hardness arose from me, from my own person. I can even imagine this: that if I had walked by its side more often in those days, as I do now, if I had granted it the right to sit down at my table, and to lie down next to me, instead of living intimately with it for several seconds during which all its proud powers were revealed, and during which my own powers seized it with an even greater pride, then we would not have lacked familiarity, nor equality in sadness, nor absolute frankness, and perhaps I would have known something about its intentions which even it could never have known, made so cold by my distance that it was put under glass, prey to one obstinate dream.[39]

This passage is so strikingly written that it largely speaks for itself. Although it sets out in the extreme material conditions (hardness, opacity) that can be applied to a thought, the passage ultimately attains an exquisite ethical sensibility, one hardly inimical to deconstruction's purview. The narrator maintains an intimate rapport with this bizarre thought-thing (with certain affinities to Kafka's Odradek),[40] yet finds, on deliberation, that he did not grant it enough time to realize itself fully. He would have needed an even greater intimacy and deliberation with this thought to acknowledge *its* freedom and to fully come to terms with it. A meditation on the remoteness and opacity of our thoughts transforms (or revolutionizes) itself into an ethical meditation on the incipient violence of thinking.

> I did not have to take another step to know that there was someone in that room. That if I went forward, all of a sudden someone would be there in front of me, pressing up against me, absolutely near me, of a proximity that people are not aware of: I knew that too. Everything about that room, plunged in the most profound darkness, was familiar to me; I had penetrated it, I carried it in me, I gave it life, a life which is not life, but which is stronger than life and which no force in the world could ever overcome. That room does not breathe, there is neither shadow nor memory in it, neither dream nor depth; I listen to it and no one speaks; I look at it and no one lives in it. And yet, the most intense life is there, a life which I touch and which touches me, absolutely similar to others, which clasps my body with its body, marks my mouth with its mouth, whose eyes open, whose eyes are the most alive, the most profound eyes in the world, whose eyes see me. May the person who does not understand that come and die. Because that life transforms the life which shrinks away from it into a falsehood.[41]

In the second instance, the narrator retreats to his hotel room to retrieve Nathalie, who will become, in the second segment of the narrative diptych, his beloved. Although the room is pitch-black, the narrator encounters the life within it, whether we define this life as the character Nathalie, a woman, the life of a space with a person in it, the life of a particular room, the life inhering to the dimension of space, or life itself. In the blind compartment of space, the narrator encounters both the life of his beloved, the life toward which his life force verges, and the life motivating his inscription of the scene, the articulate inscription of that life. As the passage indicates, the two lives meet, intertwine, and contest each other. With everything against him, Blanchot inscribes this life, in all its impossible conditions. Derrida was not in the least indifferent to the question and status of life.[42]

Hegel, *Glas*, and the Broader Modernity

1. *Glas* is nothing if not an exceptional book, a book whose architecture and scope place it at the farthest reaches of book culture. Yet its highly singular bicolumnar format not only establishes a textual modality of reverberation, supplementarity, chiasmatic reversal, and constriction. In its persistent recurrence back to Hegel as synthesizer of a Western metaphysical mainstream and to Genet as the poet of an amoral and homoerotic counterculture, whose text nonetheless interweaves many of the images and figures pivotal to the Hegelian enterprise, this outlandish book on the verge of being a nonbook also brackets two decisive if not definitive limits to the broader modernity. In no empirical way, *Glas* delimits a certain epoch in the history of Western culture(s) at the same time as it stages a tympanic modality of reversal and echoing evident in all textual articulation and elaboration. In this chapter, I would like to explore and elaborate what *Glas's* historical remark might be.

2. The consummate performative irony of *Glas* is that certain of the metaphors that Hegel appropriates in consolidating a cluster of attitudes

defining a secular, modern "mainstream" of Western culture are common
to the figures that Genet explores in elaborating the "other," sensational
facet of the same tradition. Language, whether the language of poetic figures or logic, is expansive enough to entertain antipodal, radically different
polysemic significations of and scenarios for common terms. *Glas,* in its
typographic architecture and its motifs of splitting, reverberating, ringing,
and castrating, to name a few, performs the relation between the ideology
of Western culture(s) and its margins, the reflexive achievements of speculation and the mirror's tain,[1] the dialectical, organic, and consummate fate for
the West that Hegel envisioned and Genet's gay-criminal "underworld."

Glas's purview, the term of its "validity," is "eternal" and it isn't. We
can surmise some vague Derridean "universality" characterizing the tension
between a general ideology at play in all cultures, times, etc. and its linguistically "organized" undercurrent. We can hypostasize some ideologically
structured center to every culture, at whatever stage of technology, during
whatever historical period, wherever located, and however exclusively oriented to idealism. And of all philosophers, Derrida most elaborately enu-
merated the remains that cannot be appropriated by this "center," even if
this focal "site" is itself, as in Chinese and South Asian civilizations, differentiated and fragmented. Yet supplementing this general, ongoing play between ideological machine and linguistic byproduct, a play whose
nondialectical nature Derrida went to great pains to reinforce, is the "time
specific" drama of idealism in Hegel's philosophy and the particular cultural
epoch it characterizes. Hegel imposes specifications upon Western cultures
at the same time and in the same act as he imposes them upon organico-
dialectical philosophical discourse. The brilliant, I'm tempted to say "comprehensive," job of reconstructing and extrapolating Hegelian ideology that
Derrida performs in *Glas* includes among its elements: Christian humanism
as opposed to Judaic (and graphic) formalism and death; altruism as the
single legitimate model of love and social interaction; and an altruism-based
sacrifice of the familial, particular, and idiosyncratic in the interest of an
overarching social good. These metaphysical attitudes more or less buttress
Western ideology(ies) from Hegel's late Enlightenment moment until they
go out of fashion, just before or during the moment of Genet.

This is all by way of saying that there is an implicit architecture of history
in *Glas,* a historiographic accompaniment to the knell by which ideology's
appeal sounds its silent echo. And on this architectural blueprint, Hegel and

Genet are (intertwined, reverberating) columns framing a certain (epistemological and cultural more than historical) epoch. There is some utility in
characterizing this epoch as the major span of the broader modernity, which
can be defined as the age in which subjectivity achieves an irremediable
splitting and suspension between multiple and often conflicting obligations,
and in which linguistic and poetic facility both epitomize and constitute the
only available means of circumventing, suspending this (losing) predicament. Projected into time, the architecture of *Glas* may be read as the historiographic map of an epoch—under certain of whose conditions and
delusions we still labor, even in the endeavor of intellectual work. My aspiration for this essay is to explore the broader modernity, whose extremes
Glas so innovatively and unforgettably delineates.

3. There is a tendency in *Glas* for Derrida to glide between language-
and subject-based models in his account of Hegel, Genet, and the ideological and cultural baggage they carry with them, to which we will turn our
attention below. But for now it is sufficient to note that, within the framework of the Derridean project, an enterprise of thinking culture at a remove
from entrenched Western metaphysical assumptions regarding ideals, origins, purposes, identities, and the like, the trajectory of a single grapheme,
a molecule if not an "atom" of language, does better than a grandiloquent
account of an age, an epoch, a "movement." The syllable is a unit of singularity implicated countless times in a network of language that twists, dou-
bles, reverts, and repeats upon itself endlessly.

4. *Glas* is Derrida's most architectural work. Its bicolumnar structure
represents his most solid architecture. A distinctive stability and proportion
are embodied in the equilibrium of its two typographic columns. The architectural structure formed by this blueprint is a house, a home, in the sense
that the Freudian uncanny arises in the defamiliarization of the *heimlich*, the
homey.

Glas is Derrida's most elaborate construction project. Architecture is crucial both to the columns and to the strained equilibrium with which they
relate to each other. In addition, more so than in any other work, Derrida's
reading of his "subject matter," Hegel and Genet, concentrates on a reconstruction of a tradition and a counterculture out of key images, narrative
and argumentative styles, and keywords. The deconstruction of *Glas* consists less in the disclosure and unleashing of a repressed countercurrent in

works' putative significations and cultural values than in the sustained dissonance between the two columns, each combining the constitutive elements
of the same (Western metaphysical) tradition, but with a radically different
nuance.

In *Glas,* Derrida pulls no unexpected rabbits out of hats. The bulk of the
energy, interpretation, and rhetorical resources are devoted to a *constructive*
effort, in one column, the assembly of a major, Hegelian retrospective on
Western values. In the opposite column, Derrida assembles no less con-
structively the underside of the same spiritualized, if secular, teleological
vision out of swatches of text appropriated from Genet.

Glas is thus a construction project in two senses. To the degree that its
argumentative plan emphasizes the sustained dissonance between the mainstream and the alienated undercurrent of modern Western values rather
than the disclosure of repressed marginality (as is the case, say, in the readings of Rousseau in *Of Grammatology* and Heidegger in *Margins of Philosophy*), its construction project extends to both columns. But there is, of
course, also the tendentious sense in which the left column, as an amalgamation of the positivity of Western aspirations, at least as Hegel formulated
them, is more "constructive" than its counterpart on the right-hand side,
which devotes so many resources to Genet's subversive reiteration of the
same ideology.

Glas sustains a bicolumnar *Klang,* or reverberation. The infrastructure of
chiasmatic binary tension, no matter how dynamic, is crucial to its read-
ing(s) and commentary. Yet each of the two architectural supports making
this infrastructure possible is itself in an ongoing state of fragmentation and
decomposition. I'm referring here to Derrida's tendency to add splits (*coups*)
to each column in the form of marginal additions, or in some cases spliced
countertexts (e.g., Hegel's correspondence with his sister and her care-
takers). *Glas*'s *Klang* echoes across the abyss in its typographical format, yet
the architectural supports are in an ongoing condition of textual dissemination and dissolution. Cumulative, strategic fragmentation is thus as much
an element in *Glas*'s construction as is architectural planning.

5. Hegel, after the theological texts that Derrida also includes in his reconstruction project, demands, in a secular context, a human self-genera-
tion of knowledge, speculation, ethical values, and the cognitive faculties
by which these achievements are produced. Human wonder, knowledge,
sensibility, and institutions are to be exclusively human productions. An

organic dynamism, endowed with the qualities of life, is to prevail within speculation itself and between the various faculties and stages involved in the generation and evolution of human sensibility.

It may not, occasionally, be beyond Hegel to invoke the animal (the cows all gray in the night, whose culinary habits in "Sensible Certitude," the very first chapter in *The Phenomenology of Spirit*, bespeak an easier attitude toward negation than human scruple). Yet the project of Enlightenment, wherever we consult its enabling legislation, is first and foremost a human affair.

6. What are the Hegelian elements that Derrida recombines in his retrospective assemblage of post-Enlightenment Western ideology's high-road? (Remember that this gathering is too unconcerned with conclusiveness, coverage, symmetry, or design to qualify as modernistic bricolage.)

The alliances of the conventional family and their imaginary (or speculative) correlatives; Christianity's sense of its urgent, particular mission, above all in relation to a Judaism interpreted as legalistic, formalistic, and lacking in spontaneous altruism; the figure of Antigone as the epitome and bad girl of Western metaphysics; the system's epiphenomena—including fetishism and the enigmatic figures of light, sound (*Klang*), and the gift—which derange it while serving as its uncanny, unforgettable talismans. These are the materials out of which Derrida fabricates and recreates post-Enlightenment Western culture's ideological high road. The left column of *Glas* reconfigures this tradition and system in a manner that acknowledges the persistence and social utility of certain repressions brought about by systematic constraints and prohibitions at the same time—precisely in its modality of reconstruction—as it underscores and questions the arbitrariness of this repression, pointing up the stress lines in the application of closure. The left-hand column debunks in an act of assembly, while it constructs the architecture of a system that can be "experienced" only as confining by its indwellers, who are projected into a position shared by the implied residents in Piranesi's prisons.

It is commonly thought that Derrida points the way to some exit or escape from the prison of Western values so entrenched as to have become transparent, invisible. Yet Derrida's demonstration, in the left-hand column of *Glas*, aims to affirm the inescapability of certain cornerstone Western values as much as skeptically to debunk them. The *assemblage* of *Glas*'s left-hand column should give pause to anyone wishing to accuse Derrida of facile escapism or mega-cynicism. Nowhere in the column is there the least expectation that religion can be eliminated, voice can be quelled into writing, phallocentrism be transformed into the acceptance of a continuum of sexual possibilities. *Glas* thus constitutes Derrida's guarantee regarding the contrapuntal nature of deconstruction, its perdurance as sustained dissonance within the Western system and between its elements, rather than as a definitive dismantling or debunking.

7. Genet's philosophical poetry can be adequately appreciated only to the degree that it is read against the backdrop of the mainstream post-Enlightenment Western ideology, whose terms it borrows, empties, subverts, and reconfigures. Derrida's reading of Genet's drama, fiction, essays, and poetry indubitably joins his most suggestive and in his own singular sense *impossible* literary analyses; it alone comprises an ample response to detractors who claim that deconstruction violates even the most minimal allegiance to the literary pretexts for criticism. One possible explanation for the left-hand column is that it records the conceptual groundwork necessary before the Genet exegesis is possible. In preparation for my own appreciation of this wonderful and inspiring reading, I want to review a certain number of the left-hand column's discursive registers.

8. On the Hegelian side, discourse is held together by "one thread" (4a):[2] "It is the law of the family: of Hegel's family, of the family in Hegel, of the concept family according to Hegel" (ibid.). If Derrida's most notable essays tend to be "organized" by "master" tropes: the *pharmakon* of "Plato's Pharmacy," the hymen of "The Double Session," the sun and its heliotrope in "White Metaphor," then the choice of the family as the tissue connecting the Hegelian discourse of *Glas* is interesting, to say the least. The family, much as it may be translated into rhetorical and logical functions, is equally a sociological and psychoanalytic unit. Derrida's work on the family in *Glas* stands out because his other distinctive master tropes—gifts, fabrics, membranes, crypts, and so on—display linguistic and logical operations and assumptions to the exclusion of metaphysical "attitude." This avoidance of metaphysical assumptions regarding subjectivity, identity, and purpose, to name a few, is in keeping with an overall deconstructive design of rearticulating the traditions of Western philosophy and onto-theology from the perspective of the logical and linguistic processes that become constrained, limited, "bent" to the demands of idealism and ideology. As opposed to the *pharmakon,* the membrane, or the crypt, the family overflows with implications of a subjective, sociological, and teleological nature at the same time

as, in Hegel's texts and elsewhere, it functions as a syllogism and semantic generator. The Derridean focus upon family matters in a critical reconstruction of a major metaphysical position enables the left-hand column to freely pass between conceptual paradigms oriented, on the one hand, to language, and, on the other, to subjectivity. I suspect that this "opening up" of the deconstructive purview in *Glas* to subject-oriented frameworks and mythology, as in Derrida's commentaries on Freud, occurs very much by design. A quasi-systematic deconstruction needs to address the distorting effects of ideology, wherever found. The drawback to the family's pluralistic receptiveness to the metaphysics of identity and society, as well as to the dynamics of representation and communication, is the obscuring of the contrapuntal line of demarcation between language- and subjectivity-based models. In *Glas*, Derrida more than restores attention to this dynamic borderline in the ongoing tension and dance between the Hegel ("mainstream") and Genet ("marginal, textual, deviant") columns, but the intramural battles that prevail in the literary and philosophical professions have entered into a remorseless repetition compulsion on the basis of relative unclarity with regard to the essential differences between language- and subject-based paradigms, and the relative attitudes and "results" that can be expected from them.

For all the family's relative breadth of nuances in comparison with other Derridean master tropes, Derrida initially places its importance within a syllogism:

> Now within *Sittlichkeit*, the third term and the moment of synthesis between right's formal objectivity and morality's abstract subjectivity, a syllogism in turn is developed.
>
> Its first term is the family.
>
> The second, civil or bourgeois society (*bürgerliche Gesellschaft*).
>
> The third, the State or the constitution of the State (*Staatsverfassung*). (4a)

The Hegel column in *Glas* may well extrapolate in comprehensive fashion the metaphysical values prevailing during an epoch of Western culture not yet definitively terminated, but it remains true to Derrida's philosophico-linguistic field and style of intervention. He brings the family to our attention initially both as a syllogism and because of its characterization by and participation in dialectical process. The family plays a certain role in the emergence and reinforcement of the ethical (*Sittlichkeit*); the ethical is in

turn a microcosm, a synecdochical insignia (or fetish) of the Hegelian mainstream of post-Enlightenment Western ideology in general.

> The family is a *party to* the system of the spirit: the family is both a part and
> the whole of the system.
> The whole system repeats itself in the family. *Geist* is always, in the very
> production of its essence, a kind of repetition. Coming to, after losing itself in
> nature and in its other, spirit constitutes itself as absolute spirit through the nega-
> tive process of a syllogism whose three moments are *subjective spirit* (anthropol-
> ogy, phenomenology of spirit, psychology), *objective spirit* (right, morality,
> *Sittlichkeit*), and absolute spirit (art, religion, philosophy). (20a)

9. There will never be any definitive escape from this system: at most
there will be the playing, in the sense of a musical accompaniment, a *Klang,*
of an ongoing counterpoint to the system's determinations and pretensions.
There will never be a decisive victory by the knowing involutions of writing
over the spiritual immanence of voice, by the barbarians over the citizens,
by the margin over the mainstream. *Glas,* while inventively, "comprehensively" staging the play between modern Western ideology and its other(s)
also asserts the perdurance of the logocentric "foreground."

> Is it by chance that, in the paragraphs of the *Philosophy of Right* that present the
> concept *Sittlichkeit* . . . an almost proverbial or legendary citation appeals to the
> father and the son's education? It is a Remark following a paragraph. Education
> is also a constituting/deconstituting process of the family, an *Aufhebung* by which
> the family accomplishes itself, *raises itself* in destroying itself or falling (to the
> tomb) as family. *As* family: the *as,* the *comme,* the *as such* of the essentiality, of the
> essential property or propriety, since it raises only in crossing out, is itself the *as*
> only insofar as other than what it is; it phenomenalizes the phenomenalization it
> discovers. . . .
> The father loses his son like that [*comme ça*]: in gaining him, in educating him,
> in raising him, in involving him in the family circle, which comes down, in the
> logic of the *Aufhebung,* to helping him leave, to pushing him outside while com-
> pletely retaining him. The father helps his son, takes him by the hand in order
> to destroy the family in accomplishing it within what dissolves it: first bourgeois
> or civil society (*bürgerliche Gesellschaft*), then the *State* that accomplishes *Sittlich-
> keit* in "relieving the family and bourgeois society," in magnifying them.
> The family is the first moment of this process. (13–14a)

Given our knowledge of Hegel, both through Derrida and historically, the
family's dialectical position as a threshold between childhood and cultiva-
tion, between allegiance to the private and to the civil or public, comes as

no surprise. There is an odd similarity between the father's double bearing to the son, the family's "constituting/becoming" relation to itself and the Freudian *"fort-da"* of fundamental human ambivalence (here I myself cross the frontier between the philosophical and the psychological). But there is no doubt in this context that Derrida and his readers have a vital stake in education, even where this function and institution harbor metaphysical twists and biases. Having backed ourselves into affiliations with education and institutions, *we,* including Derrida, participate in the economy and metaphysics of voice and logocentrism, regardless of how decentering we would hope the effect of our pedagogy would be. The family, the state, education, public welfare, and morality—these are some of the embarrassing, domestic contracts to which we subscribe all the more by virtue of our compulsive thinking and writing. (Critics of gender and culture have been studying the contrast between this domesticity, its sublime other, and the values attached to them with the most productive results.[3]) Nowhere in his writing did Derrida more forthrightly address the potentially stultifying tangle of these ties, of course in the interest of his own philosophical thinking, than in the left-hand column of *Glas.*

10. Yet there is a moment, as I have suggested above, when even the left-hand, "mainstream" column begins to fragment and crumble. This dissolution is in anticipation, in the logic and rhetoric of Hegel, of the systematic upheaval celebrated in the literature of Genet. For all that the Hegelian high road manifests an extreme predictability as it extends from one complex of metaphysical values to another, this system, whose pronounced overdetermination resides at an extreme, harbors a violence that will lead to its loss of momentum and self-certainty. Derrida demonstrates how, through such figures as the gift and the resonance of *Klang,* the system harbors within itself the seeds and processes of its own dismantling. If the Genet column sketches out the realization of this implicit metaphysical violence or self-destruction, the *Klang,* the gift, and the treacheries of Hegelian architecture constitute a seed of the Genet column "planted" in the Hegelian reconstruction. Although both columns of *Glas* never end, in the sense that the narrative of *Finnegans Wake* turns upon itself, it is in the elaboration of figures like resonance that the left-hand, "mainstream" column comes as close as it does to any apotheosis or conclusion. The remainder of my comments on the Hegel column will be oriented to these "pre-Genet" figures,

but by way of a couple of "way-stations" still within the established complex of metaphysical images and values.

11. One is struck by the splitting that pervades Derrida's reconstitution of Hegelian religion. Translated into Genet's underworld, the hits (*coups*), splits, separations, and gaps that Derrida observes as setting the tone for Christianity will be sexualized into thrusts, penetrations, and climaxes. The purpose of Western onto-theology, according to Hegel, is to reconcile certain unavoidable and predetermined splits: in order for healing reunion to take place, a precondition of radical conflict has to be endemic, systematic. "The Hegelian reading of Christianity seems to describe a reconciliation, in order to say everything in two words: between faith and being, *Glauben* and *Sein*" (91a).

The splits of Modernity resound at a major juncture in Derrida's recounting of Hegelian Christianity:

> The cleavage—which attains its absolute in absolute religion—is the need of/for philosophy. Philosophy is descended, as its own proper object, from Christianity of which it is the truth, from the Holy Family which it falls under (whose relief it is [*dont elle (est la) relève*]. "The Need of Philosophy" . . . (that is the subtitle of a text nearly contemporaneous with *The Spirit of Christianity*) upsurges in the *between* [entre], the narrow gap [*écart*] of a split, a cleavage, a separation, a division in two. One divides itself into two, such is the distressing source of philosophy: "*Entzweiung ist der Quell des Bedürfnisses der Philosophie.*" Therefore reason proceeds to busy itself thinking the wound, to reduce the division, to return this side of the source, close by the infinite unity. . . . The progress of culture has led oppositions of the type spirit/matter, soul/body, faith/understanding, freedom/necessity, and all those deriving from these back toward the great couple reason/sensibility or intelligence/nature. . . . Now these oppositions are poised as such by the understanding that "copies (*ahmt*)" reason. So this enigmatic relation, this rational *mimesis*, organizes the whole history of philosophy as the history of need, the history of reason's interest in relieving the two. (95a)

In terms of *Glas's* gestic treasury and the rhetorical and logical implications of such acts, there is no more prevalent gesture in this book, on both columns, than cutting, splitting, cleaving, dividing, and so on. In terms of Derrida's ongoing philosophical project, this act underlines the resolving function that certain philosophical works and ideological institutions would implement, in accordance with their design. The role of philosophy, in terms of Derrida's ongoing endeavor, is to point up both the (infra)structure of division and the acts of repression performed in the name of its reconciliation. The passage cited names reconciliation as the repressive act of philosophy in the name of advancing Western ideology even as it changes, evolves. The primary thrust of the Derridean demonstration is logical and rhetorical, treating the splits and cleavages that pervade philosophy as logical structures and rhetorical possibilities.

But Derrida's own rhetoric opens up a secondary field for the splits and wounds he chronicles, one that I would describe as both historiographical and psychoanalytical. Conditions of subjectivity, over the broader modernity, in which linguistic facility and artistic intuition become transcendental values, appropriated by a few extraordinary men, are also characterized by multifaceted splitting and ineradicable wounds. Whether by design or not, Derrida characterizes conditions of subjectivity over a period marked by a bewilderment of multiple jurisdictions and obligations demanding personal commitment. The "wound" that reason keeps thinking in this passage bears a striking similarity to the fundamental "narcissistic wounds" at the core of a number of syndromes characterized by contemporary object-relations theorists as conditions of subjective fragmentation and the nonintegration, the noncommunication between fragments, affective states, and acts.[4] So the process of psychotherapy, as staged by object-relations theory, would yearn, like "mainstream" Hegelian philosophy in the passage cited, for the reconciliation ("integration") of split-off moods, tempers, states.

Hegel defines a series of splits, of ones becoming twos (or more) as a pretext for modern, Hegelian philosophy. Philosophy, in turn, will resolve these disquieting discrepancies in fulfilling its mission. As Derrida was intensely aware, religion and art, on the philosophical side, play strategic roles in addressing this predicament of fragmentation, splitting, and, systematic bad faith, which under certain conditions can be made good only through linguistic, artistic, and intellectual facility.

Even more than Hegel, Kant establishes the protocols by which the artist serves as a representative and medium for the transcendence of the systematic, radical splitting that pervades modern philosophy and subjectivity. The artist becomes a particularly critical figure in a post-Enlightenment world in which extrinsic theological and political institutions have undergone a severe reduction in their stature and imputed legitimacy and efficacy. Careful reading of Kant's *Critique of Judgment* and its relation to its predecessors suggests that the Kantian artist is the priest in a secular religion of art to replace established creeds such as those analyzed by Hegel in *The Philosophy of Right,* "The Need of Philosophy," and *The Spirit of Christianity.*[5] The Kantian artist is also, as Derrida would say, a term in a syllogism. The argument runs: if the artist can transmit certain elements of the universe's transcendental design to the human and empirical world by means of (atheological) intuitions and representational facilities, then it is possible to imagine a universe with transcendental and empirical strata conceived and designed in human terms. This project, as is Hegel's, is in keeping with Enlightenment ideology: furnishing an account of knowledge and human conditions based on human abilities and faculties alone; also, endowing the human-generated systems of knowledge with human qualities, creating, in effect, human simulacra in a discursive medium or, if you will, discursive robots.

Both the Kantian and Hegelian systems fall under the purview of this vast Enlightenment project (or culture contract). Kant's design sacrifices human dynamism in the names of comprehensiveness and perspectival lucidity. A certain eighteenth-century heritage may show through in Kant's emphasis on mapping, but his work on the players in the process of human knowledge (including faculties, categories, intuitions, powers, and language), and the interplay between different perspectives and levels of understanding is immaculate. Kant is content with observing the complicated interaction between faculties, powers, and so on, within the perspective provided by a single frame or dialectical cell (hence Derrida's focus on the Kantian notion of the frame in "Parergon"). The Kantian framework, as Derrida would say, is structured by a single encompassing duality, the transcendental/empirical, perhaps a distant descendant of another duality, between soul and body.[6]

Hegel, by contrast, leaves behind the precision and comprehensiveness afforded by a more spatial, stabilized purview in the interest of infusing the framework of knowledge with the organicism and dynamism of its human sources. Consciousness, collective and individual, meanders along the course of its progressive development. Yet both Kantian and Hegelian systems require, at a certain point, the intervention of a meta-human (what Nietzsche will eventually call the *Übermensch*) to embody the humanness of human-based systems of authority, to bear this humanity into the world.

12. The dénouement of the "Hegel story" in *Glas* is the (Heideggerian) dis-closure of the seismic instabilities underlying even so authoritative and

sound an iteration of Western cant as Hegel's. The Hegel column of *Glas,* it turns out, is sitting on quicksand; it is in a state of its own perpetual dissolution and fragmentation. Even Hegel is subject to the metaphysical fate that Derrida has extrapolated with more philosophical rigor and lucidity than anyone else. The very language with which Hegel would cement an ideological mainstream of Western post-Enlightenment thought betrays him, "whipsaws" him, undermines his politico-intellectual purpose and intent.

In Derrida's version of the horror story that can be inferred from the rapport between the empirical and the transcendental in Kant, the monster language of which the rationalistic and high-minded scientists were presumably in search is decisively victorious over its "users." The designs of Hegel, like those by any of the agents of the ideal toward whose writings Derrida has directed his scrutiny (e.g., Plato, Rousseau, Freud), will be done in and frustrated by the very terminology that was their articulate medium.

(It is possible that deconstruction imputes enormous power and even brilliance to language in its resistant and destabilizing functions; even possible that language owes some of this magic to scenarios of secular, human-originated transcendence that evolved over the span of the broader modernity, as articulated, among others, by Kant, Goethe, the Schlegels, Wordsworth, Hölderlin, the Shelleys, and Hoffmann. To see the parallelism between the nuclear power of language in deconstruction and certain *human,* subjective potentials that become liberated in Romantic discourse and literature is to begin to assemble some historical [or epistemological] context for deconstruction without in any way *containing* its discoveries.)

13. We can say of *Glas*'s bicolumnar architecture or its resonant counterpoint that the Hegel text situates a certain inwardness or interiority of Western idealism at a certain broad epoch in its "history" and that the Genet countertext traces out, assertively, the emptying or in-difference of the "same" tradition. I have elsewhere posited one useful way of thinking the postmodern as a similar emptying, decontraction, and dispossession of a number of experiments associated with modernism (here narrowly defined as an aesthetic movement predominant in Europe and the Americas roughly from 1890 to 1945.)

The writing of Genet, and its remarkable reconstruction and interpretation by Derrida in *Glas,* may well play the tain of the mirror to Hegel's version of the high Western metaphysical road (or church). And to my mind, the modality of this playful but earnest engagement includes moves and attitudes inextricably associated with the postmodern (in the most productive terms in which its discussion may be couched). It would thus be possible to assert that the Genet column of *Glas* embraces the postmodern supplement, emptying, and in-difference to the (linguistic *and* subjective) conditions of a very broad modernity that prevailed in the West at least from Shakespeare, Luther, Calvin, and Descartes through Romanticism and its defensive aftershocks. In terms of my own earlier work, then, Genet joins a group of postmodern writers including, among many others, the late Kafka and Joyce, Stein, Beckett, Blanchot, Barnes, Adorno, and Bernhard.[7] Whatever commonality may be extrapolated from these writers' script, I have argued, is distinguished at least in part by a certain monologic self-sustenance, a slowdown or blackout in the referential field and functions, and a pronounced indifference to exaggerated distinctions of identity and gender and to permutational games of structure, which comprised, in their context, appropriate responses to the claims of Romantic and post-Romantic theory. Derrida's generative reading of Genet establishes, among other things, that an in-different other to a historical or epistemological stage of *doxa* can consist of the same images (or material) of which the metaphysical base position is constructed. Derrida demonstrates as well in *Glas* that the relationship between the institutionalized Western base position—in this case, modernity—and its other is characterized by supplementarity, the re-mark, chiasmatic duplicity, and constriction.

14. To indicate the possible (but never realized) way out of modern Western complacency, above all as formulated by Hegel, Genet would have to do a number of things. He would have to deflower its pieties, demolish its basis in a certain kind of (bourgeois, heterosexist, altruistic) family,[8] and indicate a radical departure from its ideal-based morality, in which there is only a single "right" alternative. According to the Derridean exegesis in *Glas*, Genet performs all these acts, and with a vengeance. A radical transvaluation of values, positioning Genet in a situation analogous to (but historically different from) Nietszche's is merely one, albeit striking, strategy by which Genet brings liberal Enlightenment ideology to its marginal, postmodern efflorescence.

Within this transfiguration, the religion of flowers, which in the Hegelian onto-theology resides at a certain (Indian) moment of mass or public

spirituality (2a, 240a, 246–47a), becomes, in Genet's underworld, a rhetorical and taxinomic system for queers (13b, 17b, 31b, 35b, 47b, 57b, 187–
88b); the bourgeois division of labor—predicating an entire metaphysics of
sexual difference, whereby the brother departs the family in public service
while the sister (e.g., Antigone) defends the hearth and its "natural" laws
(86a, 96a, 110–14a, 125–30a, 142–50a)—becomes the in-difference of homosexual bondings, with their theatrical, "assumed" roles (25–27b, 38–40b,
74–76b, 82–86b, 103–6b, 128–42b); the prevalent Hegelian dynamic of
sublimated violence or instinct (a close variation upon *Aufhebung*), by which
consciousness advances itself and culture evolves, becomes, in a "Genetic"
environment, a highly explicit, demonstrative theater of perverse (from the
perspective of conventional mores) sex acts: erections, ejaculations, imper-
sonations, castrations, and the like (2b, 11–12b, 17b, 21–25b, 47–57b, 77b,
86b, 108b, 111–14b, 118–28b, 132b, 136–42b, 149b, 167–73b, 202b, 210–
16b, 223–29b). A Nietzschean transvaluation is involved in the *détour* from
Hegelian conventionality to "Genetic" perversity, but this act describes
only one relation between the system and its manifold of supplemental
values.

15. If Hegel's *Phenomenology* presumes the self-generated rise of human
(individual and collective) consciousness from "sensible certitude" to cultural articulation, then the countersystem that Derrida so cleverly assembles
out of Genet's fiction and drama pursues a parallel degeneration from an
excessively rigid social code to the inarticulate, the glottal ejaculation, knell,
or *Glas* in which attempts at systematic articulation ultimately issue. The
double columns of *Glas* are free-standing, but if any hinge or bridge links
them, akin to the ultimate Proustian feedback loop joining the Guermantes
and Méséglise ways, it is the resonance between the Hegelian *Klang* and the
"Genetic" ejaculation.

Derrida marks a contrapuntal echoing within the pivotal trope of efflorescence itself:

> Thus the stamin, *l'étamine. Etamine*—the whore's rose, a verge's homage to
> Mary and taboo of the hymen rendered to the fag petal [*pétale*]—names not only
> the light material in which nuns are sometimes veiled, or through which precious
> liquids are filtered. But *étamine*, stamen, is also the male sex organ of plants:
> according to the *navette* [shuttle, rape]—that's the word—running between the
> textile code and the botanical code. Situated around the style and its stigma,
> stamens generally form a thin thread [*filet*], or filaments (*stamina*). Above the

thin thread, a connective with four pollen sacs (microsporangia) that "elaborate and disperse the pollen seeds": the (interring) anther. . . .

The flower is hypogynous when the ovary dominates the rest [*reste*] of the flower. Sometimes the stamens are glued by their thin threads into one or more "fraternities," or else they become concrescent with petals (these are sometimes prolonged into spurs and carry nectariferous glands) or with the gynoecium: that's the case with orchids. (250b)

Flowers figure not only in Hegel's comparative religious imagery and in Genet's homoerotic underworld. In terms of their "internal" metonymy, linking spiritual innocence to sexual fecundity and arousal, they comprise a striking trope (as also noted in "White Mythology") for Derrida's wider philosophical project. Flowers partake of indifferent, amoral sexuality at the same time as they are spiritualized into icons of chastity. Flower arrangements, as Proust also notes, assume the form of textual webworks and interlacings. It is for this reason that in this passage Derrida devotes his attention to the interweavings of stamens and styles. The language of flowers, on both sides of the Hegel-Genet divide in *Glas*, is a textual script that is both the source and limit of ideals and other totalizing constructs. Tresses of flowers surround and qualify Western ideals in a manner analogous to the critique that deconstruction delivers to sanctioned Western-ideal based and oriented disciplines and intellectual procedures. The language of flowers exercises this role as an anti-idealistic proto-writing on both sides of *Glas*'s bicolumnar architecture. This may well be the only "nature" attributable to flowers: they flourish on both sides of the Derridean guard rail or fence.

Glas is Derrida's most explicitly sexual work at the same time as it is his most sonorous and musical. It is but a short step from the insemination of flowers to the fertilization on the periphery, if not at the "heart," of all sexual behavior. For all of Derrida's well-founded skepticism about psychoanalysis and the metaphysics of the subject that it legitimates, the treatment of sexual symbolism in *Glas* uncannily assumes the tone of the sexual division of labor in classical psychoanalysis and its clinical and literary offshoots. This is to say that, in both its columns, *Glas* conspicuously professes Western culture's biases in sexual ideology (heterosexuality and homophobia) and in symbolism as a point of departure and contrast *against* the countereconomies of writing and Genet's underworld. On the Genet side of things, then, the rhetoric of flowers *entrains* (in the French sense of the word) the

classical Western heritage of sexual mores and its always-persistent
supplement.

Thus the flower (which equals castration, phallus, and so on) "signifies"—
again!—at least overlaps virginity in general, the vagina, the clitoris, "feminine
sexuality," matrilinear genealogy, the mother's *seing,* that is, the Immaculate
Conception. That is why flowers no longer have anything symbolic about them.
"They symbolized nothing."

Demonstration. For castration to overlap virginity, for the phallus to be re-
versed into a vagina, for alleged opposites to be equivalent to each other and
reflect each other, the flower has to be turned inside out like a glove, and its style
like a sheath [*gaine*]. *The Maids* pass their time reflecting and replacing one sex
with the other. Now they sink their entire "ceremony" into the structure of the
glove, the looking glass, and the flower. The onset is supported by the signifier
"glove." *Glove* is stretched as a signifier of artifice. First words "Those gloves!
Those eternal gloves!" . . . But these gloves are not only artificial and reversible
signifiers, they are almost fake gloves, kitchen gloves, the "dish-gloves" with
which, at the close of the ceremony, the strangling of Madame is mimed, and
which, in sum, circulate between places. . . . *The Maids* are gloves, the gloves of
Madame. They are also called "angels." At once castrated and castrating (spiders
or umbrella case), full and void of the phallus that Madame does not have. . . .

But between these pairs of gloves, flowers, only flowers, too many flowers.
Their displacement is like the law, the metronome as well, nearly inaudible, the
lateral cadence, dissimulated, of each gesture. . . .

In both cases, the gladiolus, *gladiolus,* little glaive, of the iris family (Provençal:
glaviol; to the common gladiolus other therapeutic and nutritional powers have
often been accorded; the gladiolus of the harvests used to pass for an aphrodisiac
and emmenagogue). (47b–52b)

Flowers run roughshod over the sexual division of labor, the male and female stereotypes, that seem to define their place. Derrida remains ambiguous in his neutralization of this sexual tradition, on the one hand, and, at
the same time, his appeal to it, in the footsteps of Hegel and Genet. This is
in part because he elected, in the writing of *Glas,* to suspend, hold in reserve,
the distinction between language-based models, in which flowers are signifiers caught in a network with other flowers and other signifiers, and subject-oriented models such as psychoanalysis, which sustain a process of

identification through symbolism, whether of a sexual, socioeconomic, ethnic, or other nature.

Flowers are thus characterized in two of their supplementary aspects in the above passage, whose typographical "strange interlude" corresponds to the explicit design of *Glas.* Before the break, flowers neuter a systematic sexual division of labor, which they both epitomize and predicate. After the gap, itself a sexual symbol, they join a network of signifiers, and their role consists in the variations of form and meaning they assume in an arational, nonideational cluster of signifiers (210b, 212b, 222b), whose principles of interrelation are linguistic rather than logical or metaphysical. Below the gap, it is of much greater consequence to flowers that they cluster around the letter *g* and the combination *gl* than that they contain, deface, or neutralize innocence. Through the careful reading of which *Glas* is a consummate example, a wreath of flowers, ultimately beginning and ending with the uncanny French signifier *glas,* can be woven out of gladioli, gloves, swords (French: *glaives*), sheaths (*gaines*), and irises (*glaviols*). This chaining is not merely an exercise in ingenious etymologies. It is a concrete and precise demonstration of something fundamental to Derrida's philosophy, namely, that the manifold accretion of language is just as legitimate a source to plumb for the history and values of culture as canonical ideological statements. Surely the work of Nietzsche, especially as glossed by Heidegger, anticipated this position, but it took Derrida, and specifically the Derrida of certain demonstrations (the *floreligium* of *Glas* and "Plato's Pharmacy" stand high on my list), to allegorize the accretion of nuances and values in a rigorously linguistic setting in an *explicit* and compelling manner.

In the supplemental economy and bicolumnar architecture of *Glas,* then, syllables with no meaning in themselves count for more than ideas and culturally mediated symbols. This is because their chaining out to like entities is truly cultural and sexual. Understanding the impasses of Hegelian philosophy and its twentieth-century commentary/disfiguration by Genet hinges more on the pursuit of syllables and the gathering of clusters of meaning than on the "history of ideas" or the "anxiety of influence." The volume *Glas* is thus more a tribute to the sign and sound *gl* than an appreciation or commentary on Hegel, Genet, or Western philosophy of the broader modernity, although Derrida argues by performance that a more significant appreciation of these entities can be reached through the pursuit of a seme and its affinities than through the extrapolation and paraphrase of concepts.[9]

The letters and resonances of *glas* help Derrida to articulate a philosophy of marks and remarks more than of concepts and their logical relations.

> And as if all this galley-slaving had worn itself out with emitting (the word *emitting* strikes me as interesting but unsatisfying, it would also be necessary to say annointing, inducing, enjoining, smearing)

> GL
> I do not say either the signifier GL, or the phoneme GL, or the grapheme GL. Mark would be better, if the word were well understood, or if one's ears were open to it; not even mark then.
> It is also imprudent to advance or set GL swinging in the masculine or feminine, to write or articulate it in capital letters. That has no identity, sex, gender, makes no sense, is neither a definite whole nor a part detached from a whole

> gl remain(s) gl falls (to the tomb) as must a pebble in the water—in not taking it even for an archigloss (since it is only a gloss morsel, but not yet a gloss, and therefore, an element detached from any gloss. (119b–120b)

I want to emphasize the thingly quality of the grapheme *GL*. This passage constitutes Derrida's principal frame for the language-thing that, more than the notion, accounts for the "nature" of texts and culture. At two points in the passage, Derrida frames the *GL*-thing by centering it in the lines in which it appears. He amply attests to its ambiguous character: signifier, phenomenon, grapheme—exactly—it is not. Captioning it as a mark comes close to the point, but then veers away from the mark. The image Derrida selects, a pebble in the water, may be as a propos as anything to describe the mark, in this instance assuming the "form" *GL*. A pebble is a thing of nature. A pebble interrupts, but also articulates, a continuous flow of water, an element whose transparent and relatively tasteless quality mimics the attributes by which certain transcendental entities and values in Western thought are identified, such as God or being. As a concept-thing, the mark that Derrida set in relief here, the mark of writing, would disrupt the seemingly natural and ongoing flow of Western systematicity in a fashion similar to the manner in which a mere thing, a pebble, would divert but heighten the flow of a stream.

The slippage of the grapheme *GL* describes a polymorphic dissemination that may be figured as sexual thrusts or shudders, the ejaculation of semen, or the evaporation or calcification of viscous liquids. Derrida took it upon himself to exhaustively explore a nonlinear cluster of meanings emerging from the grapheme *GL*. In the following extract, *GL* pursues a meandering path, passing from one semantic field to another with unpredictability, impunity, speed, and seeming arbitrariness (that is, the arbitrariness is "always already" installed in the language network itself). The *GL*-thing meanders from birds (the raptor) to bodies, from the ear to the throat, from physical and vocal fluidity to freezing and stammering, from warmth to cold, from the sperm to the fetus, and in the genre to which the passage belongs, from poetry to Teutonic philosophy. Merely for culture's discourse (and the university's) to embrace this stutter-stepping is tantamount to a revolution, an unmistakable sea change in the constitution and protocols of knowledge.

> the imperial flight of a raptor swoops down at one go [*d'un coup*] on your nape, the gluing, frozen [*glacé*], pissing cold name of an impassive Teutonic philosopher, with a notorious stammer, sometimes liquid and sometimes gutturotetanic, a swollen or cooing goiter, all that rings [*cloche*] in the tympanic channel or fossa, the spit or plaster on the soft palate [*voile du palais*], the orgasm of the glottis or the uvula, the clitoral glue, the cloaca of the abortion, the gasp of sperm, the rhythmed hiatus of an occlusion, the saccadanced spasm of an eructojaculation, the syncopated valve of tongue and lips, or a nail [*clou*] that falls in the silence of the milky say [*la voix lactée*] (I note, in parentheses, that, from the outset of this reading, I have not ceased to think, as if it were my principle object, about the milk trademarks Gloria and Gallia for the new-born, about everything that can happen to the porridge, to the mush of nurslings who are gluttinous, stuffed, or weaned from a cleft breast [*sein*], and now everything catches, is fixed, and falls in galalith). (120b–21b)

In entirely liquid fashion, this textual glue or semen flows, above all, into itself. Yet it is but a short step from thick fluid to fluid membrane. Linguistic viscosity thus implicates the membranous qualities of texts, which can be figured as fabrics, skins, and physiological membranes, such as the hymen, themselves.

> Sperm, saliva, glair, curdled drool, tears of milk, gel of vomit—all these heavy and white substances are going to glide into each other, be agglutinated, agglomerated, stretched out *(on)to the edge* of all the fixtures and pass through all the canals.
>
> The word "*glaviaux*" ["globs"] will not be uttered until later, after invisible assimilation and deglutition, after elaboration, agglutinated to "*glaïeul*" ["gladiolus"].

But even before being presented in the text and blooming there right next to the flower, the word animates with its energetic and encircled absence the description of spit. (139b–40b)

> gl tears the "body," "sex," "voice" and "writing from the logic of consciousness and representation that guided these debates. While ever remaining a bit-effect (a death-effect) [*effet de mors*] among others, gl remarks in itself as well—whence the transcendental effect, always, of taking part—the angular slash [*coupure*] of the opposition, the differential schiz *and* the flowing [*coulant*] continuum of the couple, the distinction *and* the copulating unity (one example, of the arbitrary and the motivated). It is one of, only one but as a party to, the de-terminant sluices, open closed to a rereading of the *Cratylus*.
>
> Socrates feigns to take part. For example: "And perceiving that the tongue (*glōtta*) has a gliding movement (*olisthanei*) most in the pronunciation of l (*lambda*), he made the words (*ōnomase*) *leia* (level), *olisthanein* (glide) itself, *liparon* (sleek), *kollōdes* (glutinous), and the like to conform (*aphomoiōn*) to it. . . .
>
> It is not a word—gl hoists the tongue but does not hold it and always lets the tongue fall back, does not belong to it—even less a name, and hardly a *pro-prénom*, a proper (before the first) name. (235b–36b)

It is in no silly sense, then, that I can claim *Glas* as Derrida's tribute to a linguistic object so small that it is subsyllabic. Following Derrida's hint, let us call this minute language-thing a mark. For the high road of Western culture to truly acknowledge its blindnesses, biases, and points of closure, it need only reorient itself to the smallest of things. In this, of course, lies the immense enterprise Derrida only begins—masterfully but inconclusively—to trace out in *Glas*.

16. Yet the performance of *Glas* is too intricate and persistent to allow us to take leave of it in this "spirit" of textual ascendance. In what is perhaps Derrida's most masterly and fully realized performance of the disclosure and liberation of idea-oriented culture's linguistic substratum, he does not neglect to implicate himself in the process, to take responsibility for his role in the critique and its cultural reception. In the work in which it would be easiest for Derrida to conceal his interest in the process of cultural deconstruction, Derrida marks his presence by attaching his name, by leaving the trace of his own signature. More precisely, Derrida attaches his signature to his enterprise at a point where Genet assumes the same responsibility, where Genet, in the marvelous French tradition of the philosophy of writing, elaborated most fully by Blanchot in addition to Derrida, inscribes his own John Hancock:

The emblem, the blazon open and close (noise and strict-ure of the valve) the jerky outpouring of a wound. The whole *Studio* works (over) this wound. "There is no other origin for beauty than the wound—singular, different for everyone, hidden or visible—that every man keeps in himself. . . . The signature is a wound, and there is no other origin for the work of art. . . . Giacometti's art seems to me to wish to discover the secret wound of every being and even of every thing, so that the wound may illuminate them." . . . The signature's hidden wound, the bleeding [*saignant*] cryptogram, is the morseling of Osiris. But the economy of the signature never interrupts its work. It finds in the remain(s) of infirmity a supplementary apotrope, a sort of reseda. As Stilitano bands erect a little more for being one-handed. As Querelle from squinting. (184b)

To remark the cynical character of the paraph, one must see the photograph of the sculptor, full-face, at the beginning of the book (every trait falls [*tombe*] from it, as from a beaten dog); but above all the signature of
    [Genet's signature is reproduced at this point in *Glas*]
    the other. (184–85b)

Ineffable and intricate though the involutions, dissimulations, and materials of writing may be, at a certain point, the true writer inscribes him/herself in the mess. Genet does so at the point of reporting on his visit to Giacometti's studio, also in locating himself within the "little band" of queens and other perverts assembled in, among other texts, *Our Lady of the Flowers*.

To the degree that the act of writing constitutes a return to the scene of a crime, the writerly writer, the writer who specifies his/her relation to the materials, exigencies, costs, and *jouissances* of writing—whether a Sterne, a Nietzsche, a Proust, a Genet, a Blanchot, or a Derrida—leaves a tangle of traces that will link him/her inextricably to the transgression. Genet's signatory tie to his acts of writerly composition may be the subculture of homosexuality: its practices, superstition, and *argot*.

For Derrida, it is not so far from this marginal subculture to the Jewishness that will constitute a major trace of his personal past and that he will pin to the wider parameters of *Glas* as a trace of his having been there. Derrida has already discerned the outlines of a holocaust in the Hegelian dialectics of religion and the gift, and the enveloping *tissue* of the *talith* or Jewish prayer shawl serves him as an instance of what might be termed "the textuality of everyday life," in a culture supple and gentle enough to embrace, in some manner, its constituting textuality.[10]

Our-Lady-of-the-Flowers thus will have prescribed the *glas* form. "The great noc-
turnal occupation, admirably suited for enchanting the darkness, is tattooing.
Thousands of thousands of little jabs [*coups*] with a fine needle prick the skin and
draw blood, and figures that you would regard as most extravagant are flaunted
in the most unexpected places. When the rabbi slowly unrolls the Torah, a mystery sends a shudder through the whole epidermis, as when one sees a colonist
undressing. The grimacing of all that blue on a white skin imparts an obscure
but potent glamor to the child who is covered with it, as a neutral [*indifférente*],
pure column becomes sacred under the notches of the hieroglyphs." . . .

(The faithful, as you know, are enveloped in a veil. Some wear it all rolled up,
like a cord, a sling, or an untied necktie around their neck. Others, more amply
spread out on their shoulders and chest and trailing to the floor. Still others—
and, at determined moments, everyone—on the head. Sometimes the veil is
streaked in blue and white, and sometimes in black and white. Sometimes,
though almost never, as if by chance or choice, it is pure white. The dead man is
enveloped in his *taleth*—that is the name of the veil—after washing the body and
closing all its orifices.)

The Torah wears a robe and a crown. Its two rollers are then parted [*écartés*] like
two legs; the Torah is lifted to arm's length and the rabbi's scepter approximately
followed the upright text. The bands in which it was wrapped had been previously undone and entrusted, generally, to a child. The child, comprehending
nothing about all these signs full of sense, was to climb up into a gallery where
the women, and old women especially, were and then to pass them the ragged
bands.

   Meanwhile, the body of the Torah was laid out on a table, and the men busied
themselves. (240b–41b)

The reading and ceremony of the Torah marks, although in no simple way,
Derrida's stake and signature within the drama of repression, marginality,
supplementarity, and textuality that coincides with his philosophical project.
Yet he arrived at the extreme innocence in which the Torah, as cultural
introjection and fetish, is veiled, not by way of his persistent antipodal posture, his overarching skepticism in the name of marginal illumination, but
at the end of a series that has included crime, incarceration, homosexual
"banding erect," the Hegelian holocaust, and pasties (*postiche*; 138b–39b,
210b, 212b, 223b). The writer is a marked (wo)man, and Derrida made
himself no exception to this rule. Writing transpires in a multifaceted matrix of cultural conditions, including the writer's irreducible signature.

17. It is time to close this introduction to the complexities and rewards of *Glas,* a word as well as a book, one that has resonated throughout its dazzling project in unmistakably textual fashion. As a resonance and as a book, *Glas* frames the impulses and strategies characterizing both the broader modernity and the postmodern enterprise of delimiting this modernity's sway. The architecture of sometimes pristine, sometimes mutually interpenetrating, sometimes assertive, sometimes crumbling, but always supplemental and mutually exegetical columns forms a framework, a viewfinder for reading and interpretation as well as for time and cultural history. The modernity to which both Kant and Hegel are already responding arises in an uncanny, breathless sense of freedom and possibility and of the affinity between language and the claiming of these liberties. It is also pervaded, in a manner that Derrida associated with logocentrism, with a dread of this open horizon of possibility. The bicolumnar architecture of *Glas* opens a hinge in time.[11] From this phase transition[12] ensues a temporal eddy enabling Romantic liberations to swirl back to their underpinnings in the scientific self-reliance of the Enlightenment project; the monotone, but unrelenting articulation of postmodern fiction, drama, orchestral music, and opera to refer back to the permutation of colors, moods, and motifs that was the modernist rallying cry.[13]

The architecture of weights and counterweights, contractions and relaxations rehearsed in the typesetting and graphic design as well as argumentation and readouts of *Glas* may in the end fall on the side of instability. But its framework, for the book as well as for Derrida's subsequent explorations, has been meticulously designed. We encounter parallel tensions around the picture-frame corner that Derrida devises as a graphic mark of the aporias attending Kant's efforts to encompass aesthetic striving and production within a universal map and field guide to the human faculties. The picture-frame corners of "Parergon" may note stops or breaths in Derrida's engagement with the Kantian blueprint for the emergent social sciences as the Enlightenment thinker imagined them, but this typographical improvisation also marks the endless double bind in which the artwork is enmeshed:[14] between the pieties and utilities of the Prevailing Operating System and the contingency and nonmotivation of aesthetic play and transgression.

18. The ultimate outlet or issue, within a deconstructive zone or neighborhood, to the contrapuntal address to reading and mainstream systems orchestrated so meticulously and inventively in *Glas* may well be the "turn"

to the institutions, practices, and aporias of religion, politics, and culture that for so many readers highlights and distinguishes the "late" Derrida. *Glas* sets out, by this logic, in the marginal crossfire between two books, Hegel's *Philosophy of Right* and Genet's *Our Lady of the Flowers*, but it eventuates in endless dissonance or *Klang* between social systems and radically limiting and delimiting exegeses of the canonical texts that have legitimated and ensconced these systems. In this sense, *Glas* is literally the blueprint for the frame within whose compass Prevailing Operating Systems encounter the always imperative statutes of limitation ensuing from their language-immanent critique.

The bicolumnar architecture and play orchestrated in *Glas*, then, has already been embedded in Derrida's probing revisitation (or haunting) of such longstanding Western theological values and traditions as faith (in "Faith and Knowledge"),[15] self-sacrifice (in *The Gift of Death*),[16] hospitality (in "Hostipitality"), and the divine secret or mystery (also in *The Gift of Death*).[17] Far from dismissing these core Western theological precepts, as fundamental, Derrida argues, to Islam as to Judeo-Christianity, Derrida opts for the far more challenging climb: the meticulous and precise routing, on the map of rhetorical figuration rather than geographical territory, of the double binds in which each of these essential religious values is entrenched and in which it eventuates. The point at which Derrida, as much in amusement as in rancor, throws up his hands at hospitality occurs, in different and local terms, in each of the specific religious practices and traditions that he addresses. His meticulous rendering explicit of the double messages on which the edifice of Western values is founded and that mark it for immanent condemnation is a tribute, theoretically, to Gregory Bateson, however frequently or rarely his name appears on the intellectual marquees of Montparnasse. Since the moment of the cleanup immediately following the First World War, when he opposed crippling reparations levied by the Allied Powers on the German economy, Bateson militated for restraint in the production and profit extracted from industrial and commercial systems; for a vigilant caution regarding expansionist campaigns mounted by sovereign or corporate entities. His model for the delicacy that he regarded as imperative to the management of systems was the complementary, as opposed to the symmetrical model, of social relations and organizations that he observed as a young anthropologist performing fieldwork in Indonesia and New Guinea. His systematic ethics, as well as his multifaceted explorations of the genesis, structure, and outcomes, possible and tangible, of the double bind, are the crux of Chapter 9 below.

With respect to the specific double binds attending the core Western social and theological value of hospitality, Derrida writes:

> Indeed, *on the one hand*, hospitality must wait, extend itself toward the other, extend to the other the gifts, the site, the shelter, and the cover; it must be ready to welcome [*acueillir*], to host and shelter, to give shelter and cover; it must prepare itself and adorn itself [*se preparer et se parer*] for the coming of the hôte; it must even develop itself into a culture of hospitality, multiply the signs of anticipation, construct and institute what one calls structures of welcoming. . . .
>
> But, *on the other hand*, the opposite is also nevertheless true, simultaneously and irrepressibly true: to be hospitable is to let oneself be overtaken [*surprendre*], *to be ready to be not ready*, if such is possible, to let oneself be overtaken, to not even *let* oneself be overtaken, to be surprised, in a fashion almost violent, to be violated and raped [*violée*], stolen [*volé*] (the whole question of violence and violation/rape and of expropriation and de-propriation is waiting for us), precisely where one is not ready to receive . . . *unprepared* in a mode that is not even that of the "not yet."[18]

Doing nothing more formidable or tendentious than spinning out the linguistic nuances pertaining to the basic terms of hospitality, Derrida nonetheless pursues this tradition, as noble as its precepts and instances often are, into the cul-de-sac of its intrinsic impossibility. A parallel—but rhetorically and textually specific—demonstration awaits each core concept deriving from Abrahamic religion that enters the deconstructive purview on this social and institutional as well as textual phenomenon. Prominent within this subliterature of Derridean critique are the two very different senses of *religio*, in "Faith and Knowledge," at the basis of Western conceptions of faith and the major historical faiths, as well as Derrida's patient demonstration of self-sacrifice's patent impossibility, an elucidation all the more controversial in view of the premiums placed on altruism and faithful self-sacrifice in all three major monotheistic religions.

Derrida's gesture toward the aporetic impasses that he isolates in such theologically nuanced conventions as faith, ghosts and specters, mystery, hospitality, mercy, and pardon is anything but one of dismissal and denunciation. It is indeed the very impossibility of hospitality, of dying for someone else, of conferring or receiving mercy, that draws the great religious faiths toward deconstruction, toward philosophically driven close reading, and into the vortex or cleft, as we have seen in the layout of *Glas,* between the pillars of mainstream public ideology and morality and the dissolving columns of moral as well as architectural transgression and disrepair. The uplifting of the enduring religious traditions, from a deconstructive point of view, inheres in the conceptual impossibilities that they negotiate, resolutely and persistently. The Abrahamic faiths, in different ways and with different emphases, become sanctuaries for the impossibility that is the starting point to any reform, through precise elucidation, in the sense of "messianism without messianicity," that deconstructive critique might render.

> This is about the concept of concept, and this is why I suggested earlier that hospitality, the experience of the apprehension, the exercise of impossible hospitality, of hospitality as the possibility of impossibility (to receive another guest whom I am incapable of welcoming, to become capable of that which I am incapable of)—this is the exemplary experience of deconstruction itself, when it is or does what it has to do or be, that is, the experience of the impossible. Hospitality—this is a name or example of deconstruction. Of the deconstruction of the concept, of the concept of concept, as well as of its construction, its home, its "at home" [*son chez soi*]. Hospitality is the deconstruction of the at-home; deconstruction is hospitality to the other, to the other than oneself, the other than "its other," to an other who is beyond any "its other."[19]

Deconstruction, then, "is the name" for the double messages and irremediable impasses in which closed and authoritative systems inevitably eventuate. And the typography, textual architecture, and development of *Glas* chart and delimit the space within which this impossibility makes itself known, the tabula on which the impossible scores its elusive traces. The political trends and configurations that Derrida addressed as the deconstructive project widened to engage new artifacts also transpire in a zone of arbitrary and unforeseen turns, bound at the limits of totalitarian closure and, at the other extreme, of rigorously untrammeled possibility. *Rogues,* for example, liberally delves into the insanity resulting from the imputation of "rogue" status to all sovereign states and entities not subscribing to current international conventions of military engagement and finance as established and overseen by such agencies as NATO, the UN, the IMF, and the World Bank. Derrida's entire prior writerly excursion prepares him for the ironies ensuing from the "battle of proper names"[20] ignited by the imputation of "rogue" status. "There are thus no longer anything but rogue states, and there are no longer any rogue states. The concept will have reached its limit and the end—more terrifying than ever—of its epoch. This end was always close, indeed, already from the beginning."[21]

Rogues pivots on the figure of the wheel, from its most brutal and concrete to its most abstruse manifestations. National sovereignty is, in its subjective and logical as well as its territorial and diplomatic dimensions, a circular structure:

> This sovereignty is a circularity, indeed a sphericity. Sovereignty is round: it is a rounding off. This circular or spherical rotation, the turn of the re-turn upon the self, can take either the alternating form of the *by turns,* the *in turn,* the *each in turn* . . . or else the form of an identity between the origin and the conclusion, the cause and the end or the aim, the driving [*motrice*] cause and the final end.[22]

For Derrida, sovereign actions, assertions, and claims all stem from the circular reasoning not only by which might is exercised but by which selfhood as *ipseity* is constituted. It is no accident, then, that for centuries in the West the wheel constituted and executed a particularly theatrical form of capital punishment: "The torture of the wheel belongs to a long juridical and political history. . . . The subject being punished is quartered, his bound body forming one body with the wheel, subjected to its rotation."[23] In its most brutal traces, the movement, like the constitution of the sovereign state, is circular. The "reason of the strongest," the self-serving exposition by which the wolf, and its compeers among the national powers, justifies its voracity to the weak, is at its core a circular reasoning.

With a flair for the ironic twists of narrative worthy of the greatest story-tellers, whether Perrault, La Fontaine, or the Brothers Grimm, Derrida details how the self-aggrandizing conquerors among the nations are eventually attacked by the autoimmune responses by which they were constituted and called to action in the first place:

> Sovereignty neither gives nor gives itself the time. Here is where the cruel autoimmunity with which sovereignty is affected begins, the autoimmunity with which sovereignty at once sovereignly affects and cruelly infects itself. Autoimmunity is always, in the same time without duration, cruelty itself, the autoinfection of all autoaffection. It is not some particular thing that is affected in autoimmunity but the self, the *ipse,* the *autos* that finds itself infected. As soon as it needs heteronomy, the event, time and the other.[24]

In *Rogues,* Derrida has meticulously reconstructed the circular architecture, constitution, and logic through which the most aggressive nations, corporations, and related entities, whether configured by profit, national domination, ethnicity, creed, or kinship, eventually attack themselves, in a crisis of autoimmune breakdown. The account framed by the citation immediately above may be situated deep in the engine room of core Western philosophemes and tropes. In that passage, Derrida underscores sovereignty's circumscription in a moment "without duration." The primary symptom of this particular autoaffective disorder is self-absorption in the present, coinciding with obliviousness to the other. But as Derrida is quite aware, his autoaffective scenario applies to the most current and actual developments in the world economy and politics:

> The beast is not simply an animal but the very incarnation of evil, of the satanic, the diabolical, the demonic—a beast of the Apocalypse. Before Iraq, Libya had been considered by the Reagan administration to be a rogue state, although I don't believe that the word itself was ever used. Libya, Iraq, and Sudan were bombed for being rogue states, and, in the last two instances, with a violence and cruelty that fall nowise short of those associated with what is called "September 11." But the list is endless (Cuba, Nicaragua, North Korea, Iran, and so on).[25]

In the concrete vein of his mobilization and performance of rogue phenomena, Derrida pursues a sequence of aggressive incursions by U.S. commerce and agencies, including the World Bank and the IMF, under the aegis of free-market economics and ideology, whose autoimmune impact has resulted, for example, in the U.S. economic downturn of the past two years at the end of a long sequence of prior destabilizations. It is particularly striking and noteworthy that Derrida's survey of current autoimmune crises undergone by global "leaders," although characteristically situated in the operating system of basic Western philosophical categories and tropes, and although animated by intense etymological acuity and delving, could parallel, in thrust as in trajectory, the sequence of economic domino effects traced with such erudition and comprehensiveness by Naomi Klein in *The Shock Doctrine.*[26] Her sequential and richly documented tale begins with the U.S.-engineered overthrow of Salvador Allende on 9/11/1973 and refuses to relinquish its testimony until it has pursued a filigree strand of structurally parallel destabilizations, in succession, in Argentina, Bolivia, Brazil, Poland, China, South Africa, Indonesia, Malaysia, South Korea, Israel, and, most tellingly, on two separate grim occasions, Iraq. In unpredictably suggestive ways, the linguistico-critical philosopher of his age meets up with the current journalist of record tracking the socioeconomic fallout of the global late-capitalist configuration. I leave the surprising solidarity cemented by this encounter to another writerly occasion.[27]

The twin towers of *Glas* delimit the zone or *khōra* of the aporetic reversals or pirouettes defining the impossibility of the enduring Western core institutions and the traditions that they perpetuate. Such institutions include the ceremonies, rituals, and prohibitions emanating from the three Abrahamic faiths, the celebration and reinforcement of monogamy, altruism, hospitality, the sanctity of life (calibrated in a highly specific way), and scripture as "good writing," all as instances of Western core values claiming their legitimacy in canonical texts. More in a tone of playful embroidery than of belabored debunking, Derrida underscores the deep impossibility attending the institutions and sanctioned artifacts that lend the Western life-system its actual conditions and coherence.

Derrida elsewhere improvised on the format, scale, sequence, and graphic design of books and the book medium. Notable among these experiments are his globe-trotting epistolary love novel, *The Post Card: From Socrates to Freud and Beyond,*[28] also encompassing an investigation, above all, of simulation, intertextuality, archiving, and supplementarity as they vacillate between Platonic idealism and Freudian psychoanalysis. And then there is *Counterpaths: Traveling with Jacques Derrida,*[29] a second travel book, based on the pivotal journeys of Derrida's education and the remarkable sequence of interventions, on a worldwide level, that he made: the benchmark intellectual programs, wherever he traveled, at which his thinking, his bearing as a philosopher and critic, and his readouts of the moment were featured. If *The Post Card* pivots around Eros in a full range of complexities and gradations, *Counterpaths* finds flair and fascination in the give and take of friendship and collegiality. The latter volume, in its mélange of photographs and varied texts, including Catherine Malabou's running commentary and display of key Derridean citations, peers ahead into the multimedia future of the book. There is a particular resonance between *Counterpaths* and some of W. G. Sebald's most memorable hybrid fictions, works including *The Emigrants, Austerlitz,* and *Vertigo,*[30] themselves taking the itinerant trajectory of cultural reminiscence and image gathering as their starting point.

Yet it is in the virtual space of *Glas* that Derrida achieves a truly rigorous interface and follow-through linking his obverse philosophical tact or bearing, immanent tropes of thinking and figuration he was never to abandon, and the architecture and design of the book medium. *Glas* is the zone of this exceptionally fecund moment and endeavor of cultural reprogramming; a foyer where, through simultaneous innovation sustained on several multiple registers, discourse, the project named "deconstruction," encounters and embraces its full range and its own impossibility.

SEVEN

Systems, Games, and the Player: Did We Manage to Become Human?

For Richard Macksey

Systems are under siege—in their tangible capacities, their delivery, their resilience, and their conception. We find ourselves at a sociocultural juncture when reading the daily newspaper has become an ordeal. The panoply of the liberatory functions, institutions, and settings in the infrastructure of culture is in a disabling state of social marginalization, its credibility and credence seriously overdrawn. A global condition of religious hyperthyroidism is merely the symptom of a general withdrawal from freedoms of an intellectual, secular, communicative, and psychosexual dimension, constituting a stopgap solution to our world's proliferating and competing complexities (in such domains as demography, ecology, and the sustainability of the biosphere and human communities). Systems that we have delimited and deconstructed for generations, whether relatively "purer" ones, delineated by Kant and Hegel, or their more "dedicated" counterparts, configured by Marx and Freud, continue to furnish an edifying domain for thinking and writing. This is in large measure owing both to the exhilarating breadth and outreach that such constructions encompass and to the intricate intellectual organization that they entail. It is nothing less than thrilling to encounter the world through the mediation of an organizational viewfinder programmed in different ways by the above-mentioned and other systems thinkers, one simultaneously encompassing and coordinating architectural, logical, conceptual, rhetorical, structural, semantic, and subsemantic levels and elements. In the present critical and integrative exercise, we have not so much a stake in systems per se as in the correction, reprogramming, and creative dismantling and redirection that can transpire under their aegis.

Play may well emerge as one of the most productive rubrics under which to group the possibilities and strategies for assessing the give, resistance, or openness conditioning the overarchingness or inevitability that often seems to characterize systematization. It is around the notion of play that certain transvaluations in the environmental impact of systematic administration or governance occur. As Benjamin pointed out, in "On Some Motifs in Baudelaire," the one-armed bandit at the gambling casino marks the spot at which the automatic work gestures of the factory assembly line are metamorphosed into playful, and probably expensive, phantasmagoric battle against economic fate and fortune. Most games structured enough to be recognized as such are fitted out with rules, patterned interactions, and interconnected repercussions, which endow them with indispensable systemic parameters. We might say of the game, then, that it is a system tilted in a direction that affords its players the illusion of control, allowing them—to a certain degree, and the specific context of this degree is debatable—to participate in the programming and output of the system.

So play, or gaming, seemingly a frill or luxury commodity, turns out to be a core concept related to whatever freedom prevails in any number of interconnected domains: our personal liberty and a matrix of legal, professional, and administrative systems, all cybernetically implemented, that grow toward one another, as we hold on for dear life to our two or three e-addresses, our implanted identities and fixed points in an electronically wired Cartesian universe. But play may also go far in helping us conceptualize the options we exercise as critical, theoretically informed participants in the ebb and flow of information and the output of cultural artifacts. We attain our own critically nuanced perch in this vast output only by playing out our options as cultural programmers. The critical disciplines remain indispensable to an electronically wired universe of discourse and cultural memory.

We lose this always tenuous critical edge or foothold amid a sublime proliferation of output and additional controls the moment we abandon our marginal positionality as players. A hard edge attends this critical monitoring of social, judicial, industrial, technological systems that is tantamount to the exercise of our personal liberty and discretion, defining our interface with various communities or packs of cultural reception. The notion of "hard play" that I am proposing here, then, attests to the resolute and persistent dimension of what might be otherwise viewed as frivolous, nonessential, or nonproductive activity, whether the programming of uncanny artifacts (what could be, from certain perspectives, more useless than a poem?) or the undirected consumption of the cultural artifacts and adaptations emerging in the sweep of time. A notion of disciplines and sanctioned play may also go far in helping reclaim, from longstanding traditions of humanism grounded in metaphysical complexes that have undergone daunting challenges, the most vibrant possibilities for the humanity yet remaining.

Computers Without Hardware: Encore Those Rascals Kant and Hegel

The first step that I propose in assessing the range and possibilities for hard play accompanying the increased incursion of systematized knowledge and experience in everyday life is to establish that hardware is not critical to all types of systems. A system may well have an architecture, input, output, storage, and feedback, the last, if it is so fortunate, being "open-ended," in the terms of Wiener, Bateson, Wilden, and others. I would argue that, by the outset of the nineteenth century, Kant and Hegel had bequeathed to Western culture two complementary computers without hardware for aligning specifically human cognitive-psychological engines and databases. Both Kant's *Critique of Pure Reason* and Hegel's *Phenomenology of Spirit* arrange the circuitry linking the various processing engines—sensation, perception, understanding, and reason—by means of an elaborate hierarchy of cables and other shifters or interfaces, among them representations, concepts, rules, laws, principles, categories, and schemas. Even as they incorporate more or less the same components into their systems or thought machines, by varying the wiring and through matters of discourse design and stylistics, Kant and Hegel, via the systems that they configure, emerge with radically different pictures of the environment in which processing, thinking, and the programming of social institutions transpire.

Kant bequeaths us a statelier and more meticulously coordinated blueprint and model of the perspectival interplay making possible such processes as the division of labor between understanding and reason, and such artifacts as the hierarchy between local courts and supreme courts. Kant devotes as much of his penetrating attention and meticulous phrasing to the interplay of wiring and connectors, the exact nature of representational rules, laws, and principles, as he does to the various processors performing intellectual work. We might say that he overinvests in essential differences between such connectors as representations and concepts, where we would today tend to focus on their shared figurative and rhetorical features as components of language. But a very specific kind of output will ensue from this judiciously coordinated and always perspectivally acute configuration, in an extended steady state, of the elements and processes responsible for human cognition and cultural production, one markedly distinct from its Hegelian counterpart. Motion and an endless progression of different shapes, forms, and guiding notions and principles furnish a Hegelian system just as interested in the interplay of human facilities as Kant's with its distinctive keynotes. In Hegel's computer architecture, the major processors—still perception, understanding, reason, and so on—are theologically sanctioned under the oversight of Spirit, to which have been appended historical moments of cultural programming, such as stoicism and skepticism, natural and revealed religion. The Hegelian system has been wired in series, not in the Kantian simultaneous and parallel. The crux for Hegel is the invariable contradiction into which careful deliberation falls at every stage of its accomplishment and delusion, together with a battery of gestures by which these impasses are resolved. The bulk of Hegel's philosophical exposition is devoted to tracing play by play, in a constructed present, thinking's obstacles, double binds, and contrived solutions. Human consciousness or sensibility is always somewhat new in every distinct moment, and is then dedicated to a new set of intellectual problems under the aegis of an evolved guiding principle or epistemological framework.

We can say of Kant and Hegel's hardware-free systems that each predicated a different set of thought problems and experiments, and each furnished a conceptual underpinning to a different set of artifacts. We feel Kant's influence lurking behind the canvases of Friedrich, Turner, Courbet, and many others in which the possibility of the intelligible resides at the horizon—it may well be placed between the empirical domain of conventional striving and the superordinate register of the operating system of the universe, which interpenetrates, infuses, mystifies, or haunts our world. This structuring horizon in the particular extended art game to which I refer may be explicit or effaced; it may be scored across the canvas or invisible. Enormous epistemological consequences ensue from this marking or its whiteout. We are in the world of Kant when, in *Frankenstein*, Victor appropriates from the transcendental the secret of life and harnesses it with the intuitive speed of electricity (a key metaphor for Hegel, as well, in his scenario for human understanding). It is in a Kantian whaleboat that we find ourselves when Ahab pursues a living manifestation of the absolute, the white whale, purified of tint and other distracting particularities. We are more in the land of Hegel in comprehensive novels of education, which may show their heroes' fallings out and reconciliations with friends, family, and colleagues; we reside there in the relentlessly conflictual climate surrounding evolution in all its theaters, from Darwin to Spencer. Under the sway of these complementary operating systems of intellectual processing and cultural aspiration, vast amounts of nineteenth- and twentieth-century conceptual speculation and programming somehow managed to get done.

I revert to these truisms of intellectual history to underscore that systems not only conform to an architecture, involve a coordination between software and hardware even when these are not literally in play, and achieve various degrees of openness, closure, and autopoiesis; they leave a fingerprint; they are invested with a style; they imply a more or less cohesive aesthetic. At least as much of our intimate rapport with the systems with which we traffic inheres in these aesthetic and stylistic intangibles as in formal features or specifications. The representations in which each system is couched derive from a specific moment of expression and from a horizon of rhetorical possibility. The true way to a system's processing is through its incidental poetry. As programmed linguistic artifacts, whether by design or not, systems emit the whirring and noise that is the pretext for their own give and play.

The preeminent systems makers invariably take the precaution of explicitly indicating the play at play in their systems. Kant is a case in point. Be assured that this full disclosure of systematic play does not in the least inhibit the give and opportunities for perversity that others extract from the self-same systems. The example I would broach occurs when in the *Critique of Pure Reason*, after having comprehensively aligned the faculties of cognition by means of their interconnective shifters, Kant raises the specter of transcendental illusion as the distortion effect that such reasonable and philosophically informed thinking invariably produces. Logical illusion, which Kant defines as "the illusion of fallacious inference," disappears the moment such incongruities are pointed out. Transcendental illusions, by contrast, are distortion effects introduced through the momentum of reason's internal logic and hard wiring. They are at once unavoidable and unimpeachable indications of reason's success. To circumvent them would amount to sacrificing reason's many indispensable contributions to the human landscape, such as the synthesis of principles and the capacity for a critical regulation of science and law. Transcendental illusion comes about through the imputation of "objective necessity" to the "subjective necessity of a certain connection of our concepts on behalf of the understanding."[1] In its own principled operation, reason applies conceptual work performed successfully by the processing of understanding to fundamental questions regarding the universe and emerges with such postulations as "The world must have a beginning in time." Even if Kant stops short of validating and legitimizing this postulation, the philosophical wonder and ingenuity that produced it and its correlatives must number among the human tendencies he finds most endearing. Yet the derivation of such ponderous inferences brings reason to an impasse. Its very success and compelling force create an exigency for its critical connection and redirection. Kant calls this capacity for adjustment at the far reaches of speculative capacity "transcendental criticism."[2] What it corrects is "an illusion that cannot be avoided at all, just as little as we can avoid it that the sea appears higher in the middle than at its shores, since we see the former through the higher rays of light than the latter, or even better, just as little as the astronomer can predict the rising moon from appearing larger to him, even when he is not deceived by this illusion."[3] The transcendental illusion issues forth directly in the wake of Kant's successful configuration of the blueprint and assembly of the cognitive processes that link up the wiring, concepts, rules, principles, laws, and so forth.

In its blindness to the subjectivity and ultimately human provenance of its principles, reason not only errs into delusion, it introduces a disruption, a gap, a parallax, into its own blueprint and canon:

> Hence there is a natural and unavoidable dialectic of pure reason, not one in which a bungler might be entangled through lack of acquaintance, or one that some sophist has artfully invented in order to confuse rational people, but one that irremediably attaches to human reason, so that even after we have exposed the mirage, it will still not cease to lead our reason on with false hopes.[4]

Eternal vigilance is the price of untracked reason. Through its very mastery over a processing of sensation and perception, pure reason initiates a constitutional crisis of its own. It can pose questions regarding the nature and origin of the universe, the constitution and unfolding of time, with no reasonable solution. It can trump itself. It confronts its human source only with conundrums in the form of self-countering or neutralizing antinomies. The very brilliance of pure reason—in the *Critique of Judgment* Kant reformulates this as original genius—creates an irresolvable intellectual crisis. It is no exaggeration to say, therefore, that philosophy takes on a second, more dangerous mission (or is it an adventure game?) on the far side of the transcendental illusion. Philosophy becomes responsible for itself, its errors as well as its achievements. It assumes critical responsibility. This is a function not limited to correcting certain misprisions on the part of Plato, Descartes, and Leibniz. This is a self-generating, autopoietic moral imperative at the level of philosophical oversight. The emission of the transcendental illusion's uncanny light thus marks the divergence at which it folds and reverses upon itself, doubling its trajectory, doubling the wager staked on the successful culmination of reason's adventure.[5]

The uncanny gap or point of *all* return that Kant programs into his system also marks the swing or hinge of its give and play. It arises, in the architecture of pure reason, at a point analogous to where the sublime, gendered male, interrupts and dwarfs the play of beauty in the *Critique of Judgment*. It is in the quest of two deductions or proofs that Kant launches the aesthetic recalibration of reason's systems and schemes: a demonstration that communal accord regarding beauty, manifest as "judgments of taste" constitutes a limited and popular application of the synthetic a priori knowledge also responsible for scientific discoveries and paradigmatic symphonies and an appeal to the sublime as the cognitively hard-wired predilection for awe and unrelenting, multidimensional, multiperspectival complexity at the core of such cultural phenomena as monumental art and subjugation to God. The sublime turning point at which reason, in order to be self-regulating and self-programming, has to redo its exhaustive and creative labor is also the parameter at which the considerable possibility for play enters the Kantian system: where the unflinching quest after and service to the transcendental furnishes a master plot to Mary Shelley and to countless monster movies afterwards, at which Lacan, in the spirit of R. Crumb's perverse appropriation of stock Disney characters, configures "Kant avec Sade."

Systematic Chaos or Playful Systems?

It is no accident, as we can already intuit, that a vast, variegated, and growing literature of systematic processes and parameters has accumulated in and around the sciences. The variegated and polychromatic environments in which systemic speculations play endow this body of work with all the richness of a literature. In a relatively short space, we move from Wiener's enlargements upon cybernetics, informed by electrical engineering; to Bateson's deliciously variegated *Steps to an Ecology of Mind*, enlivened by other than stock Western—other in the most advanced senses of the term—models of apprehending and processing the world, a trajectory in constant need of renewal; to the often elegant physical literature, whether in the hands of Werner Heisenberg, Ilya Progogine, or Albert Einstein, regarding a universe configured by relativity, undecidability, complementarities, or complexity; to the singular cabal of scientists, designers, and artists who convened at the Macy Conferences in Cybernetics of 1946 to 1953 and who found employment at such sites as the Bell Labs and IBM.[6] Somehow, given the potentials and exigencies of the postwar moment, a cadre of thinkers and producers, including Weiner, Bateson, Margaret Mead, John von Neumann, Siegfried Giedion, Gyorgy Kepes, Roman Jakobson, Benoit Mandelbrot, and sociologist Paul Lazarsfeld was able not only to divert the dominant questions, aims, and thrusts of science and to rewire the instrumentation and storage of information and communications but also to devise its prevailing aesthetics.

At first glance, the inventive, open-minded literatures of systems, chaos, and games—in their grappling with complexity, undecidability, and strange attractors—offer badly needed confirmation to the discourse of contemporary critical theory, which sets out from the open-ended field of linguistic accidents and contingencies as the deep structure underlying all discursive investigations. But constructs such as chaos or systems themselves are embedded so deeply in the environments of ongoing metaphysical speculation that they almost immediately occasion the mutually neutralizing antinomian postulates characteristic, according to Kant, of all incursions of the transcendental. Of systems in general we can ask, as the transcendental critique asks of the world, "Do they have a beginning in time or in space; are they also enclosed in boundaries?" and we contend immediately with the response that systems have no beginning and bounds; they are temporospatially bounded. Indeed, the same indirect visual access or possibility of visualization, mitigated by mutually complementary global possibilities, is true of chaos. Indeed, the literature of chaos leaves us with only complementary images, or perhaps better afterimages, for negotiating the wider claims of systems: scope, interconnectedness, operating under infrastructures if not laws, and so forth. It may well be the ongoing Kantian split viewfinder for registering the noumenal domain that inspires Niklas Luhmann to characterize the instability constantly besetting social systems in terms of the double contingencies invariably involved in environmental relations and internal selection.

We struggle from work to work in the literature of systems, chaos, and games, and often within the parameters of the same work, vacillating between the fields of a chaos opened unilaterally and unconditionally, and a chaos invoked so that it may then be brought under some acceptable administration. The systolic-diastolic rhythm of chaos as well as systems is always already embedded in the play between the openness and closure of systems and their environments. Scientists, as in the accounts of James Gleick and Fritjof Capra, are frustrated and intrigued by the turbulence, the abrupt changes in patterns, and the withdrawal or radical redrawing of boundaries that they encounter. In keeping with the cat-and-mouse game playing itself out on the deceptive transcendental horizon of a prototypical Kantian system, the scientists are not always sure to luxuriate in the seeming contingency at play or to muzzle or quarantine it. This *fort-da* relation to chaos itself enters the picture when Gleick recreates Edward Lorenz's wonder at discerning certain patterns in the otherwise remorseless work of tracking meteorological change:

> Instead, the map displayed a kind of infinite complexity. It always stayed within certain bounds, never running off the page but never repeating itself, either. It traced a strange distinctive shape, a kind of double spiral in three directions, like a butterfly with its two wings. The shape signaled pure disorder, since no point or patterns of points ever recurred. Yet it also signaled a new kind of order.[7]

Gleick's description of data assuming the form of butterfly patterns in Lorenz's research hovers over a Mallarméan figure, the beat of a butterfly's wing between order and disorder. Almost to a person, the scientists whose strange encounters with chaos Gleick retraces find a heightened pleasure in turbulence, whether describing the swirls made by coffee cream or the fluctuations recorded in the cotton market over a millennium, whose patterns can only be described as aesthetic. At the same time, the effort to synthesize the master pattern or, in literary terms, the meta-trope, into which the daunting complexity or seemingly irreducible irregularity falls is never over. Both fractals, which inscribe turbulent patters of irregularity at widely divergent scales of activity and detail, and strange attractors, which trace the traffic patterns of complexity into intricate, asymmetrical figures determined as much by avoidance as by attraction, reign in chaos while celebrating its ever-nuanced expression.

The scientists of chaos found themselves irresistibly drawn to those moments when, through no discernible cue or trigger, a highly structured and regular pattern, say the "doughnuts" formed by water swirling in an experimental cylinder, lost their shape and went haywire. The natural habitat of turbulence is the space of phase transition, where matter radically alters its states. Mathematical physicist David Ruelle seeks out the "patterns and details" observed in liquids as their phase transitions enter chaotic turbulence.[8] In the midst of this radical transformation emerge "strange attractors," radical infrastructures or tropes of transition both signaling and structuring, in a loose and contingent way, the outcome. Reconstructing Ruelle's thought processes, Gleick formulates the scientist's suspicions vis-à-vis liquid turbulence:

> The visible patterns in turbulent flow—self-entangled stream lines, spiral vortices, whorls that rise before the eye and vanish again—must reflect patterns explained by laws not yet discovered. In his [Ruelle's] mind, the dissipation of

204 Systems, Games, and the Player

energy in a turbulent flow must still lead to a kind of contraction of the phase space, a pull toward an attractor. Certainly the attractor would not be a fixed point, because the flow would never come to rest. Energy was pouring into the system as well as draining out. What other kind of attractor could it be? According to dogma, only one other kind existed, a periodic attractor, or limit cycle—an orbit that attracted all nearby orbits. . . . For some initial conditions—those with the lowest energy—the pendulum will still settle to a stop, so the system actually has two attractors, one a closed loop and the other a fixed point. Each attractor has its "basin," just as two nearby rivers have their own watershed regions.[9]

The strange attractor is a constantly moving point of orientation—a contradiction in terms—in a system whose volatility is defined by its irregular eruptions of phase transition: "A system whose variables change continuously up or down becomes a moving point, like a fly moving around a room."[10] Even tracing the variables of turbulence that move in closed loops, derivable patterns, the strange attractor works in cahoots with a co-conspirator. This second attractor is both a partner in turbulence and a point of orientation for the first. The experience of the system is thus on a par with the double contingency stipulated by Luhmann for relationships in closed systems.[11] In both of its complementary phases, the strange attractor is invested with all the variability requisite to the transformations in phase space that it describes. Yet it is in the service of scientific law that Ruelle and his fellow chaos scientists derive this metatrope of unbridled physical instability and christen it.

Gleick's recapitulations of intricate scientific inferences and reasonings are intensely poetic throughout. He courageously traces how the rise in computer power over the phase of chaos theory that he covers coincided with scientists' ability to model and image constructs of which they had not been aware. In this account, the computer is elevated from the status of a wayward toaster to that of a cybernetic partner and not so secret sharer in the process of imaging itself. And if there is any sector of scientists' processing and inventiveness that Gleick highlights as he recreates their whale hunt for chaos, it is their uncanny knack for a certain kind of imaging, an intuitive gift affording them an esteemed place in the seating arrangements for the Kantian system.

It is precisely Benoit Mandelbrot's gift for visualization that gained him admission to the École Normale Supérieure and École Polytechnique with no formal mathematical training:

Given an analytical problem, he could almost always think of it in terms of some shape in his mind. Given a shape, he could find ways of transforming it, altering its symmetries, making it more harmonious. Often his transformations led directly to the solution of the analogous problem. In physics and chemistry, where he could not apply geometry, he got poor grades. But in mathematics, questions he could never have answered using proper techniques melted away in the face of his manipulation of shapes.[12]

It would indeed demand a special facility with shapes to discern the patterning common to widely disparate phenomena—the price of cotton, the formation of clouds, and the capillary flow of liquids, themselves thrown out of whack by abrupt turbulences. Yet it was this "intuition from scratch"[13] that facilitated Mandelbrot's synthesis of fractals. The scientists who first discerned the need for strange attractors as templates of chaos and then hunted down their configurations were also distinguished by their mental ability to perform complex manipulations of space. The name of Otto Rössler, a German nonpracticing M.D.,

who came to chaos by way of chemistry and theoretical biology . . . became attached to a particularly simple attractor in the shape of a band of ribbon with a fold in it, much studied because it was easy to draw, but he also visualized attractors in higher dimensions—"a sausage in a sausage in a sausage in a sausage," he would say, "take it out, fold it, squeeze it, put it back." Indeed the folding and squeezing of space was a key to constructing strange attractors, and perhaps a key to the dynamics of the real systems that gave rise to them."[14]

The key, according to Michel Hénon, working on attractors of greater complexity out of Nice Observatory, "was the repeated stretching and folding of phase space in the manner of a pastry chef who rolls the dough, folds it, rolls it out again, creating a structure that will eventually be a sheaf of thin layers."[15] Gleick here invokes a genius no less than French pastry in the imaging of breathtaking breakthroughs on the fronts of theoretical physics and mathematics. And from Gleick's detailed recapitulation of several parallel projects of complex inference that proceeded through visualization emerges a powerful picture of what constitutes Kantian synthetic a priori knowledge under contemporary paradigms of science.

Kant took elaborate pains to characterize artistic creativity as the most precious human intuitive facility, in itself proof of the human basis of scientific knowledge, and theological/cosmological speculation as a human achievement brought about through uncanny access by a gifted few to the transcendental operating system of the universe, consisting of time, space, and the proportions of geometry and harmony. Human beings who have been touched in a certain way so as to allow them access to these heavenly numbers are few and far between, according to Kant's speculations, but they have left a decisive and disproportionate imprint on the fields of scientific inquiry and artistic invention. Captain Ahab's lightening-bolt striations may be taken as a literary emblem of a visitation by or exposure to synthetic a priori knowledge. *Moby-Dick* is not only structured by an architecture in which monomaniacal vision or physical epiphenomena such as St. Elmo's fire emanate from a remote pinnacle. It is coded by a hegemonic ideology with racist as well as nationalistic parameters. In this sense, the quest for the white whale is the effort both to bring an untamed force of nature under control and to participate in the speculative purification, the sublime movement upward to higher faculties always in their purely intellectual state, that serves the Kantian *Critiques* as both process and aim. Kant characterizes the synthetic a priori knowledge made accessible by genial attunement and the systematic purification or upgrading of the faculties as follows: "For if one removes from our experiences everything that belongs to the senses, there still remain certain original concepts and the judgments generated from them, which must have risen entirely *a priori*, independently of experience, because they make one able to say more about the objects that appear to the senses than mere experience would teach."[16]

Many Kantian accounts of the intuitive speculative breaks in the gravitational pull exerted by sensation and concepts pivot around processes of elimination: subtraction; purification through distillation or precipitation. In this sense, a chemical apparatus of filtration is implied throughout Kantian reasoning. As Gleick's chaos hunters set about synthesizing the arbitrary trajectories of turbulence and other perturbations, they give testimony to a more vivid scenario of intuitive grasp than Kant. The performance involved in the derivation of complex physico-mathematical infrastructures is, as suggested above, one of picturing. That visualization of chaos, and of the movement through chaos to processes of scientific and conceptual reasoning, fulfills Hegel's mandate, in the wake of Kant, that "Science dare organize itself only by the life of the notion"[17]—the famous Hegelian *Begriff*— "itself." Mandelbrot illuminates modern science with the most vibrant possible flash of its Kantian heritage when he recounts:

When I came into this game there was a total absence of intuition. One had to create an intuition from scratch. Intuition as it was trained by the usual tools—the hand, the pencil, and the ruler—found these shapes quite monstrous and pathological. The old intuition was misleading. The first pictures were to me quite a surprise: then I would recognize some pictures from previous pictures, and so on.

Intuition is not something that is given. I've trained my intuition to accept as obvious shapes which were initially rejected as absurd, and I find everyone else can do the same.[18]

A Kantian intuition that is a priori and arbitrary still undergirds science's most striking and productive discoveries. But it twists the contours of the time-space continuum with the flexibility of pretzel dough.[19]

Luhmann, in his scenarios of systemic complexity and selection, traces out the open-ended communication loop between a system and its environment. The system is related to its environment by its difference from it. Ongoing system/environment communications are dedicated to negotiating this difference. "They [systems] constitute and maintain themselves by creating and maintaining a difference from their environment."[20] "The environment . . . is delimited by open horizons, not by boundaries that can be crossed; thus it is not itself a system. It is different for every system, because every system excludes only itself from the environment."[21] The environment thus plays the occasional, relative, and dispensable sidekick to the system's arbitrariness and specificity. The environment maintains a relation of complementary self-effacement and yielding to the system's symmetrical self-assertion and competitiveness. (Symmetry and complementarity are key modalities of social interaction and organization that Gregory Bateson observed and elaborated early on in his anthropological studies. We will have occasion to remark in detail their significance and implications in Chapter 9 below.) What is irreducible about the rapport between system and environment in Luhmann's work is the incessant communication and feedback by which the two are essentially linked.

The system is thus constituted, its rapport to the greater world is determined, by a rich tapestry of foreground/background shifts and displacements. The relation between elements, say, individuals or social groups, within the system proper is one of double contingency. Luhmann's account of this state of affairs draws heavily on the pivotal Hegelian notion and trope of reciprocity, updating the dialectical condition of pure undecidability through mirroring by disfiguring it.[22] By allowing the figure of undecidable reciprocity to define the rapport between entities encompassed by the same system, each one negotiating the complexity of multiple interpenetrating roles, Luhmann carries forward the ambiguity as to whether the ultimate downbeat will fall on a system's openness or its exclusionary features. A good measure of the logical force of Luhmann's formulations inheres in his susceptibility to the poetry of philosophical terms. His recalibration of contemporary systems theory in terms of its complexity, adaptation, self-reference, and autopoiesis is indicative of an ongoing attentiveness to the discourses of contemporary science, critical theory, and sociology. Luhmann is capable both of entertaining a certain jouissance entering systems in the vividness of the terms out of which they are built and pursuing the functions of selection and boundary setting that may well constitute the most material work executed by systems. A significant share of this atmospheric byplay inheres in and around the process of selection:

> To combine the problem of complexity and systems theory, as we propose here, requires a renewed treatment of the concept of complexity. In what sense can one speak of difference in complexity, difference in degree of complexity, and reduction of complexity if complexity is defined as the necessity of making selections? The literature focuses on the difficulties of measurement produced by an obviously multidimensional concept. Our problem, however, concerns the more basic question of how to relate the in itself complexly constructed concept of complexity to systems.
>
> Measurement and comparison can start with the number of elements or with the number of relations in effect among them. One can always speak of greater or lesser complexity (difference in complexity, difference in degree of complexity) if lesser complexity exists in both respects. This is so for the relationship between a system and its environment. In a narrower sense, one should speak of a reduction in complexity if the framework of relations forming a complex nexus is reconstructed by a second nexus having fewer relations. Only complexity can reduce complexity.[23]

I quote at length here, having selected a citation at once exemplary of Luhmann's systems thinking and indicative of a high concentration of its distinctive elements. Systems, in Luhmann's parlance, deal in and with complexity: they process complexity. They do so in large measure by means of selection, a mode of reduction, subtraction,[24] elimination—in practical terms, filtration. The process of selection is key, for example, to establishing the interchange between systems and their environments introduced in the above passage. "Greater complexity within systems is possible because the environment does not manifest random distribution but is structured selectively by systems in the environment."[25] Key here is the selective function that systems exercise on themselves and in relation to the environment. One of Luhmann's great contributions is to gauge systematic achievement and value within an environmental (or climatic) horizon. The interchange between system and environment—not unlike, in criticism, that between texts and contexts—is decisive not only for the orientation of systems but for the possibilities of exchange and interaction between systemic elements, such as individuals or social groups. From their broader environments, systems gain their orientation "not just occasionally and adaptively, but structurally, and they cannot exist without an environment. They constitute and maintain themselves by creating and maintaining a difference from their environment."[26]

Systems' debts to their surrounding environments are therefore considerable. Indeed, the very articulation of systems depends on the reference and self-reference emerging from differences from their environments situated at their boundaries. "Delimited by open horizons, not by boundaries that can be crossed," the environment "is not itself a system. It is different for every system."[27] Lacking, therefore, the "self-reflection or capacity to act . . . the environment receives" in this strategic interchange, "its unity through the system and only in relation to the system."[28]

The relationship between a system and its environment is therefore specific, yet it evolves in a climatic or meteorological sense, one therefore susceptible to the sort of turbulence that was tracked with such gusto and persistence by Edward Lorenz. Yet within systems prevails a set of selections whose designed purpose is to restrict and reduce complexity. This systematic orientation to complexity is evident even in the definition of this state of affairs that Luhmann supplies: "we will call an interconnected collection of elements 'complex' when, because of immanent constraints in the elements' connective capacity, it is no longer possible at any moment to connect every element with every other element. The concept of 'immanent constraint' refers to the internal complexity of the elements, which is not at the system's disposal, yet which makes possible their 'capacity for unity.' "[29]

Even as a faint boundary, the point of departure between Luhmann's environmental, interactive, and reciprocally dynamic systemic update and the thrust of theoretically motivated philosophy and literary exegesis can be discerned here. In terms of Luhmann's wider project, a derivation of current conditions of exasperating social overdetermination and congenital failures to interconnect through the status of complexity and other filtration functions, the inability "to connect every element with every other element" of a system is a source of intrigue, if not frustration, whereas the most memorable critical close readings, the ones in which the unpredictable accidents in a targeted text or bounded aggregate of signifiers both disclose and derange the operation of the systems in their environment, relentlessly pursue the impossible task of interconnecting every textual element, precisely in the face of this pronounced impossibility. The task of criticism, at least as it has been inflected by the performance of close reading at its best, then, is a systemic deviance in a Luhmannian world of systems nonetheless articulating the stakes, gives and takes, and Kantian impasses at play in a contemporary environment of precipitous hyper-systematization.

Communication and the derivation of meaning are key not only to the architecture of Luhmannian systems but to the dynamics of their immanent relations and their exchange with the environment. Indeed, for Luhmann, social systems are precisely these processes. Even given Kant's careful specifications regarding representations, concepts, rules, and so forth—that is, the interconnective wiring between the faculties—and even given Hegel's recurrent reminders, always emerging with the force of irony, with respect to the linguistic materiality of his speculations,[30] language is more persistently immanent to Luhmann's updated systems than to the German idealist "computers without hardware." Luhmann devotes minute attention to the manner in which persons, which he defines as "psychic systems that are observed by other psychic systems or by social systems" decode messages and infer situational parameters from one another. These interactions are invariably shrouded in blinds of what he calls, building upon foundational work by Talcott Parsons and Edward Shils, in their *Toward a General Theory of Action*,[31] "double contingency," the unreliable work of agents assessing their prospects on the basis of fellow agents traversing shared social contexts who are as clueless as they are. The problem, as Parsons and Shils formulate it and as it inflects Luhmann's subsequent understandings of systems, is that: "Not only, as for isolated behaving units, animal or human, is goal

outcome contingent on successful cognition and manipulation of environmental objects by the actors, but since the most important objects involved
in interaction act too, it is also contingent on their interaction for intervention in the course of events."[32] Based on Parsons and Shils's acute sense of
the partial blindness and psychological projection involved in most sociological events, Luhmann, in his systematic parameters for double contingency, elaborates a proto-sociological dynamic of unlimited and paralyzing
mirroring or reciprocity.

This is a state of mutual recognition by two hypothetical agents poised
in oppressive parity that triggers, within the longstanding draft as well as
drift of the Hegelian mastery/servitude parable,[33] an intriguing feedback
process with the other if not a definitive trial by death henceforth serving
as the rationale for social difference. Consequently, the orientation of social
systems is, for Luhmann, in spite of his timely attentiveness to the feedback
loops of communications and the autopoiesis and self-release of systems,
toward the reduction of possible outcomes through the processes and mechanisms of selection. The projective fixation on one's alter results, then, for
Luhmann, in a concession of freedom. In his terms:

> Knowing and calculating the behavior of one's partner is replaced (because it is
> unattainable) by a concession of freedom. *This reduction is*—and this is a theoreti-
> cally central hypothesis of higher integrative power—*bound to the experience of
> action* and thereby steered by the concession of freedom. The meaning unit "ac-
> tion" is constituted as a synthesis of reduction and an opening for possibilities of
> selection. Its function is to secure this and reproduce it connectively. This is why
> what happens when black boxes deal with each other appears to them as *action*.
> Action is selection attributed to the system. However it may be rationalized as
> choice among alternatives, represented as decision, or related to motives, initially
> it is nothing more than actualized contingency.[34]

Luhmann justifiedly pursues the reductive trajectory of actions as they are
selected from the panoply of possibilities. Even amid the hovering indeci-
sion of double contingency, the inconsequentiality of "black boxes" passing
in the night, the system is impelled by its momentum toward the concerted
reductionism of action. This is indeed one, but only one direction in which
systems can tend. Thinkers as diverse as Deleuze, Guattari, and Derrida
demonstrate that systems are also the interface to open-ended networks of
signification that proliferate, disseminate, verge toward no specific point or

destination. It is indeed the random dispersions and haphazard coincidences of their constitutive signifiers that make systems, at least in one of their facets, playful.

Why is the selective feature of systematization decisive to Luhmann's reconfigurations? Could this have to do with the social setting and objectives in which he installs systematic efforts and aspirations? Luhmann himself distinguishes "between the social dimension immanent in meaning and the formation of social systems."[35] Does Luhmann's social system willy-nilly eventuate, then, in the scene and performative of decision?

> Every moment of meaning offers a point of mediation for various system/environment references, a possibility for *ad hoc* integration, so to speak. . . . The social dimension of all meaning concerns the entire world, the entire extensiveness of one's own experience, and the estimated experience of others. . . . This world-wideness correspondingly must be reduced to something cared about at the margins. By contrast, social systems are formed only where the actions of different psychic or social systems must be attuned to each other because the selection of one action is the precondition for the other or vice versa. The constitution of the social dimension is a necessary, but not sufficient condition for the constitution of social systems (just as experience is a necessary, but not sufficient condition for action). The social dimension makes visible the possibility for the divergence of system perspectives contained in all meaning. What is jointly interpreted can mean something quite different for each participant. This divergence can then be used to form social systems.[36]

Perhaps, starting out from Parsons's black box theory, Luhmann has nonetheless attended to the feedback loops of Weiner; to the pulsation of closed and open systems registered, in different ways, by Bateson, Wilden, and Gleick; to the interchange between system and environment characterized in different ways by Bateson, Wilden, and Capra, whose historical paradigm may well be the at times contentious interchanges between civilians and barbarians, town and country, or nation-states and empires; to the complexity charted by Prigogine; and to the autopoiesis, "the pattern of organization of living systems,"[37] mapped by Humberto Maturana and Francisco Varela.[38] It is surely Luhmann's placement of systematic organization at the service of a social imperative, akin to the Kantian moral imperative, that orients his systems, in spite of their attentiveness to meaning processes, to the elimination of noise, static, and the tangential possibilities they resonate by means of an at times ominous selection. Darwinian natural selection has given way to contemporary systematic selection. At stake is nothing less than the free and unimpeded flow of meaning, populations, and aspirations in the contemporary world.

"*To a Child Dancing in the Wind*"

Play, then, in a universe marked by the augmented scope, efficiency, virtuality, interconnectivity, and selectivity of systems, is not merely an optional feature, an add-on, but a matter of life and death. One could argue that the playful scrambling of systematic coordinates and mechanisms in such a universe is the possibility of life itself, life not as the biological substrate of (human, animal, and plant) existence but the possibility of the radical improvisation indispensable to reconfiguring local networks (of housing, production, distribution, commerce, social service, etc.) under conditions of global warfare and communication. We are speaking here less of magisterial gestures toward the incorporation of give or indeterminacy into grand systems by their chief engineers and programmers (e.g., Kantian beauty and sublimity; Hegelian reciprocity). Rather, we invoke play, under the sway of the most far-reaching modernists, among them Benjamin, Proust, Stein, and Joyce, as an impulsive blurring between material and ideational linguistic components, an improvisational deployment of the materials at hand, however unaccustomed and arbitrary, in the opening and release of systematic momentums, leaving their outcomes unknown and unpredictable. It is under the aegis of such a notion of play that there can be such intimate solidarity between thinkers of the greatest rigor and erudition—on a par with Benjamin and Derrida—and children.

Child's play, then, is decisive, indispensable, anything but tangential. The current mythical fictive hero of record, Lisbeth Salander of Stieg Larsson's *The Girl with the Dragon Tattoo* series, not only seizes control of her relations in the world around her by dint of her cybernetic omni-capability, her diminutive stature marks her in part as a child hero.[39] The indispensability of play was not lost on the writers and artists who addressed a nascent twentieth century whose material culture, technological advances, media of communications, and networks of mass transportation were entrancing, but whose capabilities for mass warfare, death, and violent suppression were mounting. An instinctive response on the part of those artists and thinkers both blessed and cursed by an intuitive "agenbite of inwit"[40] was to invest a disproportionate share of hope for rescue and redemption from impending destructive forces in the cognitive freshness and inventiveness of children. Only this appeal to childhood, surely with roots in the Romantic moment, can explain the coincidence of the vivid images of children as readers and proto-critics in texts as diverse as Proust's *Swann's Way*, Joyce's *A Portrait of the Artist as a Young Man*, Benjamin's *One-Way Street* and *Berlin Childhood Around 1900*, and Bruno Schulz's *Sanatorium under the Sign of the Hourglass*,[41] to name only a few instances.

The shoulders of children—or rather, of the image of the child—bear a disproportionate share of the accommodation to both the wide sway of systems under advanced modernization and the innovative margins of play. Proust introduces his mega-novel of aesthetic possibility, social mores, and intertwined heterosexual and queer love not only with Swann, a composite figure of social mobility, taste, and romantic despair, but also with the young "Marcel" (the hypothetical name for the novelistic narrator). The backdrop to "Marcel's" adult sensibility is a childhood experience of Combray regularly punctuated by the dissolution of surfaces to reveal depth phenomena and the shocking disclosure of passions (Françoise's sadism, Mlle Vinteuil's lesbian love making) in neighbors to whom they would seem most inimical. "Marcel's" tormented separation from Maman occasioned by Swann's visit and his wait for the resumption of his bedtime reading is far from the only pretext in the recollected summers at Combray preparing him for a lifetime of minute sociological observation and precise cultural commentary.

Joyce's fictive account of a consummate literary artist whose despair regarding Irish domestic ideology and exasperation with its cultural obtuseness bear striking resemblances to his own does not begin with Stephen Dedalus's initial literary or oratorical interventions. At the outset of *A Portrait of the Artist as a Young Man*, rather, Joyce pays exquisite attention to the specific elements of the image-language coinciding with Stephen's earliest memories, among his most persistent and vivid. He resolves the eternal quandary as to whether art and its sensibility set out from ideas or from language decisively in favor of the latter. The artist, even as a toddler, fashions impressions out of resonant phrases and images. Some of these—for example, Dante's paintbrushes—may be linked to horrific occurrences, the familial brawl over Parnell and Irish politics at an early Christmas supper.[42]

Others may be less apologetic in their playfulness, for example, the association his young schoolmate draws between "a thigh" and his own surname, Athy.

Under the aegis of a modernism painfully aware of the incipient systematic outreach and dimensions of communications and social administration, the player-child emerges as a proto-critic (social as well as cultural), whose capacity for play is tantamount to a being not yet jaded, an access to the full panoply of cognitive faculties and sensibilities imputed to early experience. The improvisers of modernism outfit their hypothetical children with exquisite sensibility and critical discrimination before dispatching them out into minefields of Benjaminian shock. The clear implication of this tribute is that advanced technological societies will need to draw on the playful capacities and improvisation of children to correct their own swerves toward totalitarian aggression and control. It is, then, hardly surprising that I would turn to Benjamin for a final glimpse of the momentous task of playful systemic resistance that was invested in (and possibly imposed on) the child of the twentieth century:

> For children are particularly fond of haunting any site where things are being visibly worked on. They are irresistibly drawn by the detritus generated by building, gardening, housework, tailoring, or carpentry. In waste products they recognize the face that the world of things turns directly and solely to them. In doing these things they do not so much imitate the works of adults as bring together, in the artifact produced in play, materials of widely differing kinds in a new, intuitive relationship. [*Sie fühlen sich unwiderstehlich von Abfall angezogen, der beim Bauen, bei Garten- oder Hausarbeit, beim Schneidern oder bei Tischlern entsteht. In Abfallprodukten erkennen sie das Gesicht, daß die Dingwelt gerade ihnen, ihnen allein, zukehrt. In ihnen bilden sie die Werke der Erwachsenen weniger nach, als daß sie Stoffe sehr verschiedener Art durch das, was sie im Spiel daraus verfertigen, in eine neue, sprunghafte Beziehung zueinander setzen.*] Children thus produce their own small world of things within the greater one.[43]

It is crucial to note here that Benjamin's children, distinguished by their uniquely material relation to the things of culture, do not simulate the systemic features of the adult work world but evolve their own practice of composition. Children's work is the product of a "new, intuitive relationship" to things rather than the instrumental one of adulthood. The above passage is riddled with the stunning intuition that remains fresh for children but that development toward adulthood diverts and dissipates. Children "haunt" the worksites where they locate and appropriate their material treasure; the adult pursuits of construction and maintenance exercise an uncanny hold on them. Their image-world achieves a distinctive collusion between the spectral features of knowledge and insight and joyful participation in material culture.

Benjamin pursues with gusto the counter-intuitive marriages of impulses at cross-purposes to one another that childhood arranges. He aligns the search-and-capture missions on which children send their hands with the full satisfactions of adult lust:

> *Pilfering child* [Naschendes Kind].—Through the chink of the scarcely open larder door, his hand advances like a lover through the night. Once at home in the darkness, it gropes toward sugar or almonds, raisons or preserves. And just as the lover embraces his girl before kissing her, the child's hand enjoys a tactile tryst with the comestibles before his mouth savors their sweetness. How flatteringly honey, heaps of currants, even rice yield to his hand! [*Und wie der Liebhaber, ehe er's küßt, sein Mädschen umarmt, so hat der Tatsinn mit ihnen ein Stelldichein, ehe der Mund ihre Süßigkeit kostet.*] . . . His hand, the juvenile Don Juan, has soon invaded all the cells and spaces, leaving behind it running layers and streaming plenty: virginity renewing itself without complaint. [*Der Hand, der jugentlich Don Juan, ist bald in alle Zelle und Gelasse eingedrungen, hinter sich rinnende Schichten und strömende Mengen: Jungfräulichkeit, die ohne Klagen sich erneuert.*][44]

The extended simile between a child's probing hand, in search of unofficial nourishment and (possibly illicit) love, or at least active sexuality under battle conditions, may delight an adult sensibility. But the child has an answer to this benign adult wit: the passage is, after all, articulated from her point of view. Not only do the child's desires impel her toward a mastery of the object world, but the attainment of this mastery results in ecstatic joy. Decisive to this vignette is the fact that the domain of this attainment, its sensory field, is tactile. Children have a special *touch*, in other words, for the materials in their environment, conferring upon them this mastery. Their *feel* for the materials that can best enhance their play, resulting in hybrid solutions to pressing constraints and limitations, is uncanny. Their cultural experience sets out imbued with a unique and special taste, an instinct for what's important, for what has been pervaded with an aura redolent of inexhaustible possibility. It is through their touch that children realize the apprehensions and judgments of their yet-unadulterated taste. In contrast to the virginity whose taking was Don Juan's unrelenting obsession, the unique conjunction of taste and touch spurring children on in their improvisations is a renewable resource. In their haptic play, children are always on the verge of the ecstasy discovered in adult sexuality. Indeed, it is through child's play and its inexhaustible freshness that the paradoxical fantasy of renewable virginity finds its tangible expression.

Benjamin invoked child's play and invention as a hopeful statute of limitations upon the actualization of systematic outreach and coordination happening in his world. The degree to which playfulness was tangibly able to curb these tendencies may constitute yet another instance of history's getting away from Benjamin. Over a long span of his polymorphous writings, he charted a tension between the soaring edifice of systematic aspiration and the surreal, cubist alternatives playfully cobbled together from waste products in the alleys and back lots of the city. He shared this project with the most telling cultural programmers and makers of his moment. Its unresolved enigma remains a heritage and challenge for creative work today.

EIGHT

Atmospherics of Mood

The present flâneur, whose promenades these days are more often on the channels of the Worldwide Web than on the boulevards of the odd constellation of cities that he frequents, whether Buffalo, Baltimore, Berlin, Philadelphia, San Francisco, Los Angeles, London, Chicago, or Paris, poses the following questions to himself, as he sets out on an unusually chaotic route:

Why Walter Benjamin's Arcades Project? *Not only because of its elaborated themes of weather and fashion at the outset of Euro-American modernization but because of the ethics as well as aesthetics of citation that it radically sets into play. The strategies of citation itself, within an overall field of text display and discourse design, surely rank among the most powerful measures within the politics of writing. These critical options are available to every one of us as cultural citizens, and it is incumbent upon us, in the sense of the Derridean notion of responsibility, to explore and deploy them in our expression. Through the new medium of the Arcades, Benjamin addresses, with uncompromising openness, the material dimensions of textual remains. In a practice as well as a spirit of radical democracy, he allows the auratic finds of his feverish digs for telling textual nuggets to speak for themselves, placing the reader in the open-ended and precarious predicament of making sense of his erudite collection.*

Why the fascination with Chinese medicine? Not only as a conceptual and thera-peutic system, but also as embracing certain features of mood and turbulence shared by the dynamics of climate. Also, as a counter-system to certain instances of Western thinking, Kant and Hegel prominent among them, configured around the speech act of judgment. In its analogical and combinatorial configurations, Chinese medi-cine takes the full panoply of physiological and emotional conditions, even extreme ones, to be among the customary happenings of the natural order of things. In this openness, this holding judgment in reserve, the worldview and compendium of diagnoses and interventions embraced by Chinese medicine serve as an instance of what Bateson characterizes as the fluctuation between "strict" and "loose" thinking much in evidence during paradigm shifts and other momentous instances of crystal-lization. As Bateson formulates it in Steps to an Ecology of Mind *and elsewhere, this mindful fluctuation between intuition and theoretical rigor is particularly con-ducive to an ecological intelligence and creativity that are critical at the present juncture.*

Why the obsession with systems? As I hope I intimated in Chapter 7, because in our personal and social lives we have been, since the outset of the broader modernity, beset by an impossible and often conflicting overlay of them and also because, given contemporary technologies, their operating systems, the traces of their fingerprints in our personal lives, are becoming steadily less visible. The normal citizen devotes escalating amounts of time and energy to negotiating systems that are, in their irreducible configuration, arbitrary and intransigent. In this context, as the Schle-gels, Nietzsche, Baudelaire, Mallarmé, Artaud, Benjamin, Blanchot, and Barthes understood only too well, art and critique are indispensable media of noise and resistance introduced into systems whose momentum and efficiency are only too well entrenched. In terms of contemporary systems theory, deconstruction may be ap-preciated as an alliance with turbulence (or a meticulously derived and mobilized linguistic chaos) in checking the multifarious momentums of executive and judg-mental systems.

What assistance does contemporary systems theory hold out in the face of the devastating political, ecological, and cultural or literate disasters currently confront-ing us? It extends an invitation to explore hegemonic forces and apparatuses as a Prevailing Operating System, sometimes seeming occulted or ahead of us (but with which astute contemporary observers, such as Naomi Klein in her The Shock

Doctrine,[1] *occasionally manage to catch up). Also, it challenges us to an informed and unremitting effort to activate the release valves necessary to relieve the overloads and related stressors imposed by exploitative, cumulative modes of investment, urban development, and colonial conquest.*[2]

Weather, Turbulence, Mood

The mere narcotizing effect which cosmic forces have on a shallow and brittle personality is attested in the relation of such a person to one of the most genial manifestations of these forces: the weather. Nothing is more characteristic than that precisely this most intimate and mysterious affair, the working of the weather on humans, should have become the theme of their emptiest chatter. Hence for him, the deepest connection between weather and boredom.[3]

If the present chapter starts out with a commentary on the weather, we know already that it's all downhill from here. According to Benjamin, in this interpellation into Convolute D of *The Arcades Project*, by the time the conversation arrives at the weather, it has sunk to the emptiest chatter. The weather is such a pervasive feature of our ongoing environmental conditions that directly addressing it attains all the creative excitement of expatiating on the current level of our perspiration. Perhaps the most intriguing link posited by Benjamin's sentences is that between weather and boredom, climate and mood. He thereby suggests an analogy between the variability of our emotional landscape, or *Umgebung*, and turbulence, which is one of the best terms not only for the dynamic of climate but also for that of chaos.

The Arcades Project is a vast print-medium website on Paris in the nineteenth century and the modernization that took place there, with particular attention to Parisian innovations in the process. This polymorphic work and instance of the Benjaminian "dissolving book," as has been noted above in Chapter 4, preoccupied him during the last fourteen years of his life and holds more than one surprise in store for us. About 75 percent of the material in the convolutes, its thematically organized sections, consists in citations gathered from extensive reading, mostly in Paris's Bibliothèque nationale, which had increasingly become Benjamin's second address. The extracts comprising the main part of the convolutes are a patchwork of materials: some begin in the late eighteenth century and continue through the Second Empire in Paris; some are more contemporary to Benjamin's collecting sources and commentaries; some are "primary" (literary examples, legal proclamations, prospectuses for real-estate projects); some are "secondary" in the sense of being reportage and other copy generated by "primary" phenomena. As we review the materials he gathered and digested as well as the critique he synthesized, we vicariously experience the immoderation of his extended readerly feeds.

Yet a haphazard climate pervades the perhaps 25 percent of the material that comes to us in Benjamin's own words, what Carol Jacobs dubs "In the Language of Walter Benjamin." We can never tell whether these interjects, emanating a mystery and arbitrariness like a psychoanalyst's verbal punctuations in the therapeutic monologue, are distributed at the beginning or the end of a sequence of topical materials, whether they occur as staccato, singular outbursts or congregate as an interlinked cascade of meta-comments. A dynamic different from the thematic organization of the materials comprising the bulk of the convolutes may apply to the interrupted but never-flagging transcript of Benjamin's sensibility. With respect to Euro-American modernization, some of the thematic organization of the materials in *The Arcades Project* is nothing if not obvious: "Iron Construction" (Convolute F), "The Streets of Paris" (P), "Arcades, *Magazins de nouveautés*, Sales Clerks" (A), "Exhibitions, Advertising, Grandville" (G), "Prostitution, Gambling" (O). As obvious places for a cultural history of modernization à la Parisienne to start, even one whose dialectic between materiality and intellectuality is particularly problematical and rich (more on this below), we don't bat an eyelash over convolutes dedicated to Baudelaire (J) and Hugo (d), or even someone, "The *Flâneur*" (M), more properly an icon or collective extrapolation of urban wandering and shocked consciousness than any historical personage in particular. But our eyes open wide with astonishment when we discover that the very first convolute after Benjamin has introduced us to the Arcades, the new form of economic life that they initiated, and, above all, the new terminologies and street argot that they necessitated is devoted to fashion: fashion as a paradigm for the progression of cultural history as much as a prurient colonization of the female body, which it also is. "Yet fashion is in much steadier, in much more precise contact with the coming thing, thanks to the incomparable nose which the feminine collective has for what lies waiting in the future."[4] "Every fashion is to some extent a bitter satire on love; all sexual perversities are suggested in every fashion by the most ruthless means. . . . Thus, the confrontation

with the fashions of previous generations is a matter of far greater significance than we ordinarily suppose."⁵ It makes us catch our breath even more
sharply when we realize that cultural history and critique, as Benjamin practices them in *The Arcades Project*, will henceforth take into account even the
prevailing climate during a distinctive cultural configuration or constellation. It will read that meteorological climate—just as the history of science
can designate certain pathologies at transitional moments, say tuberculosis
throughout the nineteenth century or AIDS in our own—as the expression
of a mood or a temperament of the cultural climate.

Benjamin's incorporation of a certain splenetic and overcast weather pattern, an overbearing atmosphere, whether encountered in Baudelaire's
urban lyrics or Charles Meryon's allegorical engravings, into a composite
culture-gram also including Paris's catacombs and sewers, the sweeping ca-
thedrals of its newly constructed cast-iron train stations, and its dens of
gambling and the skin trade is a testament to a critical practice allowing no
telling element in the mix to disappear untold from history's time bubble.
If a critic is to touch and taste—critical senses for Benjamin—the telling
draft or wake of a moment, it is incumbent on her to rise, or rather sink, to
the inconsequential, the perverse, the contraband, and the abjectly material.
Critique and cultural history are no longer the exclusive domain of the edifying and the self-aggrandizing.

Critique, in keeping with Benjamin's long-term struggle to make it compatible with attitudes and practices of material history, is no longer the paraphrase, expiation, and distillation of telling concepts from diverse rubrics
and housings in which they have been archived, with no anticipated or fore-
gone outcome. There can be no sublimation, purification, or occultation of
the material from critique. "The materialist presentation of history leads to
bring the present into a critical state."⁶ Indeed, the discursive fragments or
inconsequential historical post-its out of which the convolutes are made are
a discursive substance or humus from which a star picture, *Sternbild*, or
constellated snapshot of an epochal configuration emerges:

> The interest which the materialist historian takes in the past is always, in part, a
> vital interest in it being past—in its having ceased to exist, its being essentially
> dead. To have certified this condition with respect to the whole is the indispens-
> able prerequisite to any citation (any calling to life) of particular parts of this
> phenomenon what-has-been.⁷

Any vitality that the diverse materials comprising the convolutes can claim is grounded in the historical alienation effect establishing them as what has been (*Verflossensein*). Citation, posting the shards of language in the display, is the beaming up of dead materiality into a context or time bubble in which it gains placement and currency, if not new life. Benjamin's extended characterization of the collector and the allegorist, who join the *flâneur* among *The Arcades Project*'s distinctive dramatis personae, describes the respective attitudes with which the critically wired cultural historian addresses these inert but invariably auratic fossils of lost time. Nineteenth-century Europe's most expressive weather pattern, as well as the mood that it ushered in, belongs to the cultural compost in which *The Arcades Project*'s constellation is rooted.

Each convolute, in keeping with the practices of cultural history and critique that Benjamin customized for *The Arcades Project*, is its own constellation or reshuffled card deck of the factors and accidents that converged to make the Parisian Second Empire into what it was. Benjamin's materialist overview of arguably the most critical concatenation of cultural, technological, commercial, administrative, and military factors still bearing on our own modernity thus starts up all over again, in a Nietzschean recurrence, every time the camera angle of its manifestly cinematic viewfinder changes. The weather, in Convolute D, "Boredom, Eternal Recurrence," thus becomes tangled in a nexus of factors whose relation to it is by no means obvious: the drapery and fabric that will define the apartment as a plush display case or treasure trove of commodities; the down time in moments of its inclemency that will become the bedrock for the urban market in penny arcades and other trivial and leisure pursuits; the attentiveness to the turbulent but generally subdued climate of mood afforded by incidental meteorological lapses in the nineteenth century's headlong rush toward profit and empire.

We unearth in every convolute turbulent nuggets, textual analagons to a railroad turntable or Grand Central Station, usually in Benjamin's own phrasing but not always, in which the materials and historical counterforces comprising a particular topical setting of the viewfinder (or a mini-climate) combine and collide with particular vividness and intensity. In the throes of a collation of materials that has dared to suggest that climate, mood, and the chaotic turbulence they share is as decisive a force for social and cultural history as industrial spreadsheets, we encounter the following passage in Convolute D:

> Boredom is a warm gray fabric lined on the inside with the most lustrous and colorful of silks. In this fabric we wrap ourselves when we dream. We are at home then in the arabesques of its lining. But the sleeper looks bored and gray within his sheath. And when he later wakes and wants to tell of what he dreamt, he communicates by and large only this boredom. For who would be able at one stroke to turn the lining of time outside? Yet to narrate dreams signifies nothing else. And in no other way can one deal with the arcades—structures in which we relive, as in a dream, the life of our parents and grandparents, as the embryo in the womb relives the life of animals. Existence in these spaces flows then without accent, like the events in dreams. Flânerie is the rhythmics of this slumber. In 1839 a rage for tortoises overcame Paris.[8]

This passage, extending to the most private and incommunicable bastion of all, the individual sheath of the personal dream, is a highly poetic taking off from (and takeoff on) the smooth crossroads established between global climatics and private atmospherics in the nineteenth century. It may concern itself less with sumptuous and richly colored interiors—the apartment, the arcade, the department store, and even the intrapsychic technicolor movie exclusively for private consumption, being the soft underbelly to nineteenth-century imperialism and urban malaise—than with the glossy *pellicule*, fabric, or skin between turbulences of the weather, the global economy, and the new city, reprogrammed in accordance with economic paradigm shifts. In this dense imagistic passage—fulfilling Baudelaire's wish for the miracle of a poetic prose and justifying Benjamin's lavish tribute throughout *The Arcades Project* both to surrealist poetics and to montage technique, as developed by Eisenstein and Pudovkin—the world economy, the emerging cosmopolis, urban interior design, and even the personal dreamscape (the last as the figment of a collective Imaginary) undergo shared cycles of manic discovery and subdued writing, incautious enthusiasm and expenditure and monotonous restraint.

By the end of the convolute, Benjamin even calls Nietzsche in as a reinforcement and official monitor of boredom as eternal return that is one of the inevitable climatic rest stops encountered in these swings. Benjamin announces here less a totalizing regime in which all levels of production and sensibility march in lockstep to the same cycles of boom and bust than a delicate climate configured by responsiveness through an aggregate of feed-back loops wired to one another. The positive or negative feedback encoun-tered by the demolition of what had been the medieval street plan of Paris, the orientalist dreams of a commercial utopia, as in Zola's *The Ladies' Para-dise,* and the vast covered horizontal spaces, for example, in train stations, made possible by iron girders and sheeting segue into one another. Benja-min's pivotal figure for this interfacing, one indicative of a feeding frenzy that had taken place in the public's taste for cashmere shawls as well as in the subdued hypoactivity of a rainy day, is the smooth fabric sheet, whether the lining to an overcoat or the plush wall coverings signaling the transfor-mation of living space, now the apartment, into a protective *etui,* or carrying case, for the commodities its proprietors have managed to amass. "The most lustrous and colorful of silks" with which we might customize the interior, whether of our bad-weather Burberry or a dismal stretch of wall space in our pied à terre, morphs into the placenta out of which the collec-tive dreams of the moment, as well as new human life, are hatched. Benja-min's dependence here and in his historiography of fashions on a distinctly feminine poetics as he gathers a composite collage of modernization in the nineteenth century is backlit in lucid profile. The deep slumber of a collec-tivity undergoing traumatic changes in the availability of critical resources and goods, information and communications, and the movement and em-ployment of peoples is the broadest climate that Benjamin has enlisted in a materially attuned practice of cultural history and critique.

There is something big-hearted or, in Benjamin's technical nomencla-ture, messianic about his incorporation of the intangibles and whimsicalities of fashion, mood, and weather into a culturally encyclopedic database of sociopolitical and economic modernization. Owing to the irreducible tur-bulence of these programmatic parameters, he cannot come out a winner by taking them into account, if winning entails mapping their interplay with other factors or their impact in any definitive way. These very different X factors are intangible and unpredictable—in a word, turbulent—in their own ways. They bespeak, in other words, the chaos that has been an over-riding concern of systems theory. It is a testament to Benjamin's critical rigor that he unleashed and accommodated such turbulence within the rhi-zomatic, smooth space of the convolutes. An uneasy alliance with and sus-ceptibility to turbulence becomes the ongoing burden of rigorous critique. It may well be the scientists who have encountered turbulence face to face—

that is, with a measure of the *faciality* we encountered above, with the assistance of Deleuze/Guattari, in Chapter 1—who have evolved one of the most a propos current terminologies for the chaos that Benjamin lived and admitted into his project:

> A practical interest in turbulence has always been in the foreground, and the practical interest is usually one-sided: make the turbulence go away. In some applications, turbulence is desirable—inside a jet engine, for example, where efficient burning depends on rapid mixing. But in most, turbulence means disaster. Turbulent airflow over a wing destroys lift. Turbulent flow in an oil pipe creates stupefying drag. Vast amounts of government and corporate money are staked on the design of aircraft, turbine engines, propellers, submarine hulls, and other shapes that move through fluids. Researchers must worry about flow in blood vessels and heart valves. They worry about the shape and evolution of explosions. They worry about vortices and eddies, flames and shock waves. In theory the World War II atomic bomb project was a problem in nuclear physics. In reality . . . the business that occupied the scientists assembled at Los Alamos was a problem in fluid dynamics.[9]

> All the rules seem to break down. When the flow is smooth, or laminar, small disturbances die out. But past the onset of turbulence, disturbances grow catastrophically. This onset—this transition—became a critical mystery in science. The channel below a rock in a stream becomes a whirling vortex that grows, splits off, and spins downstream. A plume of cigarette smoke rises smoothly . . . until it passes a critical velocity and splinters into wild eddies. The onset of turbulence can be seen and measured in laboratory experiments; it can be tested for any new wing or propeller by experimental work in a wind tunnel; but its nature remains elusive.[10]

In this diptych of extracts from Gleick's *Chaos*, turbulence, a dynamic as well as a scientific interest, moves out of engineering schools and departments, where it has been sequestered, to center stage in the scientific address of chaos. This displacement is both substantive and methodological. The interest shifts from ship propellers and airplane wings to phenomena of a more intangible nature: sudden loss of plane altitude, infelicitous arterial blood clots, unanticipated, possibly terrorist explosions. Most strikingly, sudden onsets of turbulence, the tipping points in steady states or seemingly cumulative processes, become the province of theoretical physics and fractal mathematics. Addressing the abruptness, arationality, and irreducibility of

chaos prompts a scientific paradigm shift: "Then confusion appears, a me-
nagerie of wild motions. Sometimes these motions received names: oscilla-
tory. The skewed varicose, the cross-roll, the knot, the zigzag."[11] The
science of chaos, itself an outcropping of relativity theory and quantum
physics, brings the utterly intractable and befuddling to center stage. This
is something very much like Benjamin's insistence on a discourse of climate,
fashion change, and mood within the convolutes.

There is surely no everyday phenomenon—that is, no ongoing feature
of experience or state of affairs imbued with duration—more arbitrary and
inscrutable than mood. It is no accident that music, of all the art forms,
along with motif, rhythm, and tempo, invokes mood as one of its primary
formats. We might say that mood is inherently musical because its landscapes and mini-climates are palpable and the transitions between them are
contrived, abrupt, playful, and often unmarked. This surely has to do,
among other factors, with the specific nature of its duration and its relation
to time. Mood is particularly critical to our self-conception and self-esteem
in the West because it is hard-wired into the experience of duration that is
so critical to our productivity, creativity, sociability, and the full range of
our performance indicators.

Our tendency, at the moment, to manage our moods and their transitions, along with similar conditions of attentiveness, via a range of approaches including pharmacology is redolent of the moment when physical
turbulence remained the property of the engineering school. The alternative to this would be something like a culture of mood change, emotional
climate, or explicit interpersonal turbulence or inconsistency in what Goffman calls "the presentation of the Self."[12] This is not a firmly anchored and
reinforced culture in the West. One could go on here about the grounding
of classical (i.e., Freudian) psychoanalysis, particularly its nosology and diagnosis, in a specifically Kantian model of judgment, but we'll save that for
another time.

The imponderables of mood fare better in Eastern models, such as Chinese medicine, because they are attributed to established recurrent combinations in an elemental matrix. *Qi*, the vital force or energy, passes through
the same elemental phases in all natural forms, including all "sentient beings."[13] Earth, water, wood, fire, and metal are in this sense universals at
the same time as they are energic components. Your momentary mood, as
bizarre or extreme as it may be, is a particular configuration of elements

and related organic subsystems you share with everyone. You may feel that you're skipping along the surface of Mars, but there is a place for this climatic emotional energy within the matrix of possible combinations. You do not violate a prescribed social contract, as you do in a diagnostic system modeled on Kantian judgment, when you enter this particular mood—or any other, for that matter. In this respect, it is not far-fetched to say that all psychotherapeutic regimens of treatment, including pharmacological ones, strive to get a grip on mood, if not actively to define the phenomenon. Systems of elemental process and interaction, by contrast, are already inscribed in a dynamic of turbulence both modal and atmospheric. These alternative systems cooperate with and extend the climate of mood; they establish a harmonic resonance with it.

Mutually Communicating Medical Systems

After spending a lifetime of study under the delusion that geophysical transformation is glacial and imperceptible in its progression, virtually invisible over the span of generations, we now find ourselves in an environment whose striking recent modifications are only too evident. Through the simulation of special effects, ecologically oriented documentaries such as Al Gore's *An Inconvenient Truth* may graphically highlight the current dire predicament with footage of ice caps that melt and alpine glaciers that dissolve before our very eyes. But perhaps even more importantly, such artifacts, in concert with journalistic coverage of environmental issues and crises, mobilize our first-hand testimony to uncontestable and in many respects irreversible climate change.

The world is heating up. It is drying up before our eyes. It is becoming hospitable to conflagrations and other heat events at a time when the resources that would counteract these, such as water and earth, have been compromised and drastically reduced. In a Western scientific model, including that guiding *An Inconvenient Truth*, a pathogen, a hostile intruder, a terrorist—say, carbon-dioxide emissions or greenhouse gases—can be isolated and identified. Its pernicious influence can be traced to the source, wherever situated, and then methodically pursued through its displacements, intensifications, amplifications, mutations, and ramifications into a system of coordinated infelicities, insults, or attacks. This profiling and pursuit, associated with policing by Benjamin toward the end of Convolute I, "The Interior, the Trace," is not nearly so pivotal or momentous in Chinese science. This long and tried tradition, with its basis in an integrally related and mutually moderating nexus of elements, might approach the current mega-heat happening or event as an unprecedented intensification of the fire element, unchecked by its natural governors, water and earth—but then by the others as well, wood and metal. Chinese science is no more deluded about the possibility of a sustained or perfect elemental balance—in the environment, the human body, or the political sphere—than is its Western counterpart. But the thrust of its observation and prescription, in *fengshui* as in Chinese medicine, is, on the one hand, ongoing attentiveness to elemental interactions in constant flux and, on the other, periodic interventions in the name and interest of their balanced mutual inter- and counteraction. (One paradox of the Chinese system of medicine is that fire, which Westerners associate with passion, not especially known for instilling rigor or constancy, also gives rise, in this system of analogies and sympathetic vibrations, to interpretation and explanation, above all of life processes, but also as integral pursuits of their own.)[14] The global economy's thermal warm up in other words, coincides with a massive generation, dissemination, and archiving of *information*. The two heat events are indeed by no means separable.

One additional and in all likelihood far too general premise to seed at this point concerns how an ontology and epistemology of elements interrelated both by complementarity and dialectical negation would not only program Chinese historiography but tangibly affect the outcome of Chinese events. It is a well-established taking off point for Chinese history, at least as formulated in the West, that its formative dynasties—and the classical schools and texts that they engendered—left the persisting umbrella culture with a matrix, not of elements but of political formations, onto-theological bearings, and relations to empire and secularity that would recur in different combinations throughout the unfolding of dynasties. As the historian of barbarian incursions and center-periphery shifts on a global scale, William H. McNeill, has noted, already in the Zhou dynasty Confucian decorum and the Taoist sense of mystery were configured as a play between mutually enhancing while supplementary ways of life coexisting under the aegis of

Chinese civilization. This give and take between opposing but complementary worldviews would establish itself as an ongoing feature of Chinese history:

> Confucian emphasis on decorum and self-control could not satisfy everyone. Too much was left out: the depths of human passion and the mysteries of nature had no place in a well-regulated Confucian world. . . . The existence of Taoist adepts gave a balance to the ancient Chinese world view that Confucianism alone could not supply. Moderation and self-discipline needed its complement of mystery and magic to satisfy the normal range of human needs and to express the fluctuating needs of men who lived in hard and uncertain times. By complementing each other, the one supplying precisely what the other lacked, Confucianism and Taoism constituted an unusually stable pattern of thought, which lasted, with many changes and later enrichment yet without fundamental interruption, from Confucius' time until the twentieth century of the Christian era. No other cultural transition has lasted so long and governed the lives of so many millions of men.[15]

In this accounting, the Confucian-Taoist spectrum, augmented by Legalist precisions and later by Buddhism, gave rise to a differentiated but stable palette of ways of life. The competing worldviews would later be at times, but not always, encompassed under an overarching umbrella of neo-Confucianism.[16] These multiple ways of life, can be retrospectively configured into a permutational matrix under whose aegis many of the shifts in direction, many of these in turn dramatic, of Chinese history take place. Haun Saussy encourages us to think of the functional motivations and impacts of the spectrum of organization on which Taoism, Confucianism, Legalism, and later Buddhism could be productively configured:

> I think the deeper structure looks more like this: a pole of MANAGEMENT (legalistic-Confucian statecraft and administration lore), a pole of ESCAPE (because nobody really likes to be managed, so it is a relief to imagine alternative worlds in which things are not as they are), and a pole of VALUE (in which claims are made about what is desirable. The institutions and ideologies that hooked to these poles varied from time to time.[17]

On superficial levels, as many commentators noted at the time, Chairman Mao's revolution may look like a happening unprecedented in Chinese history, with the dismantling of imperial superstructure and a stunning, rigorous indifference to organized religion. But a combinatorial model of sociopolitical functions or of prevalent theaters of ideological thinking allows us to see, even under conditions of one-party monopoly, a continuation of some of the classical variations upon Chinese government. The tropes and variegated positions for Chinese history that Chairman Mao was able to extract and translate from the canonical texts of Communism were grafted onto the yin-yang dynamics structuring so much of Chinese physics, metaphysics, biology, and government.

If the ethics of contemporary systems theory militates for a strategic decrease in pressures and logistical demands on already overstressed systems, the wisdom of Chinese history places seemingly antithetical and opposed integral systems, whether of government, commerce, or climate, on a shared spectrum (configured like a feedback loop), on which they are then free to complement and mutually decode and elaborate one another. Our task here becomes to examine what the *complementarity* of a system of elements, one whose elements relate through correspondences and analogies might have to offer chaos and turbulence, as these enter *The Arcades Project* in the form of fashions, mood, and climate. We might also recall that Benjamin's heterogeneous database and energy source is configured as a rhizomatic display or posting in visual historico-cultural space. Both the topically organized universe of the Benjaminian convolute and the comprehensive checklist of natural phenomena encompassed by Chinese medicine's correspondences, analogies, and oppositions expand outward in the embrace of a complex, diverse, and by no means coordinated zone of phenomena.

The first generation of American alternative health-care givers who encountered such practices as acupuncture directly in a Chinese setting were stunned by what was set out before them, above all by the long-standing conviction of the organism's intimate interface with the environment and its dynamic internal integration. Harriet Beinfield, who, along with her husband Efrem Korngold, was among the first to make this cultural border-crossing, wrote:

> Within the Eastern worldview, the human being is a microcosm of Nature, a smaller universe. Human beings represent the juncture between Heaven and Earth, the offspring of their union, a fusion of cosmic and terrestrial forces. . . . Sustained by the power of Earth and transformed by the power of Heaven, humanity cannot be separated from Nature—we *are* Nature, manifest as people. As a cosmos in miniature, we are propelled by the same forces. Good and bad are relative, not absolute. Life and death balance each other. Seen and unseen, soma and psyche are aspects of one continuous process, by definition everchanging and in flux.[18]

Indeed, the cosmological view of Eastern medicine, as it first dawned on China watchers in the 1970s, both recalls the heritage of spiritualized Romanticism that was on the public agenda at the time and invites a deeper analysis of systems theory on a global scale. The passage cited is fraught with organic holisms made possible by this new way—to Western thinking at the time—of situating the human organism in the terrestrial environment. But even at the level of its high-flown organicist aspiration, it is infused with a sense of multiple system-environment interactions, above all, between human physiology and the major components of the natural environment. The Chinese health system grounds its observations and diagnoses in a cosmic correspondence between what goes on along the mind-body continuum, interactions between the five phases or elements, and the processes of the encompassing natural environment. Body and mind can only be related in this configuration in a highly interactive feedback loop. The architecture of this system is rooted in the five phases or elements and all of the complementarities and oppositions that can be observed and appended between them. But the system's practical approach to any particular condition, say asthma or diabetes, is by no means either so intuitive or so organically edifying. This is how Beinfield and Korngold encapsulate the system's approach to diabetes:

> According to Chinese medicine, diabetes is described as severe *Dryness* or deficiency of *Moisture*. The reasoning is correlative and axiomatic: Dryness causes *Dryness* to manifest, *Dryness* causes deficiency of *Moisture*, a deficiency of *Moisture* may cause *Dryness*. Cause and effect are difficult to distinguish. They mutually generate one another and arise simultaneously.
>
> This system of correspondence describes the parallelism and synchronicity of events in the inner and outer world of the human organism. All phenomena are ordered according to the *Five Phases* of *Wood, Fire, Earth, Metal,* and *Water,* which represent the five evolutionary phases of transformation and correspond with five *Organ Networks,* five seasons, five climates, and five personality types. The workings of the body are associated with each of the seasonal cycles of birth, growth, ripening, harvest, and decay. Each of the five *Organ Networks* performs a function within the cycle. Analogous to the five climates and seasons in nature is the internal milieu generated by each of the *Organ Networks.* Disturbance of the internal milieu may cause the *Liver* to generate *Wind,* the *Heart* to generate *Heat,* the *Spleen* to generate *Dampness,* the *Lungs* to generate *Dryness,* and the *Kidneys* to generate *Cold.*

According to this correspondence logic, various conditions of distress are linked to each Network.[19]

Contemporary readers whose hipness and savoir faire are indebted to critical theory cannot fail to be struck by the concentrated architectural weight resting on analogy in this characterization. (Of course the same analogical thinking dominates Western element-centered medical systems, whether by Pliny or Galen.) The analogies on which the above passage is built invite comparison to the similitudes that were, for Foucault,[20] the archaeological bedrock to Western thinking and science during the Renaissance. There are parallels within the body in this Chinese physiological picture of the world to the major states achieved by the elements in the external world. Organ networks, phases (i.e., natural elements), seasons of the year, times of day, stages of life, moods, foods, and even colors are on an unalterable course of mutual synchronicity and divergence. As oppressive as this preprogrammed parallelism between disparate elements in the energic, material, and temperamental worlds may seem, the system also grounds all possible symptoms and outcomes in a matrix whose underlying mathematics is *combinatorial*. The fundamental democracy between any particular outcome and any other relieves this medical system of the judgmental and adversarial opposition to potentially detrimental stressors and pathogens characteristic of a more closed system. Any one disease, as onerous as it may be in its particular context, is at worst a variant on others. Alternate combinations of prevalent elements can be mobilized by the practitioner in order to assist the current health problem to evolve out of itself. This is a medical system, in other words, whose combinatory and elemental thrusts help keep it, in Wilden's words, "open," even where its underlying architecture may be bound up in analogical parallels.

Chinese medicine is a system, then, that can accommodate the full underlying turbulence in the phenomenon of mood, even when each mood has a context in a particular configuration of elements:

> The *Five Climates* correspond to a cycle of the seasons. When a person exhibits internal response patterns analogous to external climatic conditions, Chinese medicine postulates that a person has that condition: that climate exists internally. Cold, for example, makes things contract. . . . Chinese medicine describes a person as manifesting a condition called *Cold* regardless of whether actual exposure to external cold caused the condition. An adverse internal climate can be unrelated to outside weather.[21]

There is a permeable foyer or interface allowing extrinsic climatic conditions *into* the organism, but the organism's present state needn't represent prevailing weather conditions outside. Disease is itself an imbalance emerging within the constant interchanges or feedbacks, positive and negative, between the elements and the organ networks to which they are bound. There are no clear checkpoints in and out of disease. At any given instant, the organism is balanced and imbalanced, healthy and sick. The imbalance can be dramatic and marked at any instant if the feedback between the elements and their energies becomes turbulent. Turbulence is the ongoing condition of an organism held in an ongoing state of openness, as Wilden and other systems theorists deploy the term.

The history of multiple overlaid cold wars enables us to understand, I think, the unabashed reverence the first U.S. envoys to the Chinese medical arts felt toward the field. Eastern medicine dawned upon these privileged initial visitors with all the aura of a compelling body of lost wisdom. There is indeed something spiritual in the way writers like Beinfield and Korngold couch the tradition's grounding in and openness to the natural environment, its reverence for *qi*. Yet when they characterize the other torque or body English they took from—their conventional Western medical training, their descriptions are largely in accord with the tensions that systems theorists, whether Wilden, Deleuze and Guattari in their Capitalism and Schizophrenia diptych, or Luhmann situate in and around systems.

If their embrace of acupuncture and Chinese diagnosis and herbology betrays just a trace of over-enthusiasm, our U.S. Eastern-medicine pioneers have not lost contact with the drift of Western science and the philosophical program powering it. They can, on the one hand, be put off by the man-machine (*homme à machine*) ensuing from Descartes and its separation from the elemental universe and can feel affinity for Claude Bernard's internal climate (*milieu intérieur*), on the other, instantiating the periodic Western intuition of an imminent personal climate. (Bernard, an eminent contemporary of Pasteur with a more environmental approach to medicine, often found his takes and positions drowned out in his generation's rage for infectious diseases.) Beinfield and Korngold's background in Western science places them in a position to appreciate the body English with which Wilden jukes closed systems:

> Descartes' statement justified the ethics of symmetry by clearly stating the atomistic epistemology upon which we still depend. It is an epistemology related to

the forces and energy pushing and pulling bodies about in what was to become a Newtonian universe of attraction and repulsion in mechanical equilibrium. Additive, closed-energy models of all reality—the conception of reality as an AGGREGATE of individual bodies possessing forces, humors, sympathies, affinities, instincts, and the like, in an entropic universe—excluded those minority voices who, like Pascal or Rousseau, to some degree or another protested on behalf of the multiplicative and fractionative communicational relationships of clear and distinct billiard balls, demonstrated the danger and utility of the Cartesian epistemology. Every *cogito* was free to sell his disposable energy at the best price. . . . The Cartesian "revolution" made the crucial absolutist and analytical error (for us) of unjustifiably conferring a privileged ontological status on entities ("substance") as opposed to relationships ("attributes," "accidents"). In spite of Aristotle, Hegel, and Marx, the truth that entities do not create relationships so much as RELATIONSHIPS CREATE ENTITIES, was (and still remains) generally obscured.[22]

In Wilden's psychoanalytic field, Descartes becomes a prime suspect as the schizogenetic first mover of Western modernity. The atomically dispersed subjects who inhabit Descartes' fragmented social landscape are oblivious to the relational field and to the links and interfaces within it that have, more than anything else, created *them*. We could describe as "relationally deprived" the subjects configured, in the passage above, by the philosophes of the broader modernity. In the communicative domain whose parameters Wilden sets out in his theory of systems, the analytical monologue to which these subjects give vent with the collusion of a therapist is, more than anything else, the noise and dysfunctional static in their lives that they have not been allowed to fully experience, acknowledge, or vent, this in a universe that has radically pigeonholed and foreclosed their relations of every sort. Wilden's systems overview of psychoanalysis, both in its Freudian foundations and in its cognitive reconfiguration at the hands of Lacan, places particular emphasis on the communicative conditions in which subjects, under a variety of conditions, find themselves. As characterized by Wilden, the landscape of curtailed relations that predominates in the wake of Enlightenment ideology is a wasteland for the writerly contingency and flex evolving throughout the critical tradition, arising in literary impression and arriving at the current moment via Surrealism, the Frankfurt School, rhetorical reading, and deconstruction.

Digital Displays; Analog Responsibilities

It would be tempting to resolve this fable of East-West encounter, international cooperation, and the mutual search for hors-systemic therapies and other supplements in favor of a decisive decoupling or opening up of Western culture in the multiple dimensions of its determination, purification, schizogenesis, and digitality by the potentials inherent in an Eastern elemental system, with its dynamism, organic interconnection, and always undecided drift. This is an outcome only too familiar to my generation of aging hippies. But this edifying back door out of some of the gridlocks of flow, critical resource shortage, and civilizational friction attenuated by basic incompatibilities in market setups and informational policy is out of reach for us in the present-day world. Any reference back to a systems theory such as Wilden's will bear this out. His sustained meditation on the contemporary task of negotiating systems that are increasing in their complexity, opacity, and totalitarian ability to control us not only was ahead of its time but also managed to encompass cybernetics, information theory, psychoanalysis, semiotics, the social sciences—especially the communications-wired anthropological meta-matrices of Bateson—and philosophy within a common intellectual framework. His free-wheeling analysis mobilizes the pivotal interfaces encompassing and framing contemporary experience: analog and digital organizations, open and closed systems, positive and negative feedbacks and entropies.

It is not only that Wilden, assuming the susceptibility of the true critic, placed himself directly in the cross-currents rebounding between so many disparate and in many respects incompatible conceptual frameworks: he maintained a rigorous and formal openness to the events and phenomena he was willing to embrace within his purview, from the analog scale according to which the Tsembaga of New Guinea turn on and off husbanding and/ or slaughtering pigs, to the systemic interactions between Lacanian Real, Symbolic, and Imaginary, to the fall of Rome as all instances of systemic collapse. There is a finitude about the gradations in systemic architecture and behavior between models emanating from a bewildering multiplicity of terrains in Wilden's formulations that is never quite achieved even in Deleuze/Guattari's Capitalism and Schizophrenia diptych or by Luhmann's magisterially operational overview of systems.

Given the exceptionally high degree of complexity that Wilden admits into the interface between analog and digital computers or into systems' adaptation to the positive and/or negative feedback from the environments that they encounter, any clear-cut drift of current environmental impasses into the sphere of mutual elemental counterbalance and homeostasis is going to be unlikely. We might try to hypostatize that Chinese elemental systems, whether of health, design, or the environment, stay touchingly analog, while the West, particularly over the broader modernity, has grown ominously digital. The analog mode of organization or climate prompts the reactions we experience to Neanderthals in *Clan of the Cave Bear* on the long eve of their certain eclipse by Cro-Magnons like Ayla. We feel warmly toward its rootedness in the earth, its strong orientation toward the visible, in this sense, toward its accountability.

> The analog is pregnant with MEANING whereas the digital domain of SIGNI-FICATION is, relatively speaking, somewhat barren. It is almost impossible to translate the rich semantics of the analog into any digital form for communication to another organism. This is true both of the most trivial sensations (biting your tongue, for example) or the most enviable situations (being in love). It is impossible to precisely describe such events except by recourse to unnamable common experience (a continuum). But this imprecision carries with it a fundamental and probably essential ambiguity. . . . The digital, on the other hand, because it is concerned with boundaries and because it depends on arbitrary combination, has all the syntax to be precise and may be entirely unambiguous. Thus what the analog gains in syntactics it loses in semantics. Thus it is that because the analog does not possess the syntax necessary to say "No" or to say anything involving "not," one can REFUSE or REJECT in the analog, but one cannot DENY or NEGATE.[23]

The analog, like Charles Foster Kane as child, before being pumped up and expanded by his untold millions into the Citizen, is connected to his roots, his natural surroundings. He knows who his father is. There are many things he cannot do, but we feel a nostalgia for him in this state, just as he will be driven his entire life toward a point prior to his entry into the digitalized world of big capital through his insatiable and barely conscious quest for "Rosebud." In this passage, Wilden links the analog to passages in Wittgenstein, notably in *The Blue Book*,[24] in which private language encounters the limits of its transmissibility to others. Language in its analog modality is grounded in some anatomical or sensory-perceptual fact, that is, in materiality: this is what lends it its meaning. But it cannot negotiate the threshold to general and transmissible signification. Produced through a standardization of semantics, digital language establishes the boundaries within which all variants of signification can be messaged. It delineates a field in which my toothache can somehow be registered, but at the expense of the analog personal touch, noise, or what Barthes called "the rustle of language."[25] Wilden thus finds himself in the delicate position of recurring to his own analog nostalgia at the same time as he spins out, from an admirable diversity of perspectives and disciplinary languages, the potentials, achievements, and dimensions of digital metaphysics.

Precisely his acuity to the unique topologies of the analog and the digital allows him to avoid the pitfall of any schizophrenic dualism between the two modalities of organization. Much as they each have a distinctive torque and have left very different marks on history—Wilden associates the digital, for example, with "the rise of individualism, the invention of perspective, Protestantism, the discovery of alphabetical order for dictionaries, the ordering of practical and abstract knowledge in the *Encyclopédie*, the invention of interchangeable machine parts, the standardization of weights and measures"[26]—in his intimate understanding of their interdynamics, he is certain that analog and digital share intertwined and inseparable fates. He can thus forthrightly elaborate the persistence of the analog in digital computer architecture and in the persistence of the "human touch" indispensable for such critical discriminations as those between figure and ground, whether in Proust's characteristic midwifery of subliminal aesthetic expansion in the depths or in cognitive pattern recognition:

> In the case of the digital computer, the machine processes are analogs of mathematical formulae which are digital representations. Moreover . . . it is possible in principle to represent the behavior of any analog system or computer in a digital computer, provided only that the problem can be stated in a finite number of unambiguous "words." But some of the most common human communicational acts are probably not definable in this way and almost certainly do not involve only digital processes. The most significant examples are the phenomena involved in fringe consciousness, in attention or "zeroing in," in the distinction between the essential and the non-essential or between figure and ground, in pattern recognition . . . and obviously, in the necessary human tolerance for ambiguity which allows us to define and redefine the rules for any given situation.

At present these decisions or ways of dealing with them have still to be made by the human programmer, who perhaps provides the necessary analog component to complement the amazing brute-force problem solving capabilities of the digital computer.

Writing on the cusp of the 1970s, Wilden grasps the serious implications of digital and analog processes and operations in a way that verges on the uncanny, the "unreal." In the distant background to the passage immediately above, an impalpable "touch" or "feel" is a necessary component of auratic handiwork or childlike wonder in Benjamin's writings. This almost tactile "feel" for things is a factor as well in the depths that the Proustian narrative finds embedded in the surfaces presented by people as well as made objects. Wilden, sensing the profound implications of the digital revolution in its early stages, places the uncanny touch as indispensable to the acupuncturist as to the inventive writer in the realm of the analog. The practice of Chinese medicine is manifestly analog: diagnosis is a tracking of the energy flows of the five elements as they interact in the zones of their greatest confluence. These are the pulses, the abdomen, and the foot. There are potentially other diagnostic zones. The methods of diagnosis are analog: sight, touch, smell, questions couched in concrete language. The grounding of the organ networks in elements deriving from an ecology relatively unencumbered by engineering endows the entire practice, whether acupuncture, acupressure, or herbology, with an analog drift. Yet the full followthrough with which each energic component runs through the entire body, from head to toe, as we say, also opens up a digital dimension to the practice. One of the common strategies available to the acupuncturist is to insert a needle in a point at the farthest extremity in the body from the symptom. The continuity of an energy circuit encompassing the entire body—an energy circuit or flow transforming the organic into smooth space—allows a therapeutic effect even greater than that produced by a proximate needle, which might be painful and invasive.

We live in a world in which we cannot simply retreat from the digital back into the analog, as tempting as that might be. The analog retains some features of an opening that, for Wilden, is the persistent ethical thrust of systems and communications theory. We need to keep trying to imagine the contemporary world in its terrestriality from the perspective of that opening, whether it is expressed as the noise in the system, as Deleuze and

Guattari's bodies without organs, or as nomadic incursions through smooth space. We need to acknowledge that Euro-American and Chinese heat events are looped together; they are loopy. We can all learn a tremendous amount about this terrestrial heat event in its multiple and concurrent theaters—Wilden, following Bateson,[27] would describe it as concurrent positive feedback from too many sectors, including investment, consumption, and urban expansion—we continue to learn from the interplay of elements in classical works going back to *The Yellow Emperor's Classic of Internal Medicine*.

We Who Make Noise

A final move, as we review a range of the sociopolitical and discursive options made possible by the interplay between East and West, between metaphysical and cybernetic discourses, between open and closed systems, is to contemplate the prospects for the critical static or noise that we emit within the institutional configurations that we inhabit, whose protection we have sought. On the one hand, on the basis of the extremely rich and open-throttled treasury of critico-philosophical thinking that we have witnessed and in which we have participated, prospects for wise, multi-faceted critique with the limberness allowing it to address a shifting range of triggers and repressors should be, by this stage of institutional history, strong. When I was growing up, I was fortunate to see Hitchcock's *Vertigo* and *Psycho*, Welles's *The Trial*, Fellini's *8 ½*, Truffaut's *Shoot the Piano Player*, Antonioni's *Blow-up*, Godard's *Weekend*, and Kurosawa's *Ran* in movie houses as first-run features. The more or less adult stage of my life-long studies coincided with deconstruction's fabled marathon and the substantial and remarkable achievements in philosophy, linguistics, psychoanalysis, feminism, and the theoretical social sciences that ran alongside it. The most vivid cultural discoveries of my youth coincided with a particularly felicitous moment to interact with the rich output of the conceptual and artistic worlds.

Our task as cultural critics is exacerbated by the fact that at a certain point we are supposed to shut up; to the degree that we ourselves perform functions defined by closed systems, our persistent noise making eventually becomes a liability. We all encounter these cut-off points with a sense of crisis regarding what we really are about, and we should. Indeed, there are multiple occasions on which it is perfectly clear that the smooth functioning of the systems of which we form part, whether educational, informational, or professional, demands our compliance and that our compliance consists in giving up our noise and ceasing and desisting in our inscription. And comply we do. For it is not toward noise, or disturbance, or mutation that integral organizations gravitate. Wilden comments, on this point: "Organisms are goalseeking, or telenomic, but what they seek is stability, not change; what they reproduce is themselves, not novelties."[28]

Wilden's insight into the play of positive and negative feedbacks is a splendid vantage point from which to assess our options. If we do our job right, that is, if we make noises, if we follow traces and lines of flight, that should enable us to discern the hidden totalizing and exploitative momentums and agendas in the systems that have enlisted our services. If we persist in embellishing our uncanny taste and feel for emerging developments with strident critique, it is in the very interest of the systems in which we participate to send some unambiguous negative feedback our way, special delivery. Indeed, the more we persist in making unpleasant noises, the more negative feedback it behooves the institutions of our affiliation to direct at us. This is a bit paranoid, you might say. But as Pynchon's Slothrop understood, just being paranoid doesn't mean it isn't true. Paranoia may indeed be an embedded posture in noisy critique and open-ended systems analysis. There is indeed a noise parameter in the ecology of critical climate change. In this instance, critical silence or white noise is in no way a desired end.

The book, then, joins other environmental zones that have been threatened by a variety of factors, among them overexploitation, sharp curtailment of their eco-diversity, and immoderate increases in discursive tarifs and specialization, limiting the range of their application and the communities they serve. The various corruptions to existing systems at the hands of draconian measures that were foreseen by Gregory Bateson at the outset of the current moment of environmental awareness will be outlined in detail in Chapter 9 below. If the book is too tight at its binding, its institutional as well as its physical or categorical one, it will be impeded in its opening and expansion. If it is calibrated only toward positive feedback, it will be muffled, foreclosed in its critical tact and function of making noise.

The feedback, the public response elicited by a successful book, is not merely positive. A perverse extension to this line of reasoning would be as follows: the better the critic performs her job, if it is making noise, the more negative feedback she elicits. Not only is the negative feedback that she evokes, whether in the form of outright censure or calculated indifference, the truest indication that in her capacity as acute reader, she shorts circuits and skews messages: we remember Derrida's being declared a nonphilosopher by the Yale Philosophy Department and the uproar created by his nomination for an award at Cambridge.

Yet a further complication is that the positive feedback the critic produces, the encouragement she offers as a teacher, and the discursive spinoffs and occasions her writings generate are a double-edged sword. Anything positive she accomplishes might amount to an untenable and schizogenetic pressure added to a system already heated up considerably beyond the safety level of its participating members. Not only does the critic elicit decreasing supplies of positive reinforcement as she persists in her relatively unrecognized work, but she needs to be increasingly vigilant about the pressures that her rarely on-target conceptual sallies have imposed on the relatively few observers monitoring them. As dialectically treacherous as the feedback loops of positive and negative feedback in Wilden's extrapolation may be, nothing is more devastating and indeed terminal than compliance with the negative feedback that suggests, however politely, that she shut up. The critic, when she relinquishes her bearing as a critical noise maker and unwelcome addition to sound pollution, abandons her cultural mission.

The inherent paradoxes of the play of positive and negative feedbacks—that negative feedback will elicit recalcitrance and rage while positive feedback can add to a system's overload and nudge it toward the brink of novalike implosion—extend to the bearing of openness and our deeply conditioned sympathy for it. Who doesn't want the legal, social, communicative, and marital systems that we truck in on a daily basis to be as open and responsive as possible? Positive feedback both opens a system to the mutation and adaptation that might transform it and it overrides systematic equilibrium with new-found pressure and momentum. As Wilden painstakingly demonstrates, a morphogenetic model, one whose selectivity, homeostatic stability based on feedback from the environment, and self-generated artificial intelligence prepare it for the wonders of learning, memory, simulation, and self-replication, is on a higher level than a closed feedback loop, even the one by which we stay on our course while sailing.[29]

The maintenance of an open bearing to the environment—and who among us doesn't want to be perceived to be open?—is not without its own economic and calculated interest. Part of the system's very openness is its resistance to the mutating static and noise that are the critic's walking papers, her less than reputable edition of the social contract:

> These disturbances may be the result of learning, of mutation, of the impending dissolution of the environment of the system, of disturbances in the environment, of collision with another system, of the splitting of the system, or of similar factors. Since all open systems in themselves are primarily conservative of structure, the necessity of a change of structure in order to survive cannot be the result of deterministic laws of evolutionary development. If the open system is determined by anything, it is determined by the goal of STAYING THE SAME. Only when the system enters positive feedback does this determination change. In nature but not in history, the loss of control described by the term positive feedback is always and essentially the result of error or accident (for the given system). It cannot be triggered by the control processes of the adaptive system itself.[30]

The critic, in the rhetoric of apocalyptic endless warfare, flies in under the radar, maintains her stealth. In the language of astute systems theory, she whispers her unsolicited critical noise lest it avalanche into a positive feedback event. Yes, the moment the critic discerns that her elaborate message has been elicited, solicited, or in some way commissioned by the institutional context, the disciplinary occasion at hand, she knows that its material environmental impact has already been blunted. The message, by the time it has been commissioned, has already outlived any generative surprise it might have worked by means of its unannounced, unsolicited, possibly unwelcome communiqué. Hard work this criticism, indeed, and even harder nowadays to find it. Yet it is situated in the very systole and diastole of movements and conditions making systems possible and enabling the environmental discourse that would seem to lend them coherence.

Thinking Flat Out: Back to Bateson

Back to Bateson

Nowadays, we would characterize "Marcel's" grand revelation in *Time Regained*, the culminating volume of Proust's *Remembrance of Things Past*—a discovered conjunction between two landscapes, moods, and mini-climates, if you will, which the narrator had always considered mutually distinct—as a feedback loop on a very high plane of computer design. This is not the place for an exhaustive review of the geological rift articulating the landscapes of the Île de France around Illiers, the basis for the imaginary Combray in Proust's biography. For "Marcel," even during his youthful wanderings, the terrain is forever divided between the Guermantes way, with its tranquil riverscape redolent of one of Monet's *Water Lilies*, and its more wooded and pastoral Méséglise counterpart, in which he will experience his shocking sexual initiation at Montjouvain. In terms of a geographical ontology established from the outset of the mega-novel and lasting until its very end, ne'er shall the divergent routes meet.

In an odd but nonetheless compelling way, we owe a significant share of the tropes and scenarios by which we can articulate and conceptualize the continuity between the Guermantes and Méséglise ways to studies conducted over many years and in a bewilderingly wide range of fields by Gregory Bateson. Whether we understand these pathways (or loops) as symmetrical and complementary in relation to one another or perhaps, respectively, as analog and digital, their relations and interconnections were charted out and placed in the dense overlay of their logical, anthropological, genetic, psychoanalytical, and cybernetic contexts by this highly improvisational social scientist. Bateson's retrospective *Steps to an Ecology of Mind* is a veritable sourcebook if not Bible for twenty-first-century thought. In tribute to his anthropological formation, Bateson always regarded the interactions among people, animals, plants, and the various artifacts resulting from these interchanges from the perspective of the communications and exchange of information that they involve.

As Proust teaches us (and as Derrida and Deleuze/Guattari reinforce, by means of radically different terminologies), paths tend to join up, even after spectacular digressions. Through the inborn perversity of our wiring, whether we attribute it to neurological architectures or the imponderables of the Freudian archive, nothing gets lost: submerged, blurred, arbitrarily crossed with other data stores and value systems, perhaps, but not lost. I want to recall here a moment from my own intellectual formation, before a delirious and empowering *excursus* into French philosophy and criticism, and into the foundational texts, from a range of discourses, for which these schools rendered sorely needed elucidation and radical updating, when the possibilities of theorization itself were for me associated with the social sciences as they were then practiced in North America.

Such names as Walter Benjamin, Roland Barthes, and Claude Lévi-Strauss first became known to me less in the literary classroom than in the context of coursework I did at Brandeis in the late 1960s in sociology and social psychology. (The exception to this rule was the then-unattributed exposure and access to the writings of Martin Heidegger I gained under the aegis of Allan Grossman's eccentric but compelling poetics.) Social science, as it was practiced in those days, still allowed itself to be informed, at least to some degree, by anecdote and other sources indicative of data's nonobjectivity, by avowed observer bias, and, by implication, the limited point of view inherent in all acts of interpretation. The confusion between different frames of observation and interpretation was on the verge of becoming an explicit, discipline-wide project. Even the inchoate thrust of flow itself had left its mark on the diversity of social scientific thinking.

The classrooms I visited under the tutelage of such humanistic social scientists as Gordon Fellman and Jerome Boime were cartographic studios as much as they were ports to specific bodies of methodology and erudition. As ateliers of learning, these classrooms placed study in a more collective and indeed public sphere than did my graduate studies, with their professional emphasis. The product of a semester's reading and discussion was a map or flowchart of the interactions and influences between such newly acquired intellectual resources as Marx, Freud, Weber, Simmel, Arendt, and Löwith. In certain respects, I learned the terrains on which the thinkers of classical sociology, the Frankfurt School, and French structuralism could be placed in meaningful interaction before I became conversant in any profound or significant way with their writings. The humanistic social sciences had charged themselves with surveying a smooth space, long before Deleuze/Guattari coined this term,[1] in which the shocks, incongruities, and impasses of modernity and late capitalism could be registered within the discourses of society and experience, personal and collective. As I subsequently learned, this was both a facility and structural liability in my early formation.

Bateson's elaboration of the double-bind theory of schizophrenia showed up on the syllabus of an upper-level social psychology course I took with Gordon Fellman in 1967 or 1968. I can vividly remember noting at the time the accord between this model of undermining and its repercussions in dyadic family structure and my personal experience of family life. I could see even as a very inexperienced student that Bateson's account achieved the profundity of insight that my first readings in Freud opened up to me without the psychomachy and stage machinery of personal metaphysics.

When forty years later I met up with Bateson again, it was on a very different trajectory, as distinct as the contrasting landscapes that "Marcel" attributes to Guermantes and Méséglise. It was in the context of a systems theory course I had crystallized out of two ongoing strands in my own intellectual interests: Romantics, specifically Kant's and Hegel's systems making as a framework for a broad range of nineteenth- and twentieth-century aesthetic and cultural epiphenomena; and encyclopedic novels from the same time frame, whether Melville's *Moby-Dick*, Kafka's *The Trial* and *The Castle*, Joyce's *Ulysses*, Proust's mega-work, or Pynchon's *Gravity's Rainbow*.

As I began shoring up the substantive philosophico-literary core of the course with a range of readings in psychoanalysis, cybernetics, visual design, and the theories of chaos, games, and systems, I collided with references and appeals to Bateson at every turn. Given Bateson's extensions of his own communications theory to computers and social systems, it was hardly surprising to encounter serious acknowledgment of his originality in such works as Wiener's *The Human Use of Human Beings: Cybernetics and Society* or Gleick's overview, *Chaos.*[2] But in violation of the basic laws of physics, the testimonials continued unabated as the inquiries and treatments meandered farther from Bateson's academic home bases. Gyorgy Kepes's and Reinhold Martin's design classics, respectively *Language of Vision* and *The Organizational Complex* are graphic visual examples.[3]

That Bateson traveled as far afield as his own early Balinese ethnographic studies is evidenced by Deleuze/Guattari's spirited efforts, in their wildest and most speculative decodings of latevcapitalism, at catch-up ball with this Anglo-American phenomenon. As the citizen of a terrestriality whose codes have been hopelessly scrambled and whose potential for organized knowledge and experience is lost, Deleuze/Guattari's schizo, above all in the Capitalism and Schizophrenia diptych, walks out of the pages of Bateson's double-bind studies. The symmetries and asymmetries that Deleuze/Guattari track in their phantasmatic, playfully psychotic architecture of movements and relations under late capitalism—a language of assemblages, parastrata, and epistrata[4]—clearly derives from Bateson's lifelong obsession with (and hope for) complementary, as opposed to symmetrical, relations. One of the oddest quirks of Deleuze/Guattari's Capitalism and Schizophrenia diptych is their fascination with critters, such as lobsters and ticks, that manage to be symmetrical and asymmetrical at the same time. (The axial structure is balanced, but the claws don't match.)[5] Such an obsession, along with their fascination for "planes of symmetry,"[6] could only drift or derive from Bateson's investigations into the codes and distributions of evolutionary biology. (His father was an eminent geneticist.)

In the broadest sense, Bateson's placement of a broad spectrum of social phenomena—from social competition to schizophrenia to alcoholism to phenotype diversity—under the umbrella of communications theory empowers Deleuze/Guattari in their project of designating language as a crucial but not necessarily exclusive code in the configuration of institutional structures. This may well constitute the enduring contribution of their joint studies, a diversified overview of the signifying systems, wired in parallel, collectively forming the partly elusive Prevailing Operating System behind social reality under any particular social regime or formation. This goes as far back in their particular historical purview, thanks to Leroi-Gourhan and others, as Lascaux, and embraces such "dark ages" as "nomadic despotism."

It is no surprise, then, that Bateson traveled from his early far-flung ethnological studies to the historically significant Macy Cybernetics Conferences of 1946 to 1953 in New York, where much of the aesthetics and stylistics, as well as the mathematics, ergonomics, and even ethics of the computer age were codified, by an assembly of the leading logicians, mathematicians, social scientists, designers, and artists of the postwar period. Bateson's insistence on communication as the key underlying dynamic of biology and commerce as well as of social structures served as the discursive foundation stone for the Information Age. Indeed, his explorations have always been at home in the discourse of systems theory, from its foundations in John von Neumann's work on games,[7] Wiener's elaborations of cybernetics, and Ludwig von Bertalanffy's *General System Theory*,[8] to Wilden's crucial update at the outset of the 1970s and Luhmann's authoritative overviews of the field.[9] As variegated, nuanced, and seminal as Wilden's 1972 *System and Structure* may be,[10] a lion's share of its moment and inevitability derive from the textual crossfire (or frontier) between Bateson and Lacan on which Wilden draws heavily for his models, inferences, extrapolations, and prescriptions. Indeed, the apparently odd coupling of Lacan and Bateson is at the heart of many of *System and Structure*'s uncannily prophetic anticipations. Lacan himself must take enormous credit for rewiring psychoanalysis to embrace cognitive science, the linguistics as well as architecture of cybernetics, and the ecology of system-environment interactions.

In view of philosophy and theory's long-established and well-founded skepticism concerning the moral imperative, Bateson's work is grounded in a persistent and focused ethics, one that I'd describe, in keeping with his terminology, as an ethics of restraint in the cumulative stress imposed on systems. For Bateson, the truly unfortunate turns in human affairs—wars, dysfunctional families, clinical schizophrenia—all bear the signature of the schizzes that systems, under undue pressure, engender. The persistence of this homespun ethics, a direct outgrowth of Bateson's psychiatric as well as his anthropological fieldwork, is all the more remarkable given the rich diversity of interests and discourses in which he trafficked. With respect to this ethics, Bateson's accounts of family meltdown, alcoholic sprees, Germany's transformation from the key losing party of World War I into the global monster of the 1930s and 1940s, and ecological and environmental catastrophes we have begun to encounter on a regular basis are parallel.[11] Excessive and mutually reinforcing stressors and stresses imposed on any environment will eventually produce such results as implosion, social revolution, or anomie. We need not only to moderate the force of the stresses arising from consumption, energy use, urban development, and finance imposed on our environment at any given moment but also to modulate the interplay and simultaneity of these exploitative vectors. Bateson's ethics of modulation anticipates the problematic and performance of finitude that would become such a distinctive feature both of postmodern aesthetics (disability in Beckett; uncertainty in Blanchot) and post-structuralist theory. His urgent sense that the overstressed infrastructure of twentieth-century life would remain in immanent danger until demand could be ameliorated or alternative delivery devised anticipated the didactic thrust linking a broad spectrum of seemingly disparate theoretical experiments. What the abstruse reasoning and performances of deconstruction and rhetorical reading share most in common with possibly more issue- and interest-oriented models such as postcolonial theory or gender studies may well be their gravitation toward the relaxation and opening of systems in a state of protracted rigidity and stagnation.

It is indicative of Bateson's perversely polymorphous but also relentless project that he chose, as the designation of his "finds" or telling crystallizations, the term *steps*, as in the title of his retrospective compilation volume or reader. A step is the barest part or unit of a journey, as would befit a widely traveled cultural anthropologist. But there is also something provisional, limited, or unsystematic about a step. There is no telling where it may lead, whether it will culminate in a definitive exploration or in an inconsequential neighborhood jaunt. A step is a way of approaching science in its smaller grain. Divvying up the progression of his broader realizations into steps gives the introduction to the first edition of Bateson's self-configured retrospective a homespun, local feeling. The modest scale of aspiration conveys to readers the sense that significant revelations are forthcoming in one's immediate environment and that, while some training is necessary in the deployment of indispensable implements, the tools are at hand. This is the dialect in which my first exposure to the social sciences was couched, my initial contact with such names as Marx, Freud, Comte, Weber, Simmel, Benjamin, Lévi-Strauss, and Barthes. In the introductory prose to *Steps to an Ecology of Mind*, it sounds like this:

> It was only in late 1969 that I became fully conscious of what I had been doing. With the writing of . . . "Form, Substance, and Difference," I found that in my work with primitive peoples, schizophrenia, biological symmetry, and in my dis- content with the conventional theories of evolution and learning, I had identified a widely scattered set of benchmarks or points of reference from which a new scientific territory could be defined. These benchmarks I have called "steps" in the title of the book.
>
> In the nature of the case, an explorer can never know what it is he is exploring until it has been explored. He carries no Baedecker in his pocket, no guidebook which will tell him what churches to visit or at which hotels he should stay. He has only the folklore of others who have passed that way. No doubt deeper levels of the mind guide the scientist or the artist toward experiences which are relevant to those problems which are somehow his, and this guidance seems to operate long before the scientist has any conscious knowledge of his goals. But how this happens we do not know.[12]

This passage, in its frank acknowledgement of the blind in which original research, as well as open-throttled writing, take place, is characteristic not only of Bateson but of the social scientific milieu in I gained my first expo- sure to methodological considerations. There were going to be no quick fixes to entrenched intellectual problems, whether akin to Kantian antino- mies or to deconstructive aporias.

It is not entirely gratuitous that the title of the essay Bateson completed in time for the theoretical epiphany described in this passage was "Form, Substance, and Difference." Differences of grain and articulation mark a significant frontier common to the methodologically acute social sciences and what would come to identify itself as rigorous critical theory. There is no question that, to Bateson, difference betokened several varieties of scien- tific impasse and result. In *Steps*, the gamut of the nuances of difference runs from modulations in a decorative pattern largely unnoted by outsiders to the milieu in which the pattern was produced, to the distributions in a range of genetic and structural possibilities, to the very medium out of which effects arise in communication. The problematic of difference serves

strategically as a threshold where a social scientific inquiry whose methodological overview has evolved out of fieldwork encounters certain limits and
passes the baton to a theoretical operating system whose philosophical configuration and primary allegiances are explicit.

In certain respects, difference marks the boundary of a theoretical Prom-
ised Land Bateson and compeers were never to claim as their own. When
Derrida, in certain of his key early essays, designates *différance* as a meta-
trope for language's intransigence to itself, a contingency, inexactitude, and
resistance limiting even the truth claims and authority of philosophy,[13] he
ups the theoretical ante to a production of difference that Bateson encountered in every domain of his variegated studies. There can be no faulting
Bateson for the drama and centrality that he accorded to the dynamic of
difference. If deconstruction successfully stages the profundity of difference's conceptual underpinnings and the outreach of its effects, it may well
do so as the *digitalization* of tropes and other epiphenomena initially encountered in an *analogical* (relatively more empirical) field; this may well be
the thrust of all theoretical upgrades as dislodgings of phenomena from the
materiality and contingency in which they were initially encountered and
marked.

Thinking in the Raw

Viewed through the lens of the ethos of rigor that has dominated theoretical
speculation over the last four decades—whether applied to philosophical
concepts or rhetorical tropes—Bateson's open acknowledgment and even
profession of the "loose," moments, the intuitive analogies and other rough
suppositions, pivotal to his "steps," if not his major breakthroughs, strikes
us as both remarkably modest and forthcoming. When one reads Bateson's
retracing of his ongoing allegiance to loose as well as rigorous thinking,
one is reminded of Derrida's insistence, in spite of his own uninterrupted
affiliation to philosophy as a social as well as academic institution, on surfing
the undertows of his interests and arguments that ensued from the linguistic
accident and density of the textual artifacts that he explored so meticulously.

Indeed, a systolic-diastolic rhythm sets into Bateson's thinking almost
from the outset, enabling his elaborated findings, whether of enforced egali-
tarianism among the Iatmul, systemic mutual undermining as the pretext

for schizophrenia (at least as phenotype), or "alcoholic pride," to retain their grounding in crystallizations and realizations that often emerge suddenly, after years of empirical encounters and randomly sifting through the evidence. Given that one of the few overarching thrusts in Bateson's work is toward the extreme restraint that must be exercised on impulses to push systems toward their limits (what he describes as "extractive" or "cumulative" societal tendencies), it is striking that he maintains his indebtedness to the loose swerves in his trajectories of thinking.

Bateson's lifelong mission was to explore how the systematic arrangements of societal life (whether military or marital) could be rendered more humane (i.e., with greater equanimity, with less polar contradiction and strife) through the reduction of conflict and the opening up of noncompetitive models of endeavor and participation. For him, anthropology was less a matter of gathering information about lands and peoples remote from the imperial centers of power and commerce than a quest for alternatives to the schemata of logic, social administration, and profiling that he associated with the West. In retrospect, we can argue that he practiced and elaborated anthropology as a medium for the emergence of deconstructive supplements to Western metaphysics. Derrida confronted this potential social-scientific module for deconstructive study in his encounter with the *Tel Quel* group, particularly in its appeal to Maoism and the past traditions of Chinese philosophy on which it drew. Already in the early 1970s, Derrida chose to limit his interventions to the immanent study of works of Western philosophy and the mutations that their ideological figurations underwent, above all in literature but to some degree in the visual arts and architecture as well. Derrida's decision undoubtedly had to do above all with his practices of philosophical critique and literary exegesis, but it also involved the positionings of his work and atelier within the French and American academies. It is important to note that there were repercussions to what amounted to a strategic choice and drift regarding the appeal to non-Western cultures as they would be transcribed and documented by the social sciences. Derrida did not again direct his reading and interpretation in a way that could be readily accommodated within the traditional social scientific division of labor until *Circumfession* and *Specters of Marx*.[14] As institutional comparative literature now takes up the inquiry into what might constitute world literature, as exemplified by studies such as Haun Saussy's splendid *Great Walls of Discourse and Other Adventures in Cultural China*,[15] it begins to retrace certain of the initial steps taken by Bateson and *Tel Quel* toward the West's others, in the full ambiguity of this claim, as sites of deconstructive apprehension or inkling.

Among the many striking features of such early studies as "Experiments in Thinking about Observed Ethnological Material" (1941), "Morale and National Character" (1942), and "Bali: The Value System of a Steady State" (1949), is the coincidence between the quest for non- (or less) dialectical modes of thinking and social administration in putatively non-Western communities and the theorization of the indispensability of loose moments in thinking and conceptual work if they are to be conducive to paradigm shifts and other creative breakthroughs. It is as if hunches and loose analogies, whose role in Bateson's findings is frankly acknowledged in "Experiments in Thinking," are tantamount to the unhinging of the determinants of Western logic and science, made possible not only through fieldwork in remote cultural arenas but also, by Bateson's enumeration, in art, humor, and certain mystical and esoteric experiences (some of which will be associated with Learning III).[16]

Bateson's bearing and commitment as a social scientist involve certain positions untenable to uncompromising and full-throttled critical practices such as deconstruction or rhetorical reading. As a clinician, Bateson can only cheer his alcoholic clients on to the mystical apprehensions and alliances with the Lacanian "Big Other" that would gain them a handle on their substance abuse. Mystical totalization and fusion are red herrings for a reading practice as conceptually grounded as deconstruction (though they have a place in Deleuze and Guattari's systems theory, given its debt to Bateson).[17]

[Early in his writings, Bateson begins retracing the steps back to his major observational-inferential breakthroughs, even when these include gaps of utter uncertainty or conceptual rawness. As a young anthropologist, he was astonished to discern "lateral" alternatives to conventional top-down rule and recrimination among the practices of the Iatmul, a New Guinea people. Their "social system differs from ours in one very essential point. Their society completely lacks any kind of chieftainship, and I phrased this matter loosely by saying that the control of the individual was achieved by what I called 'lateral' sanctions rather than by 'sanctions from above.' . . . I found further that in general the subdivisions of the society . . . had virtually no means of punishing their own members."[18] Not only is the lateral architecture of social cohesion, one avoiding "top down" regulations and transferences among the Iatmul, a refreshing change for the young Bateson, it furnishes him with a spatial metaphor for an alternative social system to those prevailing closer to home. Indeed, the shape and contours of the symmetrical and complementary relations that will be so momentous to him emerge from "a set of stricter words and diagrams, in terms of which I could try to be more precise in my thinking about the Iatmul problem. . . . I found that the 'hunch' worked. I found that so far as opposition, control etc. between the clans was concerned, the relations were reasonably symmetrical, and further . . . though there were considerable differences, these followed no serial pattern."[19] Bateson finds from the outset of his work that conceptually dense and complex relationships can ensue from casual, seemingly fortuitous spatiotemporal apprehensions. There is a close parallelism between according the results of this "loose think-ing" their due and making suggestive sense of phenomena encountered far off the customary path, especially when insisting on making the "frame analy-ses" that will preclude a priori, ethnocentric devaluation of cultural alterity.[20] Until the intricate circuitry of power, exchange, deference, and symmetrical as opposed to complementary patterns in a culture emerges, what Bateson calls "the feel of a culture" suffices: "I was especially interested in studying what I called the 'feel' of a culture, and I was bored with the more conven-tional study of the formal details. I went out to New Guinea with that much vaguely clear."[21] Acknowledgment of his hands-on relationship to his concep-tual "handles" as well as his material could hardly be more explicit.

Not only does Bateson derive full benefit in his ethnographic studies from figural and analogical "takes" on prevailing relationships, he gains the capital insight that quasi-science, science in its unproven, analogical con-figuration, can be the basis for highly efficacious regimes of healing, diet, and so on (e.g., Chinese acupuncture and herbology). "I want to emphasize . . . that, as a matter of fact, considerable contributions to science can be made with blunt and crooked concepts."[22] My own exposures to shiatsu massage, a form of acupressure, as well as to Ayurvedic medicine,[23] have led me to the same insight. Bateson is aware that confusions at the level of class-member distinctions can enter such figure- and analogy-based thought processes,[24] but this does not negate their generative value. He does not conceptually overvalue the physical tension between a river and its banks, but it nonetheless helps him discern some of the rapports between ethos and societal structure:

I pictured the relations between ethos and cultural structure as being like the relation between a river and its banks—"The river molds the banks and the banks guide the river. Similarly, the ethos molds the cultural structure and is guided by it." I was still looking for physical analogies, but now the position was not quite the same as when I was looking for analogies in order to get concepts which I could use in analyzing observed material. I was looking for physical analogies which I could use in analyzing my own concepts, and that is a very much less satisfactory business. . . . When one is seeking an analogy for the elucidation of material of one sort, it is good to look at the way that similar material has been analyzed. But when one is seeking an analogy for one's own concepts, one must look for analogies on an equally abstract level. However, these similes about rivers and banks seemed pretty to me and I treated them quite seriously.[25]

Bateson was aware early on that his overall struggles to remedy bipolarity in social institutions and procedures, to relieve industrial and urban configurations of some of the stress imposed upon them, and at least to theorize the supplanting of regimes of rigidity with continuums of flexibility placed him in implicit opposition to the Prevailing Operating System in its multiple sites and theaters: "My attack on the system was to suggest that there might be other forms of comparability."[26] His profound misgivings regarding the double binds and other rigidities imposing lockstep conformities and producing schizophrenics were tantamount to a technical receptivity not only to "loose thinking" but to systematic noise, static, and interference, in its multiple forms. Bateson's avowed openness to certain forms of mystical apprehension may date him as a wizard of the 1960s, but mysticism joins art and humor as domains of systematic expansion and reconfiguration that he found particularly productive. Indeed, as suggested above, some disruptive mystical apprehension is crucial if Bateson's Learning II (in "The Logical Categories of Learning and Communication"), already involving some productive adaptation on the part of its learners, is to progress to Learning III.[27] One of Bateson's favorite examples of the reconfiguration taking place at this level, which happens to be where addicts liberate themselves from their self-destructive dependencies, is the Zen koan, in which the conundrum is solved not by a logical solution but through a radical shift of field (or frame) that the formulation, functioning as a "strange attractor,"[28] fosters.

Through an opening to this particular mysticism, Bateson gains a vantage point on the alternation between loose and strict thinking in scientific thought:

But the more mystical phrasing of the matter was what I vaguely learnt, and it was of paramount importance. It lent a certain dignity to any scientific investigation, implying that when I was analyzing the pattern of partridges' feathers, I might really get an answer or a bit of an answer to the whole puzzling business of pattern and regularity in nature. . . . Thanks to this mystical belief in the pervading unity of the phenomena of the world, I avoided a great deal of intellectual waste.[29]

Whenever we pride ourselves upon finding a newer, stricter way of thought or exposition; whenever we start insisting too hard upon "operationalism" or symbolic logic or any other of these very essential systems of tramlines, we lose something of the ability to think new thoughts. And equally, of course, whenever we rebel against the sterile rigidity of formal thought and exposition and let our ideas run wild, we likewise lose. As I see it, the advances in scientific thought come from a *combination of loose and strict thinking*, and this combination is the most precious tool of science.[30]

While the telling advances in science gain a great deal from fluctuations between the mini-climates of unremitting rigor and loose thinking, no authoritative weather pattern can be extracted from or imposed upon these interactions. Indeed, the highest aesthetic value emerging from Bateson's thinking—and art is a privileged domain for testing and delimiting systematic claims—is the psycho-cultural pleasure that can be taken from asymmetries in conceptual work, inconsistencies in the grain or scale of inquiry, and disruptions to trains of thought that are too consequential.

I would say first that we ought to accept and enjoy this dual nature of scientific thought and be willing to value the way in which the two processes work together to give us advances in understanding the world. We ought not frown too much on either process, or at least to frown equally on either process when it is unsupplemented by the other. There is, I think, a delay in science when we start to specialize for too long either in strict or loose thinking. . . .

I think we might do something to hasten matters, and I have suggested two ways in which it might be done. One is to train scientists to look among the older sciences for wild analogies to their own material. . . . The second method is to train them to tie knots in their handkerchiefs whenever they leave some matter unformulated—to be willing to leave the matter so for years, but still leave a warning sign in the very terminology they use, such that these items will forever stand, not as fences hiding the unknown from future investigators, but rather as signposts which read: "UNEXPLORED BEYOND THIS POINT."[31]

Tying knots in handkerchiefs, that is, marking certain current voids in articulation as well as conceptualization for revisiting in the future, is hardly the technique favored by hi-tech, equipment-critical physical science. Yet once again, on a level remote from the horizon of his theoretical oversight, Bateson has accessed a figure for the rawness, spontaneity, and contrivance at play in the advances of his thought.

Between Symmetry and Complementarity

We have already begun to retrace the steps by which Bateson, through his early ethnological studies in New Guinea and Bali, first accessed tangible alternatives to the bipolar logic, reciprocal competitiveness, and acquisitive, exploitative attitude toward the environment that he regarded as his Western legacy. Through the tentative figurative process that he detailed in "Experiments in Thinking about Observed Ethnological Material," Bateson early on arrived at two counterpoised meta-sociological attitudes toward otherness and the environment—what he called the symmetrical and complementary—that served him for many years as a loose platform for his deliberations on these matters and their wider, sometimes systemic, implications. Although Bateson's readers encounter an early exuberance about the complementary as the relief valve for tit-for-tat competition, the enabling legislation for difference in the division of labor, and the ethos of unmotivated activity (as in "art for its own sake"), Bateson acknowledges that schismogenic stress can emerge from the complementary as well as the symmetrical. There is no simple either/or or on/off switch relating these two complexes of social attitudes and thought-processes:

> Both complementary and symmetrical relationships are liable to progressive changes of the sort which I have called "schismogenesis." Symmetrical struggles and armaments races may, in the current phrase, "escalate"; and the normal patterning of succoring-dependency between parent and child may become monstrous. These potentially pathological developments are due to undamped or uncorrected positive feedback in the system, and may—as stated—occur in either complementary or symmetrical systems. However in *mixed* systems schismogenesis is necessarily reduced. The armaments race between two nations will be slowed down by acceptance of complementary themes such as dominance, dependency, admiration, and so forth, between them. It will be speeded up by the repudiation of these themes.[32]

Whether Bateson was aware of it or not, both symmetrical and complementary bearings, as he formulates them relatively early on (in "Morale and National Character," 1942), are ramifications of the pivotal "Master and Bondsman" fable in Hegel's *Phenomenology of Spirit*.[33] As I have attempted to elucidate this pivotal text elsewhere in terms of the operative logical and rhetorical tropes making it possible,[34] what Bateson designates as the symmetrical corresponds to the fable's initial impasse, an intolerable standoff of parity between two proto-subjects equal to each other in every respect, mirroring one another in every move, and in all likelihood quite curious about which one might be better or stronger. Bateson's early way of characterizing this situation is as "*symmetrical* patterns, in which people respond to what others are doing by themselves doing something similar."[35] Hegel introduces the parable of lordship and bondage in part to answer the question, at the level of world history recast in terms of the cognitive and logical advances making its "higher" productions possible, concerning how social stratification is first introduced into history and society, both as a possibility and as a map of social distinctions or differences. In order to answer his own query, Hegel hypostasizes in the fable a struggle to the death between systematically identical and mirroring entities, in the wake of which one exercises power and privilege over the other. It doesn't take a Marx or a Kojève to extract from this speculative text that the business entrepreneur or investor of civil society occupies a role metaphorically akin to the life-risking partner in the timeless struggle.[36] As a philosophical parable, "Master and Bondsman" chronicles the metamorphosis of an intolerable standoff of reciprocity into a functioning social hierarchy.

In line with this reasoning, we can say that Bateson's notion of complementarity corresponds to the aftermath of the duel and risk crisis, a configuration in which collaborators tolerate, even capitalize, on the differences between them. "Here the stimulus which evokes greater striving in A is the vision of greater strength or greater striving in B";[37] "Among the complementary motifs we have mentioned only three—dominance-submission, exhibitionism-spectatorship, and succoring-dependence."[38] Complementary relationships play themselves out on what might be described as continuums of differentiation. Curiously, in their structure, Bateson's three examples of spectrums along which cooperation and true division in labor can be established demonstrate the duality characterizing all Freudian instincts. Freud is incapable, in fact, of discussing sadism or exhibitionism in any context other than of masochism or scopophilia.[39]

The New Guinea Iatmul, it turns out, trump conventional Western societies in the symmetrical pressure they generate, even (and precisely) when they dispense with vertical configurations of power. Among the Balinese, by contrast, complementarity forms the always loose context in which Bateson's "discoveries" emerge with a palpable sense of relief and release from the imperatives of Western dialectical logic. These finds vary from the "lack of climax . . . characteristic for Balinese music, drama and other art forms,"[40] rehearsed in a flirtation game Balinese mothers play with their sons, to the fact that "There are very few Balinese who have the idea of steadily maximizing their wealth or property; these few are partly disliked and partly regarded as oddities."[41] Balinese rules of etiquette and propriety do not derive from some higher authority or reflect the interests of elite castes or classes. Their violation, rather, entails a confusion or misrecognition of contexts. "It is wrong for a casteless person to address a prince in other than the 'polished language.' . . . The prince or the deity may express annoyance, but there is no feeling that either the prince, the deity, or the casteless person made the rules. The offense is felt to be against the order and natural structure of the universe rather than against the actual person offended."[42]

In keeping with the "close reading" Bateson advocates in the evaluation of a 1935 memorandum by the Social Sciences Research Council,[43] he is loath, in his exegesis of any culture, to leave any significant anthropological detail unturned. He is, for example, profoundly struck by how:

> The Balinese are markedly dependent on spatial orientation. In order to be able to behave, they must know their cardinal points, and if a Balinese is taken by motor car over twisting roads so that he loses his sense of direction, he may become severely disoriented and unable to act (e.g., a dancer may be unable to dance) until he has got back his orientation by seeing some important landmark."[44]

Even this singular and incongruous detail regarding the Balinese has a place, once Bateson has begun reading the culture as a system. The overall tack of Bateson's gloss on the Balinese is to read their society as a culture-wide resistance to the splits and schisms of schismogenesis. Within this context, the seemingly odd compulsion to stay on top of one's topographical coordinates plays an important role in a broad sense of balance that the

Balinese struggle to maintain. It is in the name of this balance that they are so resistant to hierarchical etiquettes and extractive relations to the economy and natural environment. "Further, in our analysis of the Balinese ethos, we noted recurrent valuation: (a) of the clear and static definition of status and spatial orientation; and (b) of balance and such movement as will [be] conducive to balance."[45]

The Balinese capacity to engage seriously in unmotivated activities, endeavors whose value is intrinsic to themselves, is striking in regard to aesthetic and ceremonial activities, but it also pervades the life-system. Bateson includes it among the factors conducive to a complementary bearing and worldview. He had, of course, been exposed to configurations in which art and religious experience were tantamount to the suspension of purposive striving long before his fieldwork in Bali. In Kant's *The Critique of Judgment*, the experience of the aesthetic amounts to a critical questioning of purpose itself;[46] this skepticism is magnified by the disruptive realm of the sublime in its varied manifestations. The question of purpose and the complementary posture that improvisational artistic processes and self-sustaining critical intervention demand haunt all of us whose work demands creative reconfiguration, translation, and the scrambling and unscrambling of messages amid the domestic arrangements of institutional employment and intellectual "career."

> It is common to find that activity . . . rather than being purposive, i.e., aimed at some deferred goal, is valued for itself. The artist, the dancer, the musician, and the priest may receive a pecuniary award for their professional activity, but only in rare cases is this reward adequate to recompense the artist even for his time and materials. The reward is a token of appreciation, it is the definition of the context in which the theatrical company performs, but it is not the economic mainstay of the troupe. . . . Similarly, in regard to the offerings which are taken to every temple feast, there is no purpose in this enormous expenditure of artistic work and real wealth. The god will not bring benefit because you made a beautiful structure of flowers and fruit . . . nor will he avenge your abstention. Instead of deferred purpose there is an immediate and immanent satisfaction in performing beautifully, with everybody else, that which it is correct to perform in each particular context.[47]

Balinese society creates a rich preserve for activities whose "beautiful performance" is its own reward. These take place on the substratum of a general societal "penny wisdom" amounting to a basic reverence for material resources. That they are at a remove from the economy of reward and compensation and the circuitry of positive reinforcement makes them a crucial factor at play in the complementary world view. It is indeed the tendency in the West for fundamentally unmotivated and self-legitimating activities—the arts and cultural appreciation, for example—to be mediated by considerations of professional advancement and institutional affiliation, which dislodge them from the complementary into the competitive stock market of the symmetrical. A double bind worthy of Batesonian schizophrenia emerges from the partnership between creativity and the symmetrical: in effect, considerations of professional advancement destroy the meditative, non purposive conditions under which aesthetic and critical syntheses transpire. Institution cannibalizes artwork, if not the artist herself, who remains the polarized shell of what drew her to her calling. Although Bateson himself does not make this extrapolation, it cries out for articulation amid the concussions between symmetrical and complementary bearings.

Bateson progresses from the modest and dispassionate observation of anthropological fieldwork to the highly theoretical elaboration of the Iatmul and the Balinese as fluid social systems. The Iatmul are strongly schismogenic; the Balinese their unlikely counter. Bateson's ability to theorize his fieldwork and to recast his systematic extrapolations into the prevalent techno-dialect of his day is particularly noteworthy, even in the context of the explicit linkage he draws, in "Experiments in Thinking about Observed Ethnographic Material," between loose figurative thinking and "high" conceptual abstraction. It is by dint of his fluid and highly suggestive crossover between empirical specificity and systematic interconnectedness that he is acknowledged as a seminal contributor to so many diverse fields, among them cybernetics and evolutionary biology.

What is readily apparent in the following extract from "Bali: The Value System of a Steady State" are the following long-term characteristics of Bateson's discourse: (1) an ability to schematize the day-to-day interactions in an observed community into what may be called, for lack of better terms, a life-system (a term slightly displaced from the multiple sectarianisms conveyed and implemented by the world's "major religions"); (2) "routes of communication" as the wiring or infrastructure of systems emergent through the painstaking observation that is at the heart of the experience of alterity. The rootedness of Bateson's systems making in communicative processes allowed his work to travel so well in its day, even to the European academy, where, among others, he speaks to Lacan, Deleuze, Guattari, and even Derrida (to the latter, of course, on difference, but also on the constitutive role of "slash marks");[48] (3) the continuation of what Deleuze and Guattari will term "schizzes" (the products of Batesonian schismogenesis) as impasses in human affairs conducive to the lamentable outcomes of violence, psychological derangement, and social exclusion (I recognize that value judgments, or an ethos, are implicit in this attitude); (4) the vibrant interface Bateson sees between certain processes relegated, in the academic division of labor, to the "social" or sociological and to the cognitive or psychological; and (5) the close intimacy between the observer, in this case the anthropologist, and the organizational patterns of the life-system being witnessed, indeed, the unavoidable *inflection* of the observer's "thought-process" and inscription by the communications loops being traced.

> It therefore follows that such a schismogenic system [in this case, the Iatmul] is—unless controlled—liable to excessive increase of those acts which characterize the schismogeneses. The anthropologist who attempts even a qualitative description of such a system must therefore identify: (1) the individuals and the groups involved in the schismogeneses and the routes of communication between them; (2) the categories of acts and contexts characteristic of the schismogeneses; (3) the processes whereby the individuals become psychologically apt to perform these acts and/or the nature of the contexts which force these acts upon them; and lastly, (4) he must identify the mechanisms or factors which control the schismogeneses.

The degree to which the cognitive and interactive processes of the anthropologist have been structured by the communicative processes into which he has been drawn (or inserted himself) is evident here. Interacting with a society that splits off from itself countless times, as Bateson observes among the Iatmul, the anthropologist and her transcript are susceptible to the schizzes structuring the social differences and divorces at hand. Closely in tune with this observational process is the fact that personal psychology, in such a communications-critical context, is far more an outgrowth of patterns of speech act and gesture than the residue of inbred mechanisms such as drives or even of cognitive faculties. (It is in this sense that Bateson is monitoring "processes whereby the individuals become psychologically apt to perform these acts.")

Bateson's systematic approach to the patterns that he observes in a community continues as his speculation ventures toward the therapeutic. He takes up possible remediation of the escalation of splits:

> These controlling factors may be of at least three distinctive types: (*a*) degenerative causal loops may be superposed upon the schismogeneses so that when the latter reach a certain intensity some form of restraint is applied—as occurs in Occidental systems when a government intervenes to limit economic competition; (*b*) there may be, in addition to the schismogeneses already considered, other cumulative interactions acting in an opposite sense and so promoting social integration rather than fission; (*c*) the increase in schismogenesis may be limited by factors which are internally or externally environmental to the parts of the schismogenic circuit.[49]

There is something of the "messianic without messianism"[50] in Bateson's hope that the extrapolation of systemic parameters from the tangle of messages ensuing from a community far off the Western beaten track might yield some guidelines for the remediation of avoidable polarizations and conflicts, whether on the battlefield, in the halls of diplomacy, or in the home. In this passage, Bateson reaches for the governmental or institutional "speed governors" that can be applied to a precipitous buildup of schismogenic stress. It is precisely as such a circuit breaker or release valve that psychotherapy, in a context of rigorous communications critique, can be applied to family systems as to individual thought processes. As the reader of Bateson's seminal analyses of schizophrenia and alcoholism in terms of double binds, escalations in competition, and other intractable communications situations cannot avoid noting, psychotherapeutic intervention is tantamount to a meticulous analysis of messages and the rerouting of the channels (or "web") along which the messages run. In its didactic thrust, it is a strategic dissipation of systematic pressures that have, through unbridled and ill-considered aggression, accumulation, and manipulation, mounted to the point of threatening the integrity of the "victim" or an expendable community.

Tight Predicaments

It is then both as a fieldworker—one whose boots are never free of dust and who has a unique flair for observing material circumstances—and as a canny systems theorist, capable of abstracting tangible processes into intricate loops of reinforcement and feedback, that Bateson syntheses analyses of such phenomena as schizophrenia, dysfunctional families, alcoholism, and the impending ecological disaster now engulfing us (the last more or less on schedule). Something in both the impromptu nature of his "steps" and the explicitness of their recounting keeps these open-ended thought experiments in social theory still fresh.

The openness of Bateson's thinking is nowhere more evident than in his reconstitution of the impasses in family life that result in schizophrenia and severe personality disorders.[51] Bateson again proves remarkably light on his feet in dancing between concrete empirical descriptions of schizophrenic communications and wide-reaching systematic characterizations of the condition overall:

> When a person is caught in a double bind situation, he will respond defensively in a manner similar to the schizophrenic. An individual will take a metaphorical statement literally when he is in a situation where he must respond, where he is faced with contradictory messages, and when he is unable to comment on the contradictions. . . . Schizophrenics also confuse the literal and the metaphoric in their own utterance when they feel themselves caught in a double bind. For example, a patient may wish to criticize his therapist for being late for an appointment, but he may not be sure what sort of a message that act of being late was—particularly if the therapist has anticipated the patient's reaction and apologized for the event. The patient cannot say, "Why were you late? Is this because you didn't want to see me today?" This would be an accusation, and so he shifts to a metaphorical statement. He may then say, "I once knew a fellow who missed a boat, his name was Sam and the boat almost sunk, ... etc." Thus he develops a metaphorical story and the therapist may or may not discover in it a comment on his being late.[52]

> Typically, the schizophrenic will eliminate everything from his messages that refers explicitly or implicitly to the relationship between himself and the person he is addressing. Schizophrenics frequently avoid the first and second person pronouns. They avoid telling you what sort of a message they are transmitting—whether it be literal or metaphoric, ironic or direct—and they are likely to have difficulty with all messages and meaningful acts which imply intimate contact between the self and some other.[53]

The empirical and linguistic precision of these formulations, grounded in empirical fieldwork with psychiatric patients at a Palo Alto veteran's hospital, in no way preempts Bateson's ability to map the systemic conditions of

schizophrenia with a rigor drawn from his grounding in the philosophy of
logical analysis. The confusion between the metaphoric and literal in schizo
communications and their elision of markers of agency are capital linguistic
observations, founded in interpersonal interactions in a clinical setting.[54]
Bateson gains a "foothold" in the sensibility of the patient who transmutes
his disappointment at a delayed session with his therapist into a fanciful tale
of "Sam's missed boat" both by extrapolating the working principles of
schizo narratology and by tracking the displacements in one of its particular
instances. In keeping with the invariably measured bearing of his pronouncements, Bateson reminds us that "normals" will behave schizophreni-
cally when they err into double-bind situations and that we negotiate at
many turns the "schizophrenia of everyday life."

Bateson's extrapolation of the rise of double-bind conditions, those
forming the parameters of schizophrenic speech acts, is an assemblage of
propositions like those comprising Wittgenstein's *Tractatus Logico-Philo-
sophicus*. These include:

2. Repeated experience. . . .

3. *A primary negative injunction*. This may have either of two forms: (*a*) "Do not
do so and so, or I will punish you," or (*b*) "If you do not do so and so, I will
punish you." Here we select a context of learning based on avoidance of punishment rather than a context of reward seeking. There is perhaps no formal reason
for this selection. . . .

4. A secondary injunction, conflicting with the first at a more abstract level, and
like the first enforced by punishment or signals which threaten survival. This
secondary injunction is more difficult to describe than the primary for two reasons. First, the secondary injunction is commonly communicated to the child by
non-verbal means. . . . Second, the secondary injunction may impinge on any
element of the primary prohibition. . . .

5. A tertiary injunction prohibiting the victim from escaping from the field.[55]

Bateson's recreation of the double-bind situation at the basis of what we
might call schizophrenic artifacts contains all the elements of what he and
others will characterize as a "closed system": a set of variables with no extrinsic or "objective" standards for prioritization or resolution and no
egress from the stigmatizing situation. Bateson makes it completely under-
standable that "Almost any part of a double bind sequence may then be

sufficient to precipitate panic or rage" on the part of the subject,[56] who has been recast as the "victim." Bateson characterizes this "muddle," a key term in the endearing "Metalogues" with which his volume begins, as a rein-forced standoff between mutually undermining injunctions with neither ad-judication nor escape in sight. For all his deep involvement in such situations and their repercussions, Bateson is not oblivious to the deep in-justice that they entail. In another essay, he characterizes the double bind as "an experience of being punished precisely for being right in one's own view of the context."[57]

Surely family life, whether in indigenous communities or in advanced technological societies, is no stranger to the configuration of mutually un-dermining injunctions without an escape route that characterizes the double bind. Again and again Bateson's all-encompassing study of exploitation, particularly by interests and agents that will not let up on the coercion they apply to fragile social structures and physical ecologies, finds itself at logger-heads with nature and its sociological vestiges. What could be more funda-mental than the family or social infrastructures evolved by communities seemingly vastly removed from the world capitals of information and tech-nology? Yet many of the evils to which Bateson's multifaceted projects are calibrated have arisen at home. Were Bateson formulating the following account of the impasses encountered by the child of the schismogenic fam-ily today, he would no doubt not take for granted the gender of the incrimi-nated parent (in those days, the notorious "schizophrenogenic mother"). Indeed, the child in the hypothetical situation might not necessarily be a son.) The scenario, though excessively tied to the figure of a mother, vividly captures the treacherous shoals of the dysfunctional family, its struggle to maintain a foothold in the community while being seriously at odds with itself.

> We suggest that the double bind nature of the family situation of a schizophrenic results in placing the child in a position where, if he responds to his mother's simulated affection, her anxiety will be aroused and she will punish him (or insist, to protect herself, that his overtures are simulated, thus confusing him about the nature of his own messages) to defend herself from closeness with him. Thus the child is blocked off from intimate and secure associations with his mother. How-ever, if he does not make overtures of affection, she will feel that this means she is not a loving mother and her anxiety will be aroused. Therefore, she will either punish him for withdrawing or make overtures toward the child to insist that he

demonstrate that he loves her. . . . In either case in a relationship, the most important in his life and the model for all others, he is punished if he indicates love and affection and punished if he does not; and his escape routes from the situation, such as gaining support from others, are cut off. This is the basic nature of the double bind relationship between mother and child.[58]

If we can accuse Bateson himself of in any way cornering his readers in a double bind, it is because of his dual ability to characterize a human impasse with compassion, empathy, and clinical patience yet to analyze complex loops of communication and feedback with a very different impersonality and detachment. Such a broad and vivid range of intellectual articulation in no way needs, however, to throw us into a state of inchoate, thwarted expression.

The family (or something very much like it) is also the breeding ground for alcoholism. The drama of resistances and capitulations to the addictive pathogen magically sustains itself: "The friends and relatives of the alcoholic commonly urge him to be 'strong' and to 'resist temptation.' . . . He believes that he could be, or, at least, ought to be 'the captain of his soul.' "[59] What is particularly stunning about Bateson's diagnosis of and prescription for alcoholism is that he can pursue its phases and variations along the feedback loop between symmetry and complementarity. Alcoholism is such a formidable demon for community and the individual alike because it adapts to both of these supplemental complexes of relational possibility, themselves spliced together in a Möbius strip.

> There is a very strong tendency in the normal drinking habits of Occidental culture. Quite apart from addictive alcoholism, two men drinking together are impelled by convention to match each other, drink for drink. At this stage, the "other" is still real and the symmetry, or rivalry between the pair is friendly.
>
> As the alcoholic becomes addicted and tries to resist drinking, he begins to find it difficult to resist the social context in which he should match his friends in their drinking. . . . As things get worse, the alcoholic is likely to become a solitary drinker and to exhibit the whole spectrum of response to challenge. His wife and friends begin to suspect that his drinking is a weakness. . . . Gradually the focus of the battle changes, and the alcoholic finds himself committed to a new and more deadly type of symmetrical conflict. He must now prove that the bottle cannot kill him. His "head is bloody but not bowed." . . . Meanwhile, his relationships with wife and boss and friends have been deteriorating. He never

did like the complementary status of his boss as authority; and now as he deterio-
rates his wife is more and more forced to take a complementary role. . . . His
symmetrical "pride" can tolerate no complementary role.[60]

This pilgrim's progress of the alcoholic can arrive at the final station of
Hegel's Master/Bondsman fable, the characteristic setting of a Charles Bu-
kowsky novel, whose barflies endeavor to outdo one another glass for glass.
Bateson's overview of diverse alcoholic postures, viewed from the symmetrical side, bears all the residue of his direct contact with the clinical population of which he speaks. Yet his encapsulation of the range of alcoholic
possibilities is also the flowchart of an addictive system. Indeed, when Deleuze and Guattari monitor late capitalism's flows in their Capitalism and
Schizophrenia diptych, gambling and credit as well as drugs will figure as
addictions that this particular Prevailing Operating System fosters.[61]

In this scenario of symmetrical competition, the alcoholic becomes ad-
dicted as much to the social environment of drinking, with its reciprocal
dynamics, as to the substance itself. His family struggles as much with his
"home away from home" as with the effects of alcoholism. The adversarial
other switches from being the partner in an escalating round of drinks to
"the bottle" itself, the metonymic figuration of the substance he is battling,
in terms mock-heroic as well as maudlin. The habitual drinker's accelerat-
ing social ills shuttle between the family, where his wife is dislodged from
her role as a partner, to work, where his boss cannot function as a true
friend. Bateson is meticulous in extracting the full symmetrical nuance of
the drinker's precipitous decline within the matrix of his social relations.
Yet the carefully plotted stages, or steps, of the alcoholic drama spill over to
a complementary setting in which the habitual drinker, by now a pronounced solitary, makes drinking its own art form, drinks for its own sake.
Bateson offers his exemplary drinker "an alternative" to his symmetrical
battle against the bottle and "this uncomfortable state—he can get drunk.
Or, '*at least*,' have a drink":[62]

> With this complementary surrender, which the alcoholic will often see as an act
> of spite—a Parthian dart in the symmetrical struggle—his entire epistemology
> changes. His anxieties and resentments and panic vanish as if by magic. His self-
> control is lessened, but his need to compare himself with others is reduced even
> further. He feels the physiological warmth of alcohol in his veins, and, as in many

cases, a corresponding warmth toward others. He may be either maudlin or angry, but he has at least become again part of the human scene.⁶³

The above characterization rings true, for example, to the mood swings undergone by Charlie's "protector" in Chaplin's *City Lights*. With a narrative ease belying the allegory's underlying logical rigor and cultural erudition, Bateson has mapped alcoholism within the prevalent formation, with sociopolitical and economic as well as psychological determinants, that produces it. What he says may apply to no single personal case history. But the account is compelling for the same reasons for which we continue to read Hegel's early encyclopedic treatises today: the coincidence in authenticity between its specific prognostications and its systematic logic.

Looping Complexities

There is no more compelling illustration of Deleuze and Guattari's notion of smooth space than the fluidity with which Bateson translates, in the Benjaminian sense, and reconfigures his acute observations and schematizations from field to field of twentieth-century exploration and endeavor. One senses, over the long haul of his diverse papers, a particularly strong parallelism between his technological fascination with machines capable of governing, correcting, and reprogramming themselves, and the ethical posture of self-correction indispensable to applying controls and brakes to accumulative and exploitative social planning run amok. Bateson played a large and impressive role in surveying the still-open field that begins with social communities, small and "complex," monitoring by different devices their intrinsic competitiveness and acquisitiveness and then proceeds—from mechanical models of governing and homeostasis to learning models of reinforcement, positive and negative, to cybernetic feedback and its circuits—in a sequence now culminating in artificial intelligence, mechanisms of turbulence, and autopoiesis in the theories of chaos and games. Cybernetics fascinated Bateson less because of what machines could accomplish or what devices could be devised using its technology than as a field or domain of communications and the circuits in which messages, meanings, and contexts are routed. He didn't approach ecology as an environmentalist. He saw, rather, that even entities as complex as systems and their environments are engaged in communicative processes that can eventuate in their mutual enhancement or depletion. These eventualities are what motivated his ecological explorations.

Bateson's legacy in large measure consists in the tremendous room he left for thinkers and scholars to fill in and refine the various message sets he deposited across a bewildering range of disciplines. Writers as varied as Wiener, Deleuze, Guattari, Wilden, and Manuel de Landa[64] (the latter by way of Deleuze and Guattari) would have abandoned major formulations in the wilderness had not Bateson opened up, however incompletely, the formats for their interventions. One manifestation of the calls for complexity and flexibility resounding throughout Bateson's later works is an ability to deposit incomplete and noncomprehensive contributions, to remain an anthropological outsider to and guest of the systems that one has confronted. Part of Bateson's enduring contribution is his willingness to "peak out" as an avid amateur in a broad spectrum of disciplines rather than enshrine himself as a devotee to any master system, whether communications theory, psychoanalysis, or philosophy. His elucidations may lack the aura of consummate mastery we have come to expect of work at the cutting edge of disciplinary formations. But in place of the authority that derives from intimate affiliation with one master discipline or another, claiming a vantage point in the "operating system," as it were, Bateson, from a complementary posture and in keeping with his own ethics of the defusing of cumulative exploitation and pressure, opens up a panorama on his miscues as well as forward steps, spins his yarn in homespun fabric rather than synthetic, a transcript of his thinking flat out. This biodegradable material is user as well as eco-friendly.

I would like to touch on a few more of Bateson's distinctive mini-climates of formulation. I appeal to them not only to fill out a certain picture but to allow myself the pleasure of retracing a few more of my own steps.

> A "bit" of information is definable as a difference which makes a difference. Such a difference, as it travels and undergoes successive transformation in a circuit, is an elementary idea.
>
> But, most relevant in the present context, we know that no part of such an interactive system can have unilateral control over the remainder or over any other part. The mental characteristics are inherent or immanent in the ensemble as a whole.

Even in very simple self-corrective systems, this holistic character is evident. In the steam engine with a "governor," the very word "governor" is a misnomer if it be taken to mean that this part of the system is under unilateral control. The governor is, essentially, a sense organ or transducer which receives a transform of the *difference* between the actual running speed of the engine and some ideal or preferred speed. This sense organ transforms these differences in some efferent message, for example, to fuel supply or to a brake. The behavior of the governor is determined, in other words, by the behavior of the other parts of the system, and indirectly by its own behavior at another time.[65]

This passage arises at a strategic situation both within the development of Bateson's work and in the subsequent drifts of contemporary critical theory. It is founded on the pivotal apprehension that information, to the degree that it is in any way meaningful to us, is an expression of difference. Information as difference is the data driving all sorts of communicative systems, ranging from physiological or mechanical ones (the eye or the mechanical speed governor) to the cogs and wheels of government and justice. Input may come from outside or may derive from internal stimulation. Needless to say, this point was not lost on twentieth-century phenomenology. The archi-trace and the trace become Derrida's most intransigent marks of difference as he subverted a tradition of unhinged experience into a configuration in which writing is the very program of thought. Whether open or closed, systems amount to circuits of difference. The only dimension of the above passage that might sound outmoded today might be its holism. The insistence on an integrality in which each adjustment to the system has an impact on every other element may be more the expression of a sentimental wish than the confirmation of an architecture rigorously contoured to *différance*.

It is clear that systems become an increasingly prevalent landscape for Bateson's analyses as the field or domain in which philosophy, cognitive science, psychoanalysis, and even biology confront their intrinsic momentums toward closure and their uncertainty, their tendencies toward rigid determination and flexibility, their exclusion of and their opening up to complexity. As Luhmann also acknowledges, the intrinsic and external impacts on circuits function like foreign affairs between systems and their environments. Paradoxically, a system's ability to remediate excessive pressure generated by its elements is tantamount to the restraint that it can implement.

Such systems are, however, always *open*: (*a*) in the sense that the circuit is energized from some external source and loses energy usually in the form of heat to the outside; (*b*) in the sense that events within the circuit may be influenced from the outside or may influence outside events.

A very large and important part of cybernetic theory is concerned with the formal characteristics of such causal circuits, and other conditions of their stability. Here I shall consider such systems only as sources of *restraint*.

Consider a variable in the circuit at any position and suppose this variable subject to random change in value (the change perhaps being imposed by impact of some event external to the circuit). We now ask how this change will affect the value of this variable at a later time when the sequence of events has come around the circuit.[66]

Close reading, in the context of a discourse in which systems comprise the domains in which differences arise, circulate, and mutate, is tantamount to meticulousness in the pursuit of circuits and what transpires along their compass, as well as acuity with regard to the architectural housing of systematic components. In his cybernetic and ecological writings, Bateson ushers in an ethics of attentiveness to Prevailing Operating Systems and to the transactions and exchanges taking place along their circuitry. This bearing, although situated with respect to specific technologies and environmental events (to wit, cybernetics and global population growth, critical resource depletion, and so forth) bears uncanny affinities to deconstruction's contrapuntal bearing. It is not entirely untoward, then, that in "Pathologies of Epistemology" Bateson should issue the *Grundprinzipe*, in effect, the Ten Commandments, impinging upon all systems.

1. The system shall operate with and upon *differences*.

2. The system shall consist of closed loops of networks or pathways along which differences and transforms of differences shall be transmitted (What is transmitted on a neuron is not an impulse, it is news of a difference.) . . .

3. The system shall show self-correctiveness in the direction of homeostasis and/ or in the direction of runaway. Self-correctiveness implies trial and error. Now, these minimal characteristics of mind are generated whenever and wherever the appropriate circuit structure of causal loops exists. . . . But that complexity occurs in a great many other places besides the inside of my head and yours.[67]

If we can accuse Bateson of any teleology in his systems thinking, it is in the thrust toward self-correction that he believes can be implanted, through meticulous thinking, into machines, whether their configuration happens to be mechanical, cognitive, cybernetic, or ecological. Bateson stakes a considerable portion of whatever intellectual capital he has accrued through his tortuous sequence of steps on this self-maintenance, which is also a form of self-redemption. This messianic aspiration marks the point at which the writing of systems (the program with which they have been uploaded) swerves unmarked into the metaphysics of ethical perfectibility and redemption. It is as if systems, if they could only carry over (in Hegel-talk, *Aufheben*) the best qualities of humanity (in the Eastern sense, as intensification of vital force rather than within a categorical logic of exclusion), could help orchestrate this transition to a more self-corrective configuration.

Bateson's trail of picturesque stutter-steps eventuates in systems attentive enough to maintain and even enhance their equilibrium, in ecologies whose cognitive and conceptual processing is as much part of their character as, say, annual rainfall or incipient levels of toxicity. The only way this give can be worked into the system is with adequate margin of flexibility (along with appeals for complexity, the ethical leitmotif toward the end of Bateson's writings).

> The healthy system . . . may be compared to an acrobat on a high wire. To maintain the ongoing truth of his basic premise ("I am on the wire"), he must be free to move from one position of instability to another, *i.e.*, certain variables such as the position of his arms and the rate of movement of his arms must have great flexibility, which he uses to maintain the flexibility of other more fundamental and general characteristics. If his arms are fixed or paralyzed (isolated from communication) he must fall.[68]

Kafka's trapeze artist, in his parable "First Sorrow," is a neurotic caricature of the segmentation that must be achieved for the perfection of sectarian art forms, each defined by an ingrained set of parameters. Bateson's acrobat, by contrast, is able to maintain his equilibrium by dint of his encompassing gesture toward the open. He is not merely a paragon of self-governance, he ventures willingly into the environment of turbulence, to which he reaches out with a commitment of creative autopoiesis.

Such a human reconciliation with the environment can only transpire if we participate in the cognitive as well as "bioenergetic" programming that

shapes ecologies and subclimates. We take responsibility for the environment around us, thus realizing a further ethical potential, only by acknowl-
edging the degree to which it is the result of patterns of communication
and thinking that we have evolved in multiple contexts—government, urban
planning, and commerce among them.

> First, let us consider ecology. Ecology currently has two faces to it: the face
> which is called bioenergetics—the economics of energy and materials within a
> coral reef, a redwood forest, or a city—and, second, an economics of information,
> of entropy, negentropy, etc. These two do not fit together very well precisely
> because the units are very differently bounded in the two sorts of ecology. In
> bioenergetics it is natural and appropriate to think of units bounded at the cell
> membrane, or at the skin; or of units composed of sets of conspecific individuals.
> These boundaries are then the frontiers at which measurements can be made to
> determine the additive-subtractive budgets of energy for the given unit. . . .
> Moreover, the very meaning of "survival" becomes different when we stop talk-
> ing about the survival of something bounded by the skin and start to think about
> the survival of ideas in circuit.[69]

It is only in ecologies configured to the relatively free circulation of "open
systems" that we have any hope of survival. Here Bateson equates survival,
amid the ecological, sociopolitical, and critical resource trends that he sees
mounting around him, with a shedding of skin, with a repudiation of skin
concepts in all their ramifications in favor of circuits allowing a free play
of messages and positions. Only amid the circuitry of open and complex
communication for which he has militated over a long and storied journey
can communities maintain their vigilance over unfortunate ideas. At the
synthetic moment of his explorations, Bateson is particularly mindful of
the tangible ecological impact of excessively rigid, exploitative, and self-
promoting thinking:

> There is an ecology of bad ideas, just as there is an ecology of weeds. . . . When
> you narrow down your epistemology and act on the premise, "What interests me
> is me, or my organization, or my species," you chop off consideration of other
> loops of the loop structure. You decide that you want to get rid of the by-prod-
> ucts of human life and that Lake Erie will be a good place to put them. You
> forget that the eco-mental system called Lake Erie is part of *your* wider eco-
> mental system—and that if Lake Erie is driven insane, its insanity is incorporated
> in the wider system of *your* thought and experience.[70]

Throughout his career, Bateson struggled to afford us the tools requisite to preserving our environment. He spared himself no expense or dislocation in gaining the perspective demanded by this task. His own circulation through subclimates of social organization and intellectual striving afforded him, by the end of his extended meditation, a unique perspective on what was already in the works. A visionary if not a prophet, Bateson synthesized some of the key admonitions worthy of taking into account not too long after the initial Earth Day. How well we listened, as we say, became history, setting the agenda of many of the most pressing crises and challenges currently besetting us:

> That the population explosion is the single most important problem facing the world today. As long as the population continues to increase, we must expect the continuous creation of new threats to survival, perhaps at a rate of one per year, until we reach the ultimate condition of famine. . . . We offer no solution here to the population explosion, but we note that every solution we can imagine is made difficult or impossible by the thinking and attitudes of Occidental culture.[71]

PREFACE: REACHING FOR THE BOOK

1. Henry Sussman, "The Phenomenology of Jetlag," *Modern Language Notes* 124 (2009): 1031–47.

1. INTRODUCTION: AROUND THE BOOK

1. How fascination with the book extends to its materiality becomes evident when we encounter Kevin McLaughlin's *Paperwork* (Philadelphia: University of Pennsylvania Press, 2005). McLaughlin's focus on the dissemination of paper as a widely available resource in the nineteenth century enables him to link in a productive manner Benjamin's account of the Parisian Second Empire in *The Arcades Project* (which McLaughlin has translated into English) and elsewhere, the rise of photography, and fictive accounts of the mounting U.S. empire rendered by Poe and Melville. McLaughlin assembles an up-to-date bibliography of resources on the history and technology of the book medium.

2. Gilles Deleuze and Félix Guattari, *A Thousand Plateaus*, trans. Brian Massumi (Minneapolis: University of Minnesota Press, 1987), 61.

3. James T. Siegel, rendering tribute to the enduring freshness of Georg Simmel's approaches to fundamental questions, also comes face to face with the question of faciality. In an unusually meditative essay, he appeals to Simmel in accounting for a remarkably placid and blank facial expression that he encounters in a Japanese subway ad. From this taking-off point, he adumbrates, in ways compatible with Deleuze/Guattari's approach to faciality, the manners in which limbs and body language often assume the conventional tasks of facial expressiveness, even extending his analysis to the cultural burden of facial expression often placed on animals. See James T. Siegel, *Objects and Objections of Ethnography* (New York: Fordham University Press, 2010).

4. For the *objet petit a*, see Jacques Lacan, *The Four Fundamental Concepts of Psychoanalysis (Seminar 11)*, trans. Alan Sheridan (New York: W. W. Norton, 1978), 17–18, 76–77, 83, 103–5, 112–13, 116, 118, 142–43, 145–48, 151, 159,

168, 180, 182–86, 194–96, 198, 209, 239, 242–43, 256–58, 265–70, 272–76, 282.

5. Deleuze/Guattari, *A Thousand Plateaus*, 170.

6. Ibid., 167. For more references to the "white wall/black hole" system, see 177–78, 182.

7. Ibid., 168.

8. Ibid., 22.

9. Ibid., 170–71.

10. Derrida *might* invoke this term (becoming-writing), but he would probably not, owing to the force and momentum of his own deconstructive tropology. I improvise this term in order to suggest a possible site at which some of the legitimate firewalls between the two philosophers' investigations grow thin.

11. Deleuze/Guattari, *A Thousand Plateaus*, 60–61.

12. See, e.g., Melanie Klein, "A Contribution to the Psychogenesis of Manic-Depressive States," in *Essential Papers on Object Relations*, ed. Peter Buckley (New York: New York University Press, 1986), 40–51, 59–65, 68–70.

13. Jacques Derrida, *Of Grammatology*, trans. Gayatri Chakravorty Spivak (Baltimore: Johns Hopkins University Press, 1976), 15.

14. Franz Kafka, "First Sorrow," in *The Complete Stories*, ed. Nahum N. Glatzer (New York: Schocken, 1971), 446–48.

15. Derrida, *Of Grammatology*, 86–87.

16. Jean-Luc Nancy is in accord with the pivotal notion that the book is a display, an open-and-shut de*liv*ery system of articulation and inscription, an ongoing story far beyond its final chapter, even where its history is to a certain degree electronic. See his splendid *On the Commerce of Thinking: Of Books and Bookstores*, trans. David Wills (New York: Fordham University Press, 2009).

17. Surely among the highpoints of this history are: Elizabeth L. Eisenstein's magisterial studies *The Printing Press as an Agent of Change* (Cambridge: Cambridge University Press, 1979) and *The Printing Revolution in Modern Europe* (Cambridge: Cambridge University Press, 1983); Marshall McLuhan, *The Gutenberg Galaxy* (New York: New American Library, 1969); Walter J. Ong, *Orality and Literacy: The Technologizing of the Word* (London: Methuen, 1982); Robert Pattison, *On Literacy* (New York: Oxford University Press, 1982). Not only the tradition but also the metaphysics of the book are on Derrida's mind in *Of Grammatology*, 1–26. In the thrust of his study and selection of an encompassing keyword, Derrida is keying off of I. J. Gelb's *A Study of Writing: The Foundations of Grammatology* (Chicago: University of Chicago Press, 1952).

18. The notion of the surprise comes as close to any tangible political upheaval or revolution as Derrida can countenance. Yet this construct, as Derrida rigorously develops it, is by no mean devoid of revolutionary consequences. See, above all, Jacques Derrida, *Specters of Marx*, trans. Peggy Kamuf (New York: Routledge, 1994), 51–56, 59, 84–87, 89–92.

19. Wilden, *System and Structure*, 373.

20. The recent primer to the unavoidable opening of classical systems to such epiphenomena as chaos, turbulence, feedback, and autopoiesis is Bruce Clarke and Mark B. N. Hansen, eds., *Emergence and Embodiment: New Essays on Second-Order Systems Theory* (Durham, N.C.: Duke University Press, 2009). This is an essential textbook for all those rethinking the systematic dimensions, features, and impact of theory, society, science, and technology.

21. I attempted to propose and elaborate a contractual notion of both the transactions involved in aesthetic fashioning and the histories of art, literature, and intellectual work in my *The Aesthetic Contract: Statutes of Art and Intellectual Work in Modernity* (Stanford: Stanford University Press, 1997), 165–205.

22. Here and throughout this study, I am positing "Prevailing Operating System" as the term, in an age of cybernetic thinking as well as processing, display, storage, etc., that can best capture the sense of overarching ideological encryption and embedding toward which a sequence of past terms for this relation strive. Among the established terms now subsumed under "Prevailing Operating System" would be: "hegemony," whether deployed by Gramsci or Laclau and Mouffe; "Ideological State Apparatus," as developed by Althusser; or *épistème*, the key operative term in Foucault's archaeology.

23. I specifically extrapolate the systems theory and parameters emerging from Borges's practice and ethos of *ficción* in "The Writing of the System: Borges's Library and Calvino's Traffic," in *Literary Philosophers*, ed. Jorge J. E. Gracia et. al. (New York: Routledge, 2002), 150–59.

24. Deleuze and Guattari, *A Thousand Plateaus*, 18.

25. Ibid., 21.

26. Ibid., 188.

27. Ibid., 5.

28. Deleuze's interest in Bergson and appeal to him as a model and predecessor in making philosophical discourse more responsive to experience and becoming were long-standing. His *Bergsonism*, first published in France in 1966, is a meticulous effort to achieve precision on such key notions as the *élan vital*, duration, memory, and intuition. It is, however, a slightly different Bergson who needs to be accessed in the task of elucidating his role as an inspiration for Deleuze/Guattari's Capitalism and Schizophrenia diptych. See Gilles Deleuze, *Bergsonism*, trans. Hugh Tomlinson and Barbara Habberjam (New York: Zone Books, 1991).

29. Henri Bergson, *Matter and Memory*, trans. N. M. Paul and W. S. Palmer (New York: Zone Books, 1996), 104.

30. Ibid.

31. For Niklas Luhmann's scenario of the system/environment difference and how systems make use of it, see his *Social Systems*, trans. John Bednarz, Jr., with Dirk Baecker (Stanford: Stanford University Press, 1995), 7, 16–17, 25, 29, 73–74, 88, 102.

32. Bergson, *Matter and Memory*, 75–76.

33. Deleuze/Guattari, *A Thousand Plateaus*, 53–54.

34. Ibid., 3–4.

35. See, e.g., the simultaneity of radically disjunctive manufacturing processes and their sharply differential rates of speed and acceleration in Karl Marx, *Capital* (London: Penguin Books, 1990), 1: 283–300, 367–74, 461–72, 492–508, 544–53, 557–61.

36. The Angel of History arises in section 9 of Walter Benjamin, "Concepts of History," *Selected Writings*, vol. 4, *1938–1940*, trans. Edmund Jephcott et al. (Cambridge: Harvard University Press, 2003), 392.

37. The latter term, of course, derives from Michael Hardt and Antonio Negri's suggestive and multifaceted exploration of the same name. See their *Empire* (Cambridge: Harvard University Press, 2000).

38. See: Sarra, *Fictions of Femininity*, 224–38; Norma Field, *The Splendor of Longing in the Tale of Genji* (Princeton: Princeton University Press, 1987), 251–57.

39. There is also a profound meditation on the tradition, parameters, and range of the book medium in Greenaway's *Prospero's Dream*, his filmic adaptation of *The Tempest*, in which the Shakespearean wizard dwells amid a fabulous book collection.

40. A critic who shares my enthusiasm for Greenaway as an afficionado of books and a theorist of film's interactive role among the media is Timothy Murray. For an authoritative overview of the interface between the humanities and the digital media, as well as a powerful reading and appreciation of Greenaway's oeuvre, see his *Digital Baroque: New Media Art and Cinematic Fold* (Minneapolis: University of Minnesota Press, 2008).

41. Sei Shōnagon, *The Pillow Book*, trans. Meredith McKinney (London: Penguin Books, 2006), 108. I'm fortunate to have the benefit of this recent and superbly annotated edition. The scholarship it incorporates is the basis of much that I know of the inner workings of the Heian court.

42. Roland Barthes, *The Empire of Signs*, trans. Richard Howard (New York: Noonday Press, 1989); Jacques Derrida, "The Double Session," in *Dissemination*, trans. Barbara Johnson (Chicago: University of Chicago Press, 1981), 183–84, 212–18, 237–39, 249–53, 260–61, 270.

43. See Shōnagon, *Pillow Book*, 316–17. Translator Meredith McKinney furnishes a full and most helpful gloss on the Captain Tadanobu episode.

44. Shōnagon, *Pillow Book*, 68.

45. Ibid., 96.

46. I mean this, of course, in Michel Foucault's sense. For his notion of biopower, see his *The Birth of Biopolitics: Lectures at the Collège de France, 1978–79*, ed. Michel Senellart, trans. Graham Burchell (New York: Palgrave Macmillan, 2008).

47. The most lurid, imaginative, and Real contemporary account of the skin trade, at least in fiction, is William T. Vollmann, *The Royal Family* (New York:

Viking, 2000). Vollmann delves deeply into the archive of myth and folklore in tracing the complexity and outreach of prostitution in a contemporary U.S. city.

48. Christian Metz, *Film Language: A Semiotics of the Cinema*, trans. Michael Taylor (Chicago: University of Chicago Press, 1991), 56.

49. E.g., Shōnagon, *Pillow Book*, section 2, in which there are no fewer than three mentions of the scenes the narrator is observing: "I remember seeing a large group of senior courtiers and others standing about near the Left Gate Watch Guardhouse. . . .Witnessing such a scene, of course you sigh and wonder just what sort of people they must be" (4). Similar scenic references and configurations can be found in sections 98, 115, 139, 145, 180, 183, 230, 273, and 329.

50. The film's ongoing narrative elements, Nagiko's romance with Jerome and her revenge plot against Yagi-san, lend what might be called a conservative counterweight to the play of filmic layers, codes, legends, and inscriptions that Greenaway athletically sustains over the course of the film. Without the linear development furnished by the apparatus of the film's embedded ongoing narratives, including Nagiko's biography, it would morph into a different, far less lucrative genre: "experimental film."

51. A question to pose here would be: Could Alain Resnais, as celebrated by Christian Metz, achieve commercial success under today's film-production conditions with the open-ended lyricism characterizing such works as *Last Year at Marienbad* and *Hiroshima mon amour*?

52. Derrida includes the broader definitions of writing, signifiers, and traces among the earliest of the theoretical parameters that he devises in *Of Grammatology*. Among the definitive passages is the following: "And thus we say 'writing' for all that gives rise to an inscription in general, whether it is literal or not and even if what it distributes in space is alien to the order of the voice: cinematography, choreography, of course, but also pictorial, musical, sculptural 'writing.' One might also speak of athletic writing, and even with greater certainty of military or political writing in view of the techniques that govern those domains today" (9).

53. See the Freud section of my *The Hegelian Aftermath: Readings in Hegel, Kierkegaard, Freud, Proust, and James* (Baltimore: Johns Hopkins University Press, 1982), 159–207.

54. This distinction is a fundament of contemporary systems theory. For a clear and helpful introduction, see Anthony Wilden, *System and Structure: Essays in Communication and Exchange* (London: Tavistock Press, 1972), 202–5.

55. *Ukigino* is, no doubt, her married name. Greenaway's giving Nagiko a family name different from her customary one, Kishihara, in these lines is an indication of the remarkable detail he lavishes throughout the film.

56. Shōnagon, *Pillow Book*, 205.

57. Here Shōnagon joins Friedrich Nietzsche, who in *Human All Too Human* and other works correlates literate style in communications with a society's

claim to culture. See, e.g., in *Human All Too Human: A Book for Free Spirits*, trans. R. J. Hollingdale (Cambridge: Cambridge University Press, 1996): "To write better, however, means at the same time to think better; continually to invent things more worth communicating, and be able actually to communicate them; to become translatable into the language of one's own neighbor; to make ourselves accessible to the understanding of those foreigners who learn our language; to assist toward making all good things common property and freely available to the free-minded; and finally, to prepare the way for that still-distant state of things in which the good Europeans will come into possession of their great task: the direction and supervision of the total culture of the earth" (2.2.87, p. 332).

58. No contemporary literary critic has run farther with the visual as well as textual display potential embedded the book medium than J. Hillis Miller. The fortuitous collision between his theoretical acumen and his collector's obsession with Victorian fiction enables him, taking as many cues from Benjamin as from Heidegger and Derrida, to extract from the phenomenon of illustration a particularly rich list of inquiries, inferences, and extrapolations. Miller's rough ride over and between the conventional boundaries separating popular media and "high" art; "high" theory and cultural studies; text and image; paintings, photographs, and engravings; and "originals" and illustrations furnishes the present study with a motive and a set of criteria, very high ones indeed. His *Illustration* is a seminal work on considerations arising out of the display both bound within the book and exceeding its parameters. See J. Hillis Miller, *Illustration* (Cambridge: Harvard University Press, 1992).

59. See, e.g., Ernst Tremp, Johannes Huber, and Kark Schmuki, *The Abbey Library of Saint Gall* (St. Gall: Verlag am Klosterhof, 2007).

60. For a delightful and suggestive compilation of contemporary assessments of and future prospects for the book, with entries by, among others, William Blake, Jerome Rothenberg, André Breton, Gertrude Stein, Edmond Jabès, Susan Howe, and Marjorie Perloff, see *A Book of the Book: Some Works and Projections about the Book and Writing*, ed. Jerome Rothenberg and Steven Clay (New York: Granary Books, 2000).

61. See, above all, Michel Foucault, *The Order of Things: An Archaeology of the Human Sciences*, trans. Richard Howard (New York: Random House, 1970), and *The Archaeology of Knowledge and the Discourse on Language*, trans. A. M. Sheridan Smith (New York: Pantheon Books, 1982).

62. Walter Benjamin, *The Arcades Project*, trans. Howard Eiland and Kevin McLaughlin (Cambridge: Harvard University Press, 1999), 63–64 (extract B1a,1).

63. The phrase is: "Who among us has not dreamed, in his ambitious moments, of the miracle of a poetic prose, musical, yet without rhythm and without rhyme, supple and resistant enough to adapt to the lyrical stirrings of the soul, the undulations of reverie, and the sudden leaps of consciousness" (Walter Benjamin, "On Some Motifs in Baudelaire," in *Selected Writings*, 4:320).

64. Benjamin, *The Arcades Project*, 460 (N1a,8).

65. Ibid., 463 (N3,1).

66. In *Friedrich Schlegel's Lucinde and the Fragments*, ed. Peter Firchow (Minneapolis: University of Minnesota Press, 1971), 175.

67. For an elaboration of this notion, pivotal in contemporary systems theory, see Fritjof Capra, *The Web of Life* (New York: Anchor Books, 1996), 95–97, 160–62, 167–68, 172, 194–96, 199.

68. For the notion of homeostasis, crucial to the capacity for self-organization manifested by certain systems, see ibid., 43, 58–59, 78, 205. Turbulence is a splendid term for the contingency that systems theory attempts to track. Its analogons in the field of contemporary critical theory include the Heideggerian *Ereignis*, or event, and the Derridean surprise. For an introduction to the role of turbulence in systems theory, see James Gleick, *Chaos: Making a New Science* (New York: Penguin Books, 1987), 67, 121–25, 158.

2. EXTRATERRESTRIAL KAFKA: AHEAD TO THE GRAPHIC NOVEL

1. The present essay is rooted in work on Kafka's animals I wrote many years ago. See, above all, "The All-Embracing Metaphor: Reflections on Kafka's 'Der Bau,'" in *Glyph 1* (Baltimore: Johns Hopkins University Press, 1977), 100–31, later published in *Franz Kafka: Geometrician of Metaphor* (Madison, Wisc.: Coda Press, Inc., 1979), 147–81. I glossed other of Kafka's animal studies, including "A Crossbreed" and "Josephine the Singer, or the Mouse Folk" in *The Trial: Kafka's Unholy Trinity* (New York: Twayne Publishers, 1993), x, xii, 6, 10, 15, 26, 36, 40–43, 70, 103, 107, 118. Kafka's experiments on the threshold between the human and the animal exerted a tremendous figurative and conceptual influence on the philosophical project Gilles Deleuze undertook in conjunction with Félix Guattari. In additional to their key notion of deterritorialization, Kafkan animality can be discerned at work in the background of such pivotal notions as nomadic flow, smooth and striated space, becoming-death, the pack, and the body without organs. See their *A Thousand Plateaus*, trans. Brian Massumi (Minneapolis: University of Minnesota Press, 1987), 149–62, 174–76, 232–309, 380–94.

2. For the notion of deterritorialization specifically in relation to Kafka, see Gilles Deleuze and Félix Guattari, *Kafka: Toward a Minor Literature*, trans. Dana Polan (Minneapolis: University of Minnesota Press, 1986), 13–15, 18–21, 35, 58, 67–68, 85–88. For a general introduction to this term, see their *A Thousand Plateaus*, 32–33, 40, 54, 61, 65, 70, 87–88, 91, 99–100, 109, 112, 117, 129, 134–35, 172, 174–91, 219–21, 291–92, 301–3, 306–7, 333–37, 345–48, 353, 432–34, 508.

3. Ibid., 53.

4. A decisive passage in which Deleuze/Guattari meld semiotics with their mega-trope of flow can be found near the outset of *A Thousand Plateaus*: "An

assemblage, in its multiplicity, necessarily acts on semiotic flows, material flows, and social flows simultaneously. . . . There is no longer a tripartite division between a field of reality (the world) and a field of representation (the book) and a field of subjectivity (the author). Rather, an assemblage establishes connections between certain multiplicities drawn from each of these orders" (22–23).

5. Ibid., 53–54.

6. I devised "complex art games" as a term for aesthetic innovation and recalibration with reference to Wittgenstein's construction "complex language-games." See my *The Aesthetic Contract: Statutes for Art and Intellectual Work in Modernity* (Stanford: Stanford University Press, 1997), 165–67.

7. Franz Kafka, *The Trial*, trans. Willa and Edwin Muir (New York: Schocken Books, 1974), 63.

8. Ibid., 141.

9. Ibid., 119.

10. Walter Benjamin, *The Arcades Project*, trans. Howard Eiland and Kevin McLaughlin (Cambridge: Harvard University Press, 1999), 104, (D1a,9).

11. Ibid., 112 (D5a,6).

12. Ibid., 116 (D8a,2).

13. Ibid., 119 (D10a,1).

14. Ibid., 460 (N1a,8).

15. See William R. Miller, Robert A. Rosellini, and Martin E. P. Spiegelman, "Learned Helplessness and Depression," and Lyn Y. Abramson, Martin E. P. Spiegelman, and John D. Teasdale, "Learned Helplessness in Humans: Critique and Reformulation," in *Essential Papers on Depression*, ed. James C. Coyne (New York: New York University Press, 1985), 181–219 and 259–310.

16. Benjamin, *The Arcades Project*, 231, (J2,1). The reference is from Gustave Geffroy, *Charles Meryon* (Paris: 1926).

17. The cinematic influences on this production surely number among them Terry Gilliam's futuristically urbane "Brazil."

18. Ben Katchor, *Julius Knipl Real Estate Photographer: The Beauty Supply District* (New York: Pantheon Press, 2000), 1.

19. Ben Katchor, *Julius Knipl Real Estate Photographer: Stories* (New York: Little, Brown, and Co., 1996).

20. See Louis Aragon, *Paysan de Paris* (Paris: Éditions Gallimard, 1953), 41–59, 62–63, 85, 97–98, 109, 111, 113, 121–22, 124–26, 195–204.

21. Luc and François Schuiten, *Les terres creuses: Carapaces* (Geneva: Humanos, 1980).

22. Luc and François Schuiten and Benoît Peeters, *Les cités obscures: L'archiviste* (Brussels: Casterman, 1987).

23. See Kafka, *The Trial*, 52.

24. Franz Kafka, "In the Penal Colony," in *The Complete Stories*, ed. Nahum N. Glatzer (New York: Schocken Books, 1971), 144–45, 161–62.

25. Luc and François Schuiten and Benoît Peeters, *Les cités obscures: La fièvre d'Vrbicande* (Brussels: Casterman, 1992), 38–39.

26. Derrida's early remarks on auto-affection as an indication of the signified's power in its absence remain among his most suggestive and illuminating on this representational dynamic. See Jacques Derrida, *Speech and Phenomena* (Evanston: Northwestern University Press, 1973), 68, 78–80, 82–83, 85–86, 95.

27. Chapter 7 of Anthony Wilden's *System and Structure* (London: Tavistock Press, 1972), 155–90, does a splendid job in elaborating the differences between analog and digital communications and the implications of this great divide.

28. Luc and François Schuiten and Benoît Peeters, *Les terres creuses: La tour* (Brussels: Casterman, 1987).

29. Franz Kafka, *The Castle*, trans. Willa and Edwin Muir (New York: Schocken Books, 1974), 40–41.

30. See Scott McCloud, *Understanding Comics: The Invisible Art* (New York: Paradox Press, 2000), 5, 7–9, 17–22, 59, 65, 68, 88, 107–17, 159, 193, 199, 212.

31. Luc and François Schuiten, *Les terres creuses: Nogegon* (Geneva: Humanos, 1990).

32. Benjamin, *The Arcades Project*, 676, 689–90. See also McCloud, *Understanding Comics*, 108–10.

33. Leo Leonhard and Otto Jägersberg, *Rüssel in Komikland* (Darmstadt: Melzer Verlag, 1972).

34. Years ago I invoked this painting—as the insignia of a world in a state of a priori deconstruction—in reading Kafka's "The Burrow" (see n. 1, above).

35. Leonhard and Jägersberg, *Rüssel in Komikland*, 35.

3. KAFKA'S IMAGINARY: A COGNITIVE PSYCHOLOGY FOOTNOTE

1. Franz Kafka, *The Trial*, trans. Willa and Edwin Muir (New York: Schocken Books, 1984), 141.

2. For the Lacanian construct of the Imaginary, see, above all, "The Topic of the Imaginary," in *The Seminar of Jacques Lacan: Freud's Papers on Technique* (Seminar I), trans John Forrester (New York: W. W. Norton, 1988), 58–59, 73–90, 137, 140–42. See also *The Seminar of Jacques Lacan: The Ego in Freud's Theory and in the Technique of Psychoanalysis* (Seminar II), trans. Sylvia Tomaselli (New York: W. W. Norton, 1988), 119–20, 152, 210, 253–55; and Lacan, *The Four Fundamental Concepts of Psychoanalysis* (Seminar XI), trans. Alan Sheridan (New York: W. W. Norton, 1978), 6, 74–75, 107, 118, 193, 205.

3. For the Kantian notion of *Einbildungskraft* ("imagination"), see Immanuel Kant, *Critique of Pure Reason*, trans Paul Geyer and Alan W. Wood (Cambridge: Cambridge University Press, 1998), 211, 225, 236–39, 257–57, 273–74, 281.

4. For the Lacanian construct of the Symbolic, see, above all, "The Symbolic Order," in Lacan, Seminar I, 220–33 and "The Symbolic Universe," in Lacan, Seminar II, 27–39. For the Lacanian construct of the Real, See Seminar

I, 58, 69–70, 80, 127, 130, 139–41, 188, 262, 271; Seminar II, 96–98, 152, 164, 182, 186, 210, 219, 225, 238–50, 253–54, 300; Seminar XI, 6, 19, 22, 36, 49, 55, 57–60, 68–69, 112, 167, 184, 186, 190, 205, 245.

5. A Kafkan taking-off point for Beckett is the quirky, sustained monologic voice in such animal parables as "The Burrow" and "Josephine the Singer." Beckett synthesizes a strikingly similar monotone, rigged with ongoing, self-effacing irony, for the protagonists of his *Trilogy* and notable works of his shorter fiction such as *The Lost Ones*. In this regard, see my *Afterimages of Modernity* (Baltimore: Johns Hopkins University Press, 1990), 178–84.

6. Reduced to the status of activist journalist with existentialist leanings by complacent cultural history, Camus was also an amazingly vivid and innovative narrative artist. Surely the viewfinder through which the narrator and protagonist of *The Stranger*, Meursault, regards the world has been conditioned by the social alienation and institutional incredulity that become everyday features of life to Joseph K. of *The Trial* and indeed of all the K. characters.

7. A more detailed discussion of Kafka's impact on Bergman appears in the final section of this chapter.

8. I subjected my poor mother of blessed memory and my sister to *Orson Welles's "The Trial"* on Mother's Day, 1962, when it had recently appeared. With its striking architectural settings (including massive offices that Welles went to Belgrade to photograph), as well as Welles's characteristic long shots and low-slung, wide-angle images, this work remains the most vivid and innovative instance of Kafka on film.

9. The process by which literary innovations are translated into music is nothing less than alchemy. The *Kafka Variations* of contemporary Hungarian composer György Ligeti speak for themselves as an example.

10. Thomas Bernhard brings the fictive Kafkan monologic voice to levels of spasmodic self-qualification even more heightened, ironic, and absurd than anything achieved by either Kafka himself or Beckett. See, in particular, his 1975 *Correction*, in which the author thematizes narrative inscription's negative capability to deactivate itself through compulsive self-correction. I've commented on this link in *Afterimages of Modernity*, 191–99.

11. Orhan Pamuk derives the template for his contemporary novel of Turkish politics and mores from Kafka's *The Castle*. Parallelisms of plot, tempo, characterization, and end results are too prominent to be overlooked.

12. Although Haruki Marukami bestows on the youthful protagonist of his *Kafka on the Shore* the name Kafka, this by no means exhausts the extent of his atmospheric, psychological, and narratological retrofittings and reprogrammings of Kafka's literary and cognitive innovations.

13. I have elaborated these aspects of the novel in *Kafka's Unholy Trinity: The Trial* (New York: Twayne Publishers, 1993), above all, 35–150.

14. Jorge Luis Borges, "Tlön, Uqbar, Orbis Tertius," in *Collected Fictions*, trans. Andrew Hurley (New York: Viking, 1998), 77.

15. See Tom Cohen, *Ideology and Inscription* (Cambridge: Cambridge University Press, 1998), 16–17, 52–54, 86.

16. For the misery that he allows to enter and tinge his picture of European fin-du-siècle life, Kafka draws most heavily on the fictive world of Dostoyevsky, one of his key nineteenth-century predecessors in crystallizing Imaginary-transformative work.

17. For the closely related notion of becoming animal, see Gilles Deleuze and Félix Guattari, *A Thousand Plateaus*, trans. Brian Massumi (Minneapolis: University of Minnesota Press, 1987), 14, 115–16, 176, 187, 240–43, 245–48, 257–59.

18. With the construct of the pack, Deleuze and Guattari reach toward a spontaneous and impulse-driven scenario for collective action outside the conventional frameworks of deliberation, public opinion, leadership, and, therefore, political process. For instances of pack movements, Deleuze and Guattari are more comfortable with animal imagery—as abounds in Kafka's animal parables and such films as *Willard*—than with conventional, subject-centered narrative. For this construct, see their *A Thousand Plateaus*, 28–37, 233, 239–52.

19. For the notion of flow, decisive to Deleuze and Guattari's joint project, see ibid., 3–4, 50, 53, 70, 112, 190, 204–5, 219, 468. I have explored this construct in my "Deterritorializing the Text: Flow Theory and Deconstruction," MLN 115 (2000): 974–96; reprinted in my *The Task of the Critic: Poetics, Philosophy, Religion* (New York: Fordham University Press, 2005), 129–51.

20. Kant furnishes an exhaustive survey and mapping of the agencies and elements involved in human thinking and knowing. He often describes the major domains of cognition (understanding, reason) as faculties (*Vermögen*). For instances of this terminology in the First Critique, see Kant, *Critique of Pure Reason*, 240–42, 249, 387–89, 444.

21. See my "The Subject of the Nerves," in *The Hegelian Aftermath: Readings in Hegel, Kierkegaard, Freud, Proust, and James* (Baltimore: Johns Hopkins University Press, 1982), 184–207.

22. In sequence, these critical (in several senses of the word) early essays appear in *Écrits: A Selection*, trans. Bruce Fink (New York: W. W. Norton, 2002), 31–106, 107–37.

23. See Jacques Derrida, "Freud and the Scene of Writing," in *Writing and Difference*, trans. Alan Bass (Chicago: University of Chicago Press, 1978), 196–231.

24. The notion of *Geworfenheit* is, of course, Heidegger's. See Martin Heidegger, *Being and Time*, trans. John Maquarrie and Edward Robinson (New York: Harper and Row, 1962), 174, 223, 321, 329–30, 399–400.

25. For the notion of *khōra* as a scene or site of writing in its full spectrality, see Jacques Derrida, "*Khōra*," in *On the Name*, ed. Thomas Dutoit (Stanford: Stanford University Press, 1995), 89–127.

26. Heidegger, *Being and Time*, 276–311, 235–40, 242–67.

27. See Jacques Derrida, "Psychoanalysis Searches the States of Its Soul," in *Without Alibi*, ed. and trans. Peggy Kamuf (Stanford: Stanford University Press, 2002), 238–80.

28. See Walter Benjamin, *The Arcades Project*, trans. Howard Eiland and Kevin McLaughlin (Cambridge: Harvard University Press, 1999), 225–27.

29. I raise this perverse possibility in "Incarcerated in *Amerika*: Literature Addresses the Political with the Help of Ernesto Laclau," in *Idylls of the Wanderer* (New York: Fordham University Press, 2007), 178–203.

30. For this crucial figure, see, above all, Gilles Deleuze and Félix Guattari, *Anti-Oedipus*, trans. Robert Hurley, Mark Seem, and Helen R. Lane (Minneapolis: University of Minnesota Press, 1983), 281. See also, *A Thousand Plateaus*, 4, 30–31, 56, 72, 149–66, 270, 479, 506–8.

31. For the pivotal figure of the dialectical image, see Benjamin, *The Arcades Project*, 388–98, 459–70, 474–76.

32. Condensation, which Freud attributes to the *Mischwort* (literally, a "mix-word" or, in the standard translation, "composite word") that is a striking attribute of jokes as well as dreams, is a pivotal element in his early grammar of consciousness. For a definitive treatment of this figure, see Sigmund Freud, *Jokes and Their Relation to the Unconscious*, trans. James Strachey (New York: W. W. Norton, 1989), 8–10, 18–36.

33. Benjamin's famous formulations in *The Origin of German Tragic Drama* run as follows: "Just as mosaics preserve their majesty despite their fragmentation into capricious particles [*Wie bei der Stückelung in kapriziöse Teilchen die Majestät den Mosaiken beliebt*], so philosophical contemplation is not lacking in momentum. Both are made up of the distinct and the disparate [*Aus Einzelnem und Disparatem treten sie zusammen*]; and nothing could bear more powerful testimony to the transcendent force of the sacred image and the truth itself. The value of fragments is all the greater the less direct their relationship to the underlying idea, and the brilliance of the representation depends as much on this value as the brilliance of the mosaic does on the quality of the glass paste. [*Der Wert von Denkbruckstücken ist um so entscheidender, je minder sie unmittelbar an der Grundkonzeption sich zu vermessen vermögen und von ihm hängt der Glanz der Darstellung im gleichen Maße ab, wie der des Mosaiks von der Qualität des Glasflusses*]" (Walter Benjamin, *The Origin of German Tragedy*, trans. John Osborne [London: New Left Books, 1977], 28–29). The ultra-fragmentation that Benjamin infuses into his inscription, its pivoting on and around kernels of citation, is accentuated in *The Arcades Project*, where he epigrammatically declares: "Method of this project: literary montage. I needn't *say* anything, merely show" (460).

34. Franz Kafka, "The Great Wall of China," in *The Complete Stories*, ed. Nahum N. Glatzer (New York: Schocken Books, 1971), 235.

35. Ibid., 243.

36. Of another auratic piece of stone surrounded by legend, the rock in the Caucasus left over when the Prometheus myth is subtracted from it, Kafka

writes: "As it [the legend] came out of a substratum of truth. it had in turn to end up in the inexplicable" (Franz Kafka, "Prometheus," in *The Complete Stories,* ed. Nahum N. Glatzer (New York: Schocken Books, 1971), 432.

37. Franz Kafka, "In the Penal Colony," in *The Complete Stories,* 142.

38. Ibid., 143–45.

39. Jacques Derrida, "The Law of Genre," in *Acts of Literature,* ed. Derek Attridge (New York: Routledge, 1992), 221–51.

40. See, e.g., Friedrich A. Kittler, *Gramophone, Film, Typewriter,* trans. Geoffrey Winthrop-Young and Michael Wutz (Stanford: Stanford University Press, 1999), 222–28.

41. A similarly degraded use of language would be spy Yu Tsun's task of eliminating sinologist Stephen Albert in Jorge Luis Borges's miniature World War I thriller, "The Garden of Forking Paths"("El jardín de senderos que bifurcan") simply for the purpose of communicating his name to the Germans. See this tale in Borges's *Collected Fictions,* 119–28.

42. See my "James Baldwin's Exile: Theory, Circumstance, and the Real of Language," in *Idylls of the Wanderer,*" 85–109.

43. Franz Kafka, *Amerika (The Man Who Disappeared),* trans. Michael Hofmann (New York: New Directions, 1996), 131–32.

44. Ibid., 134–35.

45. Marcel Proust, "Le Côté de Guermantes," in *A la recherche du temps perdu* (Paris: Gallimard, 1992), 3:122–27.

46. Franz Kafka, *The Castle,* trans. Willa and Edwin Muir (New York: Schocken Books, 1992), 349–50.

47. Borges, "Death and the Compass," in *Collected Fictions,* 156.

48. Freud's rich account of his grandson's *fort-da* game at the outset of *Beyond the Pleasure Principle* characterizes an ambivalence directed at the Real in its various manifestations at the level of object relations. See Sigmund Freud, *Beyond the Pleasure Principle,* trans. James Strachey (New York: Liveright, 1961), 8–11.

4. BOOKING BENJAMIN: THE FATE OF A MEDIUM

1. Henry Sussman, *The Task of the Critic: Poetics, Philosophy, Religion* (New York: Fordham University Press, 2005), 1–36.

2. For these texts, see: Walter Benjamin, *Selected Writings,* vol. 1, *1913–1926,* ed. Marcus Bullock, Michael W. Jennings, Howard Eiland, and Gary Smith (Cambridge: Harvard University Press, 1996), 297–369, 236–52; *Selected Writings,* vol. 2, *1927–1934,* ed. Rodney Livingstone and Others (Cambridge: Harvard University Press, 1999), 135–40 and 794–818; *Selected Writings,* 1:444–88.

3. See Hannah Arendt, *The Origins of Totalitarianism* (San Diego: Harcourt Brace and Company, 1979), 54–88, 267–340.

4. An obvious place to take up this significant strand of Derrida's thought would be "Freud and the Scene of Writing," in *Writing and Difference*, trans. Alan Bass (Chicago: University of Chicago Press, 1978), 196–231. Among the other ports of call along this trajectory would be "Ulysses Gramophone," in *Acts of Literature*, ed. Derek Attridge (New York: Routledge, 1993), 253–309, and *Paper Machine*, trans. Rachel Bowlby (Stanford: Stanford University Press, 2005).

With the appearance of his two-volume *Hitchcock's Cryptonymies* (Minneapolis: University of Minnesota Press, 2005), Tom Cohen goes to the head of the class of critical theorists thinking through the tangible impacts of the cinematic image, artificial memory, and the technocratic control, monitoring, and doctoring of information in the political and cultural spheres. Much of the foundational work that *Hitchcock's Cryptonymies* assumes was accomplished in the last six chapters of Cohen's *Ideology and Inscription* (Cambridge: Cambridge University Press, 1998). Significant additional contributions to this vital current discourse include: Friedrich A. Kittler, *Gramophone, Film, Typewriter*, trans. G. Winthrop-Young and M. Wutz (Stanford: Stanford University Press, 1999), and Avital Ronell, *The Telephone Book* (Lincoln: University of Nebraska Press, 1989).

5. In Walter Benjamin, *Selected Writings*, vol. 3, *1935–1938*, ed. Howard Eiland and Michael W. Jennings (Cambridge: Harvard University Press, 2002), 344–413. See also Benjamin, *Berlin Childhood Around 1900* (Cambridge: Harvard University Press, 2006).

6. Indeed, in Benjamin's signal "Unpacking My Library," the panorama of the cities in which he made his memorable acquisitions is inseparable from the autobiographical account of himself as a collector and the conceptual distinctions between the collector, the borrower, and the writer. See this text in *Selected Writings*, 2:492: "Memories of the cities in which I found so many things: Riga, Naples, Munich, Danzig, Moscow, Florence, Basel, Paris; memories of Rosenthal's sumptuous rooms in Munich, of the Danzig Stockturm, where the late Hans Rhaue was domiciled, of Süssengut's musty book cellar in North Berlin; memories of the rooms where these books had been housed."

7. Walter Benjamin, "The Work of Art in the Age of Its Technological Reproducibility," in *Selected Writings*, vol. 4, *1938–1940*, ed. Edmond Jephcott and Others (Cambridge: Harvard University Press, 2003), 252–56, 260–63.

8. Walter Benjamin, "On the Concept of History," *Selected Writings*, 4:392.

9. Joyce dwells, e.g., in *Finnegans Wake*, on the *Book of Kells*'s vivid and notorious Tunc page, especially on Sir Edward Sullivan's description and analysis of it. See James Joyce, *Finnegans Wake* (New York: Penguin, 1986), 119–23, 298.

10. Walter Benjamin, *The Origin of German Tragic Drama*, trans. John Osborne (London: New Left Books, 1977).

11. Henry Sussman, "Between the Registers: *The Arcades Project*, The Talmud, *Glas*," in *The Task of the Critic*, 100–28; also in *boundary* 2, 30 (2003): 169–97.

12. See one of Benjamin's signature essays, "Unpacking My Library," in *Selected Writings*, 2:492: "O bliss of the collector, bliss of the man of leisure. . . . For inside him there are spirits, or at least little genii, which have seen to it that for a collector—and I mean a real collector, a collector as he ought to be—ownership is the most intimate relationship that one can have to things."

13. For an illustration of the cover of this volume, titled in German *Der Wunderschirm: Eine Erzählung*, see Benjamin, "The World of Children's Books," in *Selected Writings*, 1:441.

14. Benjamin, "Unpacking My Library," *Selected Writings*, 2: 487.

15. Benjamin, "Old Forgotten Children's Books," *Selected Writings*, 1:406–15.

16. Ibid., 408.

17. Ibid., 408–9.

18. Ibid., 410.

19. Benjamin, "A Child's View of Color," in *Selected Writings*, 1:51.

20. Ibid.

21. Benjamin, "Goethe," in *Selected Writings*, 2:173–74.

22. Benjamin, "Goethe's *Elective Affinities*," in *Selected Writings*, 1:355.

23. See Benjamin, "On Some Motifs in Baudelaire," in *Selected Writings*, 4:330–31.

24. Jacques Derrida, *Of Grammatology*, trans. Gayatri Chakravorty Spivak (Baltimore: Johns Hopkins University Press, 1976), 66–73, 265.

25. Benjamin, "Goethe's *Elective Affinities*," *Selected Writings*, 1:333.

26. Benjamin, "One-Way Street," in *Selected Writings*, 1:446.

27. Benjamin, "Old Forgotten Children's Books," in *Selected Writings*, 1:410.

28. Derrida's construct of the Law of Genre and his fullest elaboration of it emerge in his reading of Blanchot's "Folie du jour." See Jacques Derrida, "The Law of Genre," in *Acts of Literature*, 223–35.

29. Karl Marx, *Capital*, trans. Ben Fowkes (Harmondsworth: Penguin, 1990), 1:615.

30. Benjamin, "Critique of Violence," in *Selected Writings*, 1:246.

31. Ibid.

32. Ibid., 241.

33. Ibid., 246.

34. Ibid., 243.

35. G. W. F. Hegel, *Hegel's Phenomenology of Spirit*, trans. A. V. Miller (New York: Oxford University Press, 1977), 94–96, 99–102.

36. Benjamin, "Critique of Violence," in *Selected Writings*, 1:250.

37. Ibid., 249–50.

38. Franz Kafka, "Poseidon," in *The Complete Stories*, ed. Nahum N. Glatzer (New York: Schocken, 1971), 434.

39. Benjamin, "Franz Kafka: On the Tenth Anniversary of His Death," in *Selected Writings*," 2:808.

40. Ibid., 799.

41. Ibid., 808.

42. James Joyce, *Ulysses: The Corrected Text*, ed. Hans Walter Gabler (New York: Viking, 1986), 32, 165, 378, 411.

43. Benjamin, "Franz Kafka," *Selected Writings*, 2:808.

44. Ibid., 809.

45. Ibid., 810.

46. Ibid., 809–10.

47. Henry Sussman, "The Afterlife of Judaism," in *Provocations to Reading*, ed. Barbara Cohen and Dragan Kujundžić (New York: Fordham University Press, 2005), 95–116; also in *Actualities of Aura: Textual Studies of Walter Benjamin*, ed. Dag Petersson and Eric Steinskog (Svanesund, Sweden: Northern Summer University Press, 2005), 196–220.

48. See Gershom Scholem, *Zohar: The Book of Splendor* (New York: Schocken, 1949).

49. Franz Kafka, *The Trial*, trans. Willa and Edwin Muir (New York: Schocken Books, 1968), 213.

50. Benjamin, "Franz Kafka," in *Selected Writings*, 2:798.

51. Ibid., 815.

52. See Jacques Derrida, *Sovereignties in Question*, trans. Thomas Dutoit and Outi Pasanen (New York: Fordham University Press, 2005), 22–26, 29–33, 45, 48, 50.

53. Benjamin, "Goethe's *Elective Affinities*," in *Selected Writings*, 1:355.

54. Gershom Scholem, *The Messianic Idea in Judaism* (New York: Schocken, 1995), 47.

55. Ibid., 41.

56. Ibid., 42–43.

57. Ibid., 43.

58. Ibid., 45.

59. Benjamin, "On Some Motifs in Baudelaire," in *Selected Writings*, 4:316–21, 324, 327–31.

60. Benjamin, "On the Concept of History," in *Selected Writings*, 4:392.

61. Gershom Scholem, *The Messianic Idea in Judaism*, 96–102.

62. Benjamin, "Franz Kafka," in *Selected Writings*, 2:805–6.

63. Benjamin, "On the Image of Proust," in *Selected Writings*, 2:237.

64. Benjamin, "On Some Motifs in Baudelaire," in *Selected Writings*, 4:341.

65. Kafka's "Josephine the Singer" is a precise literary instance of what Gilles Deleuze and Félix Guattari mean by a pack leader, as opposed to the head of a standard sociopolitical (and dialectically configured) organization. See their *A Thousand Plateaus*, trans. Brian Massumi (Minneapolis: University of Minnesota Press, 1987), 51–57, 233–34, 239–50, 287–88, 305–9.

66. J. Hillis Miller has written surprisingly and compellingly about the persistence and miniaturization of telling tropes in Proust, which he relates to fractals. See his "Fractal Proust," in J. Hillis Miller and Manuel Asensi, *Black Holes;*

or, Boustrophedonic Reading (Stanford: Stanford University Press, 1999), 349–77, 395, 439–49. For a brief general introduction to fractals, their structure, and their contribution, see Fritjof Capra, *The Web of Life* (New York: Anchor Books, 1996), 142–53.

67. This tack, understanding the hybrid, interlinguistic, at times exasperating patois of Joyce's *Finnegans Wake* as the preliminary dialect of a global language in the most idealistic sense, has been explored most productively by my colleague at Buffalo State College and doyen of the rich cultural life around Joyce in Western New York, Laurence Shine.

68. Jorge Luis Borges, "Tlön, Uqbar, Orbis Tertius," in *Collected Fictions*, trans. Andrew Hurley (New York: Viking, 1998), 77.

69. Also in *Hegel after Derrida*, ed. Stuart Barnett (New York: Routledge, 1998), 260–92.

5. PULSATIONS OF RESPECT, OR WINGED IMPOSSIBILITY: POETIC
DECONSTRUCTION

1. For key passages related to the dialectical image, see Walter Benjamin, *The Arcades Project*, trans. Howard Eiland and Kevin McLaughlin (Cambridge: Harvard University Press, 1999), 10, 13, 70, 150, 317, 388–92, 396, 406, 417, 459–63, 466, 468–70, 473–76.

2. See Walter Benjamin, "On Some Motifs in Baudelaire," in *Selected Writings*, vol. 4, *1938–40*, trans. Edmond Jephcott and Others (Cambridge: Harvard University Press, 2003), 327–32, 337–41.

3. I do not mean to imply that East Asian philosophy was ever an important part of Derrida's interests. But the balanced energies that distinguished Derrida both as a questing mind and as a teacher call to mind certain aspects of East Asian medical thinking. One of the best-informed overviews of the elements, energies, and organic subsystems of Eastern medicine is Harriet Beinfield and Efrem Korngold, *Between Heaven and Earth: A Guide to Chinese Medicine* (New York: Ballantine Books, 1991).

4. See, e.g., Immanuel Kant, *Critique of Pure Reason*, trans. Paul Guyer and Alan W. Wood (Cambridge: Cambridge University Press, 1998), 101, 109, 206–7, 209, 219–20, 242, 388, 397–98; see also Kant, *Critique of Judgement*, trans. J. H. Bernard (New York: Hafner, 1951), 29, 32–34, 114–16, 160–61, 164–69, 189.

5. Jacques Derrida, *Sovereignties in Question*, ed. and trans. Thomas Dutoit and Outi Pasanen (New York: Fordham University Press, 2005).

6. Jacques Derrida, *Of Grammatology*, trans. Gayatri Chakravorty Spivak (Baltimore: Johns Hopkins University Press, 1976), 10.

7. Jacques Derrida, "Limited Inc abc . . .," in *Glyph 2: Johns Hopkins Textual Studies*, ed. Samuel Weber and Henry Sussman (Baltimore: Johns Hopkins University Press, 1977), 182–84, 190–91, 199–203, 224–26.

8. Derrida, *Of Grammatology*, 18.

9. A notable exception here—in addition to two major documentary film projects about Derrida, one by Safaa Fathy and one by Amy Ziering—is the Parc La Villette, on whose conceptualization and design Derrida worked with the noted architect Peter Eisenman. For a full account of this project, narrated from multiple points of view, see Jacques Derrida and Peter Eisenman, *Chora L Works*, ed. Jeffrey Kipnis and Thomas Leeser (New York: The Monacelli Press, n.d.), 115–212.

10. For this notion, as well as the maximum positive reinforcement to writing and critique that Derrida can espouse, see his *Specters of Marx: The State of the Debt, the Work of Mourning, and the New International*, trans. Peggy Kamuf (New York: Routledge, 1994), 59, 65, 73, 85–91.

11. Jacques Derrida, *The Truth in Painting*, trans. Geoff Bennington and Ian McLeod (Chicago: University of Chicago Press, 1987), 37–82.

12. Jacques Derrida, *The Post Card*, trans. Alan Bass (Chicago: University of Chicago Press, 1987).

13. Jacques Derrida, "Plato's Pharmacy," in *Dissemination*, trans. Barbara Johnson (Chicago: University of Chicago Press, 1981), 170.

14. Since his 1998 *Ideology and Inscription*, Tom Cohen has been tracking the different inscriptions—he terms them *cinemallographics*—that Hitchcock scratches into the visual surface of cinema as an insignia of its writerly subtext. It is in the context of a tangible screen writing indicative of a crisis in the free dissemination of information and critique, one too late to head off, that he parsed the cross-hatches deposited by the title creatures of Hitchcock's *The Birds* at the "Derrida at Yale" conference in New Haven on October 14, 2005. The intervention extended a reading of the film in the "Matrixide" chapter in volume 2 of *Hitchcock's Cryptonymies*. See his *Ideology and Inscription* (Cambridge: Cambridge University Press, 1998), 169–84, 193–200; see also his *Hitchcock's Cryptonymies* (Minneapolis: University of Minnesota Press, 2005), 1:145–83; 2:82–166.

15. Benjamin, *The Arcades Project*, 211.

16. Jacques Derrida, *The Gift of Death*, trans. David Wills (Chicago: University of Chicago Press, 1995), 43.

17. See "The Fourth Abrahamic Religion?" in my *The Task of the Critic* (New York: Fordham University Press, 2005), 152–75.

18. Jacques Derrida, "Faith and Knowledge: The Two Sources of 'Religion' at the Limits of Reason Alone," in Derrida, *Acts of Religion*, ed. Gil Anidjar (New York: Routledge, 2002), 42–101.

19. See, e.g., J. Hillis Miller, *For Derrida* (New York: Fordham University Press, 2009), 55–71.

20. Jacques Derrida and Maurizio Ferraris, *A Taste for the Secret*, trans. Giacomo Donis (Cambridge: Polity, 2001), 54–55.

21. I more fully elaborate a comparative inventory of the primary discourse designs at play in memorable critique, above all poetry, philosophy, close reading, and criticism itself, in *The Task of the Critic*, 1–28.

22. See Derrida's comments on his inability to affiliate himself with any of the communal "usual suspects" emerging from his rich and complex familial, ethnic, and religious backgrounds in *A Taste for the Secret*, 26–27, 38–39, 85–86.

23. Jacques Derrida, "An Interview with Jacques Derrida," in Derrida, *Acts of Literature*, ed. Derek Attridge (New York: Routledge, 1992), 73.

24. See esp. Jacques Derrida, "Ulysses Gramophone," in ibid., 279–86.

25. Jorge Luis Borges, "Death and the Compass," in Borges, *Collected Fictions*, trans. Andrew Hurley (New York: Viking, 1998), 149.

26. Jacques Derrida, "The Double Session," in Derrida, *Dissemination*, trans. Barbara Johnson (Chicago: University of Chicago Press, 1981), 251.

27. For the figures of the resonant tympany and the waterwheel in Derrida's work (and perhaps his first bicolumnar text), see "Tympan," in Derrida, *Margins of Philosophy*, trans. Alan Bass (Chicago: University of Chicago Press, 1982), ix–xxiv. For the Derridean notion of phallogocentrism, see, among other of his works, *Of Grammatology*, trans. Gayatri Chakravorty Spivak (Baltimore: Johns Hopkins University Press, 1976), 10–16, 20–24, 50–52, 70–73; and "Freud and the Scene of Writing," in Derrida, *Writing and Difference*, trans. Alan Bass (Chicago: University of Chicago Press, 1978), 197–98, 207, 218–19, 226–27, 231–32.

28. Rodolphe Gasché, my longtime colleague in Comparative Literature at the University at Buffalo, has done a great deal to elaborate infrastructurality as the amalgamation of structures extrapolated from discursive material and patterns and the play or rhetorical figures. Gasché is particularly acute in tracking the Derridean re-mark. See his *The Tain of the Mirror: Derrida and the Philosophy of Reflection* (Cambridge: Harvard University Press, 1986), 200, 217–24, 234, 243–44, 260, 281, 288–93.

29. Derrida, "The Double Session," 251–52.

30. The *between* (French *entre*, *antre*) itself becomes one of the figures in "The Double Session" most performative of the qualities of Mallarmé's resonating poetic space. See ibid., 177, 181–83, 210, 212–15, 219–21. Not surprisingly, the spacing of the *between* figures prominently in *Of Grammatology*, where Derrida articulates the swinging supplementation between the two bearings of Western metaphysics accruing from speech and writing. For the conceptual *between* between logocentrism and its countermodality, see *Of Grammatology*, 218, 223, 238, 244, 257, 259, 262, 270, 275.

31. Both French "originals" here and, with a single exception, English translations of "Un coup de dés" derive from Stéphane Mallarmé, *Collected Poems*, trans. Henry Weinfield (Berkeley: University of California Press, 1994), 124–45.

32. Jacques Derrida, *Glas*, trans. John P. Leavey, Jr., and Richard Rand (Lincoln: University of Nebraska Press, 1986). *Glas* may contain Derrida's fullest

elucidation of the subsyllabic component of a telling signifier, the *gl* common, for example, to *glas*, *glaive* ("sword"), and *glaviol* ("iris").

33. For graphic instances of the "impossible figure," see E. H. Gombrich, "The Evidence of Images," in Gombrich, *Interpretation: Theory and Practice* (Baltimore: Johns Hopkins University Press, 1969), 61–68.

34. Jacques Derrida, "The Law of Genre," in *Acts of Literature*, 224–25.

35. Among the classics of this literature are, of course, J. L. Austin's *How to Do Things with Words* (Cambridge: Harvard University Press, 1975), and John R. Searle's *Speech-Act Theory* (Cambridge: Cambridge University Press, 1969). Derrida comments trenchantly on these works in "Signature Event Context," in *Glyph 1: Johns Hopkins Textual Studies*, ed. Samuel Weber and Henry Sussman (Baltimore: Johns Hopkins University Press, 1977), 172–97 and in "Limited Inc abc . . ." in *Glyph 2: Johns Hopkins Textual Studies*, ed. Samuel Weber and Henry Sussman (Baltimore: Johns Hopkins University Press, 1977), 162–264.

36. Were we to extract a psychoanalytical model from deconstruction, it would revere psychoanalytical tradition for its creation of a socio-clinical site for expression with complete impunity and it would hone in on such notions as everlasting memory, purity, redemption, pardon, and complete exclusivity as comprising unrealistic aspirations for mental hygiene. For the notion of a double tradition of psychoanalytical thought, see Jacques Derrida, *Resistances of Psychoanalysis* (Stanford: Stanford University Press, 1996), 19, 28, 35, 53–60; for the notion of psychoanalysis' impunity, its transpiring "without alibi," see his "Psychoanalysis Searches the States of Its Soul: The Impossible Beyond of a Sovereign Cruelty," in Derrida, *Without Alibi*, ed. and trans. Peggy Kamuf (Stanford: Stanford University Press, 2002), 240–42, 247–48.

37. Jacques Derrida, *Specters of Marx*, trans. Peggy Kamuf (New York: Routledge, 1994), 88–89.

38. Ibid., 65, 90. 168–69.

39. Maurice Blanchot, "Death Sentence," in *The Station Hill Blanchot Reader*, trans. Lydia Davis, Paul Auster, and Richard Lamberton (Barrytown, N.Y.: Station Hill Press, 1998), 167–68.

40. Franz Kafka, "The Cares of a Family Man," in *The Complete Stories*, ed. Nahum N. Glatzer (New York: Schocken Books, 1971), 427–29.

41. Blanchot, "Death Sentence," 177.

42. With regard to the pivotal importance of constructs of life for Derrida's later work, see "Majesties," the seminar on Celan's "Meridian" address, in Jacques Derrida, *Sovereignties in Question: The Poetics of Paul Celan* (New York: Fordham University Press, 2005), 110–11.

6. HEGEL, *GLAS*, AND THE BROADER MODERNITY

1. I refer here to Rodolphe Gasché's seminal study (a tongue-in-cheek predication with regard to *Glas*), *The Tain of the Mirror: Derrida and the Philosophy of*

Reflection (Cambridge: Harvard University Press, 1986). In this study Gasché elaborates the infrastructures that become prominent features in Derrida's critical rethinking of key metaphysical and ontological dimensions of Western philosophy. Infrastructures are tropes that manage to evade form and formalism, philosophical constructs that never overcome the local flavor of their contexts while marking something compelling with regard to broader issues of language and representation. The supplementarity prevailing between the Hegel and Genet columns of *Glas*; the marking and remarking of ideational processes; the constriction that is both a moment of systematic closure and an aspect of textual-sexual dissemination: these are infrastructures of the sort explicitly or implicitly set into play by Gasché in *The Tain of the Mirror*. On the notion of infrastructures see 144, 147, 149, 152, 155–57, 172–75. Gasché has written brilliantly about *Glas* in "Strictly Bonded," in *Inventions of Difference* (Cambridge: Harvard University Press, 1994), 171–98. He has suggested the infrastructural possibilities for the movement of constriction in *Glas* to me in private conversation.

2. Jacques Derrida, *Glas*, trans. John P. Leavey, Jr., and Richard Rand (Lincoln: University of Nebraska Press, 1986). This excellent translation includes many features for helping the reader, including the incorporation, generally between brackets, of pivotal terms in the "original" French. In the extended extracts to which I refer, I retain the translators' incorporations of French terms. At the end of citations, I indicate whether material derives from the left-hand, "Hegel" column, "a," or its "Genet" counterpart, "b."

3. I think, among others, of Nancy Armstrong's ongoing domestic meditations.

4. As will be evident below, Derrida is himself aware of the writerly implications of wounds experienced on a subjective plane but figured as cuts, scars, and so on. He addresses this issue in reading Genet's commentary upon "L'Atelier d'Alberto Giacometti" (*Glas*, 184b–85b). I elaborate on the critical and aesthetic implications of the "narcissistic wound" explored by object-relations psychoanalysts, such as Heinz Kohut, in *Psyche and Text: The Sublime and the Grandiose in Literature, Psychoanalysis, and Culture* (Albany: State University of New York Press, 1993), 72–73, 77, 87, 180, 189–90, 194, 201, 204.

5. I begin this investigation in ibid., 27–43, and elaborate upon it in *The Aesthetic Contract: Statutes of Art and Intellectual Work in the Broader Modernity* (Stanford: Stanford University Press, 1997), 23–33, 84–100, 134–62, 202–4.

6. See Jacques Derrida, "Parergon," in *The Truth in Painting*, trans. Geoff Bennington and Ian McLeod (Chicago: University of Chicago Press, 1987), 17–147.

7. See Henry Sussman, *Afterimages of Modernity* (Baltimore: Johns Hopkins University Press, 1990), 161–205.

8. See *Glas*, 20a, 33–34a, 36a, 52a, 76a, 97a, 162a–70a, 175a–76a, 187a–88a, 202a–3a.

9. If I am right here, certain of Derrida's texts can better be described as tributes to subsyllabic snips of letters than as elaborations of texts and their relation to concepts or ideas. To a certain degree, the rhetoric of such infrastructures, like that of structures before it, cannot totally escape the aporia according to which consequential accounts, even of the dismantling of systems and systematicity, lapse into the ideational procedures they critique. The authoritative discourse of structures, as elaborated and exemplified by Lévi-Strauss, Barthes, and Foucault, attempted to have things both ways, playing at an ambiguity in the notion of structures between their formal and substantive aspects. The discourse of infrastructures is analogously placed between a metacritique that would allegorically incorporate the performance of its design and a critique simply adding to the available polemical thrusts within the critical literature.

10. Derrida will take up the figure of the *taleth* again in his splendid "A Silkworm of One's Own: "Points of View Stitched on the Other Veil," in *Acts of Religion*, ed. Gil Anidjar (New York: Routledge, 2002), 309–55. If his bearing toward the religious Algerian Jewish community is a bit distant and skeptical in *Glas*, he revises it with the common philosophical platform he extrapolates for the three Abrahamic religions in his religious commentaries subsequent to *Glas*. See my "The Fourth Abrahamic Religion?" in *The Task of The Critic* (New York: Fordham University Press, 2005), 176–241.

11. Quite early on, in *Of Grammatology*, Derrida introduces the figure of the hinge in order to characterize the Möbius strip, the on-again, off-again, in Freudian terms, *fort-da* posture his own critique maintains in relation to the overarching system of Western metaphysics. For this figure, see Jacques Derrida, *Of Grammatology*, trans. Gayatri Chakravorty Spivak (Baltimore: Johns Hopkins University Press, 1976), 65–73.

12. *Phase transition* is a term from chaos theory indicating change of state, "from solid to liquid, from nonmagnet to magnet, from conductor to superconductor." See James Gleick, *Chaos: Making a New Science* (New York: Penguin Books, 1988), 126. Also see, with regard to phase transition, 131, 160–61, 169.

13. I have pursued the highly interactive but also paradoxical feedback loop leading from the strident improvisations of modernism to the unremitting if subdued qualifications of postmodernism—and back again—as this movement affects a variety of art forms, including literature. See my *Afterimages of Modernity* (Baltimore: Johns Hopkins University Press, 1990), 1–20, 161–205.

14. For some of the strategic deployments of and rationales behind this striking typographical improvisation punctuating a philosophical exegesis, see "Parergon," in *The Truth of Painting*, 17–39, 51–67.

15. Jacques Derrida, "Faith and Knowledge: The Two Sources of 'Religion' at the Limits of Reason Alone," in *Acts of Religion*, ed. Gil Anidjar (New York: Routledge, 2002), 40–101.

16. Jacques Derrida, *The Gift of Death*, trans. David Wills (Chicago: University of Chicago Press, 1994).

17. See ibid., 8–17, 29–32, 53–60.

18. Jacques Derrida, "Hostipitality," in *Acts of Religion*, 360–61.

19. Ibid., 364.

20. The phrase refers to an episode recounted in *Of Grammatology*, when the young Claude Lévi-Strauss, during his fieldwork on the Nambikwara of Brazil, uses subterfuge to incite the tribespeople to "out" each other's "proper" (and rigorously private) names. See Derrida, *Of Grammatology*, 107–18.

21. Jacques Derrida, *Rogues: Two Essays on Reason*, trans. Pascal-Anne Brault and Michael Naas (Stanford: Stanford University Press, 2005), 106.

22. Ibid., 13.

23. Ibid., 8.

24. Ibid., 109.

25. Ibid., 97.

26. Naomi Klein, *The Shock Doctrine* (New York: Henry Holt and Company, 2007), 3–21, 40–115, 155–68, 283–322, 443–66.

27. In "Auto-Immunity," my entry to *The Atlas of Critical Climate Change*, ed. Tom Cohen and Henry Sussman, forthcoming.

28. Jacques Derrida, *The Post Card: From Socrates to Freud and Beyond*, trans. Alan Bass (Chicago: University of Chicago Press, 1987).

29. Catherine Malabou and Jacques Derrida, *Counterpaths: Traveling with Jacques Derrida*, trans. David Wills (Stanford: Stanford University Press, 2004).

30. W. G. Sebald, *The Emigrants*, trans. Michael Hulse (New York: New Directions, 2000); *Austerlitz*, trans. Anthea Bell (New York: Modern Library, 2001); *Vertigo*, trans. Michael Hulse (New York: New Directions, 2001).

7. SYSTEMS, GAMES, AND THE PLAYER: DID WE MANAGE TO BECOME HUMAN?

1. Immanuel Kant, *Critique of Pure Reason*, trans. Paul Guyer (Cambridge: Cambridge University Press, 1998), 386.

2. Ibid.

3. Ibid.

4. Ibid., 386–87.

5. Gregory Bateson, *Steps to an Ecology of Mind* (Chicago: University of Chicago Press, 1972). This volume is an extraordinarily helpful compilation and glossary of Bateson's multifaceted contribution over many decades of innovative intellectual work. We will have occasion to review it in detail in Chapter 9, below.

6. The rare collation of markedly different enterprises and discourses achieved by these meetings, some of whose participants are indicated in my text, was funded by the Josiah R. Macy, Jr., Foundation. Their impact is chronicled by Reinold Martin, *The Organizational Complex: Architecture, Media, and Corporate Space* (Cambridge: M.I.T. Press, 2003), 38, 55, 239n.

7. James Gleick, *Chaos: Making a New Science* (New York: Penguin Books, 1987), 30.

8. Ibid., 135.

9. Ibid., 138.

10. Ibid., 135.

11. See Niklas Luhmann, *Social Systems*, trans. John Bednarz, Jr., with Dirk Baecker (Stanford: Stanford University Press, 1995), 105–6, 110–14, 117–23.

12. Gleick, *Chaos*, 88.

13. Ibid., 102.

14. Ibid., 141.

15. Ibid., 149.

16. Kant, *Critique of Pure Reason*, 128.

17. G. W. F. Hegel, *Hegel's Phenomenology of Spirit*, trans. A. V. Miller (Oxford: Oxford University Press, 1977), 31.

18. Gleick, *Chaos*, 102.

19. Another figure accounting for the plasticity of the time-space continuum would be the notion of bifurcations introduced by Capra to characterize the sudden twists in data indicating chaotic turbulence. On the notion of bifurcations, see Fritjof Capra, *The Web of Life: A New Scientific Understanding of Living Systems* (New York: Anchor Books, 1996), 191.

20. Luhmann, *Social Systems*, 16.

21. Ibid.

22. My own earlier study of Hegel gravitated to the moments of reciprocity or dialectical undecidability at which the definitive parameters of Mind—interiority/exteriority, subjectivity/objectivity, cause/effect—are suspended and up for grabs. See Henry Sussman, *The Hegelian Aftermath* (Baltimore: Johns Hopkins University Press, 1982), 3, 5, 17, 22, 27, 30–34, 36–37, 42, 46–47, 51, 56, 79, 92, 100, 132, 134–36, 150, 156, 185, 192–93, 195–99.

23. Luhmann, *Social Systems*, 26.

24. It's worthwhile recalling here that Kant, in his *Critique of Pure Reason*, early on establishes subtraction as a vital and decisive mode of purification (the sublimation, for example, from Reason to Pure Reason). See Kant, *Critique of Pure Reason*, 114, 117, 128, 140, 389.

25. Luhmann, *Social Systems*, 26.

26. Ibid., 16–17.

27. Ibid., 17.

28. Ibid.

29. Ibid., 24.

30. I'm thinking, of course, of a series of interventions at the very outset of Hegel's *Phenomenology of Spirit* through which the philosopher installs awareness as it were on the ground floor of his philosophical edifice, to the effect that the ideational role of terms and concepts in a systematic architecture can always be undermined by the material features of discourse. I think of the duplicitous role that Hegel assigns *meinen* ("to mean, to intend" and the first-person possessive pronoun) in the seminal two chapters "Sensible Certitude" and "Perception" ("Wahrnehmung," literally "taking for true"); the fact that even animals

can partake of sensible certitude's overvaluation of immediate conditions by devouring—in dialectical terms, negating—the truth of the moment; and the breakdown of each absolute present moment into a multiplicity of heres and nows. See Hegel's *Phenomenology of Spirit*, 62–67, 70–71, 73–75, 77–78.

31. Talcott Parsons and Edward Shils, eds., *Toward a General Theory of Action* (Cambridge: Harvard University Press, 1951), 3–29.

32. Luhmann, *Social Systems*, 523.

33. Hegel, *Phenomenology of Spirit*, 111–19.

34. Luhmann, *Social Systems*, 112.

35. Ibid., 113.

36. Ibid.

37. Capra, *The Web of Life*, 161.

38. An indispensable founding text on the notion of autopoiesis is Humberto R. Maturana and Francisco G. Varela, *Autopoiesis and Cognition* (Dordrecht: D. Reidel, 1980).

39. See Stieg Larsson, *The Girl with the Dragon Tattoo*, trans. Reg Keeland (New York: Random House, 2009); *The Girl Who Played with Fire* (New York: Random House, 2010); and *The Girl Who Kicked the Hornet's Nest* (New York: Random House, 2010).

40. In Joyce's *Ulysses*, this phrase is an epithet of trenchant insight recurring in Stephen's musings to himself. See James Joyce, *Ulysses*, The Corrected Edition (New York: Vintage Books, 1986), 14, 169, 199, 200.

41. With its dog-eared mail-order catalogue, its magical stamp album, and its tribute to the childhood discoveries of unforgettable summer evenings, this novel is an underappreciated classic of modernism's strategic alliance with childhood. See Bruno Schultz, *Sanatorium under the Sign of the Hourglass*, trans. Celine Wieniewska (New York: Penguin Books, 1979), 3–9, 28–35, 40–47, 85–87. See also, in this regard, "Modernist Night: Distortion, Regression, and Oblivion in the Fiction of Bruno Schulz," in my *Idylls of the Wanderer: Outside in Literature and Theory* (New York: Fordham University Press, 2007), 152–77.

42. See, in these connections, James Joyce, *A Portrait of the Artist as a Young Man* (New York: Penguin, 1977), 7–12, 16–17, 24–25, 27–39.

43. Walter Benjamin, "One-Way Street," in *Selected Writings*, vol. 1, *1913–1926*, ed. Marcus Bullock and Michael W. Jennings (Cambridge: Harvard University Press, 1999), 449–50.

44. Ibid., 464.

8. ATMOSPHERICS OF MOOD

1. Naomi Klein, *The Shock Doctrine: The Rise of Disaster Capitalism* (New York: Henry Holt and Company, 2007).

2. The present essay originated in my contribution to a conversation between American and Chinese colleagues, organized under the auspices of IC3

(Institute for Critical Climate Change) by Prof. Tom Cohen of the University at Albany and Prof. Wang Fengzhen of the Chinese Academy of Social Sciences that took place on June 7 to 12, 2008, outside Beijing. The wider IC3 project is an effort to reorient contemporary critical theory to some of the critical ecological, climatic, demographic, socio-political, systematic, logistical, representational, and archival mutations and transformations taking place at the current juncture. No one holds this complex map of interrelated X factors in his mind more vividly and trenchantly than Tom Cohen. I've learned an enormous amount working along with him on the IC3 project.

3. Walter Benjamin, *The Arcades Project*, trans. Howard Eiland and Kevin McLaughlin (Cambridge: Harvard University Press, 1999), 101–2 (D1,3).

4. Ibid., 64 (B1a,1).

5. Ibid., 64–65 (B1a,4).

6. Ibid., 471 (N7a,5).

7. Ibid., 363 (J76a,4).

8. Ibid., 105–6 (D2a,1).

9. James Gleick, *Chaos: Making a New Science* (New York: Penguin Books, 1987), 122.

10. Ibid., 122–23.

11. Ibid., 124.

12. As in Erving Goffman, *The Presentation of Self in Everyday Life* (New York: Anchor Books, 1959).

13. The multivalent term *qi* is famously untranslatable, since it transcends (or maybe better, confounds) familiar modern Western dichotomies between physical and mental, matter and energy. *Qi* is the basic stuff of the universe and undergoes transformation according to the five phases, yet it is palpable as something as simple as breath in the body (through which *qi* also circulates along the meridians used in acupuncture). *Qi* can also refer to emotions or even be an quasi-aesthetic quality, as in referring to the quality of words. Recently Arthur Goldhammer, translating François Juillen's French, has given us "breath-energy" (Juillen, *Vital Nourishment: Departing from Happiness*, trans. Goldhammer [New York: Zone, 2007], esp. 76–77). Shigehisa Kuriyama, in his excellent *The Expressiveness of the Body and the Divergence of Greek and Chinese Medicine* (New York: Zone, 2002), does not attempt a translation at all; for an example of *qi*'s range of meaning in early texts, including mood and *ciqi* ("the qi of words") see pp. 102–3. For an exemplification of the problem of translation, registering how far the term expands out from its early uses as "breath-energy," see the glossary entry in Wing-tsit Chan, *A Source Book in Chinese Philosophy* (Princeton: Princeton University Press, 1963), 784, though few would adopt his solution "material force."

14. For the element of fire's pivotal role in the interpretation of *qi* or vital force, see Harriet Beinfield and Efrem Korngold, *Between Heaven and Earth: A Guide to Chinese Medicine* (New York: Ballantine, 1991), 109–12, 177.

15. William H. McNeill, *A World History* (New York: Oxford University Press, 1999), 111–12.

16. Ibid., 224–27.

17. Haun Saussy, in personal e-correspondence with the author, February 19, 2008.

18. Harriet Beinfield and Efrem Korngold, *Between Heaven and Earth*, 29.

19. Ibid., 39.

20. Michel Foucault, *The Order of Things: An Archaeology of the Human Sciences* (New York: Random House, 1870), 17–42.

21. Beinfield and Korngold, *Between Heaven and Earth*, 63–64.

22. Wilden, *System and Structure*, 213–15.

23. Ibid., 163.

24. Ludwig Wittgenstein, *The Blue and Brown Books: Preliminary Studies for the "Philosophical Investigations"* (New York: Harper and Row, 1960), 39–41, 48–55, 59–61, 70–74.

25. As in Roland Barthes, *The Rustle of Language*, trans. Richard Howard (Berkeley: University of California Press, 1989), 76–79.

26. Wilden, *System and Structure*, 213.

27. Gregory Bateson, *Steps Toward an Ecology of Mind* (Chicago: University of Chicago Press, 1972), 496–501.

28. Wilden, *System and Structure*, 363.

29. Ibid., 373–74.

30. Ibid., 375.

9. THINKING FLAT OUT: BACK TO BATESON

1. For this notion, see Gilles Deleuze and Félix Guattari, *A Thousand Plateaus*, trans. Brian Massumi (Minneapolis: University of Minnesota Press, 1987), 352–53, 361–64, 379–85, 390, 410, 422–23, 474–92, 506.

2. Norbert Wiener, *The Human Use of Human Beings: Cybernetics and Society* (Boston: Houghton Mifflin, 1954); James Gleick, *Chaos: Making a New Science* (New York: Penguin Books, 1987).

3. Gyorgi Kepes, *Language of Vision* (New York: Dover Books, 1995); Reinhold Martin, *The Organizational Complex: Architecture, Media, and Corporate Space* (Cambridge: MIT Press, 2003).

4. Deleuze and Guattari, *A Thousand Plateaus*, 4, 7, 9, 11, 49–66, 69–73, 133–35, 141–45.

5. Ibid., 39–41, 45–49.

6. Ibid., 65, 69–70, 73, 142, 144, 154–59, 165–66, 266–72, 422–23, 506–8.

7. See John von Neumann and Oskar Morgenstern, *Theory of Games and Economic Behavior* (Princeton: Princeton University Press, 1944).

8. Ludwig von Bertalanffy, *General System Theory: Foundations, Development, Applications* (New York: George Braziller, 1973).

9. As witnessed, for example, in Niklas Luhmann, *Social Systems*, trans. Johns Bednarz, Jr., with Dirk Baecker (Stanford: Stanford University Press, 1995).

10. Anthony Wilden, *System and Structure* (London: Tavistock Press, 1972).

11. For family meltdown, see Bateson, *Steps to an Ecology of Mind* (Chicago: University of Chicago Press, 1972), 212–27, 242–43; for alcoholic sprees, see 309–37; for Germany, see 101–6; and for ecological catastrophe, see 496–501.

12. Ibid., xxiv.

13. Among other telling texts, see Jacques Derrida, "Différance," in Derrida, *Speech and Phenomena*, trans. David B. Allison (Evanston, Ill.: Northwestern University Press, 1973), 129–60; rpt. in Derrida, *Margins of Philosophy*, trans. Alan Bass (Chicago: University of Chicago Press, 1982), 1–27.

14. Geoffrey Bennington and Jacques Derrida, *Jacques Derrida*, trans. Geoffrey Bennington (Chicago: University of Chicago press, 1993); Jacques Derrida, *Specters of Marx: The State of the Debt, the Work of Mourning, and the New International*, trans. Peggy Kamuf (New York: Routledge, 1994).

15. Haun Saussy, *Great Walls of Discourse and Other Adventures in Cultural China* (Cambridge: Harvard East Asian Monographs, 2001).

16. This is the mystical, most disruptive but also most integrative stage of the learning that Bateson postulates as the necessary condition for challenging and eluding one's entrenched system-determined positions, locations, and outcome. See *Steps to an Ecology of Mind*, 283–308.

17. It remains striking that Bateson can theorize the decisive playful and nonimpressive moments in his thinking and inference at the very outset of his investigation into the qualities and inferences of symmetrical and complementary relationships. These two attitudes, addressed to one another in no simple or oppositional way, were to serve Bateson for many years as a viewfinder. Under their dual, disjointed, and by no means symmetrical projections, he was able to think through a rich gamut of possibilities for the supplementation of bipolarity, unchecked assertions of power, and simultaneous mutually reinforcing zones of acquisitiveness.

18. Bateson, *Steps to an Ecology of Mind*, 75–76.

19. Ibid., 77.

20. Indeed, the concern for perspective and observation bias manifested by the social sciences from the 1950s through the 1980s often galvanizes around the figure—and spatial metaphor—of the frame. An apotheosis of this movement is Erving Goffman, *Frame Analysis: Essays in the Organization of Experience* (New York: Harper, 1974). Also see Bateson, *Steps to an Ecology of Mind*, 184–92, 427–30. This concern for the establishment, through frames, of precise parameters of observation and bias parallels Levinas's philosophical insistence on encountering "the Otherness of the Other."

21. Bateson, *Steps to an Ecology of Mind*, 81.

22. Ibid., 84.

23. For pointed, effective introductions, see Vasant Lad, *Ayurveda: The Science of Self-Healing* (Wilmore, Wisc.: Lotus Press, 1984), and Robert E. Svoboda, *Parakruti: Your Ayurvedic Constitution* (Albuquerque: Geocom, 1989).

24. Bateson, *Steps to an Ecology of Mind*, 193, 202.

25. Ibid., 83.

26. Ibid., 80.

27. Ibid., 292–308. Although couched in terms of belief and mystical experience, the transformations that Bateson outlines in these pages in conjunction with Learning III, possibly shaking an addict out of alcoholic dependency, surely attain some of the radical alterity also characteristic of deconstructive postures and maneuvers.

28. For an introduction to this figure, operating both as a physical force and as a trope for turbulence, see Gleick, *Chaos*, 4, 133–38, 140–44, 254.

29. Bateson, *Steps to an Ecology of Mind*, 74–75.

30. Ibid., 75.

31. Ibid., 87.

32. Ibid., 324.

33. G. W. F. Hegel, *Hegel's Phenomenology of Spirit*, trans. A. V. Miller (Oxford: Oxford University Press, 1977), 111–19.

34. See "Five Hegelian Metaphors," in my *The Hegelian Aftermath* (Baltimore: Johns Hopkins University Press, 1982), 15–62.

35. Bateson, *Steps to an Ecology of Mind*, 97.

36. Alexandre Kojève, *Introduction to the Reading of Hegel*, trans. James. H. Nichols, Jr. (New York: Basic Books, 1969), 3–30.

37. Bateson, *Steps to an Ecology of Mind*, 97–98.

38. Bateson, *Steps to an Ecology of Mind*, 99.

39. Freud is particularly acute to the dual nature of the instincts in his case histories and in "Metapsychological Essays," a current of unusually speculative and free-wheeling exploration following his work on the protocols of psychoanalysis and the dynamics of the transference that was to prove decisive in establishing the regimen as an institution. A classical statement in this regard is "On the Mechanism of Paranoia," a decisive section of the 1911 Schreber case. See Sigmund Freud, *Three Case Histories* (New York: Touchstone, 1996), 135–55.

40. Bateson, *Steps to an Ecology of Mind*, 113.

41. Ibid., 116.

42. Ibid., 119.

43. Ibid., 62.

44. Ibid., 117.

45. Ibid., 125.

46. For the subtle cat-and-mouse game between purposiveness (*Zweckmäßigkeit*) and aesthetics, see Immanuel Kant, *Critique of Judgement*, trans. J. H. Bernard (New York: Macmillan, 1954), 17–31, 43–51, 73–81.

47. Bateson, *Steps to an Ecology of Mind*, 117–18.

48. Bateson's ongoing motif of slash marks in *Steps to an Ecology of Mind* verges on a communications theory encompassing the art and social organization of indigenous peoples. On this point, he clearly sees eye to eye with Jacques Derrida, in works such as *Of Grammatology* and around such infrastructural figures as the mark and the "re-mark," to the effect that inscription and difference are features of all human (and possibly animal) cultures and communities. See Bateson, *Steps to an Ecology of Mind*, 131, 413–15.

49. Ibid., 126.

50. See Jacques Derrida, *Specters of Marx: The State of the Debt, the Work of Mourning, and the New International*, trans. Peggy Kamuf (New York: Routledge, 1994), 59.

51. Here I want to suggest that, although a long tradition of genetic research has moved schizophrenia away from the psychic disorders and under the bailiwick of illnesses for which there is documented genetic predisposition, treatable more by pharmacological intervention than by psychotherapy, the considerable literature of object relations, from Anna Freud and Melanie Klein to Fairbairn and Winnicott to Alice Miller, Heinz Kohut, and Otto Kernberg, suggests a profound subtext of Batesonian "schismogenesis" underlying personality disorders, pathological narcissism, and borderline personality. There is a strong conceptual as well as etymological affinity between the stark "splitting" characterizing narcissistic and borderline personalities, in the language of Kohut and Kernberg, and the "schismogenesis" that Bateson tracks throughout his investigations. I treated the notion of splitting as it applies to personality disorders and borderline conditions in my *Psyche and Text: The Sublime and the Grandiose in Literature, Psychopathology, and Culture* (Albany: State University of New York Press, 1993).

52. Bateson, *Steps to an Ecology of Mind*, 209.

53. Ibid., 235.

54. There is a close affinity between Bateson's clinical extrapolation of schizophrenic conditions and the linguistic and rhetorical disjunctions attributed to allegory by critics from Walter Benjamin to Paul de Man. See Benjamin, *Origin of German Tragic Drama*, trans. John Osborne (London: New Left Books, 1977), 91–98, 161–67, 182–95, 207–13, 220–35; *The Arcades Project*, trans. Howard Eiland and Kevin McLaughlin (Cambridge: Harvard University Press, 1999), 205–7, 211, 351–52, 356, 365–70, 374, 377. See also Paul de Man, *Blindness and Insight: Essays in the Rhetoric of Contemporary Criticism*, 2d ed. (Minneapolis: University of Minnesota Press, 1983), 35, 173–74, 208–9, 222–28.

55. Bateson, *Steps to an Ecology of Mind*, 206–7.

56. Ibid., 207.

57. Ibid., 236.

58. Ibid., 216.

59. Ibid., 312.

60. Ibid., 325–26.

61. See, for example, Gilles Deleuze and Félix Guattari, *Anti-Oedipus*, trans. Robert Hurley, Mark Seem, and Helen R. Lane (Minneapolis: University of Minnesota Press, 1996), 34–35, 139–41, 184–87, 227–30.

62. Bateson, *Steps to an Ecology of Mind*, 328–29.

63. Ibid., 329.

64. Manuel de Landa's superimposed strata of material history arise at the intersection of "World Civilization" as a study template for global history and systems theory in a succession leading from Bateson to Deleuze and Guattari and Wilden. See Manuel de Landa, *A Thousand Years of Nonlinear History* (New York: Zone Books, 2000).

65. Bateson, *Steps to an Ecology of Mind*, 315–16.

66. Ibid., 410.

67. Ibid., 490.

68. Ibid., 506.

69. Ibid., 466–67.

70. Ibid., 492.

71. Ibid., 500.

Violence, 99, 160, 162, 171, 177, 188, 191. *See also* Benjamin, "The Critique of Violence"
Virtual reality, xix, 14, 21, 47
von Bertalanffy, Ludwig, 248
von Neumann, John, 201, 248

Weather: and the cultural or personal, 218–43 passim, 256; and Benjamin's *The Arcades Project*, 43, 56–57, 218–25
Website, 40, 41, 56, 112, 135, 220
Weiner, Norbert, 201, 212

Welles, Orson, 34, 86, 88, 105, 106, 240, 286n8
Wilden, Anthony, xviii, 9–10, 71, 196, 212, 233–42, 248, 270
Wittgenstein, Ludwig, 140, 237, 265
World Bank, 189, 191
World War I, 187, 249
World War II, 226
Worldwide Web, xii, 10, 22, 110, 218

Zevi, Sabbatai, 132, 133
Zohar, 122, 129, 132
Zola, Emile, 105, 225

DATE DUE

Demco, Inc. 38-293